I0714454

the
QUICK POSE

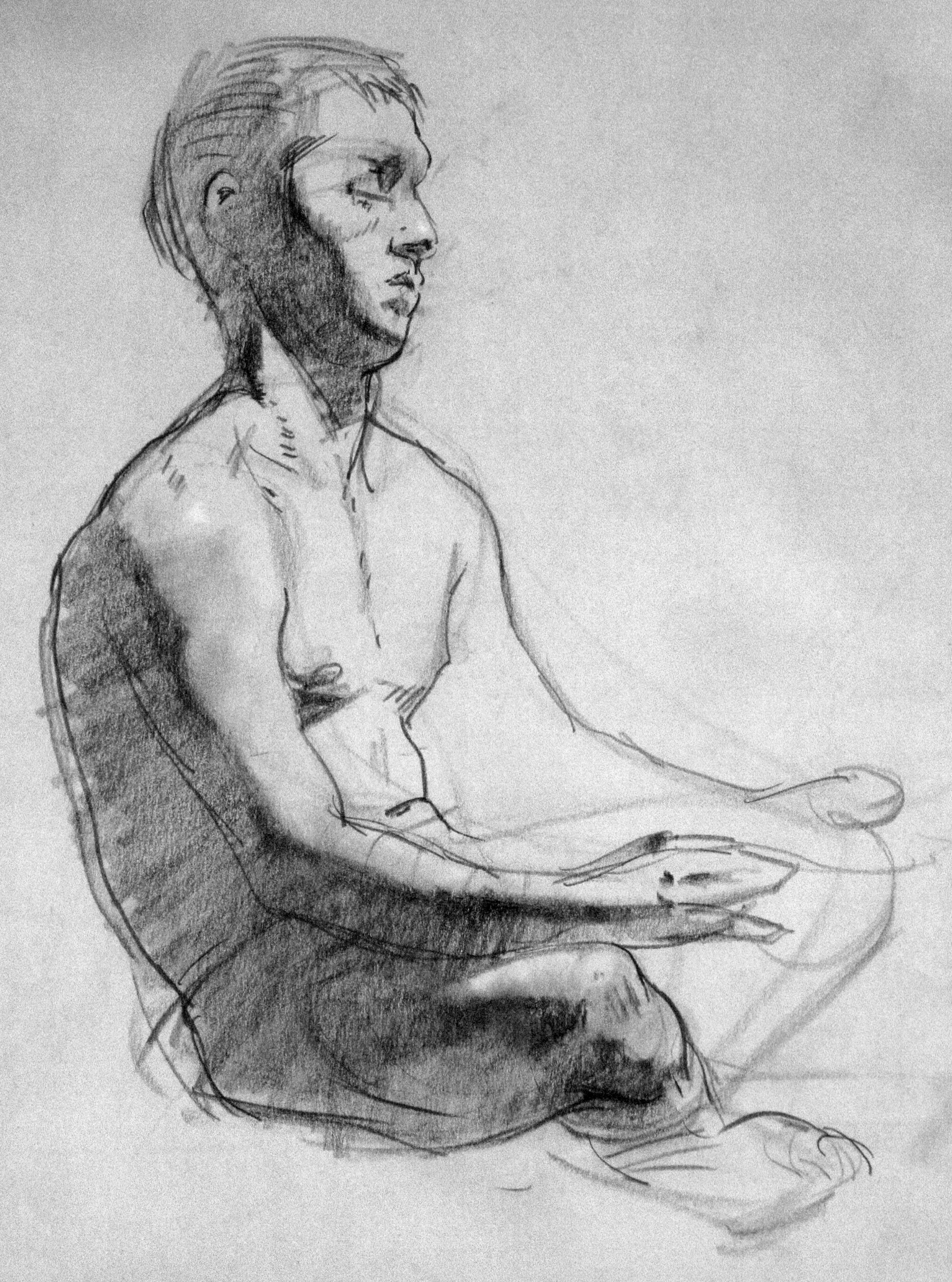

the
QUICK POSE

A COMPILATION OF GESTURES
AND THOUGHTS ON FIGURE DRAWING

Erin Meads

DOVER PUBLICATIONS
Garden City, New York

ACKNOWLEDGMENTS

Special thanks to Mary Sauer, Kristal Lindheimer, Michelle Erickson, and Amy Christensen for helping me get my thoughts into words. Thank you to the fantastic models from the Department of Visual Arts at Brigham Young University. Without them, this publication would not exist. Thank you to my students and for their patience with me. Often times I feel as though I am the student. Thank you to my teachers and to those who have taught me throughout my life. I appreciate your willingness to share. Thank you to my family and friends who always show great love and support. And lastly, thanks to my husband, Matt, for his constant love and encouragement.

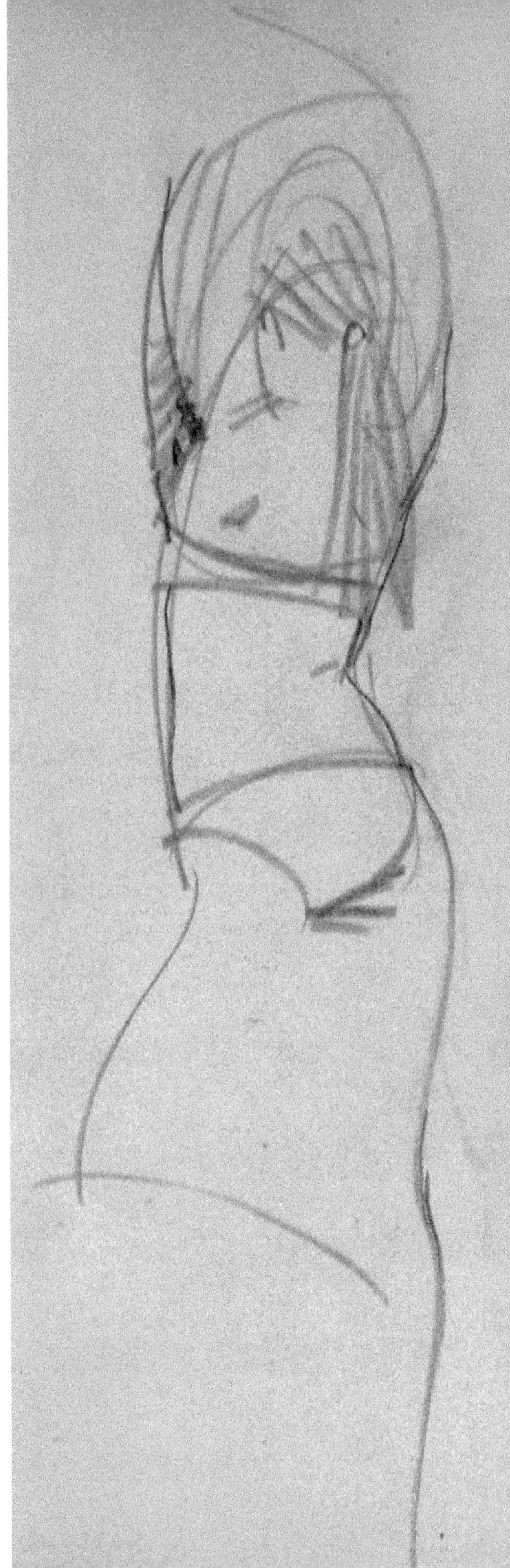

Copyright

Copyright © 2015 by Erin Meads
All rights reserved.

Artwork, text, and book design by the author.
Drawings are on 18" x 24" newsprint with conté or charcoal.

Bibliographical Note

This Dover edition, first published in 2020, is an unabridged republication of the work originally published by Erin Meads in 2015.

Library of Congress Cataloging-in-Publication Data

Names: Meads, Erin, author.
Title: The quick pose: a compilation of gestures and thoughts on figure
    drawing / Erin Meads.
Description: Garden City, New York: Dover Publications, 2020. | "This
    Dover edition, first published in 2020, is an unabridged republication of
    the work originally published by Erin Meads in 2015."
Identifiers: LCCN 2019039451 | ISBN 0486841367 | ISBN 9780486841366
Subjects: LCSH: Human figure in art. | Figure drawing—Technique.
Classification: LCC NC765 .M395 2020 | DDC 743.4—dc23
LC record available at https://lccn.loc.gov/2019039451

Manufactured in the United States of America
84136703
www.doverpublications.com

CONTENTS

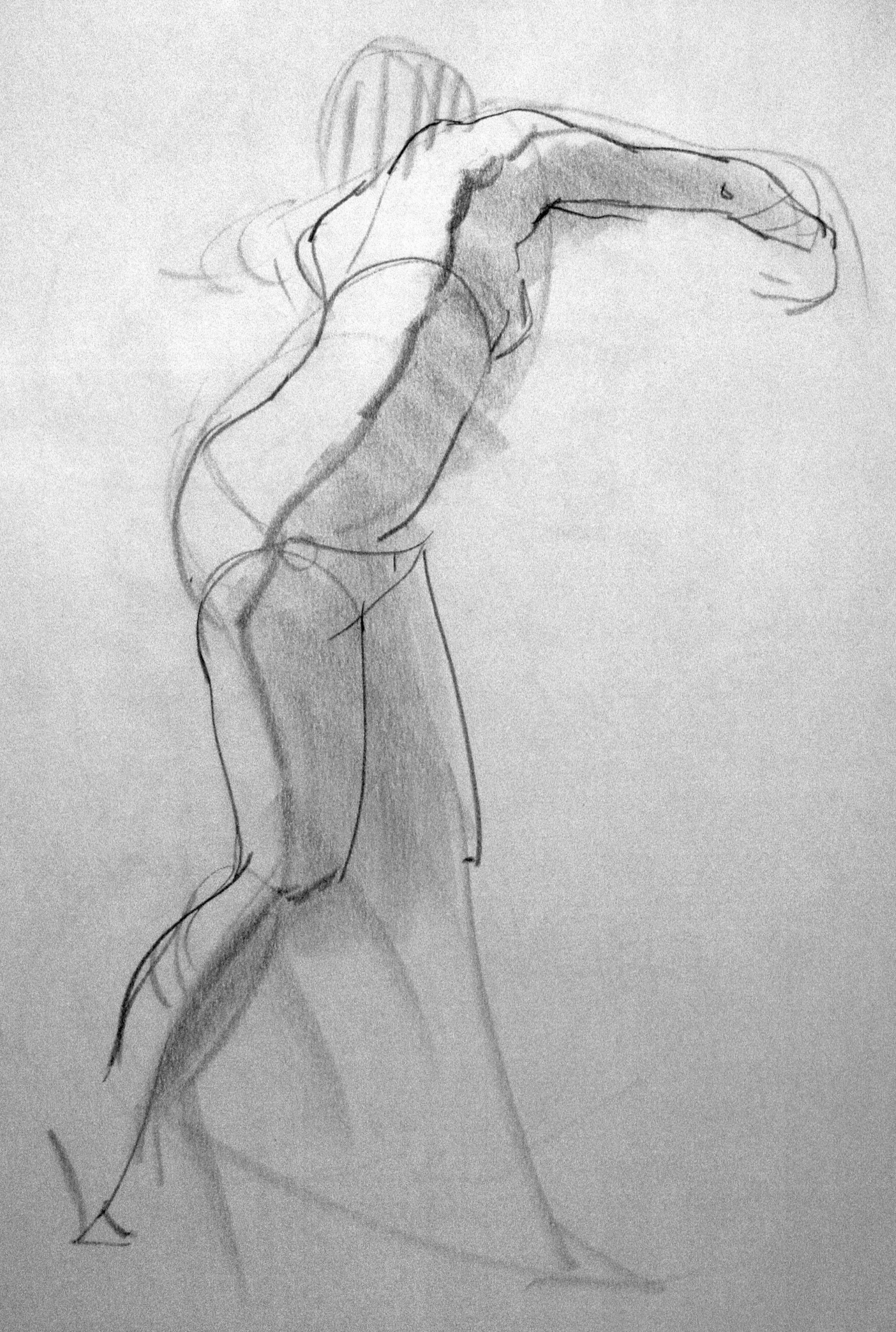

FOREWORD

by Mary Sauer

I met Erin in 2007 when she and I were both undergraduate art students. We later were apprentices together in the same studio when we were still developing as artists, in an environment rich with talented instructors and mentors. We have been in a number of workshops together over the years in locations as varied as Jackson Hole and Manhattan. As I have looked back over my art education, I see how rare great instruction to art students really is, and how difficult it can be to get a holistic understanding of traditional drawing as skill-based art diminishes in importance throughout the country. Many art teachers would rather spend time discussing the philosophical meaning of a gesture rather than the basic principles of how a drawing achieves convincibility. Frustratingly, distortion and obscurity are encouraged and emotion is valued more highly than expression with accuracy. It was my experience in art departments at universities for both my Bachelor's and Master's degrees that the only departments that valued traditional drawing skills were the illustration and animation programs. I find it amazing that many in the art world, including some art teachers, dismiss the need for strong figure drawing skills in these and all other disciplines as commercialism instead of embracing those skills as invaluable to an artist's development.

I believe that the concepts learned through drawing the figure apply to all aspects of art-making and can be interpreted by every artist differently as they develop their abilities. The figure has always been my favorite subject in art, both in painting and drawing, and building a portfolio of excellent figure drawings is, in my opinion, vital to creating everything from graphic novels to historic narrative paintings to abstract expressionist work. I have always admired Erin's talent to capture the figure, and her drawings truly are a testament to her understanding of the concepts that drive her work. Ever since I have known her, she has had an uncanny ability to translate a three-dimensional model into a two-dimensional reality and has done us all a great service by articulating her methods for doing so. I believe that artists who read this text will have the most clear and concise explanation of drawing quick poses that I have ever come across without having to take a handful of costly workshops from teachers across the country, if you are lucky enough to know which ones to take. Improved drawing does take time, but I am convinced that reading this book and utilizing its concepts will drastically speed up that process and help your drawings reach a more sophisticated level as you learn how to correct your misconceptions. But mostly, I hope that the information in this book will continue to increase your understanding of drawing the figure and feed future generations the fuel to combat obscurity of representational art.

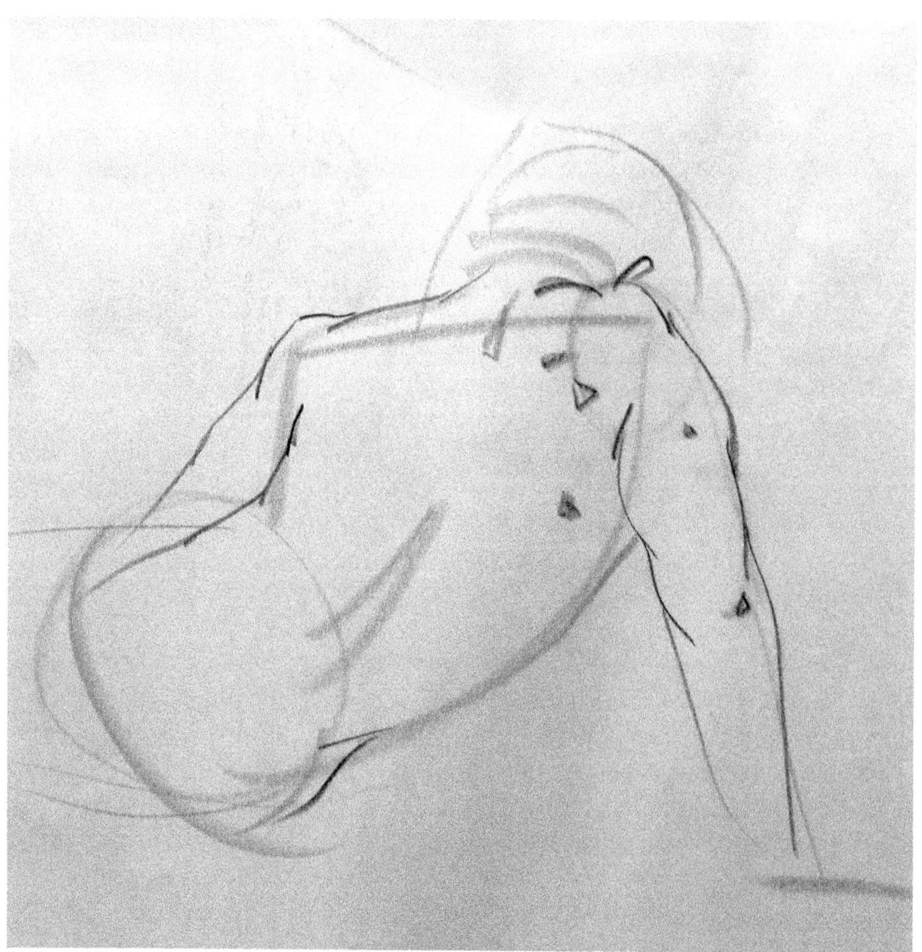

INTRODUCTION

My purpose in writing this book was not initially for instruction. I simply wanted to make some of my recent drawings accessible to those who might be interested in them. Although the idea was there, beginning work on the book got put off for over a year, mostly because I just didn't make the time to sit down and put it together. Looking back now, I'm glad for the delay because during that time frame, my ideas, methods, and confidence improved as I continued to teach figure drawing. I wanted to share how this happened, so I ended up writing a book with instruction.

Figure drawing is not an easy task. In fact, learning these concepts can be down right frustrating in many instances. From my own experience in my art education, I often gained the understanding of a certain principle when I heard it taught by more than one person. Since a standardized curriculum for art education across the country does not exist, these concepts are taught in many different ways (if even taught at all). Sometimes a principle in figure drawing that is presented by one teacher will not sink in until another teacher presents that same principle to you again. Perhaps this text will do this as I offer another perspective on figure drawing, and specifically, the quick pose.

I am lucky to have been able to study with some inspiring people. Each has given me something in the development of my own drawing method. Reflecting on their teachings has ultimately given me my figure drawing class prospectus, which is essentially the text of this book. I was surprised at how quickly the book evolved while writing, and I give credit to the people who sowed seeds of inspiration in my head. I believe every artist I have studied with has contributed in shaping me into who I am today and instilling in me methods and beliefs pertaining to art. Although it is second nature at this point, I step back from my work and realize how heavily I rely on their teachings each time I draw.

It may be important for me to note here that while progressing as an artist, it is often typical to experience what I call artistic identity crises. The question during these times is often, *whom am I supposed to draw and paint like?* The correct answer is *you*. At first it is hard to know what *you* draw or paint like. Rely on the knowledge gained from teachers, instructors, and artists you admire, and then merely seek to understand your subject. With practice and continual study, your voice will show through.

Teaching has been a great learning opportunity for me. I often tell my students that as a teacher, I am far luckier than they are because I will get more out of the class experience than they will. I say this only half in jest, knowing full well it is true. It happens every time. Not only does teaching allow me to draw and study alongside the students, but I get to learn from them as well.

I have chosen to write a book on figure drawing, and more specifically, the quick pose, which I define as drawings under 20 minutes. A large majority of the drawings included in this book took three to five minutes. The reasons I have more drawings in this range are 1) they take less time, so I can do more of them in a typical three-hour session, and 2) since they are short, models are able to do more dynamic poses, which I prefer. I like when the figure twists, bends, and stretches; and I like the challenge of getting the essence of the pose in a limited amount of time. It requires making quick decisions about what is important enough to include and, probably even more significantly, what is unimportant and should *not* be included. Some of my favorite old master drawings are simple gestures that have so few lines yet are so precise. There is something beautiful in this simplicity.

I have learned to take the pressure off myself by worrying less about producing an accurate copy or a photo-like replica of the model and more about catching the essence, spirit, or feeling of the pose instead. When drawings lack energy, they look boring even if they are perfectly accurate. Figure drawings look more like the model when they *feel* like the model.

The drawings I have chosen to include in this book come from my time teaching at Brigham Young University, where I had the opportunity to teach figure drawing for the Department of Visual Arts, specifically to Illustration and Animation majors. It is exciting to teach students who have great capacity and enthusiasm to learn. I love the atmosphere in the classroom. I love the students. I love our models. And most importantly, I love to draw.

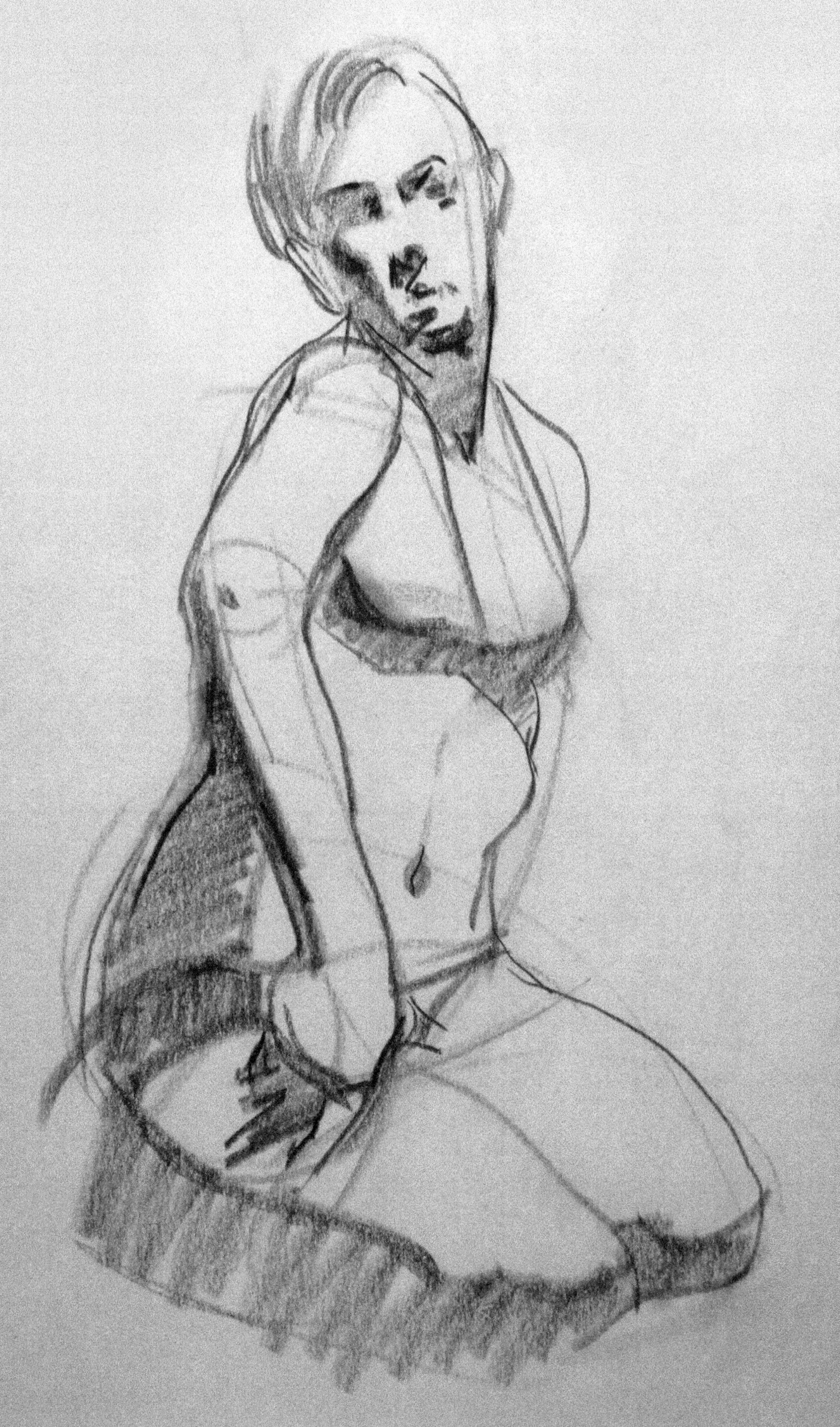

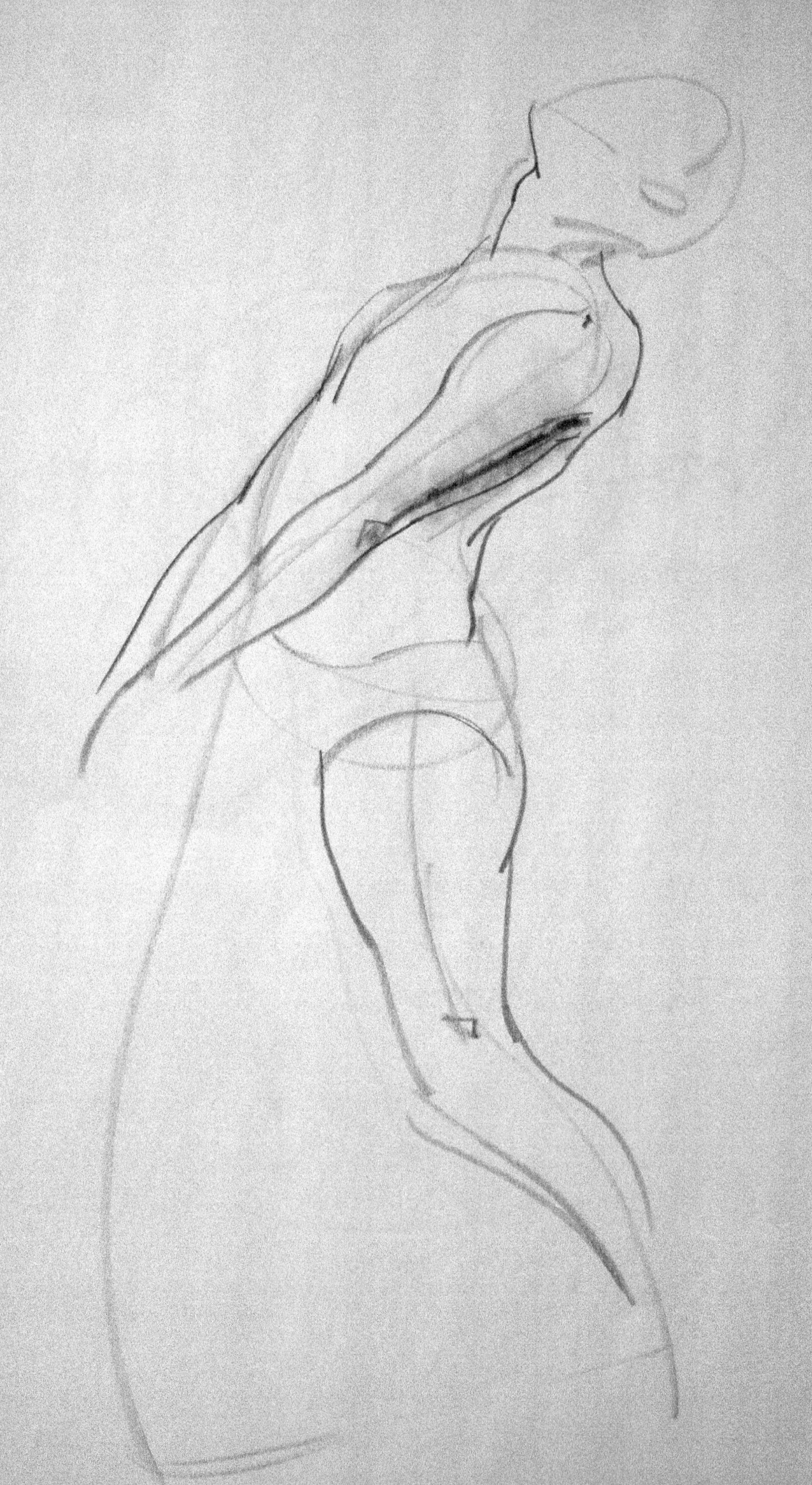

GESTURE

GESTURE

The word gesture, in general terms, refers to the communication of an idea or feeling without the use of words. In a similar fashion, gesture drawing is simply capturing the fundamental nature or feeling of the pose with a minimal amount of mark making. Gesture is the energy in a pose, and drawings that lack energy also lack interest.

When I talk about gesture in my drawing class, I start out by asking the students what the word gesture, in terms of drawing, means to them. Most of them respond with the notion that it is a very quick drawing to get warmed up. I agree with that statement but would add that a gesture can also be an end in itself. I do *not* believe a gesture drawing is a mindless waving of the arm and the conté. Instead, I believe it is very mind involved. Gesture drawings help get the brain warmed up just as much as they help to reacquaint the artist with the figure and their drawing tool. For me, it takes a good 20-minute session or two before I feel like I am fully warmed up both mentally and physically.

Before putting the conté or charcoal on the paper, make sure to take in the pose. Try to make a plan of action before beginning. I would say nearly 90 percent of figure drawing happens in the artist's head; the other 10 percent is in the hand. Each gesture should be thought out no matter the length of time given. Granted, there will not be ample time to sit, ponder, and meditate before the time is up and the model is on to a new pose. Quick decisions are required. My students are sometimes frustrated when they don't work quickly enough. My answer for them is probably even more frustrating: "keep practicing." The hard truth is that the more exposure a student has to the model and the more familiar they become with the human figure, the quicker they will be able to anticipate certain bends and stretches every human body takes. It is then that they are able to work quickly and concisely, and the fun begins.

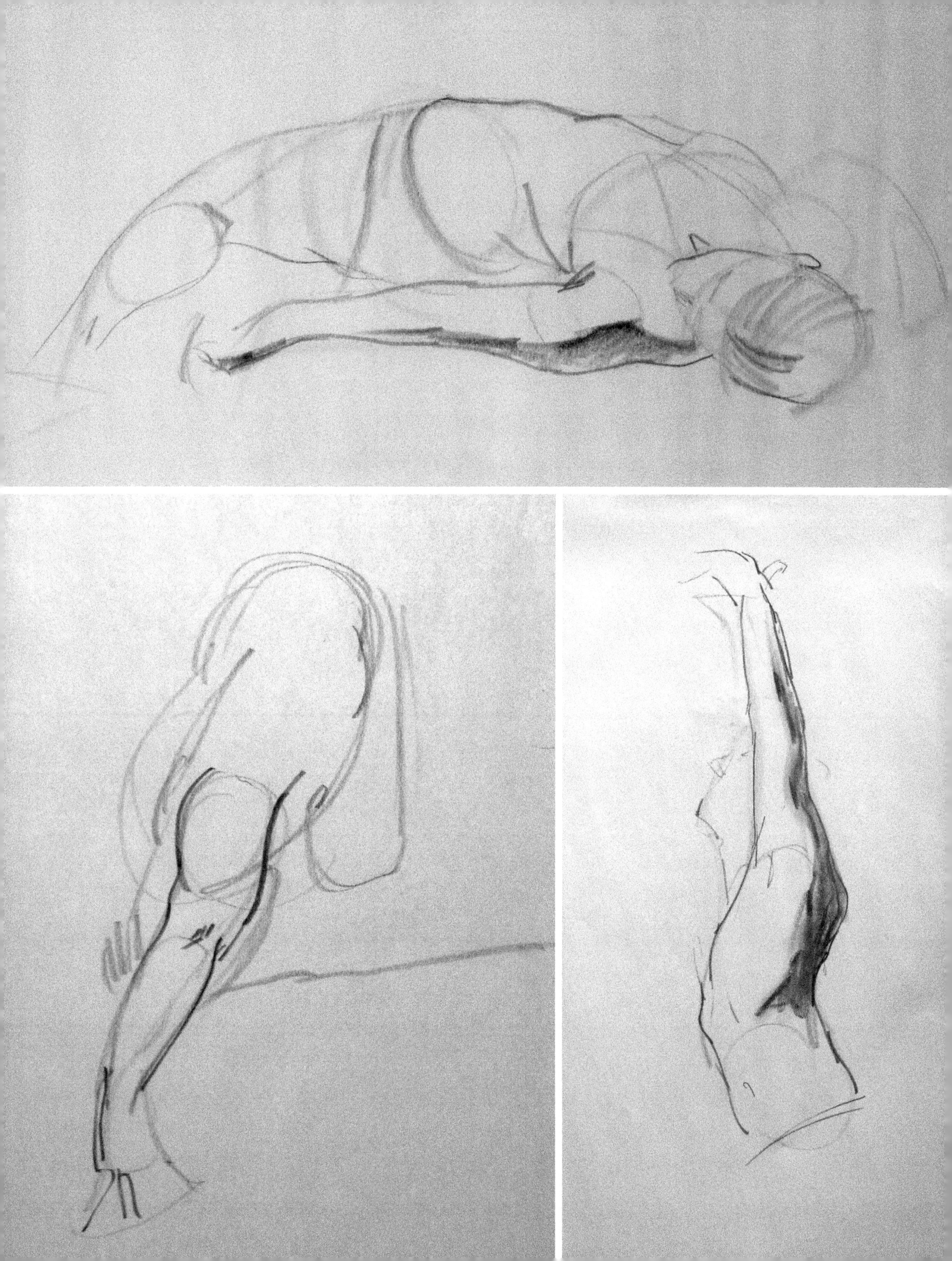

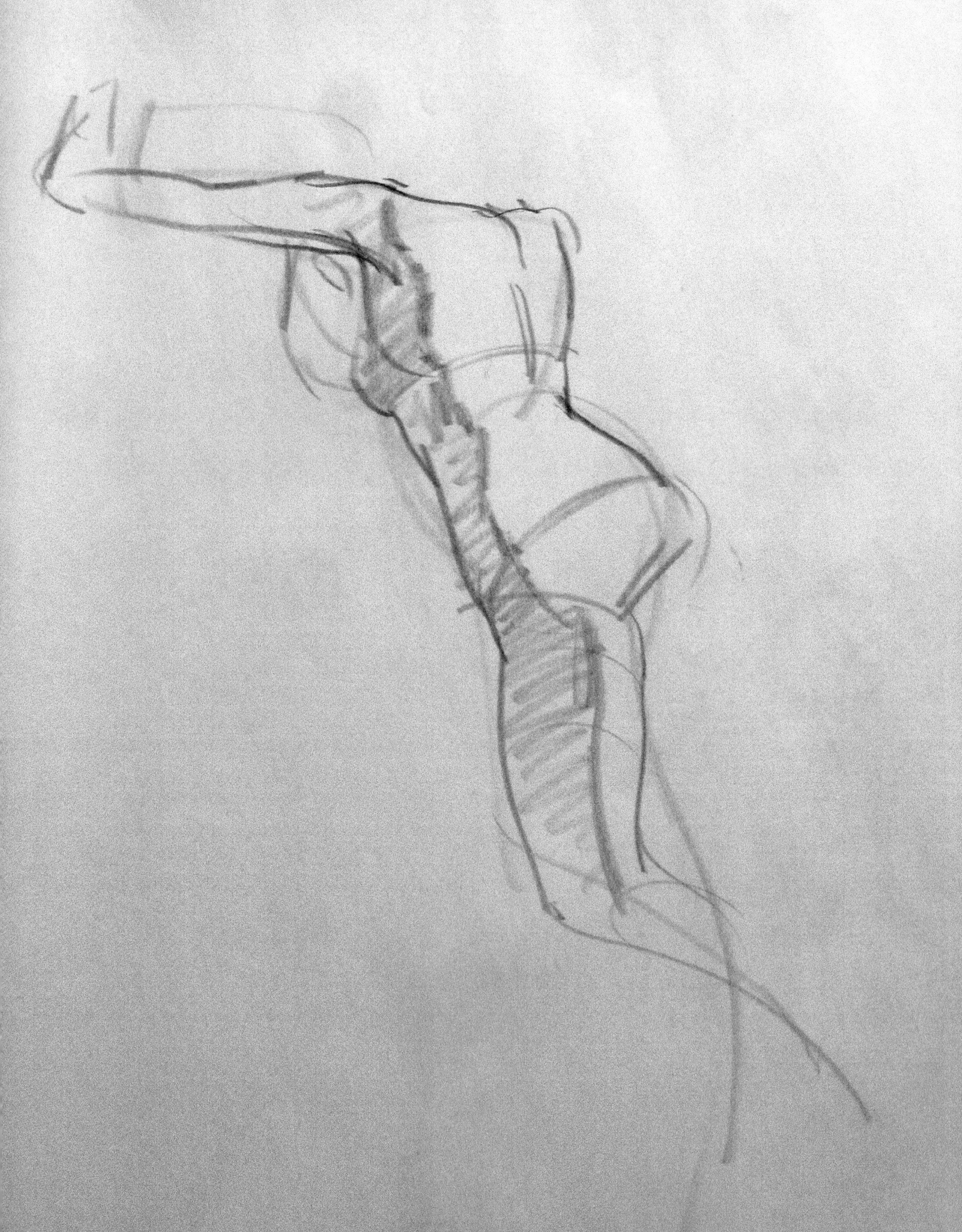

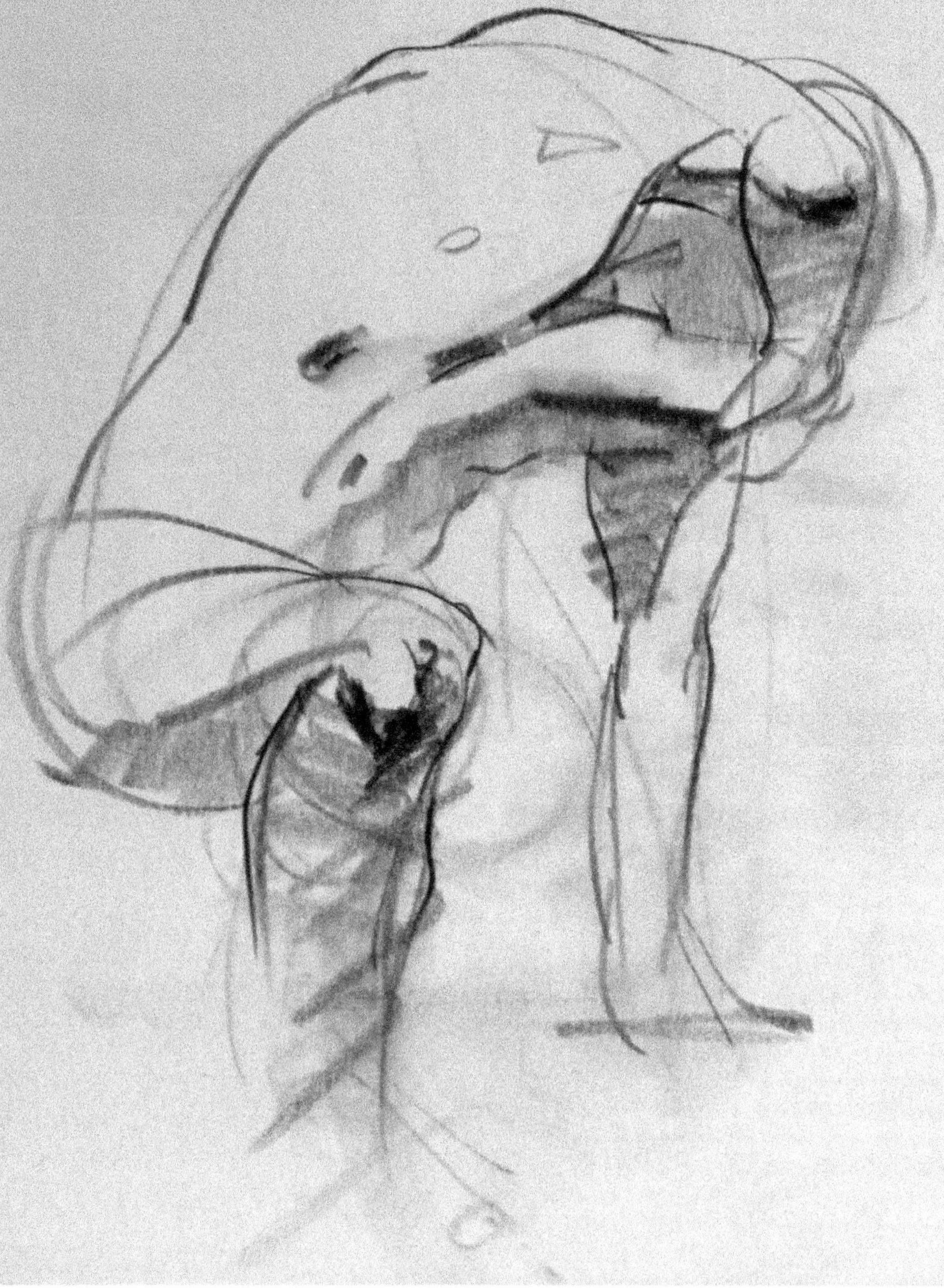

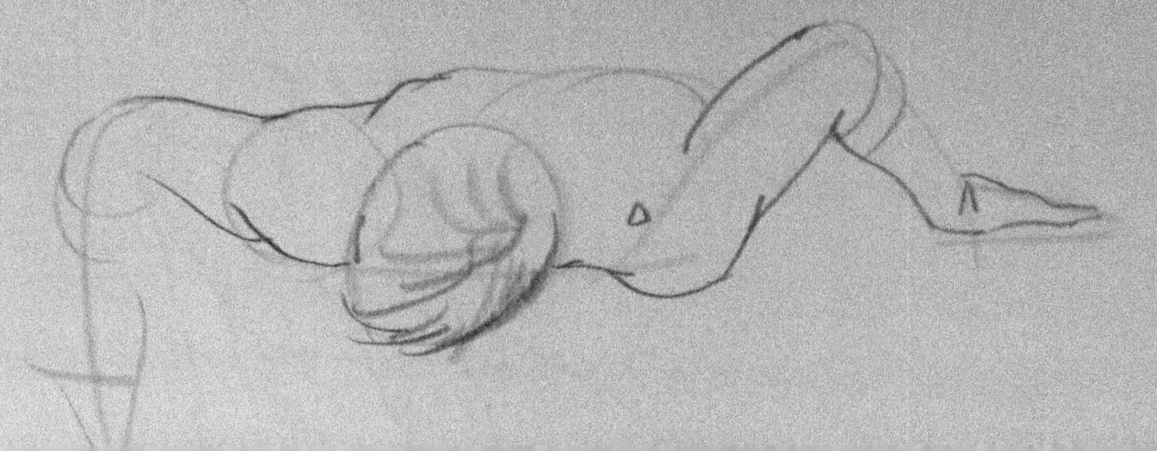

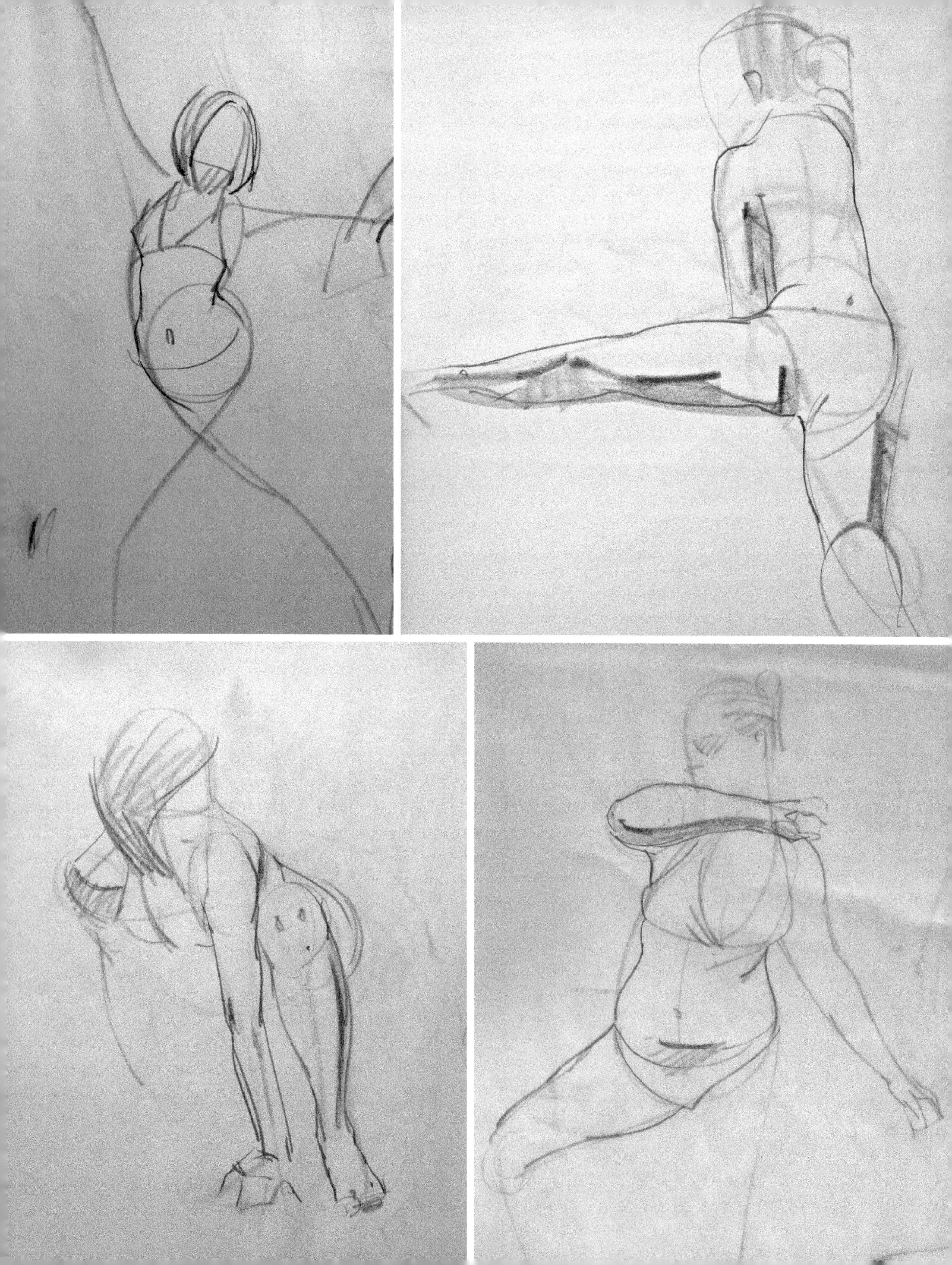

CONFIDENT LINES

New students often begin drawing gestures with lots of short, sketchy marks because they are afraid of making one long continuous line that may end up being wrong. Working this way, however, creates stiffness in the figure and uses up precious time. Instead, push for making confident, deliberate lines that take less time and create a stronger, bolder statement. Students are afraid that these confident lines will be inaccurate and their proportions will be off. Unfortunately, this may happen, but usually just in the beginning. As stated before, the more practice, the better result. As students continue to draw, apply new ideas, and become more familiar with the figure, they eventually grasp proportion by eye and can check for accuracy as they draw (additional study of proportion, aside from drawing from life, such as in a sketchbook, would also surely help). In order to improve, it is necessary to let go of what we feel is *safe*. Playing it safe all the time will never lead to improvement. Nothing will change, and growth will not occur. Be willing to take a step backward in order to eventually leap forward. Be brave enough to let go of the need to establish precise proportions and instead, focus on confident line work and capturing an accurate feel or essence of the pose. While this may be scary and uncomfortable at first, eventually it will lead to drawings with believable proportions and beautiful, confident lines.

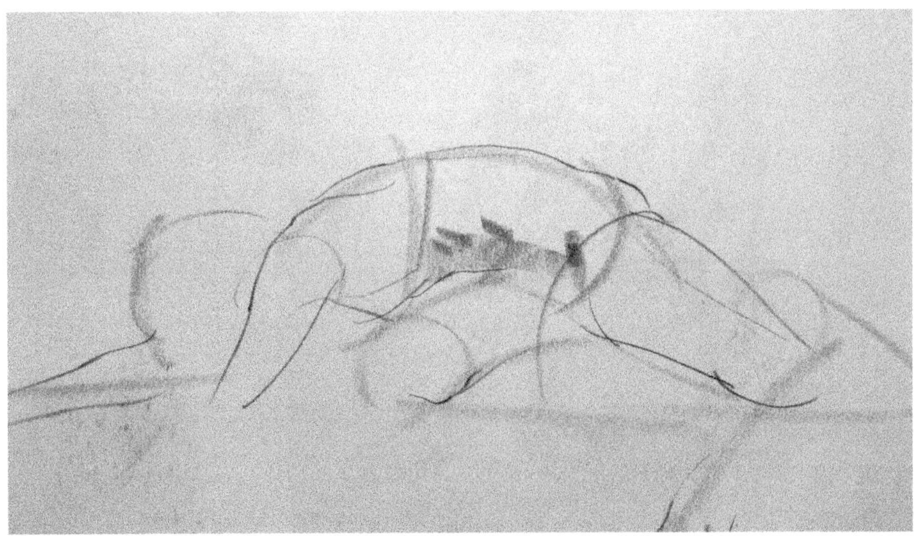

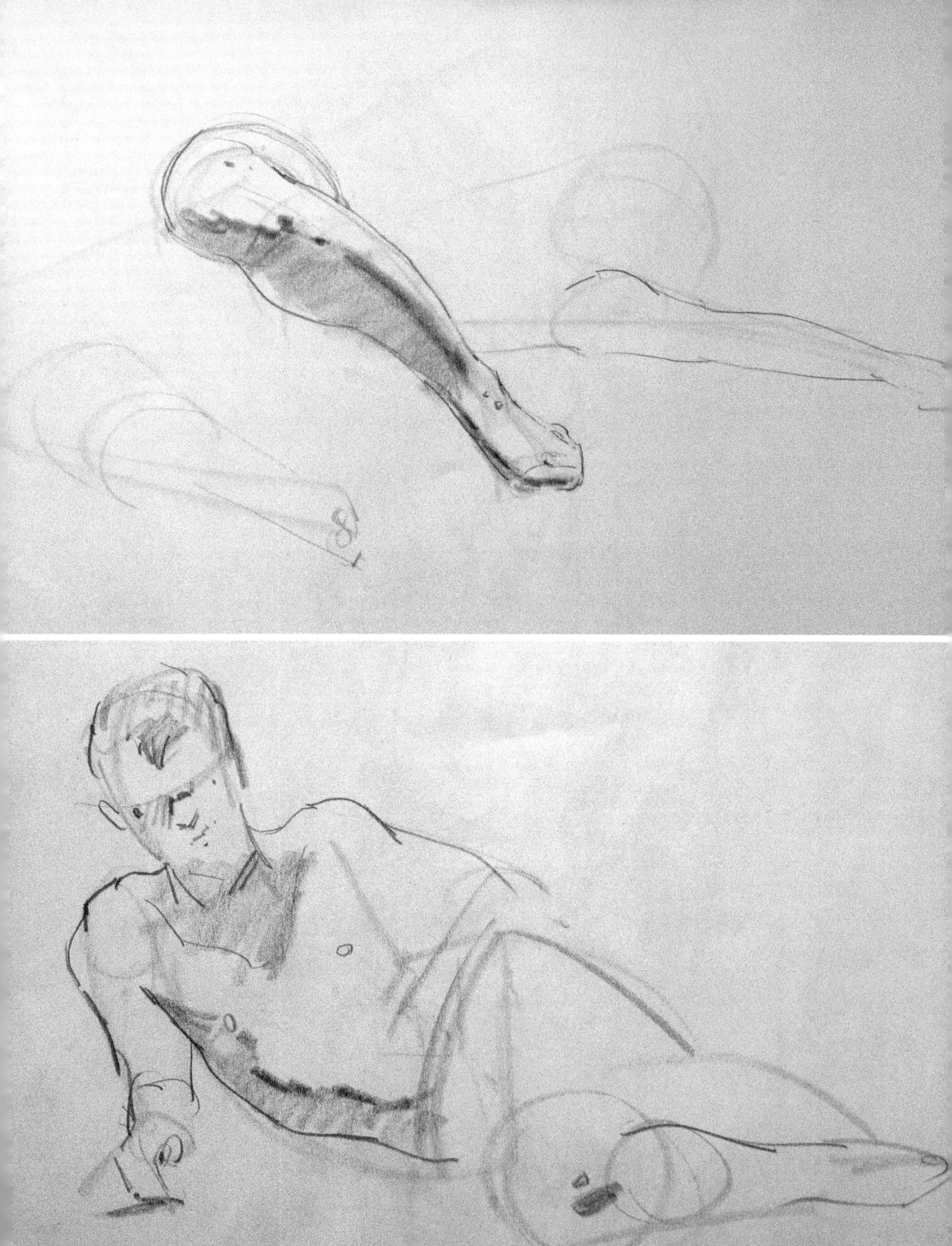

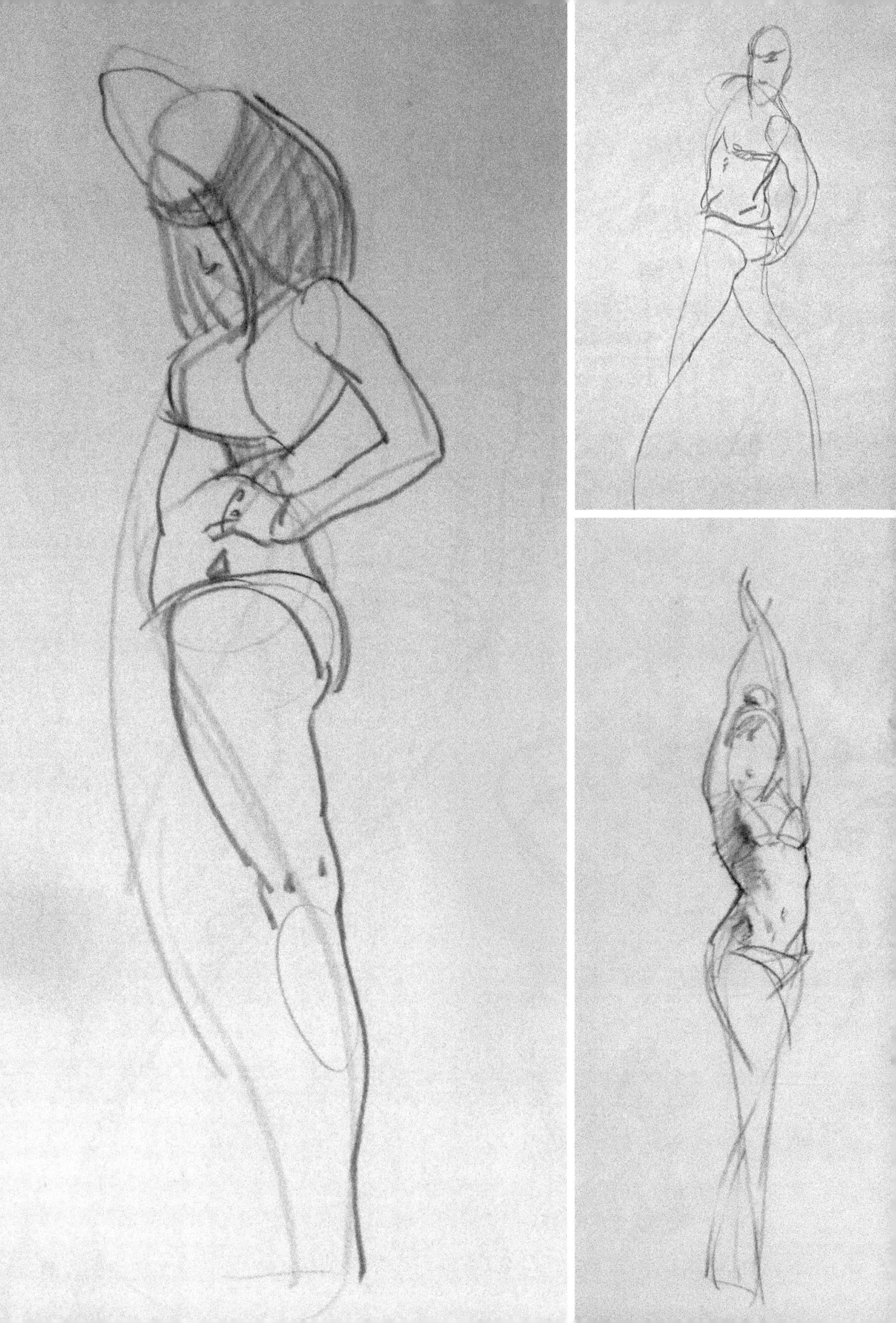

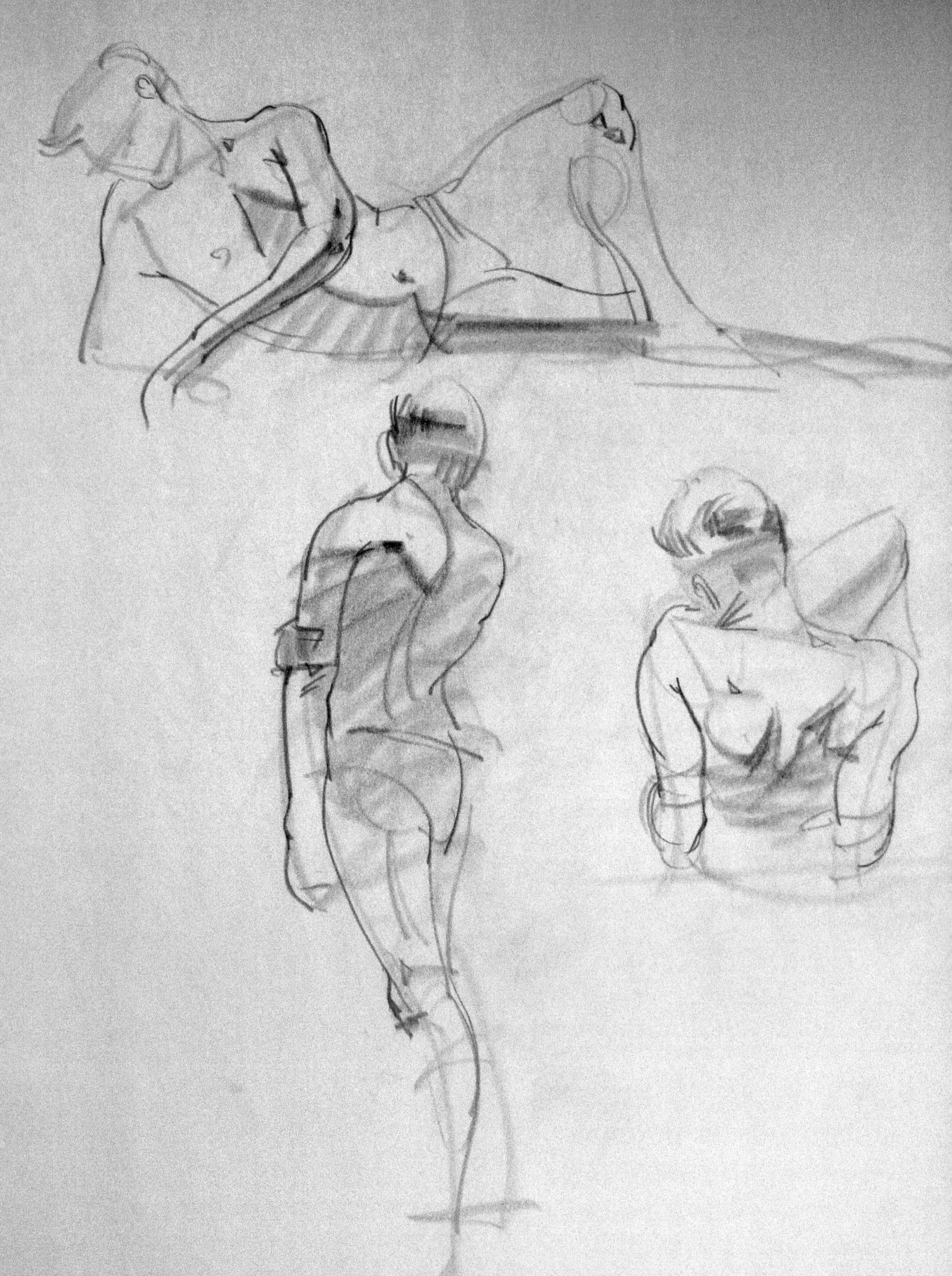

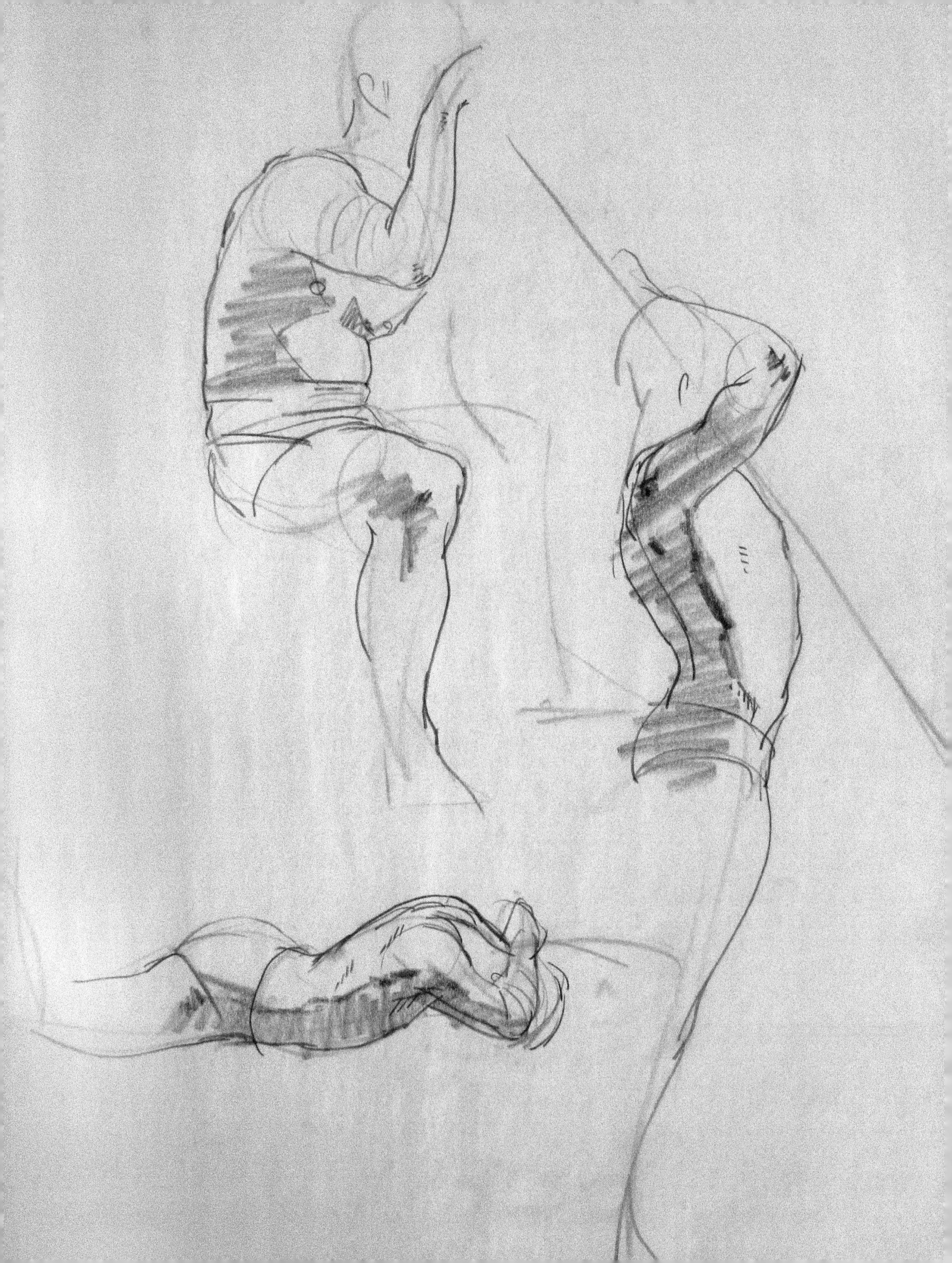

THE FIGURE AS A WHOLE

Often beginner students feel overwhelmed with trying to draw an entire figure in only one or two minutes. How is that even possible with all the intricacies and details of the human body? They are frustrated and perplexed, and they are correct in their bewilderment. There is no possible way to ever get *all* of the information comprising the human figure down on paper in one minute! Pick and choose what is important enough to include. Also decide what *not* to include (e.g., unnecessary information or anything that might distract the viewer from the real importance). This is called editing, and, as can be imagined, a lot of editing is required for one and two-minute poses.

It is also helpful to think about the figure as a whole. It sounds like a pretty simple thing to do, but it is often forgotten when faced with a short pose. For instance, a student might like the position of the head, and so naturally they start there. Before they know it, the time is up and all the student has drawn is part of the head. Instead of using a localized approach like this, aim to work from general to specific in regards to the entire body. Study the large relationships from head to toe first, and only glance briefly at everything else in-between. Work lightly. By using a soft touch in the beginning, these preliminary

lines will act as guides as the drawing progresses, and they might even seem to disappear altogether when it is complete. Using a light touch lessens the pressure to put down a perfect line in the beginning. It gives the artist a chance to ease into the pose and get a feel for the figure as a whole as they continue to edit and refine the drawing in the time allotted. It is hard for some students to grasp the concept of making light lines that are also confident. It is possible, and once this skill is achieved, the student becomes incredibly more efficient and productive in making meaningful marks.

Do not be afraid to draw through the figure, meaning that it is okay to draw on both the inside and outside of the outline (outer contour) of the figure. Working with the big relationships right off the bat helps to quickly see accurate proportions, and also helps to correctly size the drawing on the paper so it does not run off the edges.

No matter how much time is given for a pose, it is always a good idea to see the pose as a whole from the very beginning and to work from big to small. Sometimes I tell my class that they have two minutes (or more) for a drawing, but then I stop them after only one minute. While it is rather funny to me to hear them cry out with surprise and complaints when the time is called, my main reason for doing this is to stress the importance of seeing the figure as a whole early on. My hope is that they will at least have drawn in the big relationships. Upon examination of their drawings, some of the students only have the head or upper body drawn, meaning they have not seen the figure as a whole. Others have, and their drawings account for the entire figure.

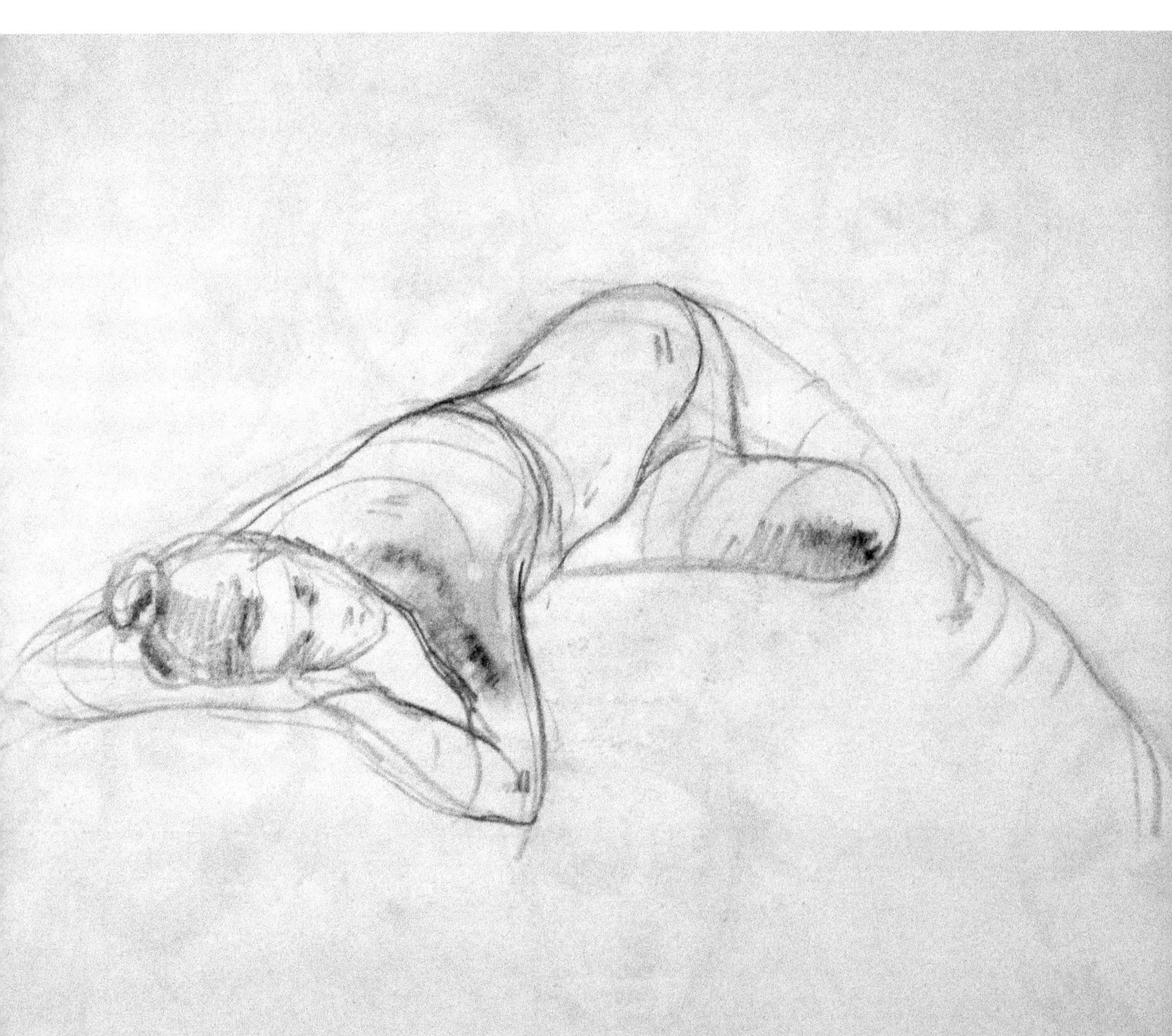

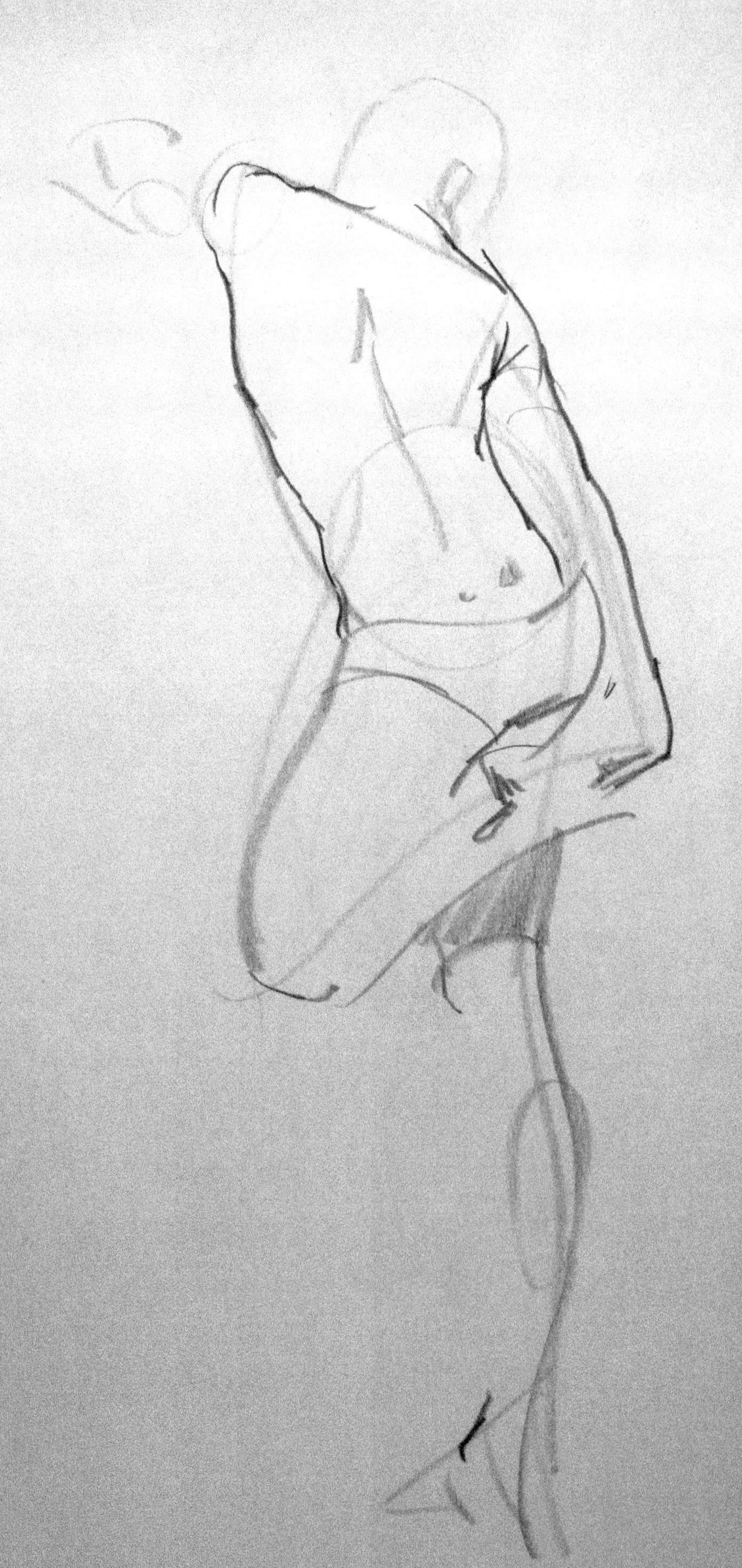

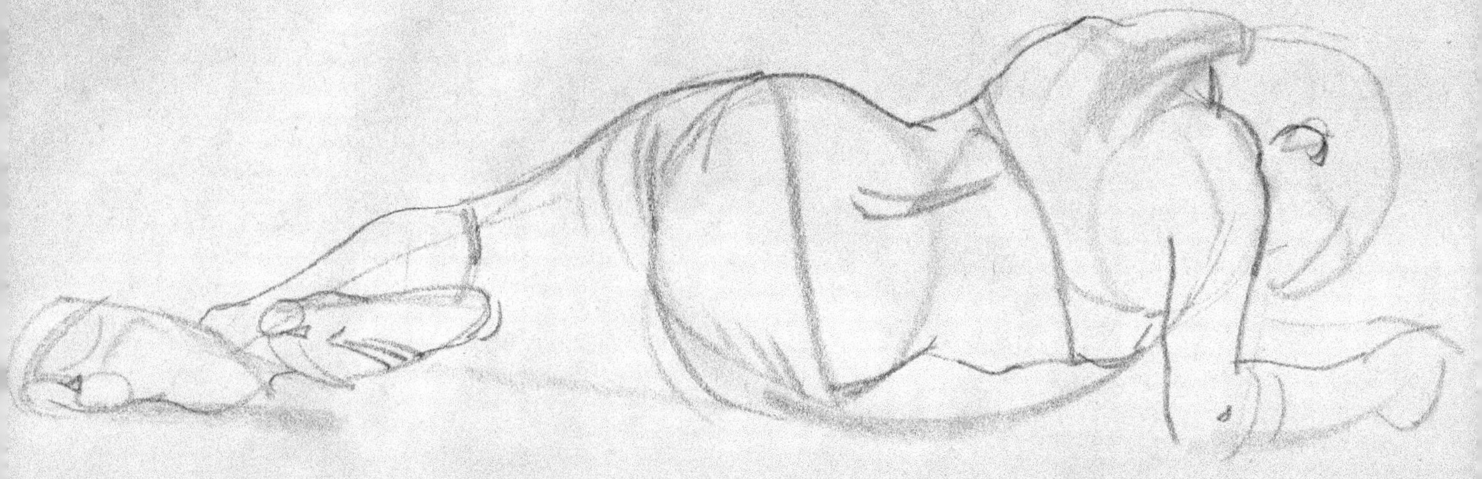

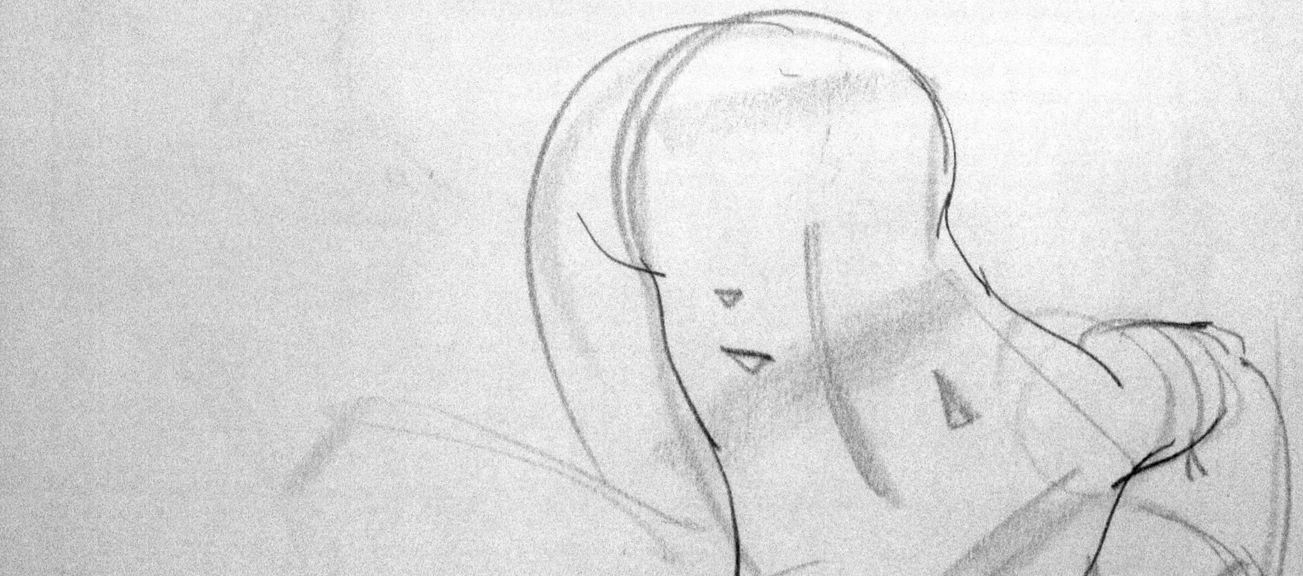

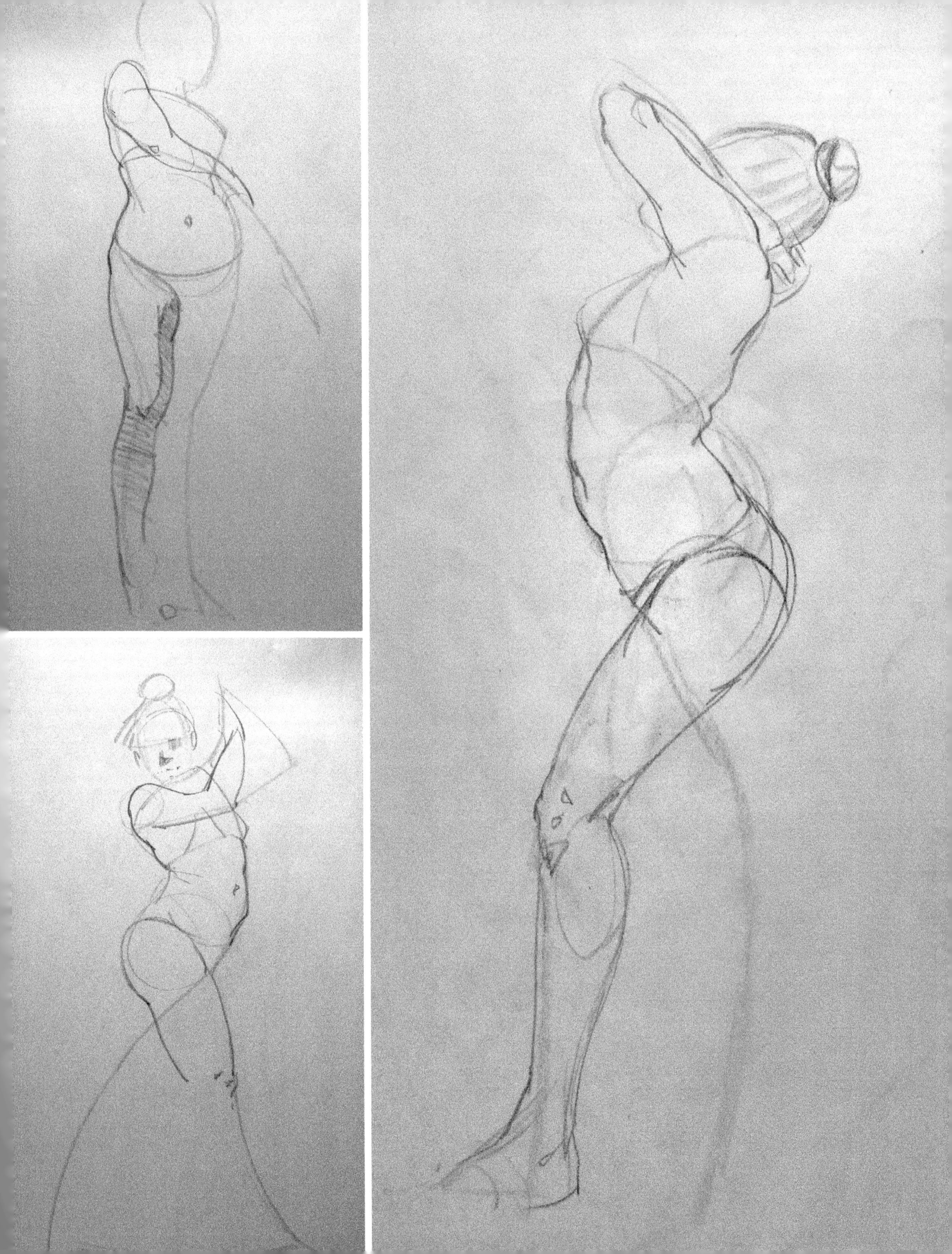

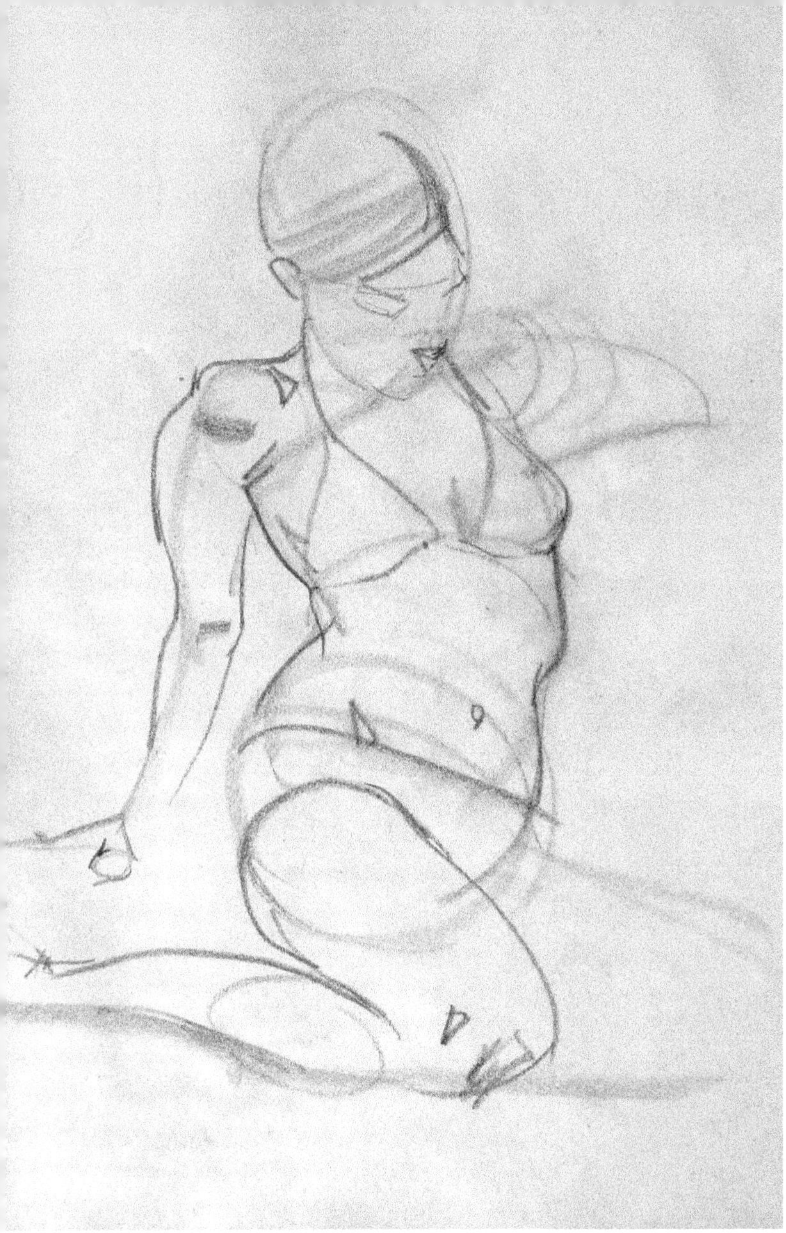

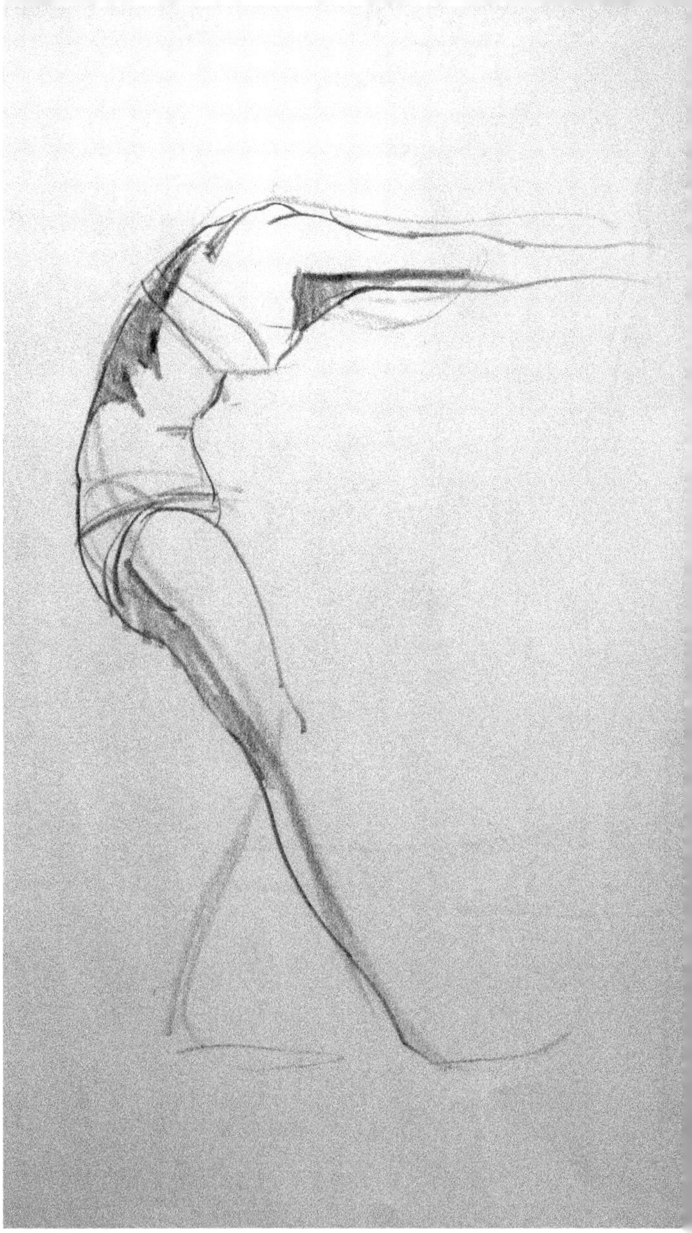

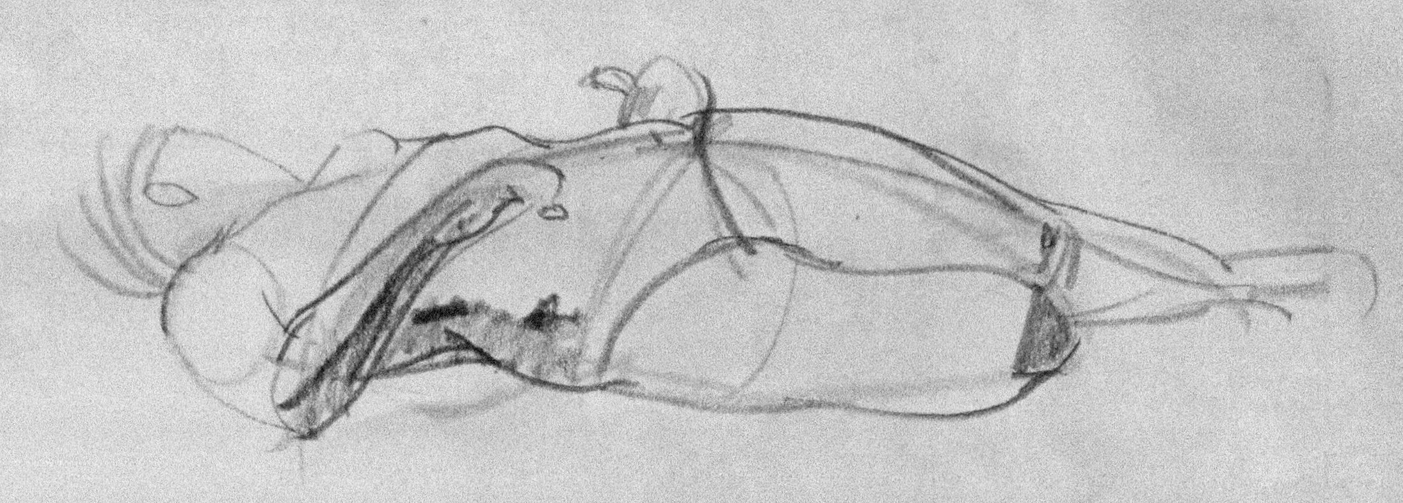

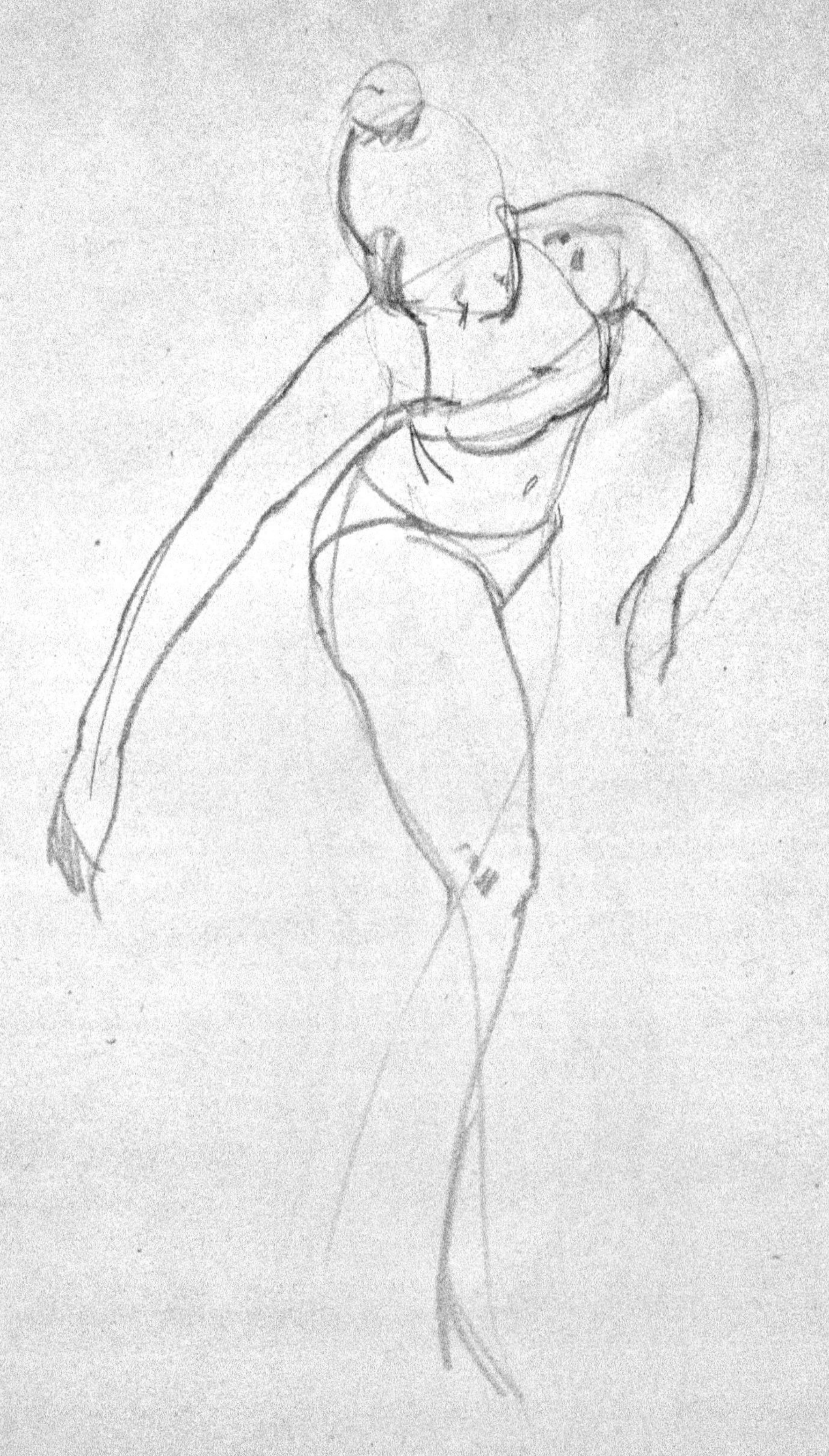

AN AREA OF FOCUS

While it is important to process the figure as a whole, it is also good to have an area of focus as long as the rest of the figure is accounted for in some way; sometimes a simple light line does the job. For example, the head and torso might be the chosen area of focus in a particular pose. In order to keep the legs and lower body at a level of finish that is slightly less than that of the head and torso, the legs might be chosen to be accounted for with a few long, light sweeping lines. While inferior, the legs are accounted for, and the drawing could be stopped at anytime and the viewer would still understand what was happening at that instant in the pose. Great gesture drawings don't necessarily have every portion of the body spelled out. Give the viewer some credit. They can assume the general existence of a foot, for example, so as long as an indication of a foot is made, it will suffice. If there is time left, attention to developing and further refining that foot can be given (remember that light touch?). Give the drawing some sense of hierarchy. It will be more interesting when the viewer knows exactly what to look at first. Eyes are focusing machines, but they can only focus on one thing at a time. Create an order of focus for the viewer to follow.

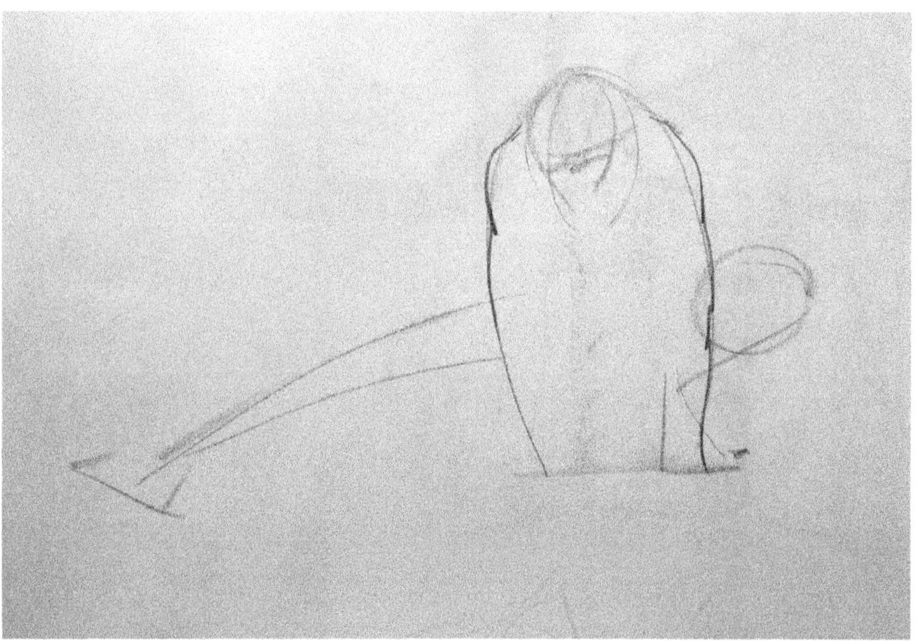

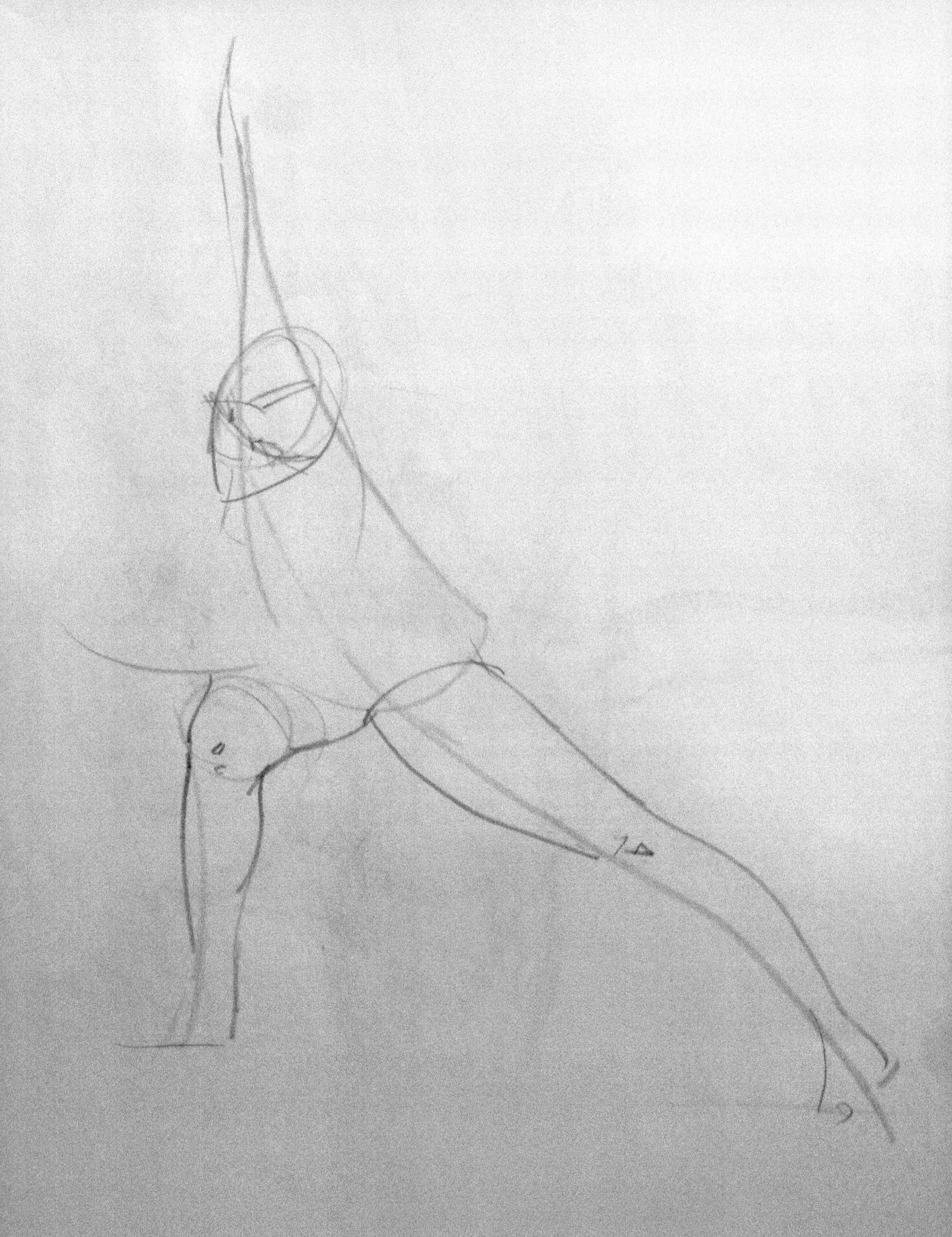

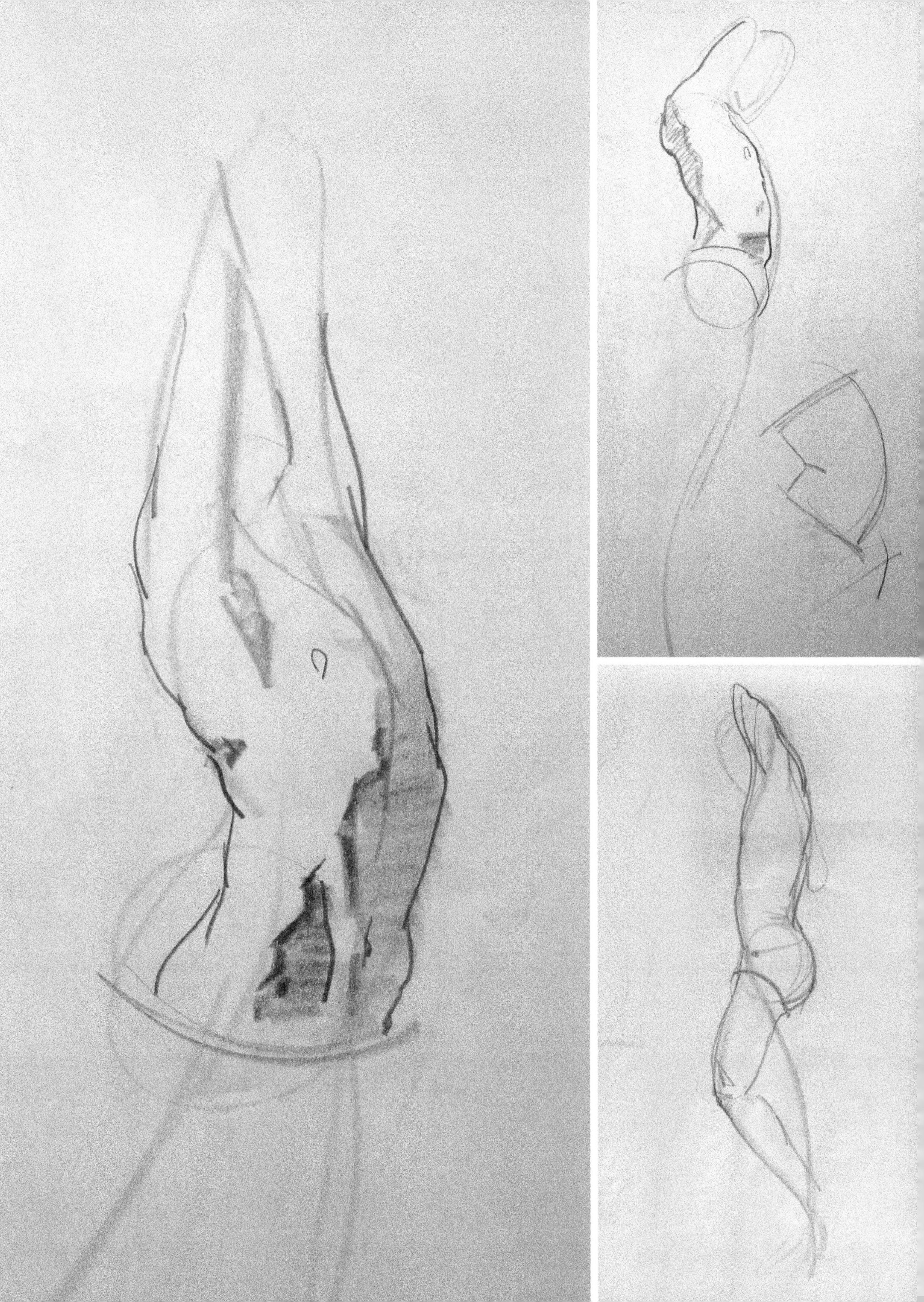

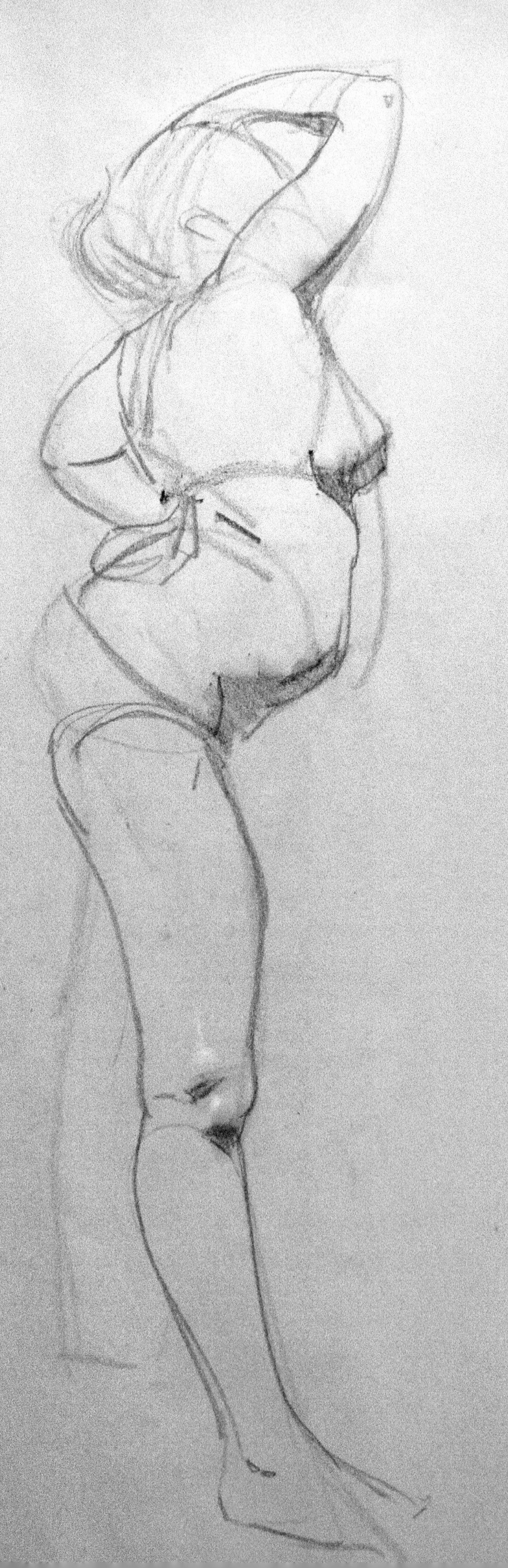

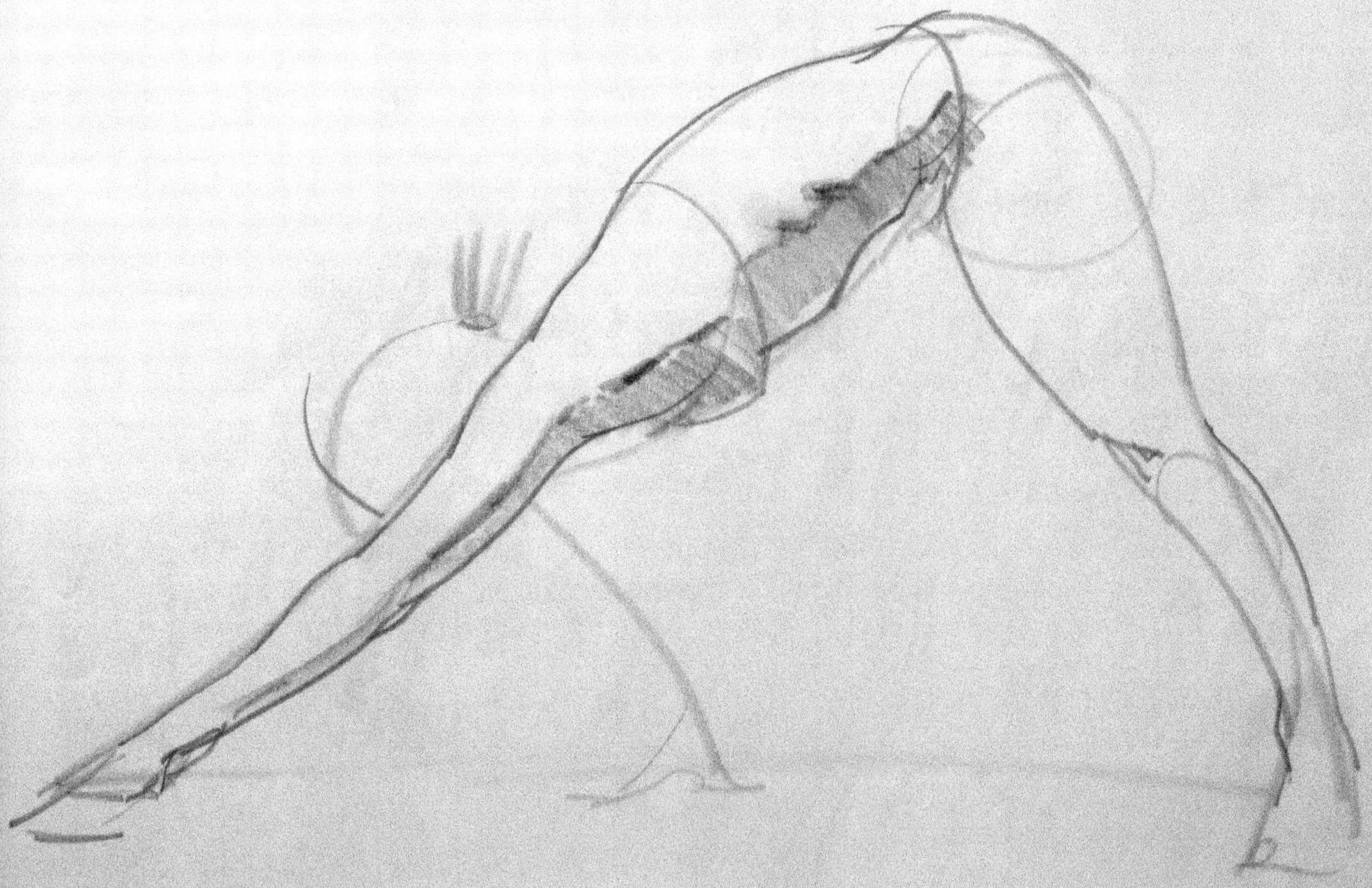

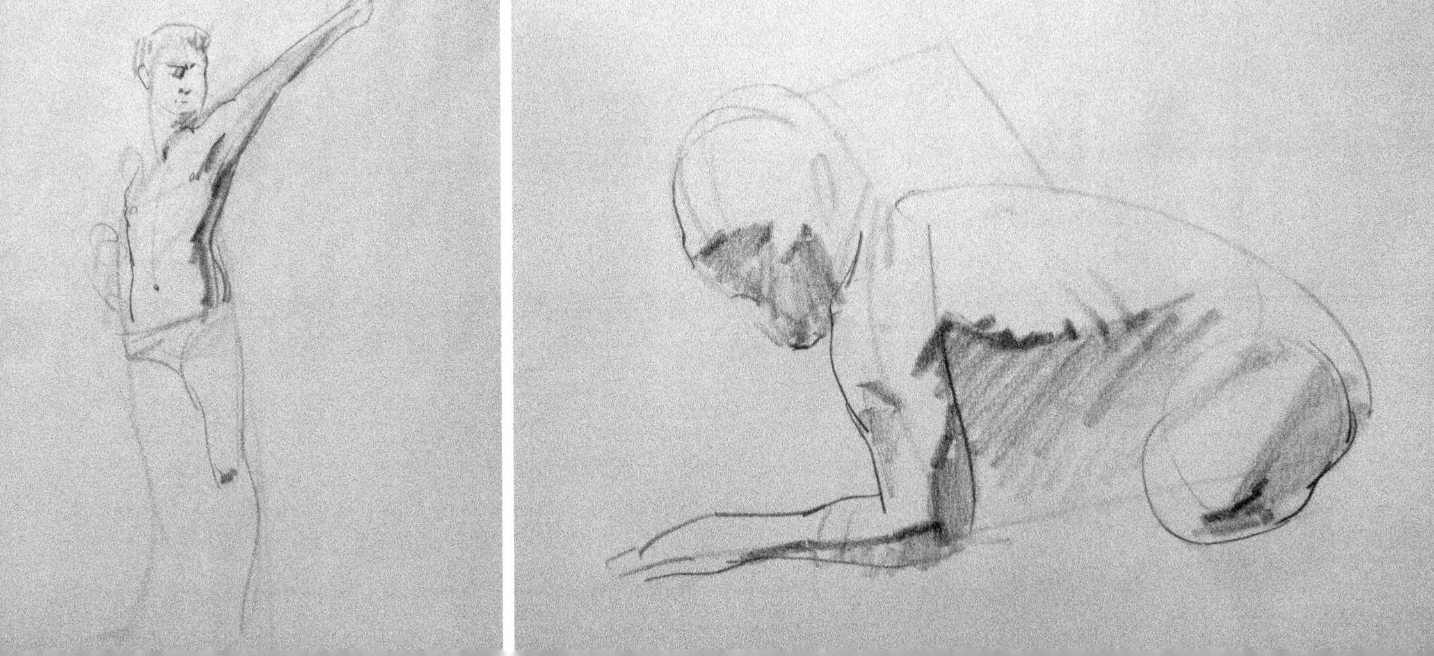

BENDING FORM

Once I began to implement it, the idea of bending form was revolutionary for me, and when my students grasp the concept, I have seen them benefit tremendously as well. Here it is: one side of the body bends as the other side stretches. It is a simple phenomenon that is worth repeating: one side bends, and the other side stretches. The neat thing is that bending form happens everywhere in the body no matter which direction the model is facing. It can be seen from the front, back, side, and almost every angle. Although there is no right answer to the question of where to start a drawing, bending form is usually what I look for first, specifically in the torso. I ask myself, which side of the torso is bending and which side is stretching? Once the bend and stretch of the torso is recognized, a large chunk of the body is taken care of.

Another interesting quality of bending form is that it can be applied to the entire body from head to toe, or it can be broken down into individual parts within.

The image directly adjacent to this text is a duplicate of the drawing on the far right. The dark, overlaid lines illustrate the bend and stretch of the torso, the leg, and the foot. These lines often act as preliminary guides when drawn in lightly in the beginning, and

they help me to remember the overall bend and stretch of the entire body. Look closely at the enlarged image on the far right and you will notice these preliminary lines subtly showing through.

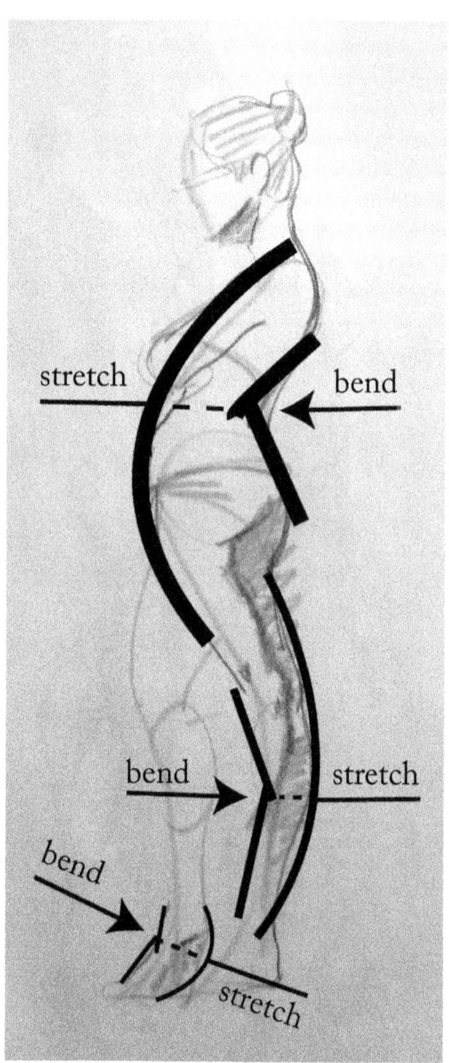

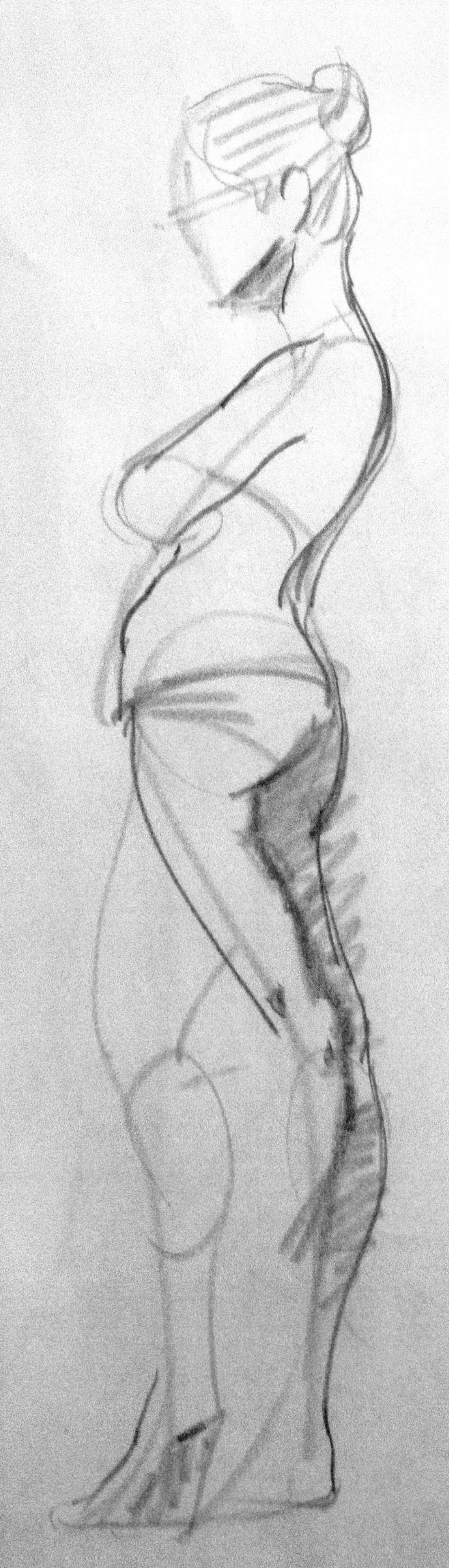

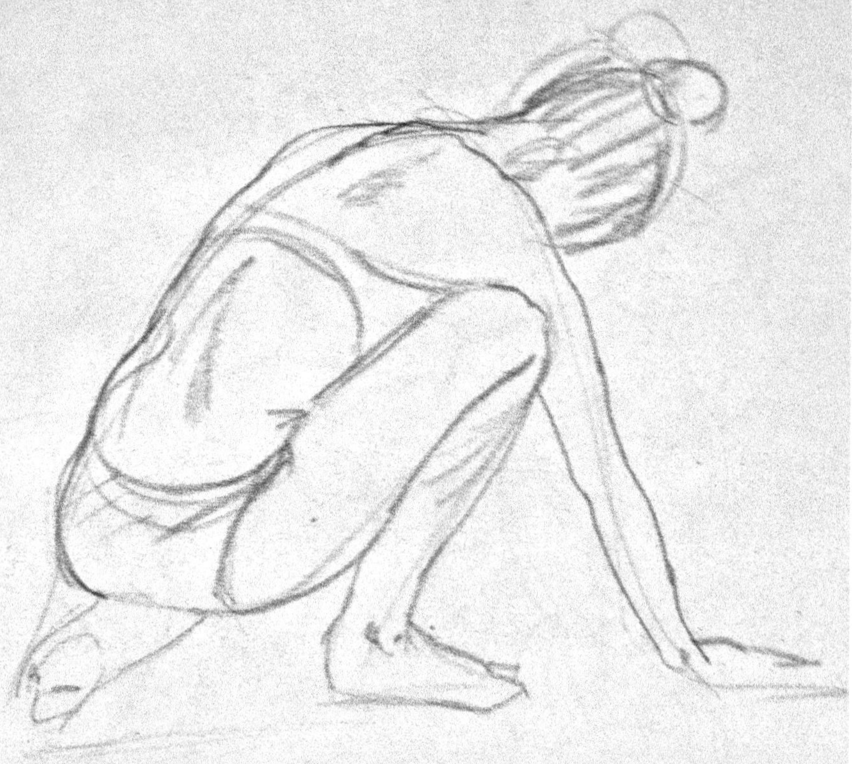

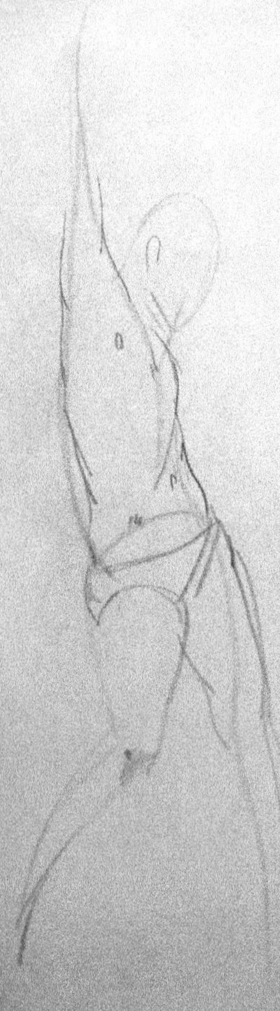

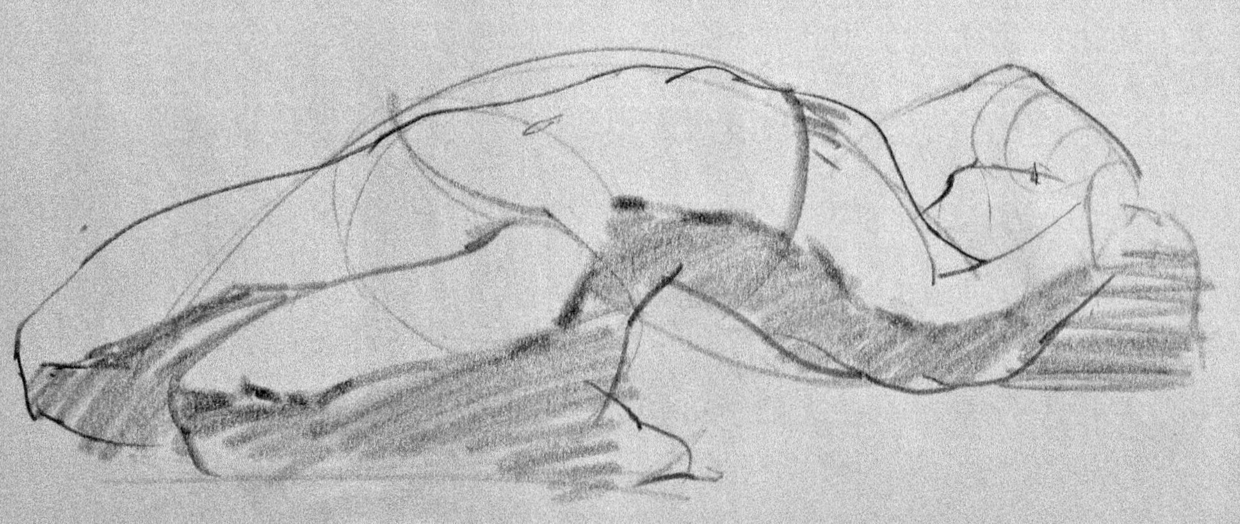

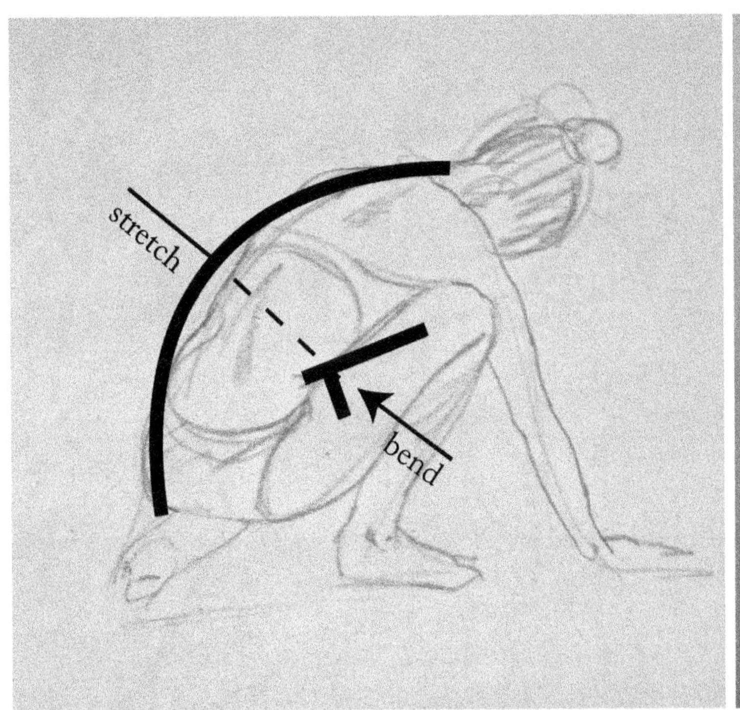

stretch
bend

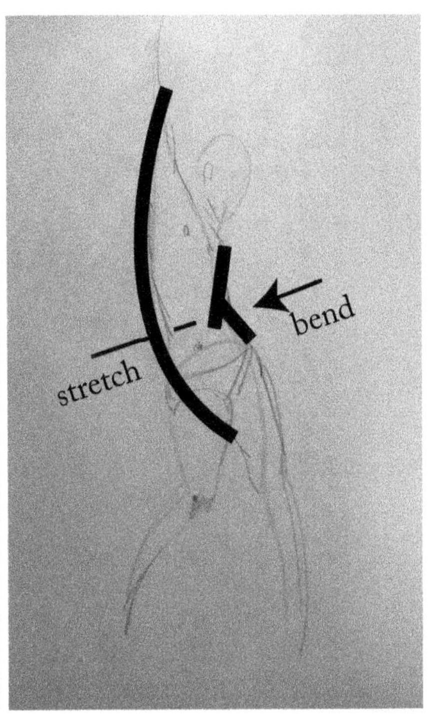

bend
stretch

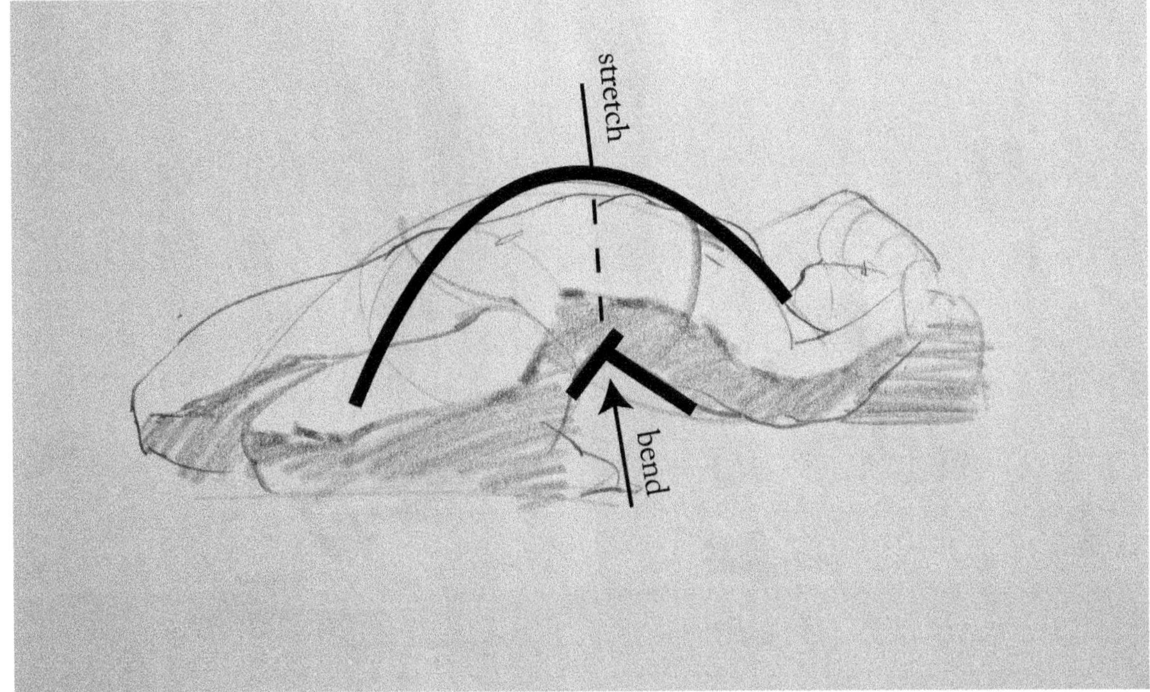

stretch
bend

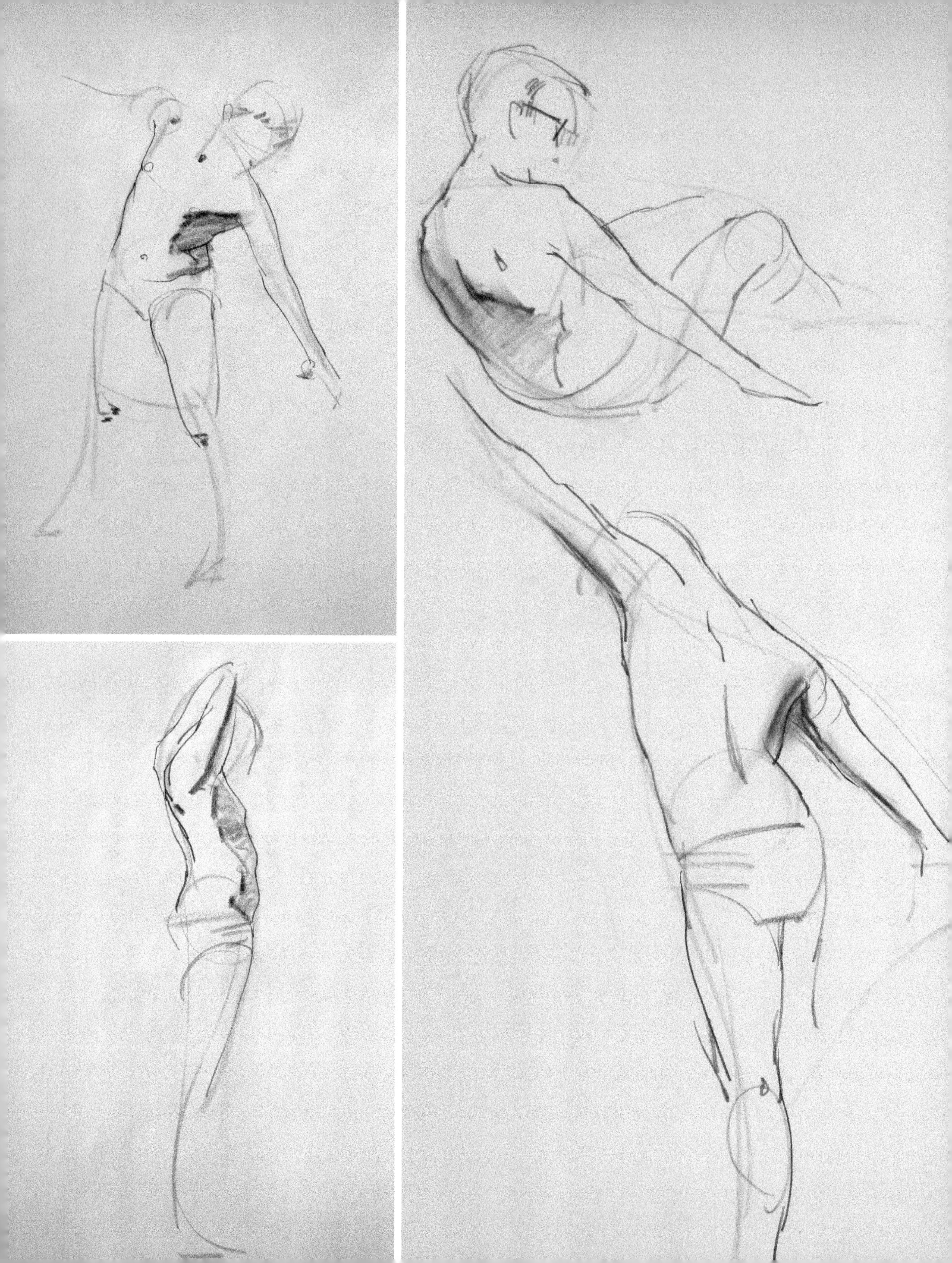

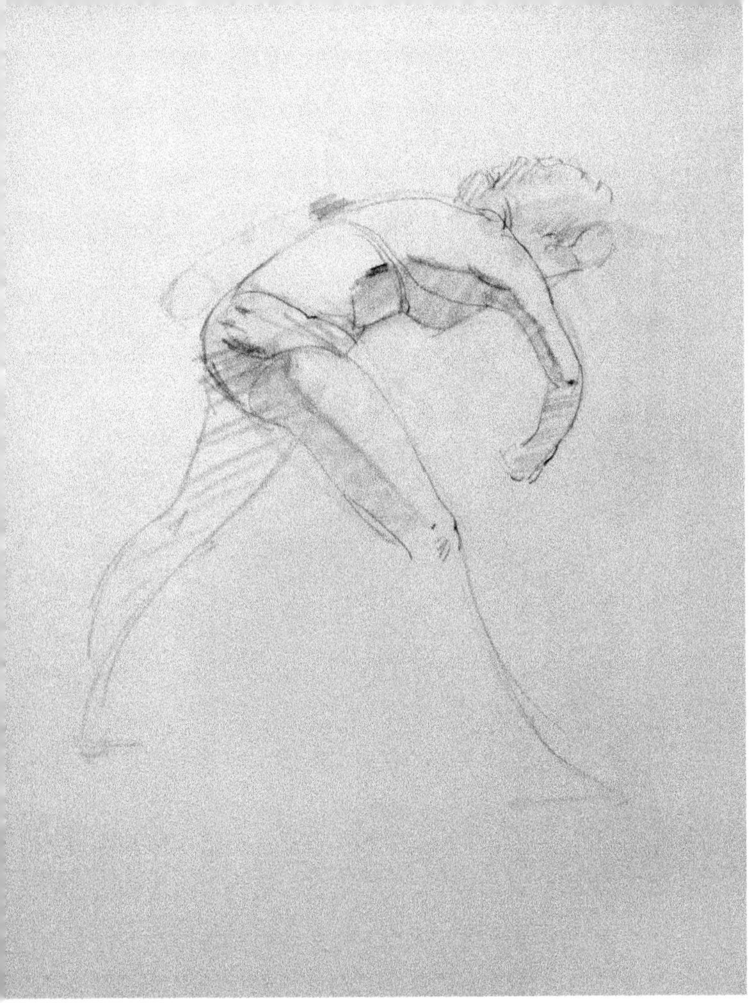

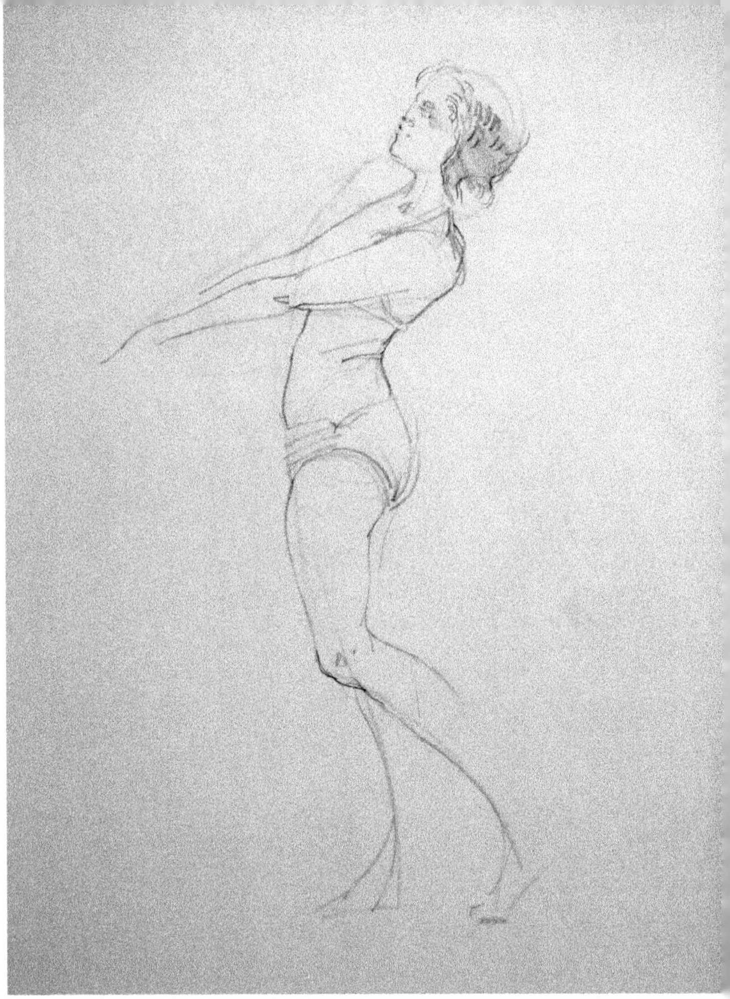

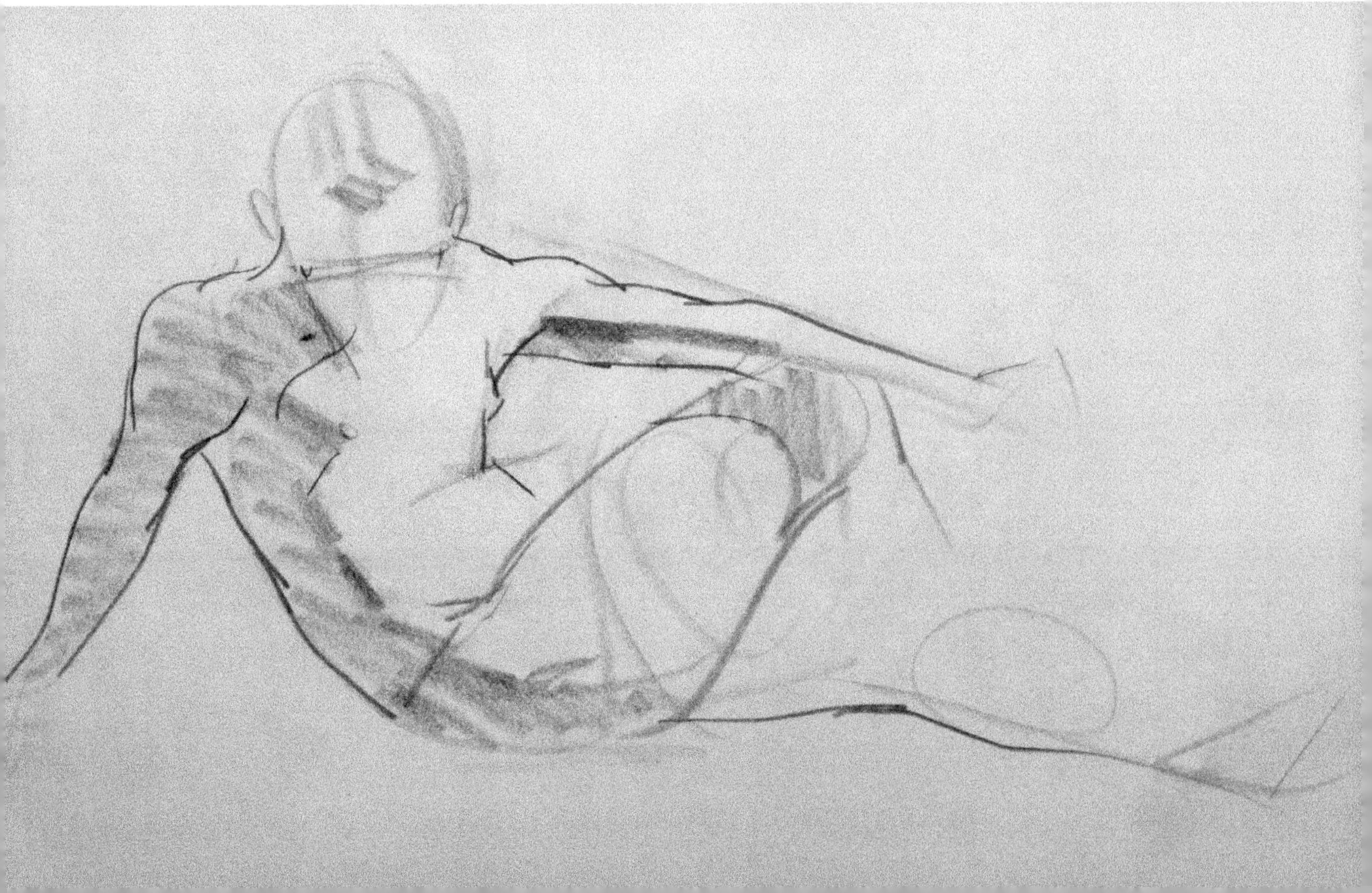

EXAGGERATION

Exaggerate the bend and stretch. The brain has a peculiar tendency to straighten things out. If something is slightly tilted, the brain subconsciously wants it upright. Purposefully push the exaggeration. Most of the time exaggerated lines end up looking more truthful than the lines that were drawn to match what was seen by the eye. Successful drawing consists of incorporating both what is *seen* and what is *known*.

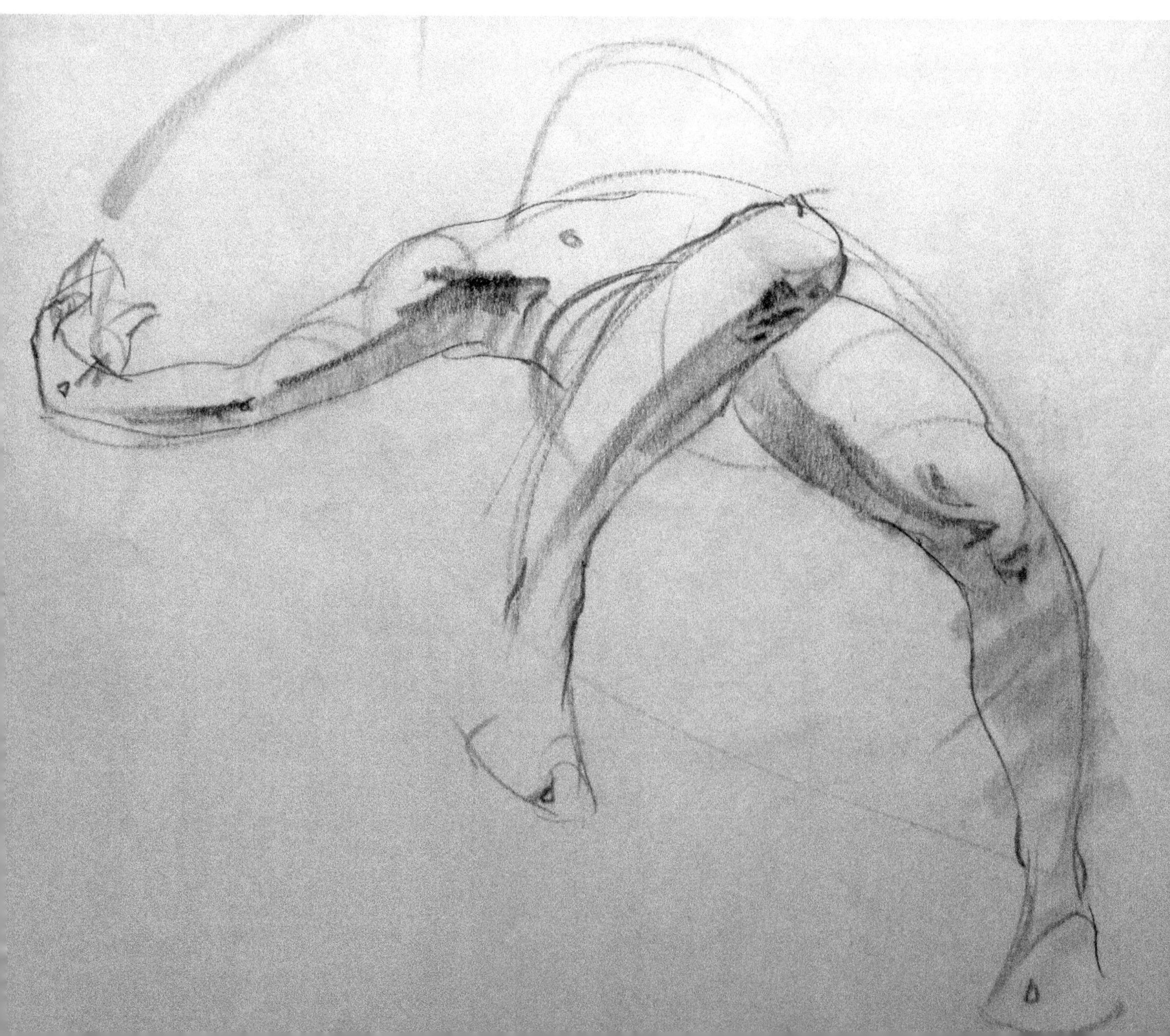

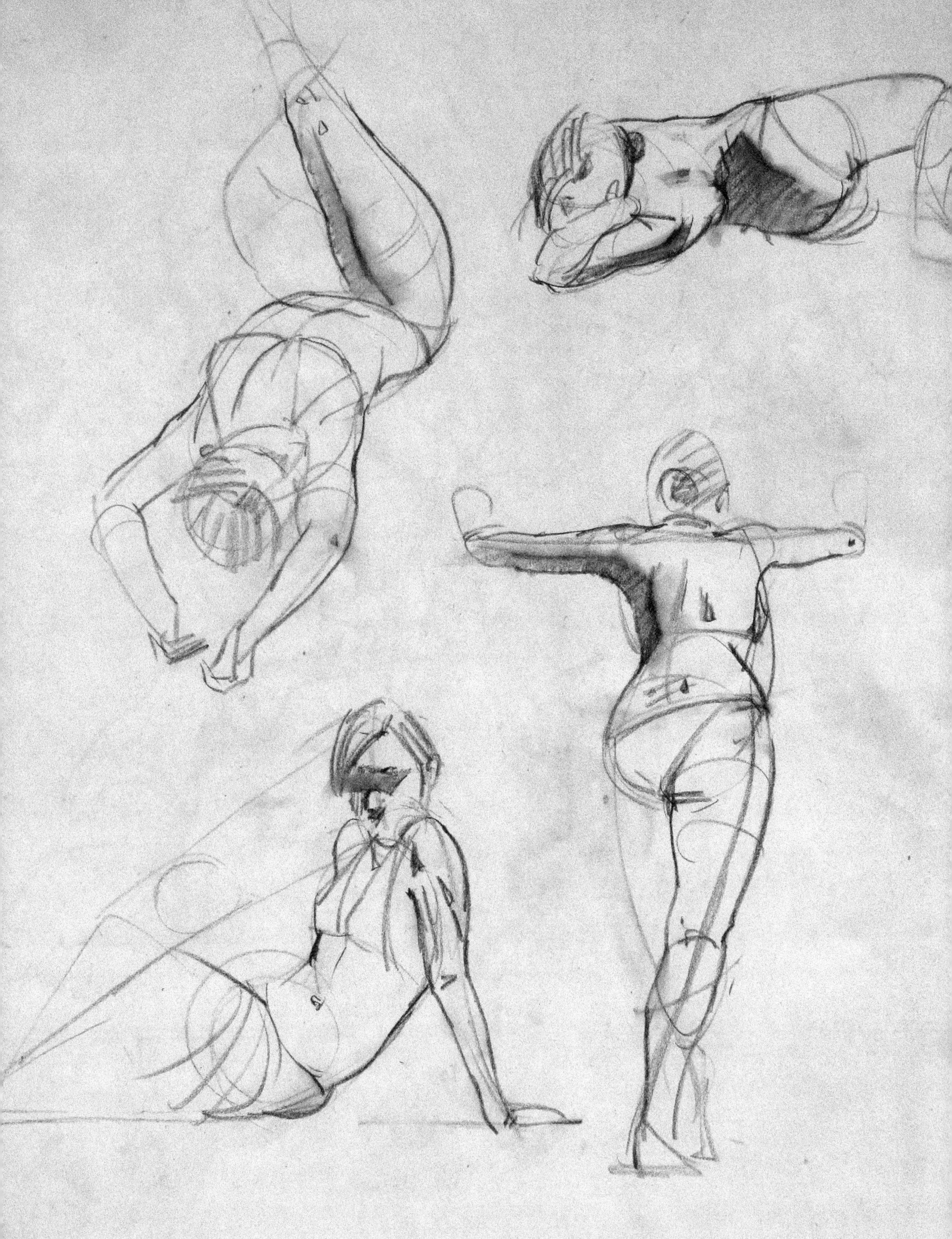

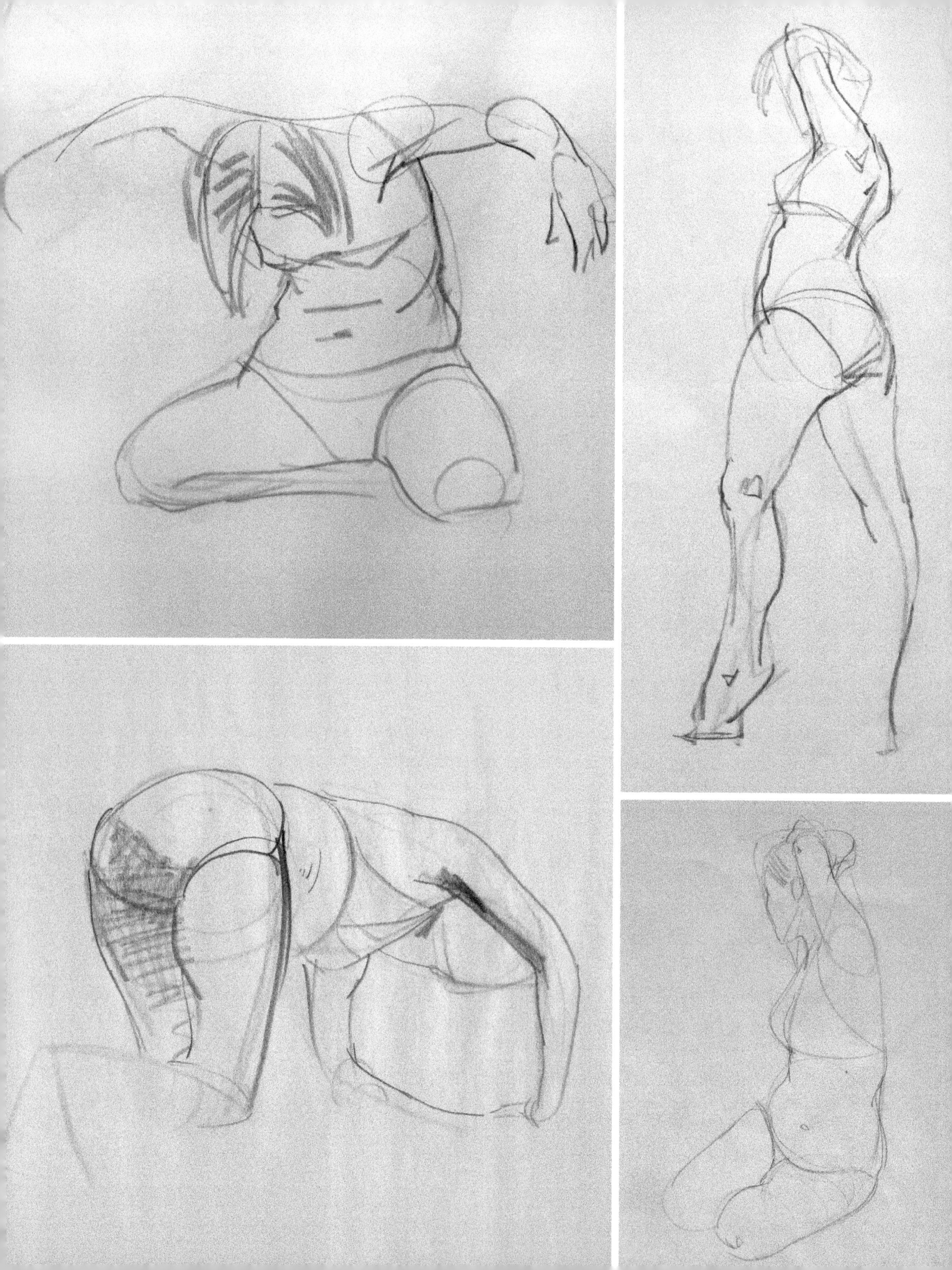

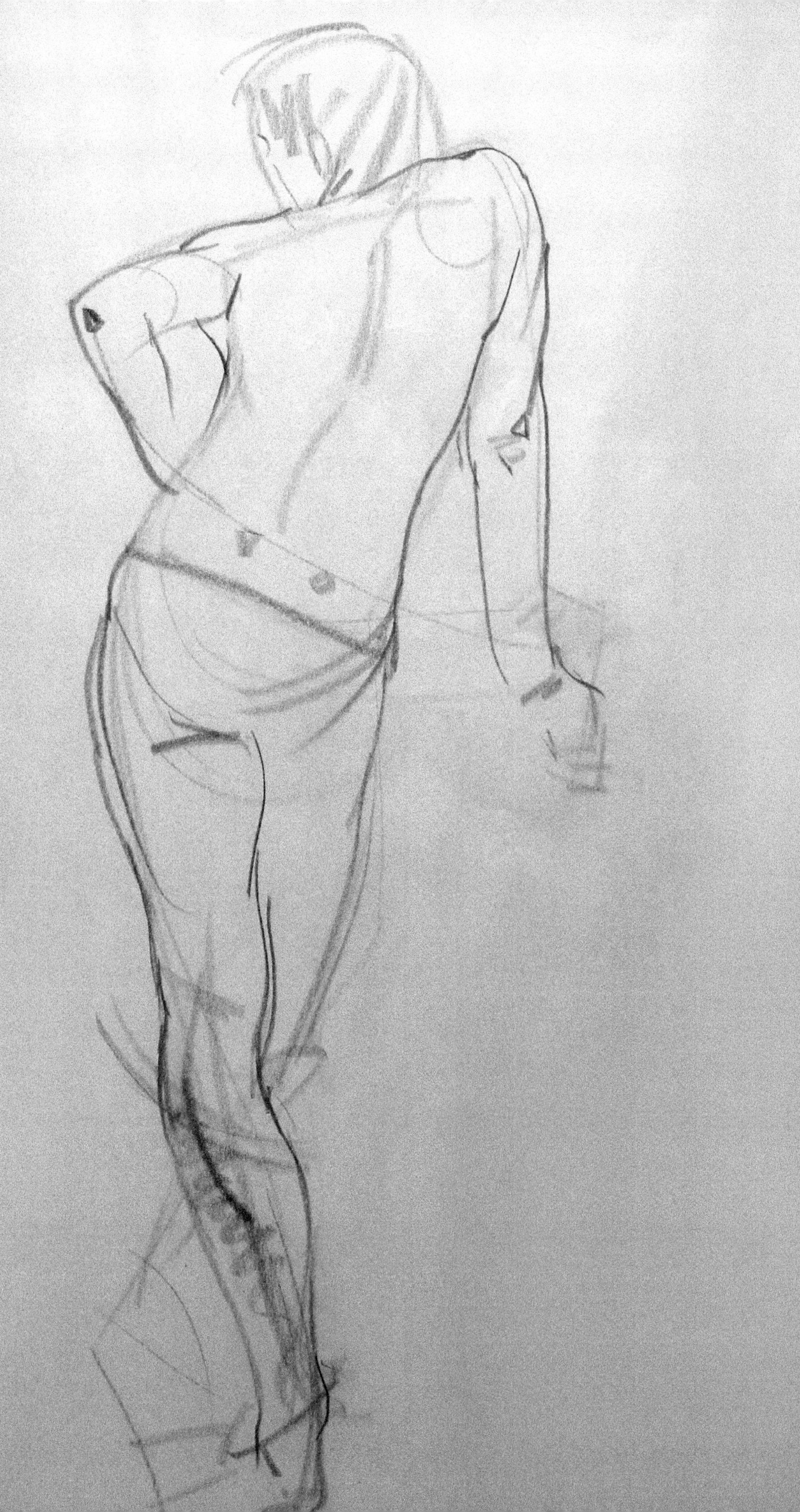

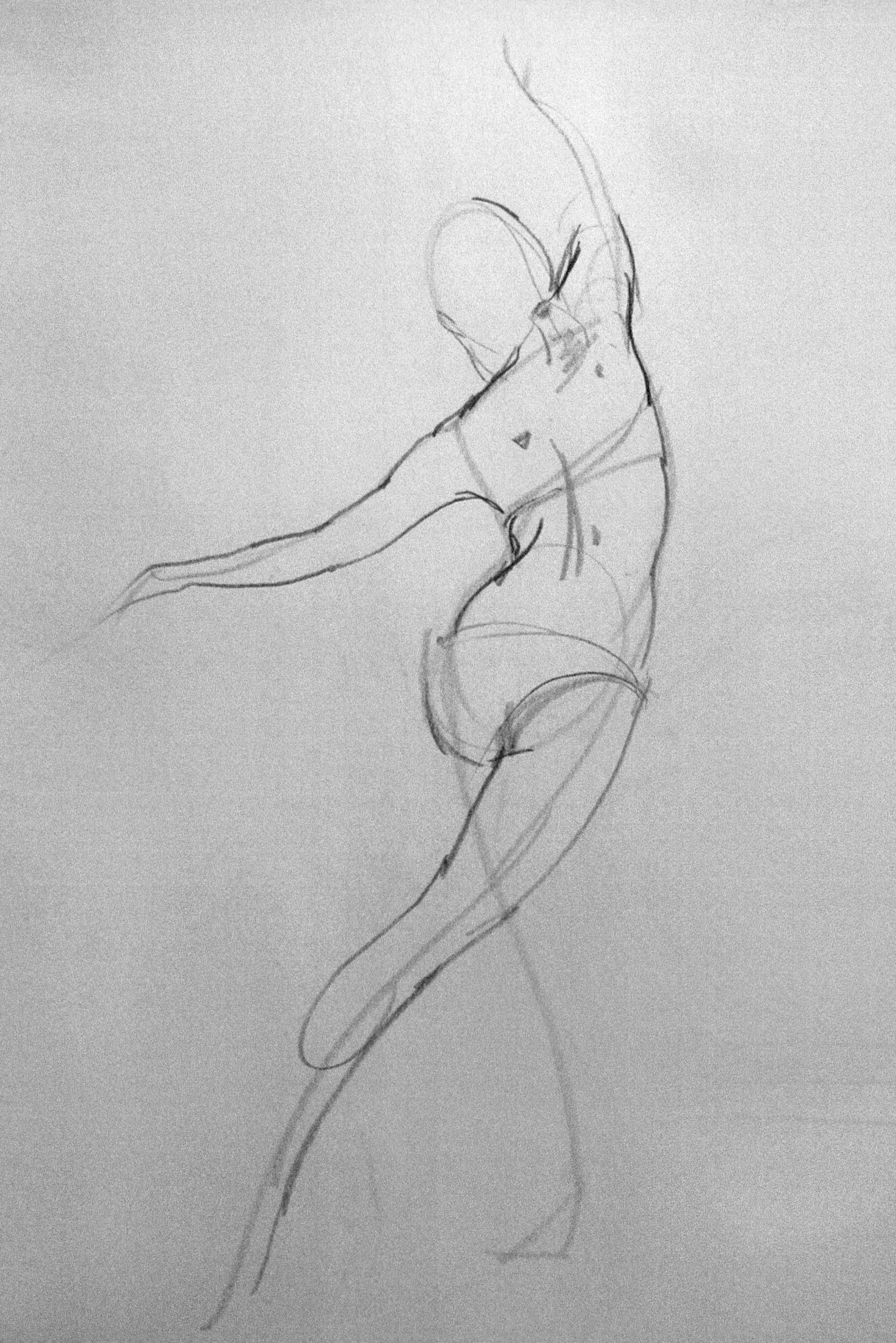

CLASS PROCEDURE

I usually start the class with one-minute gestures. After about 10 poses, I either increase or decrease the time of the poses based on the needs of the class. When the students are feeling stiff and need to remember to look at the figure as a whole, I will drop the time down to 30 seconds or even 10 seconds if need be. When the students are feeling good and loose, I will increase the time to two or three minutes for the rest of that first 20-minute session. After the break, I will gradually increase the time of the poses each session.

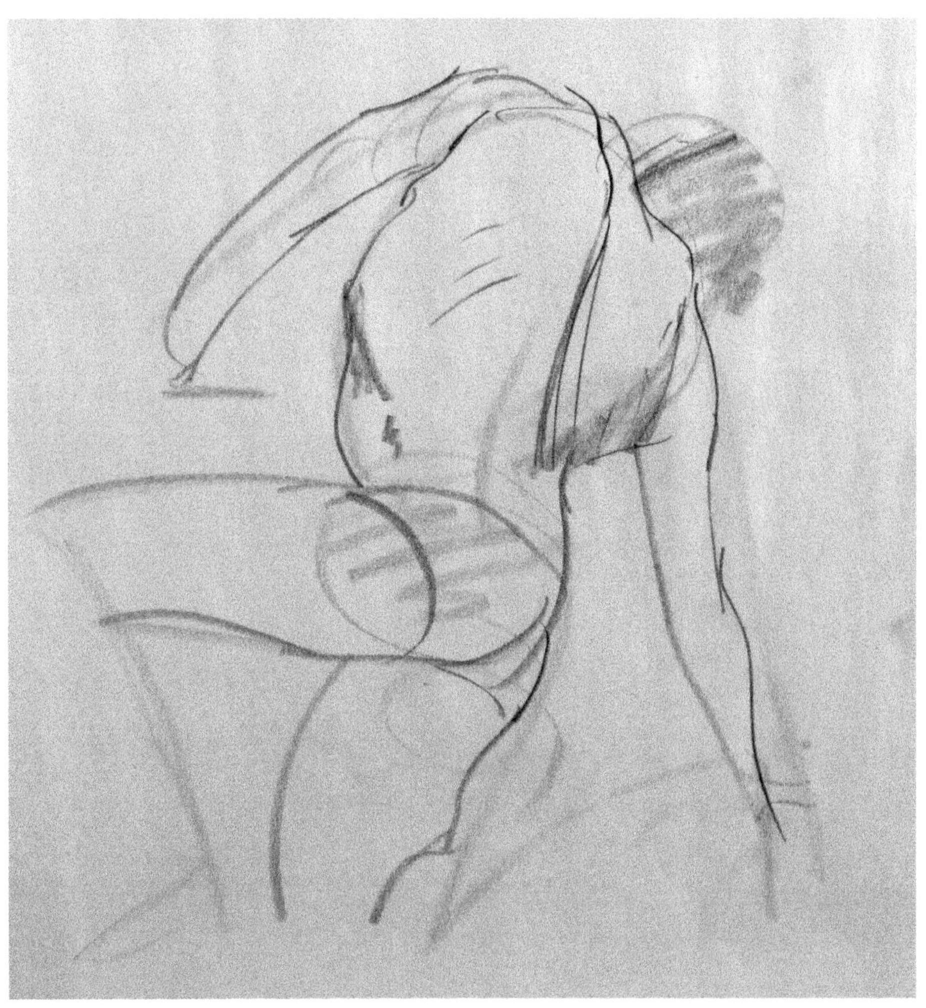

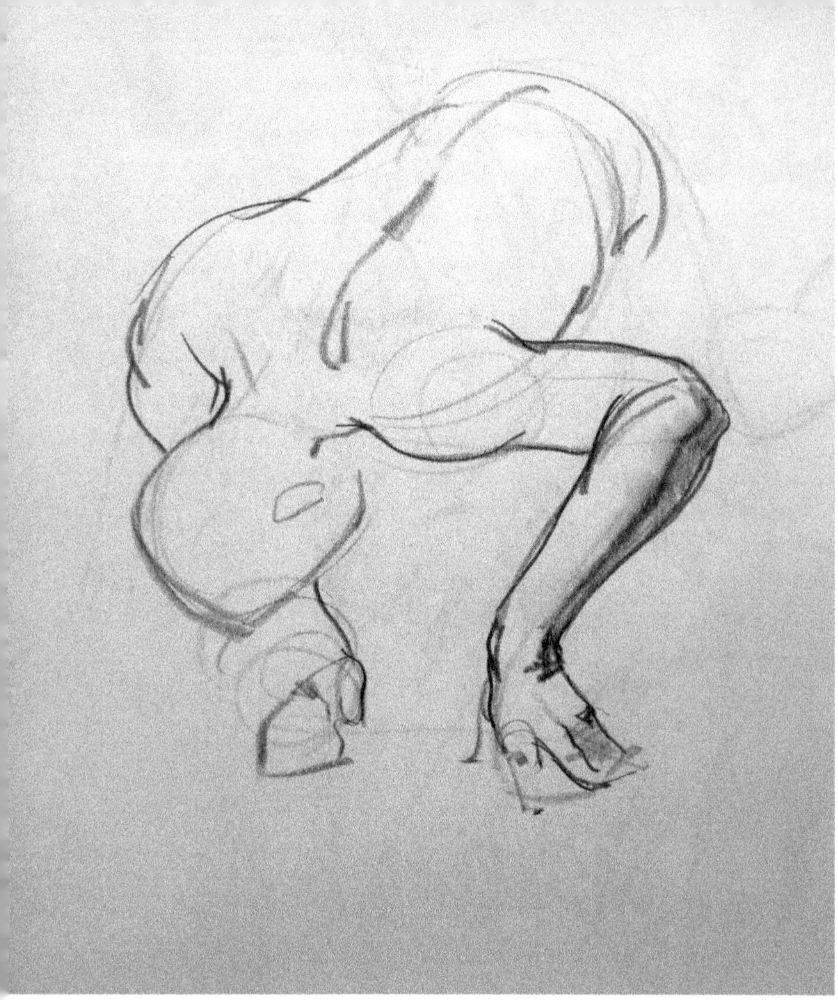

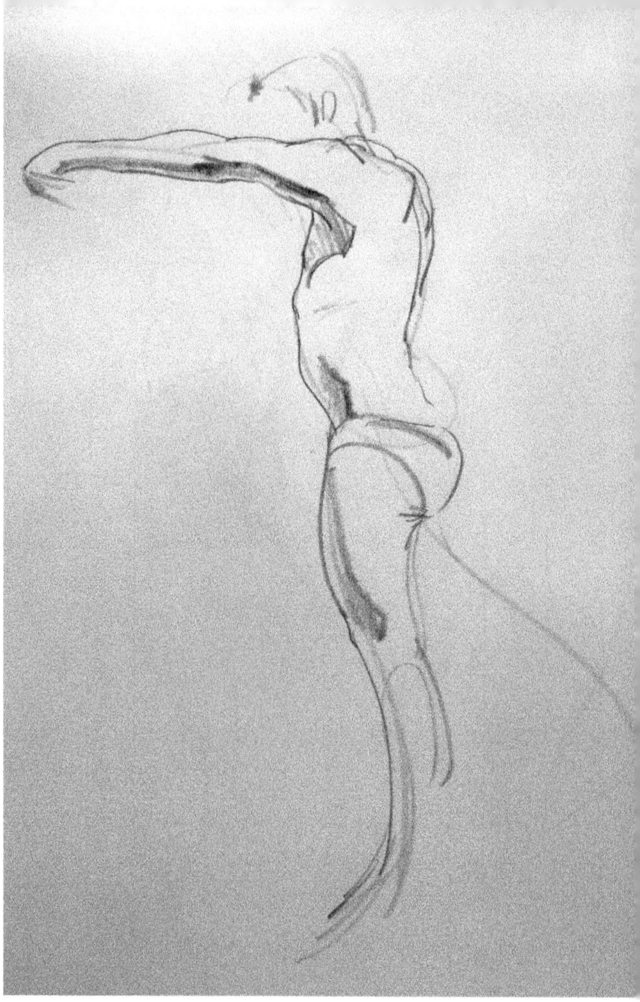

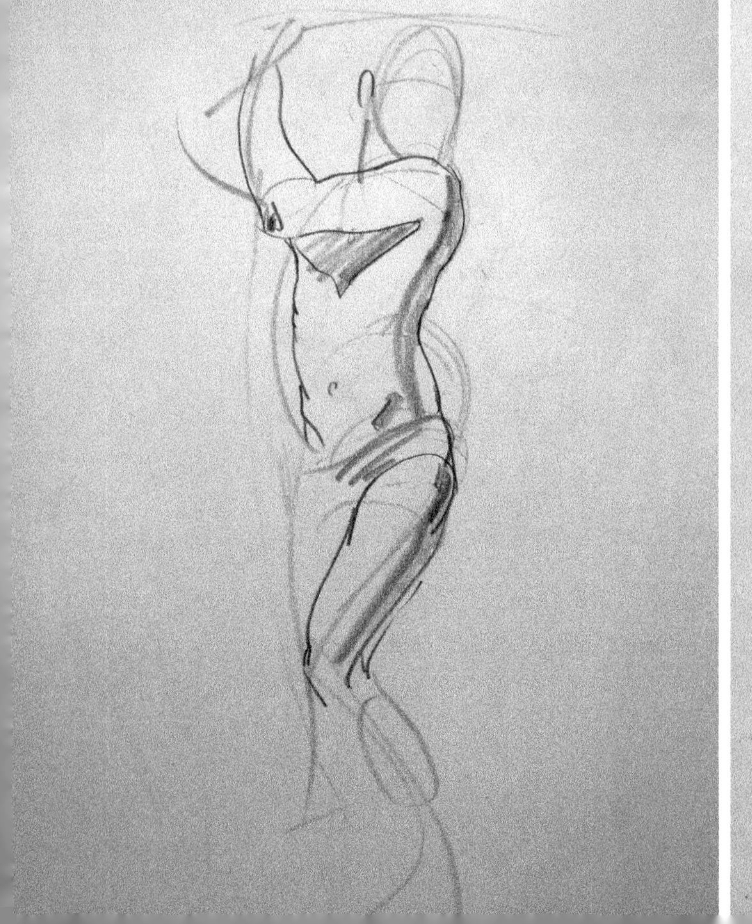
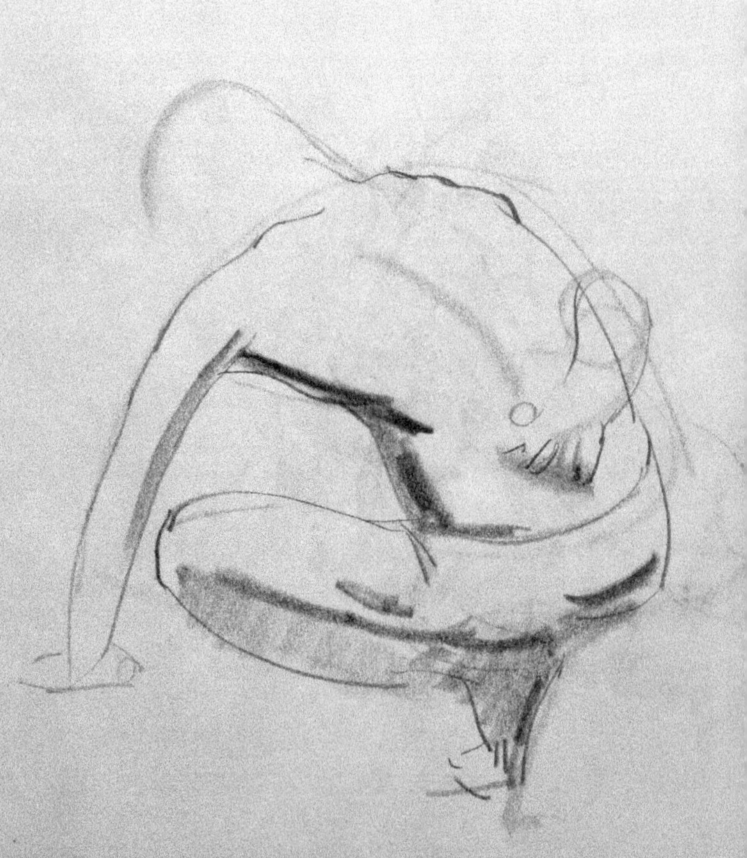

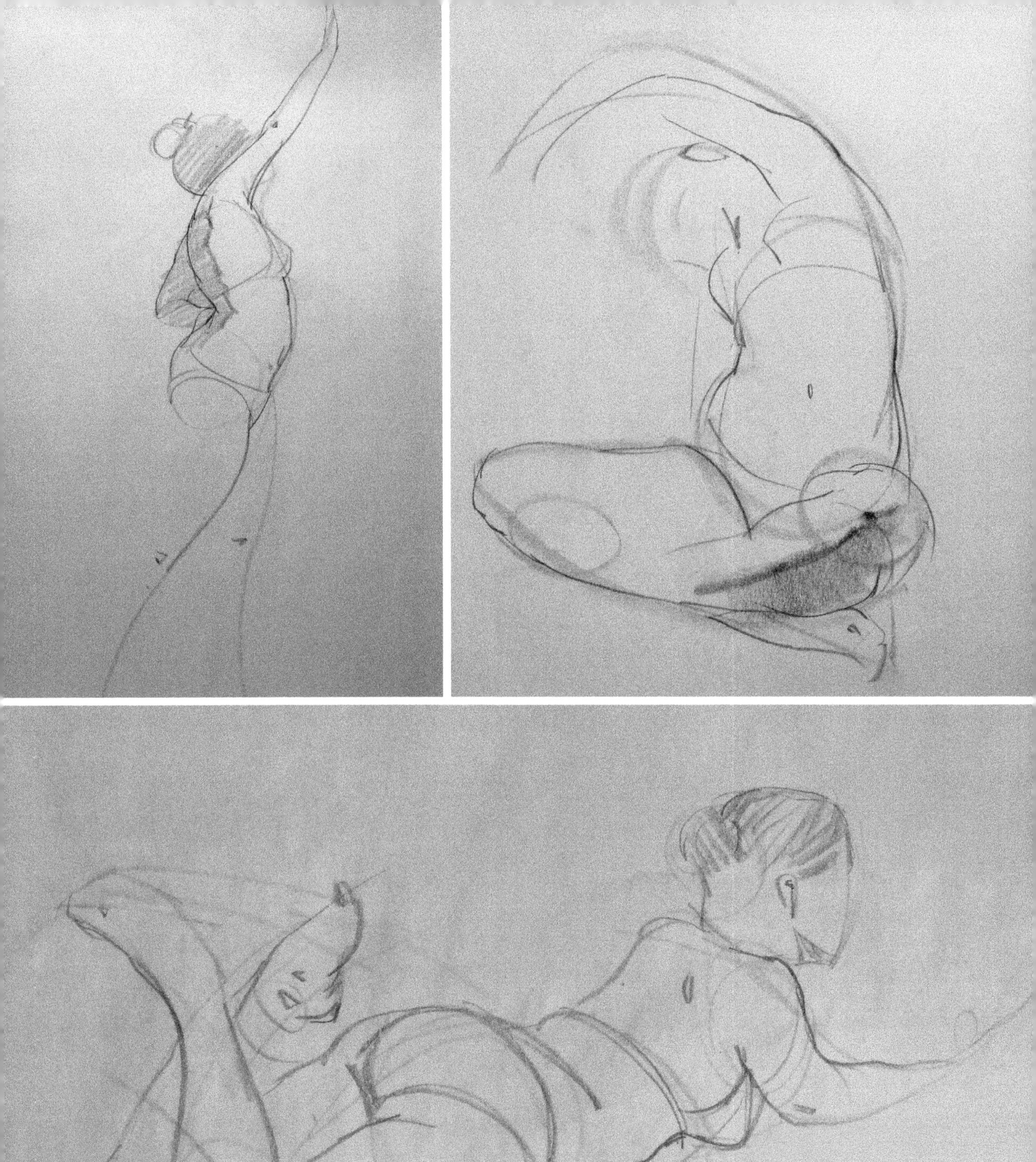

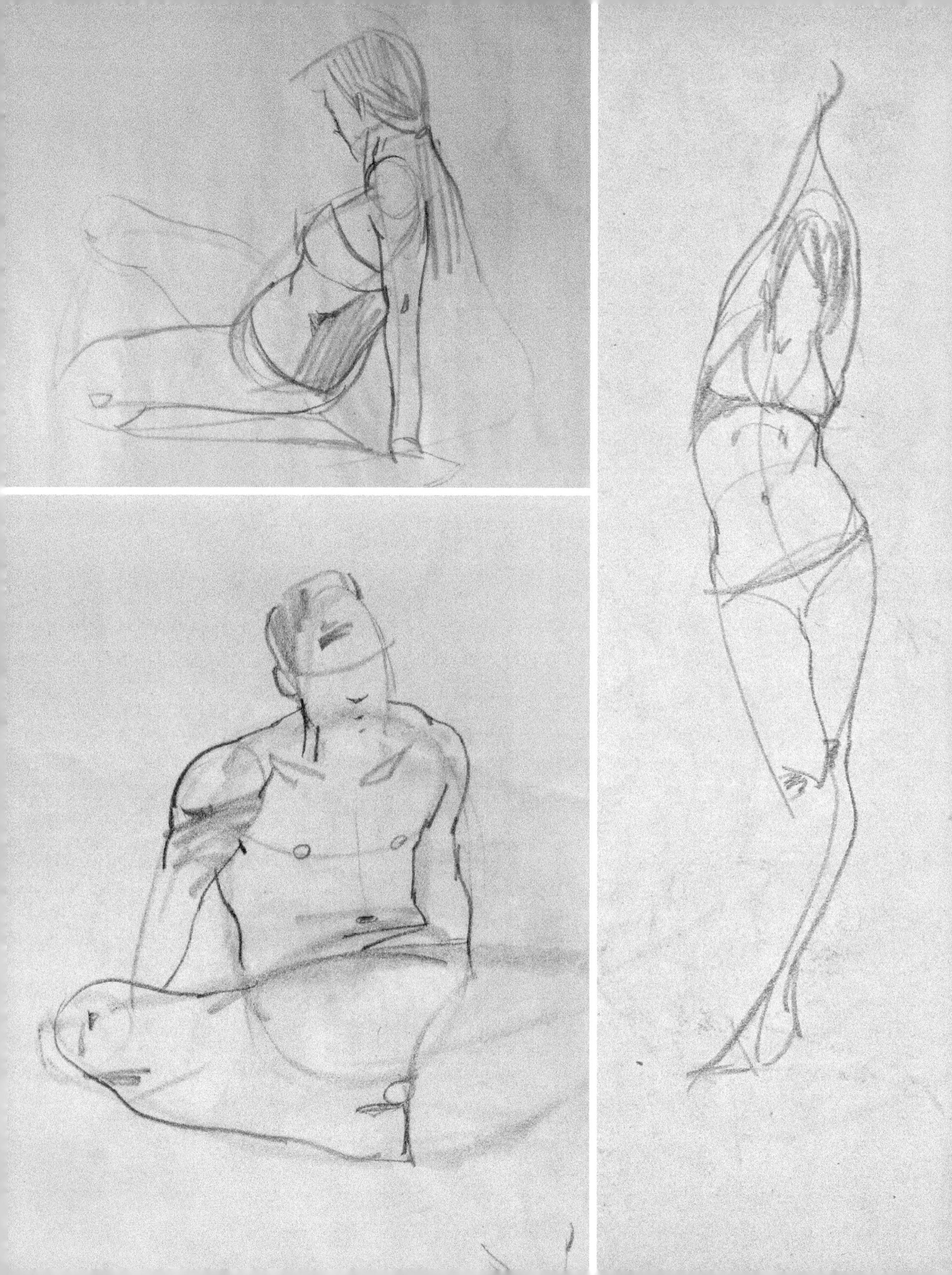

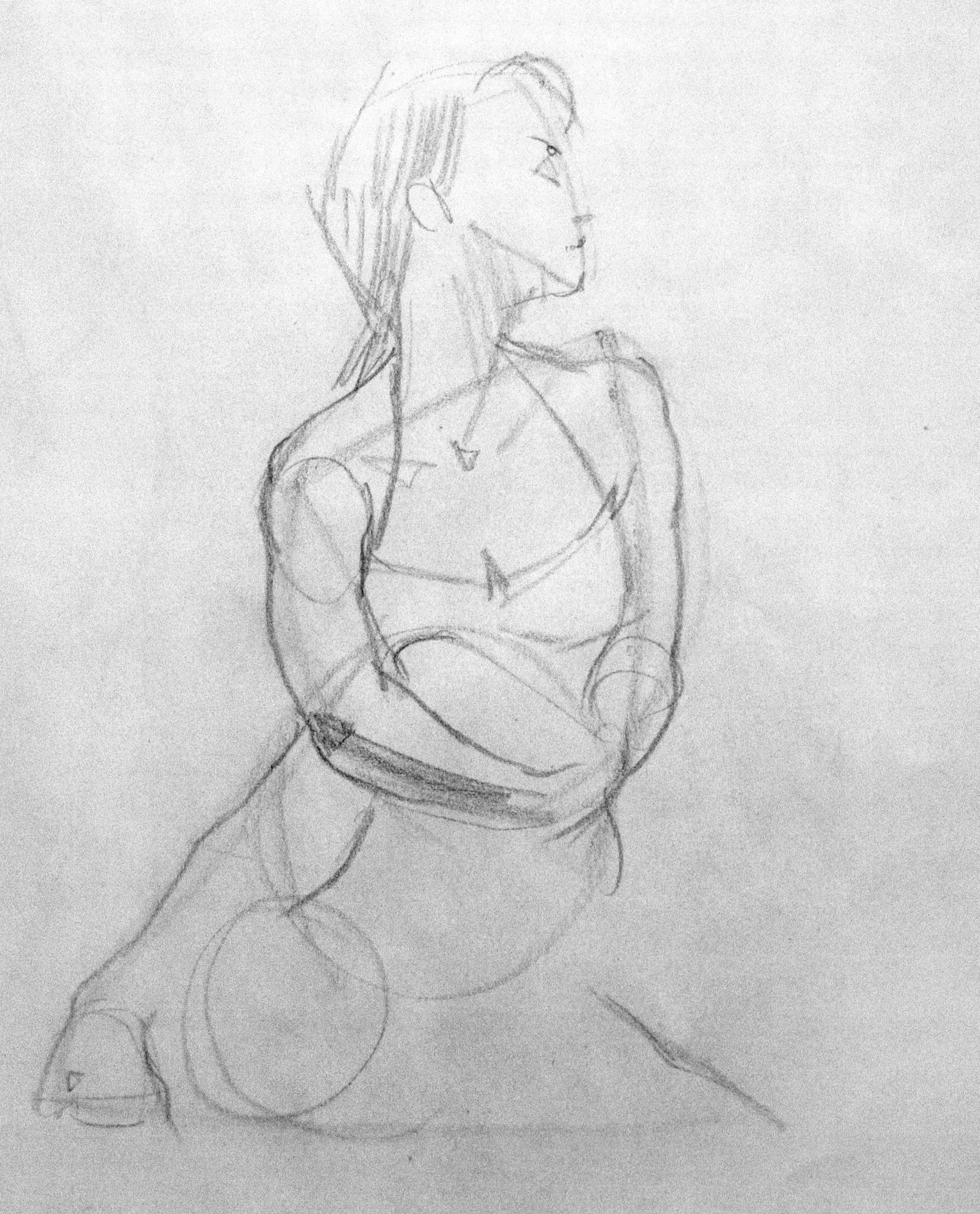

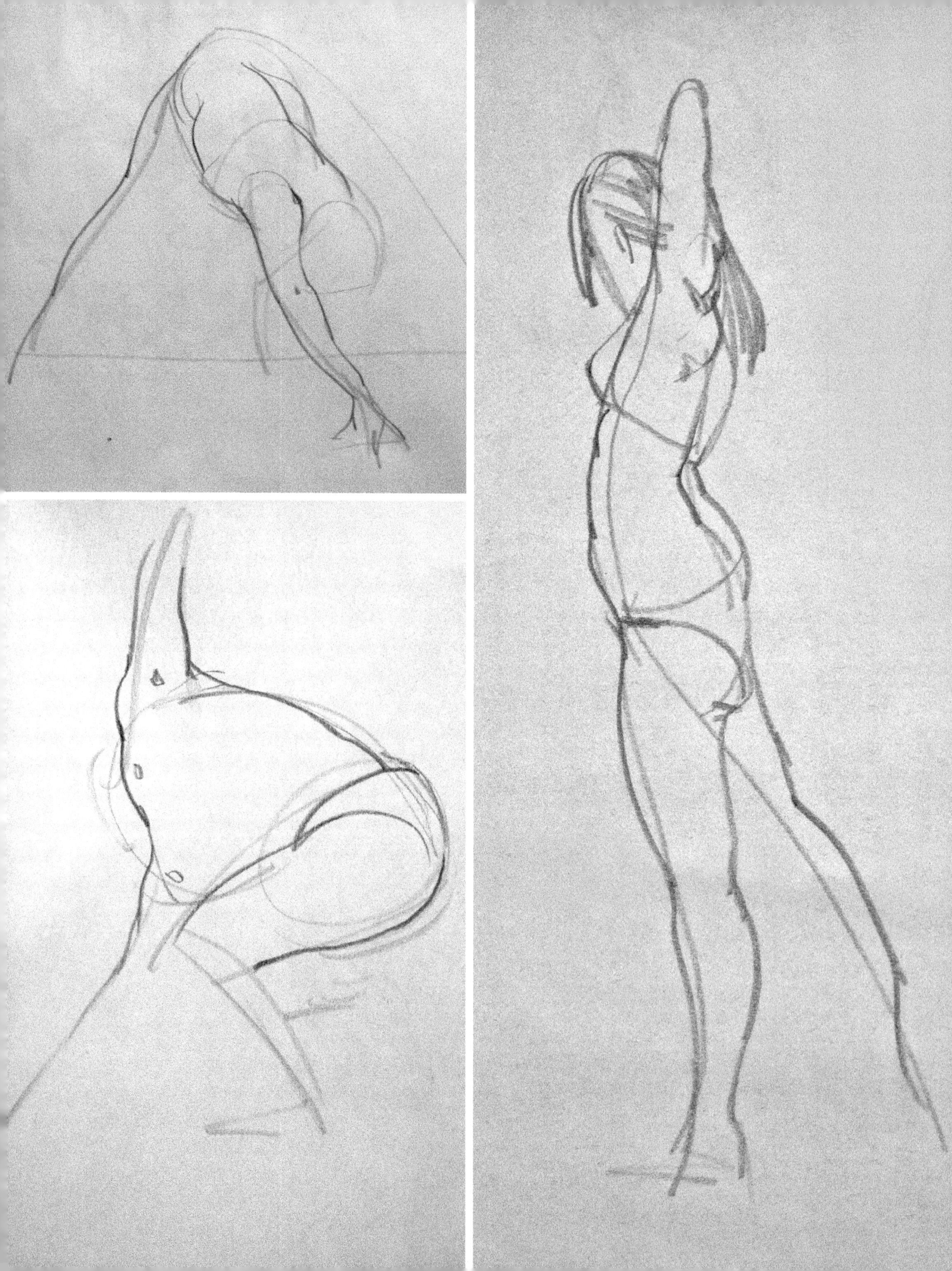

MATERIALS

It is important to use a sharp drawing tool. A sharp conté stick or pencil can do ten times more than a dull one can. Have a single edge razor blade and sanding block on hand to sand, shave, and sharpen the edges of the conté or charcoal during model breaks.

There is a learning curve that comes with the use of each particular tool. Conté is waxier than charcoal, which is more chalk-like. The pencil (whether it is conté or charcoal) can create beautifully sensitive line work. The stick (crayon) can also get beautiful lines, but is usually used more to enhance the feeling of movement with broader marks and larger masses. Make it a goal to become comfortable with the drawing tool. Get to know what it can do. Ask questions like, what kind of marks can quickly be made with it? And does it smear easily?

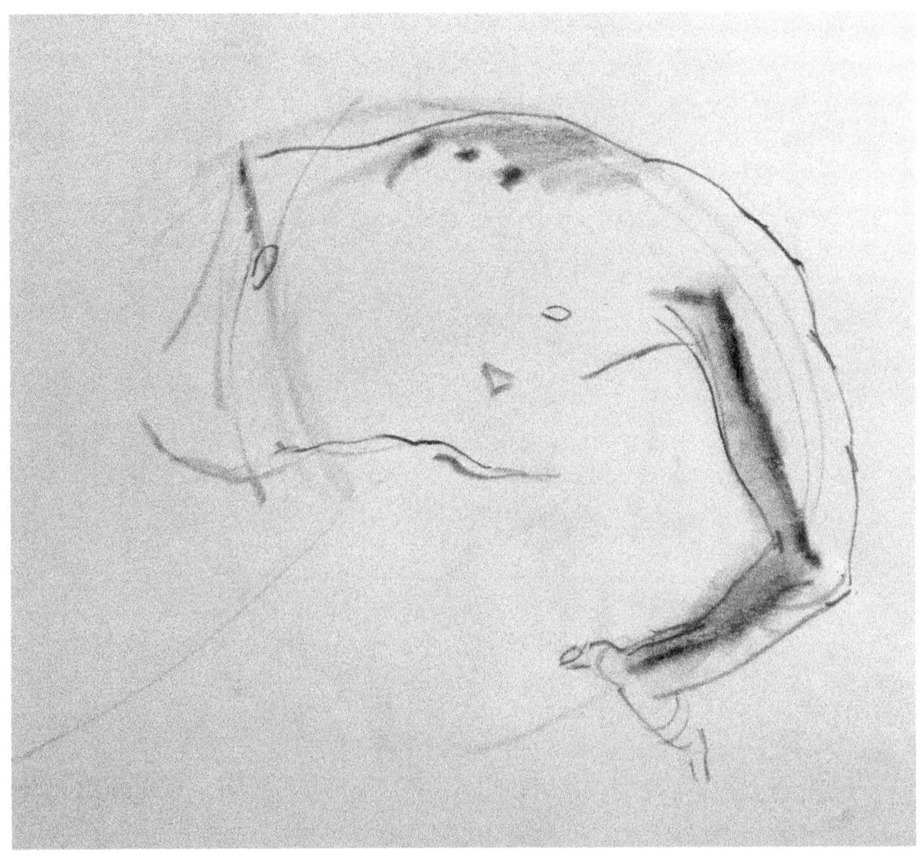

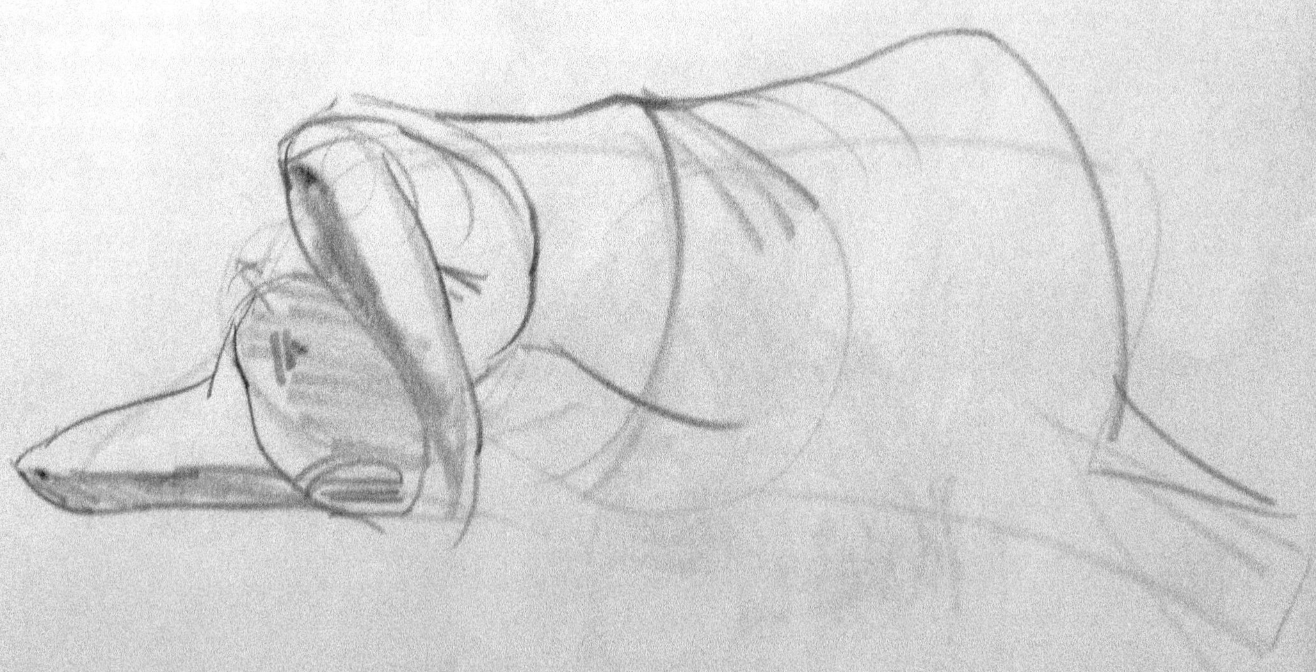

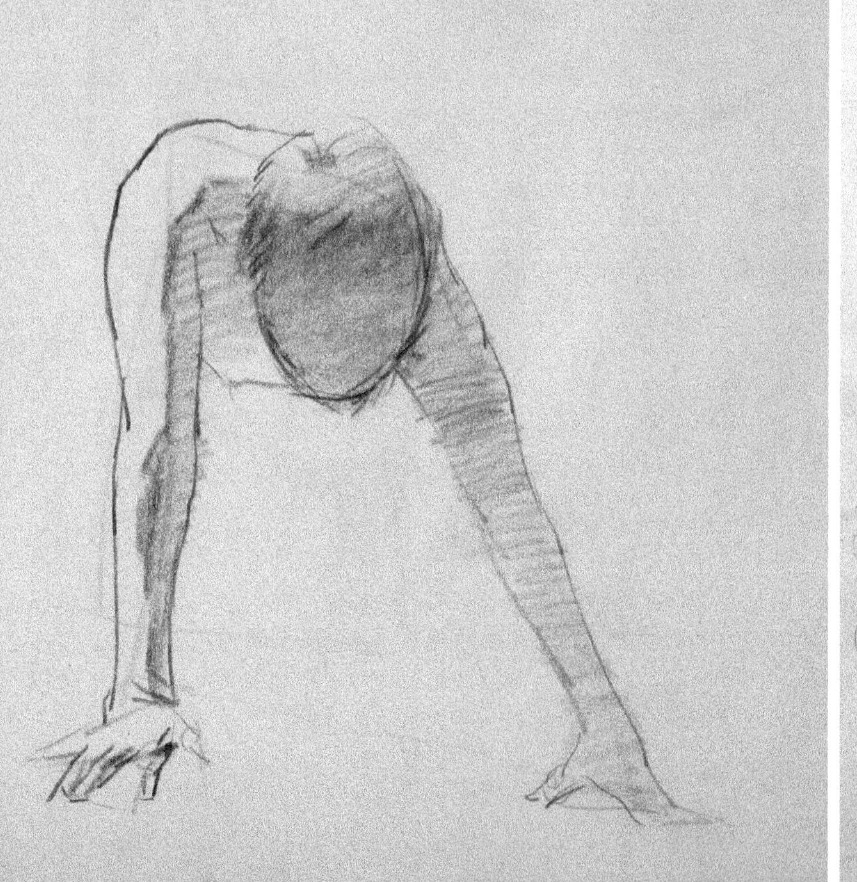
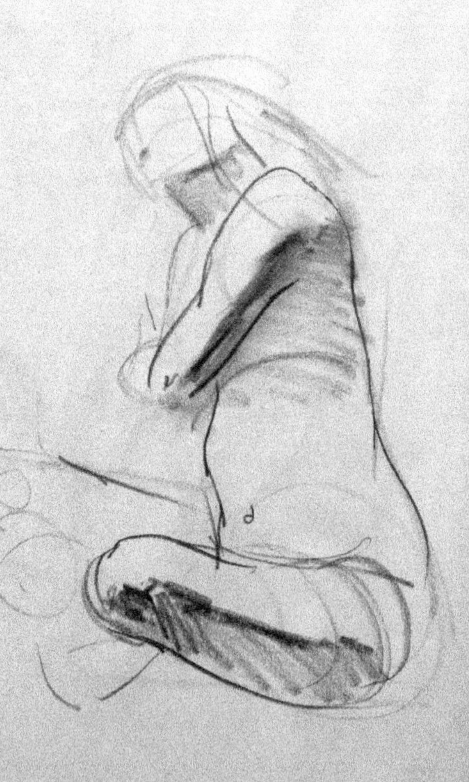

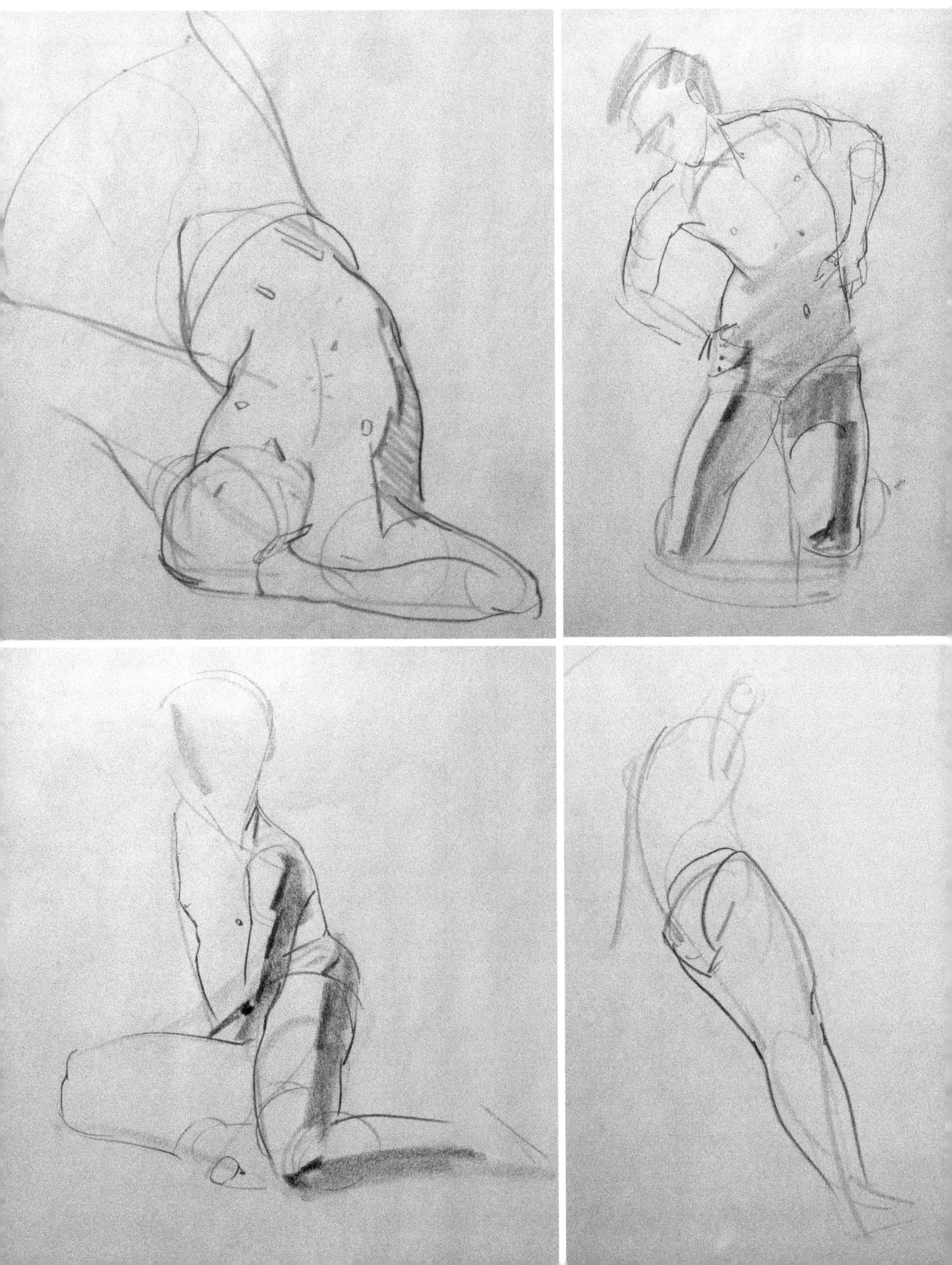

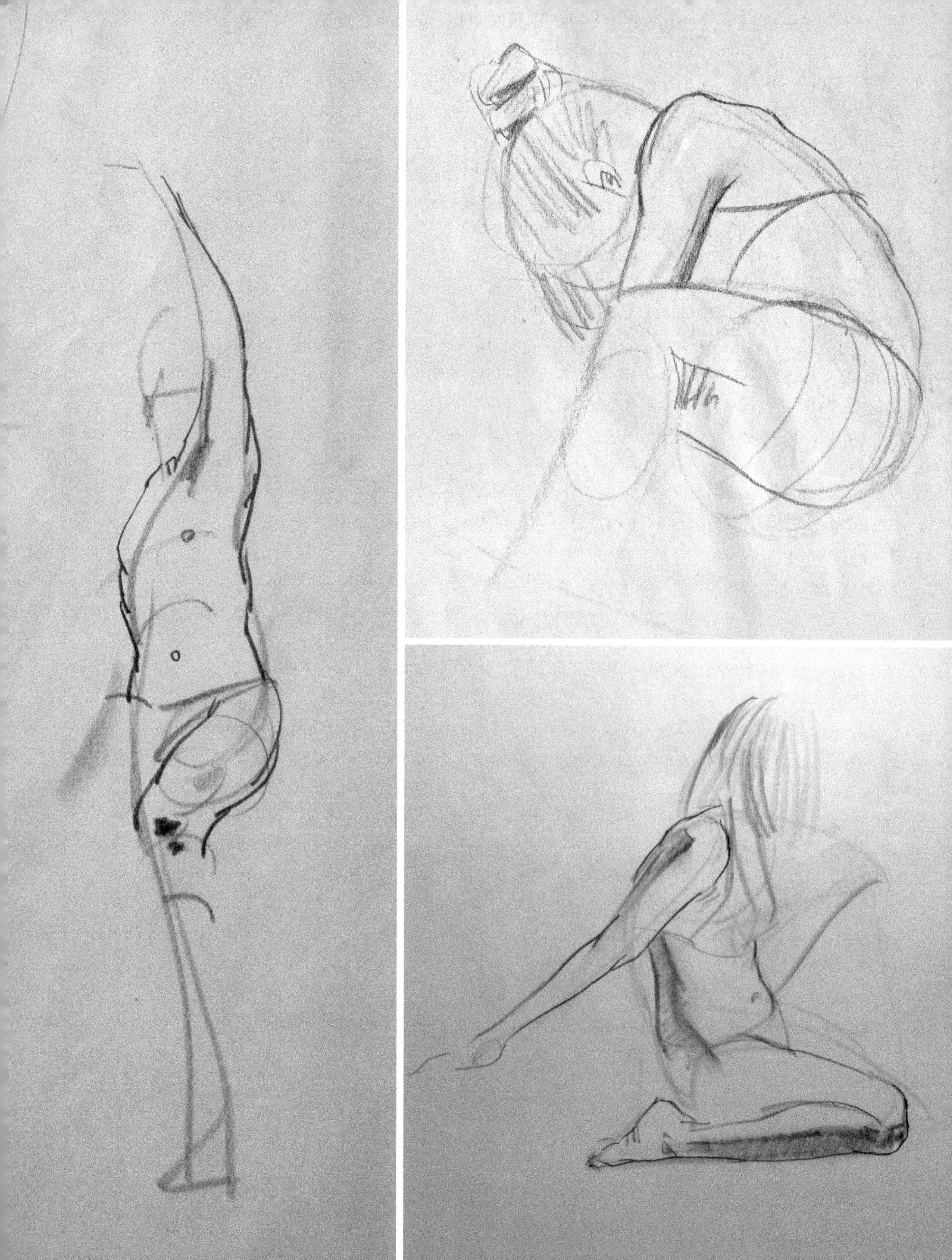

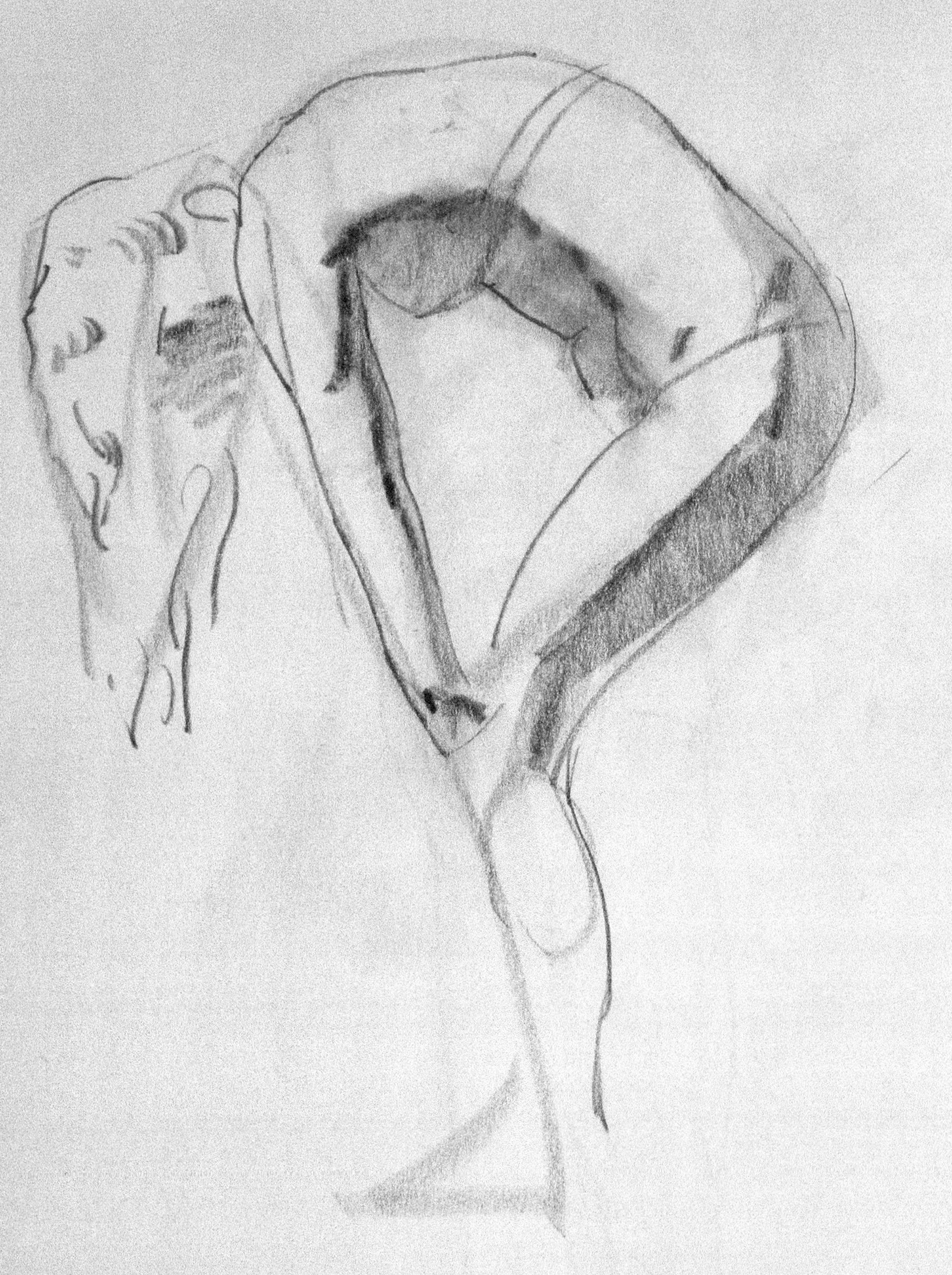

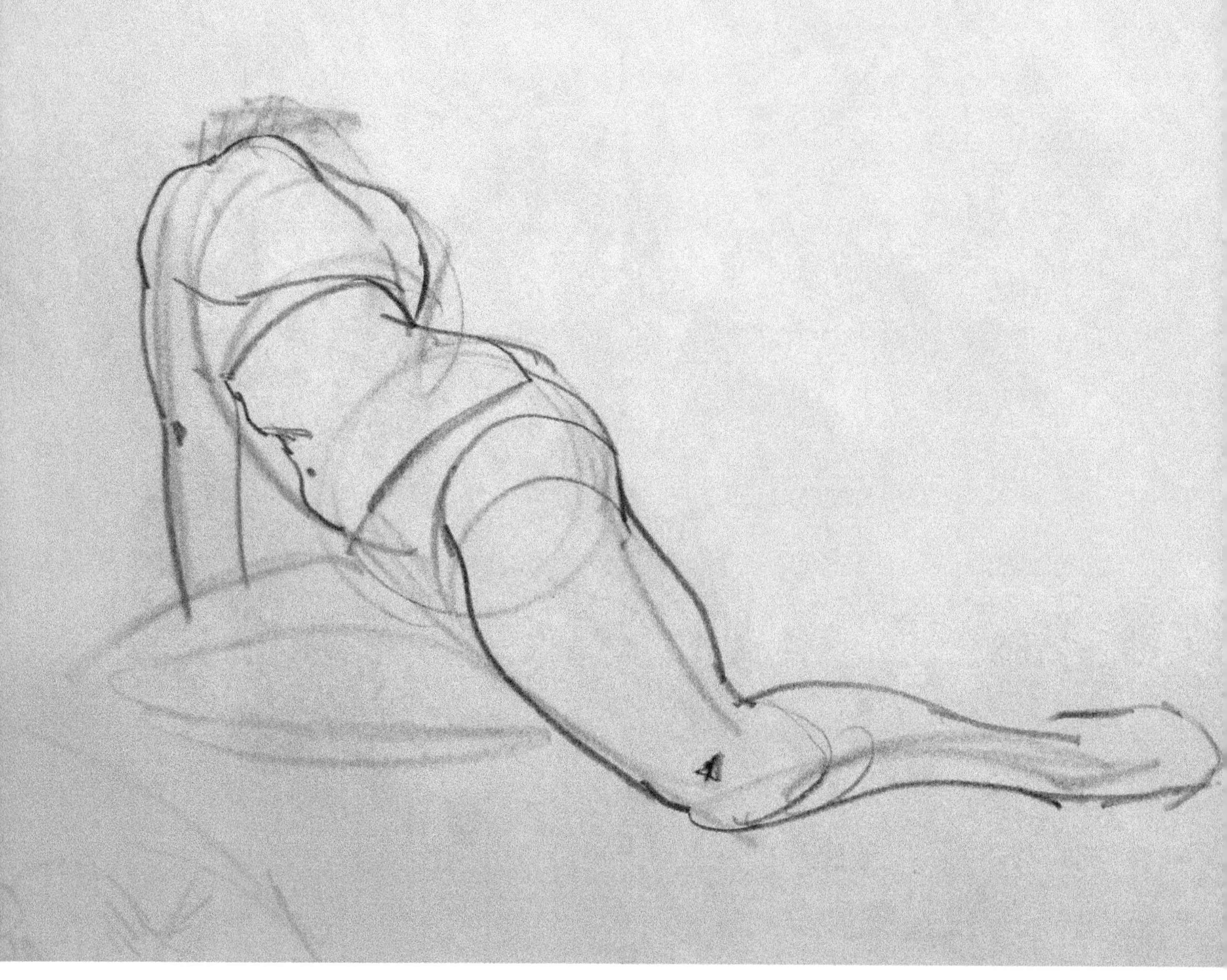

HOW TO DRAW

Most beginning artists come into a drawing class and assume they are to use the conté in the same way they would use a pen to write a letter. It is much more efficient, though, to draw with the whole arm, instead of the fingers and wrist. With the shoulder as the axis, use the whole arm to draw long sweeping lines and establish big relationships more easily and consistently. Although it seems uncomfortable at first, working this way will actually give the artist more control of line quality and placement.

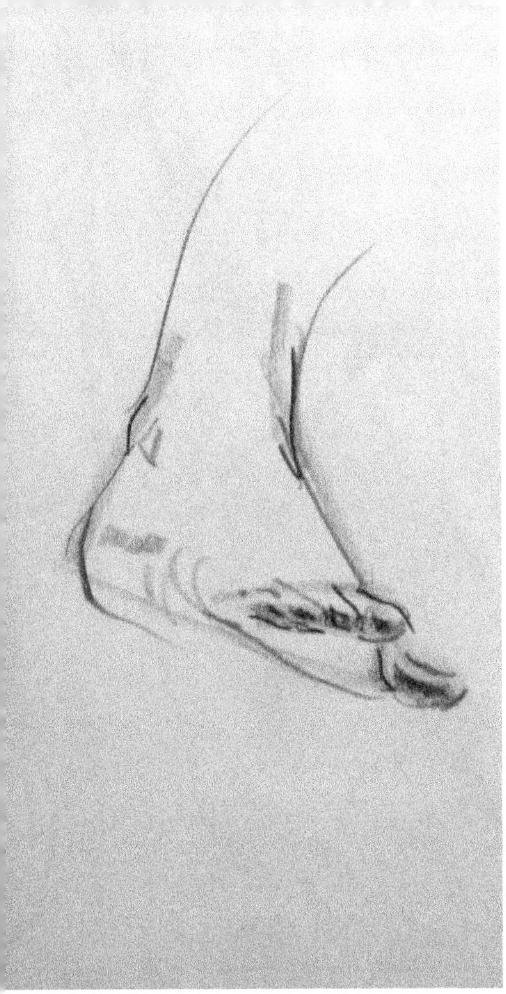

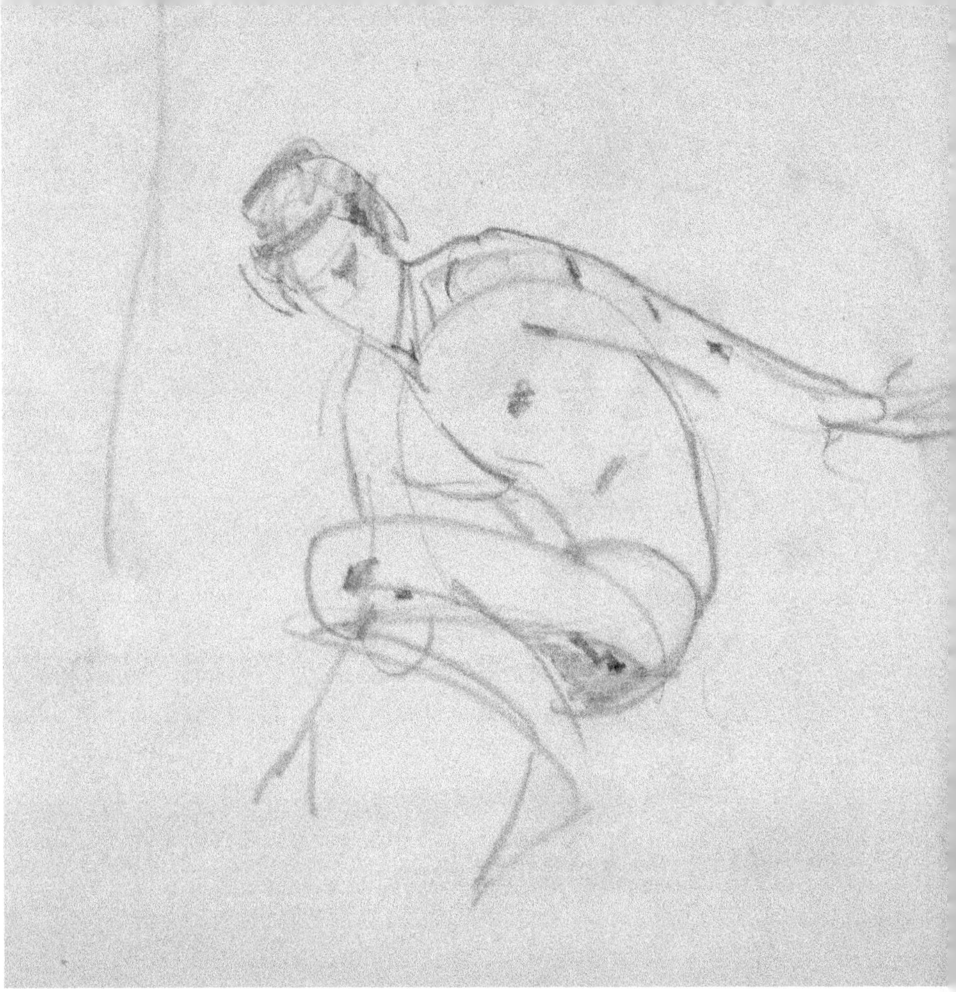

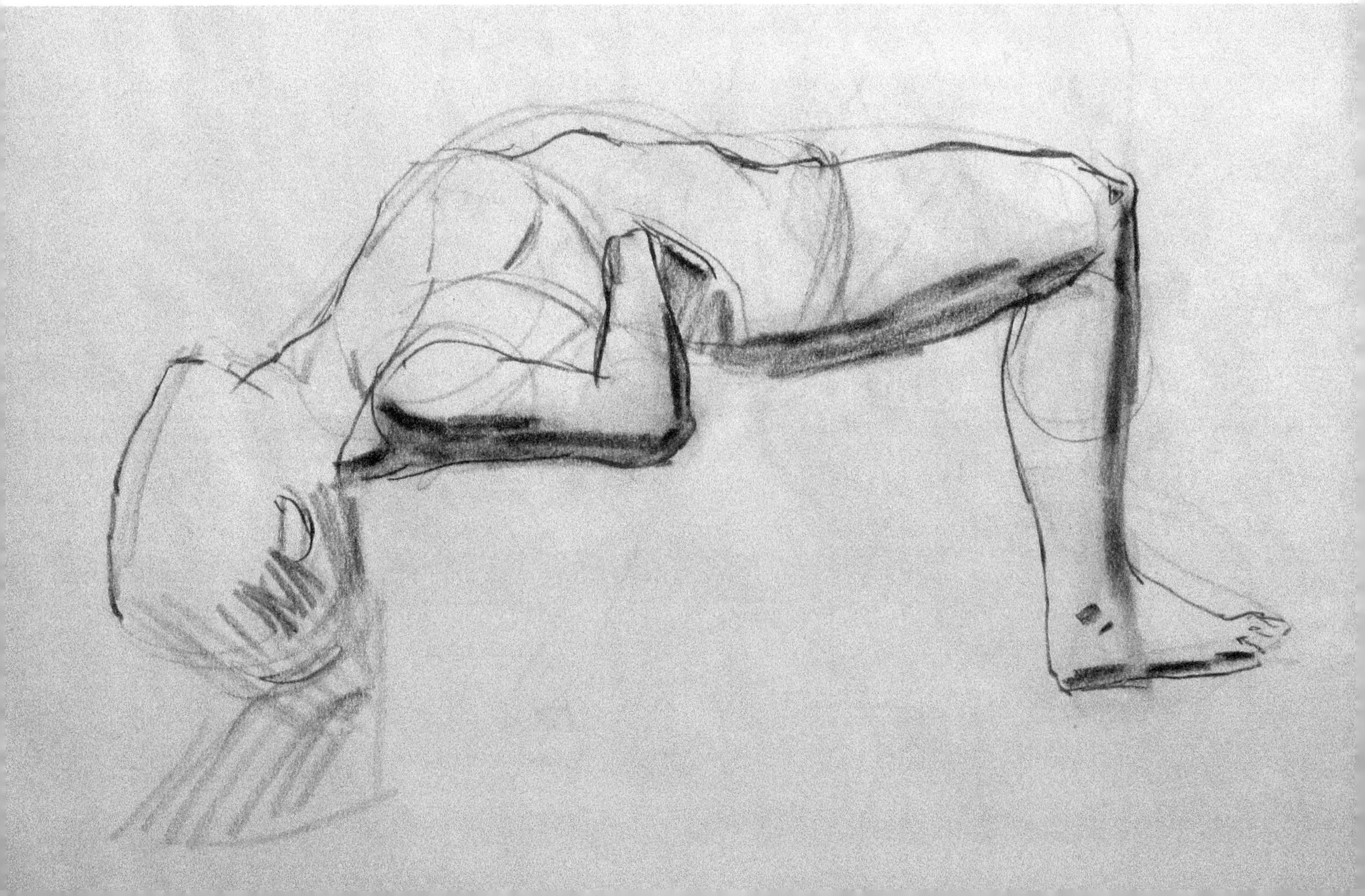

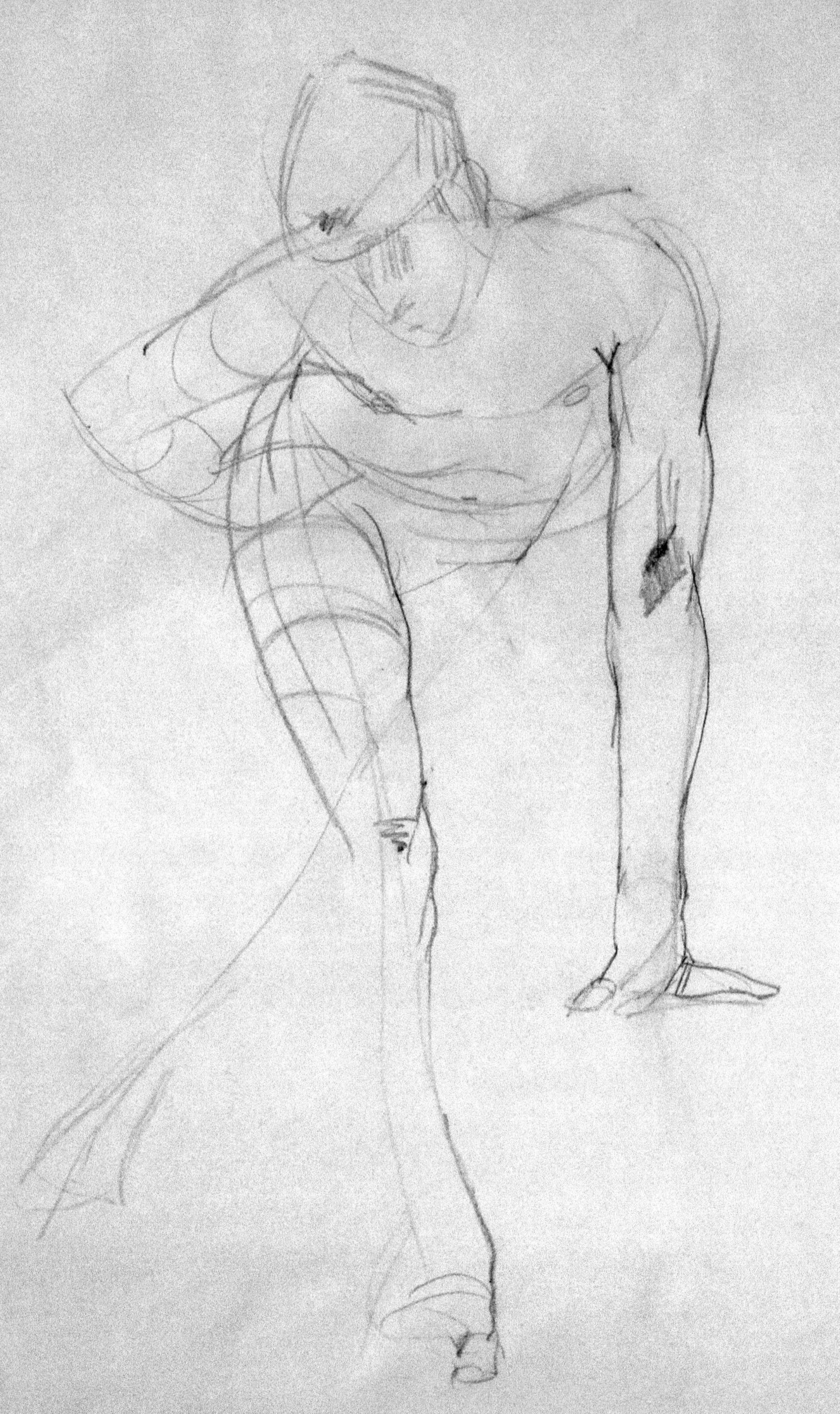

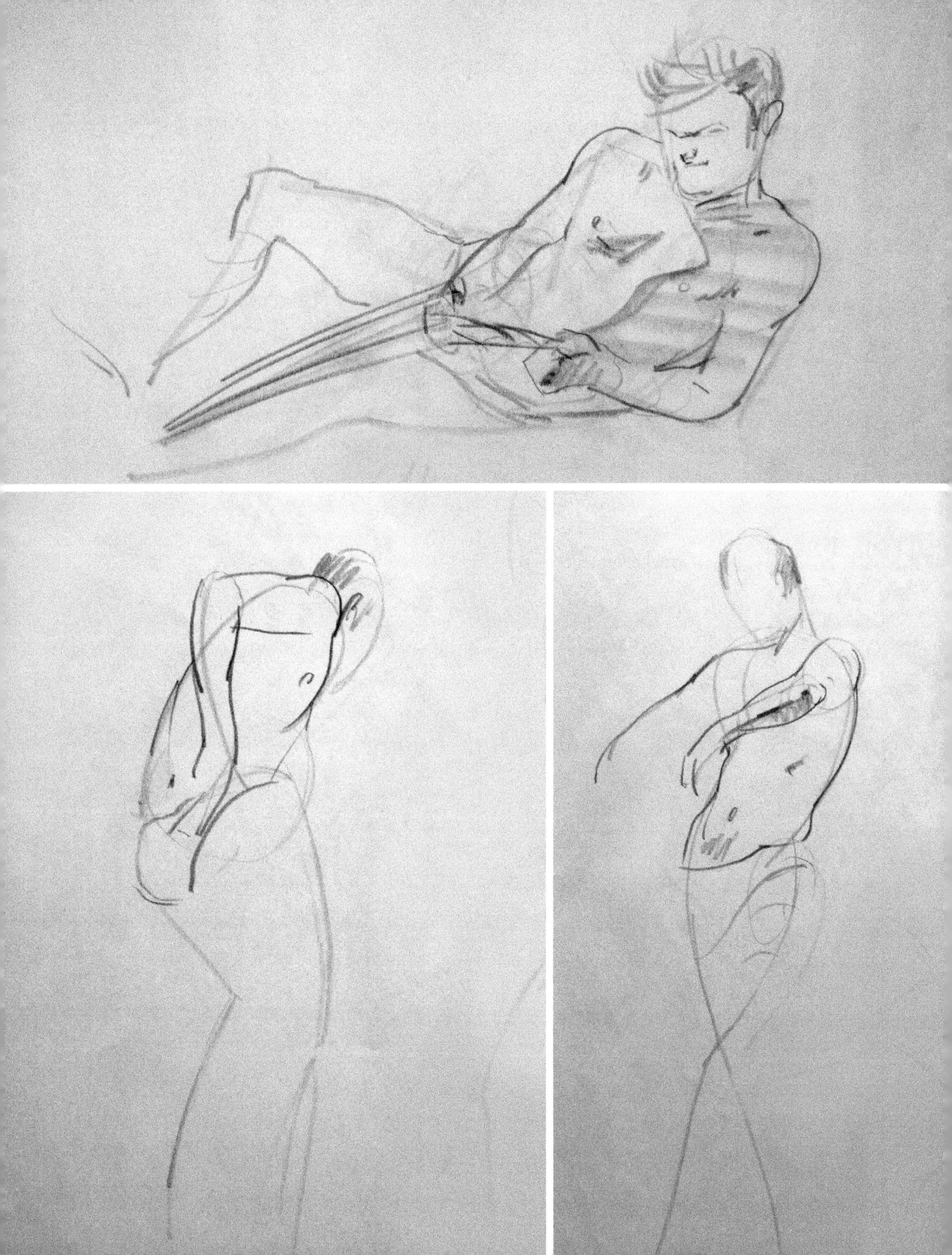

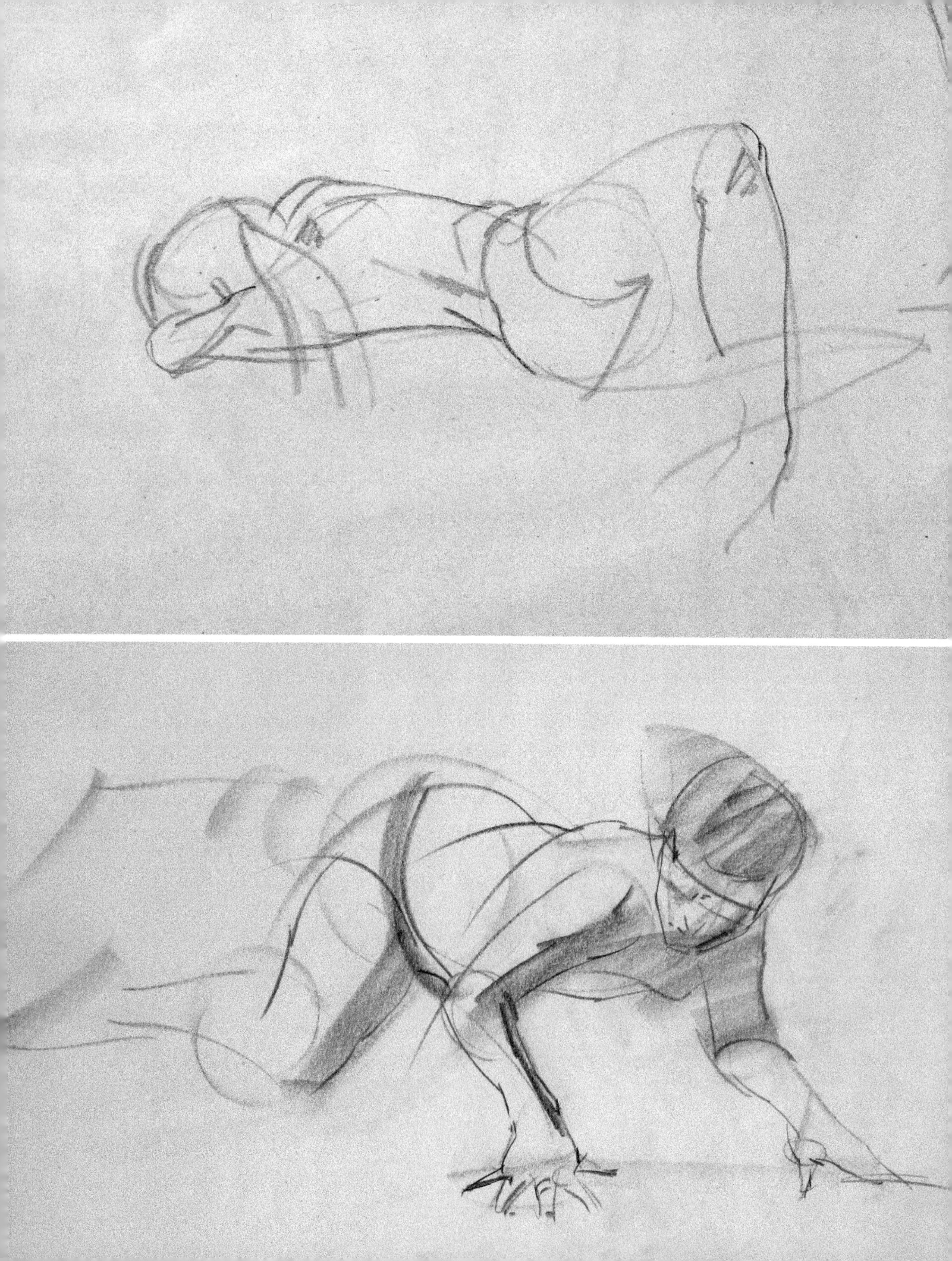

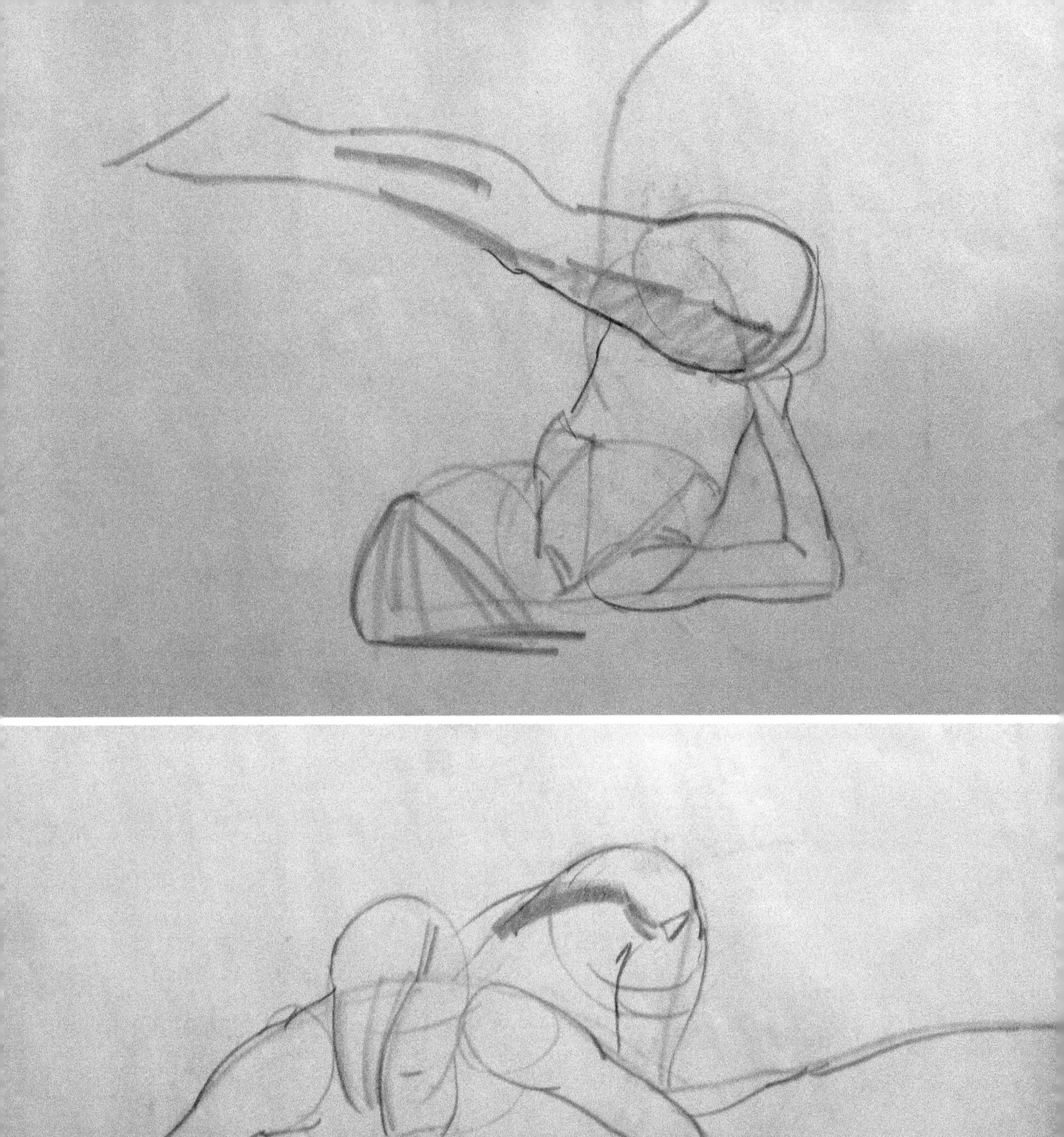

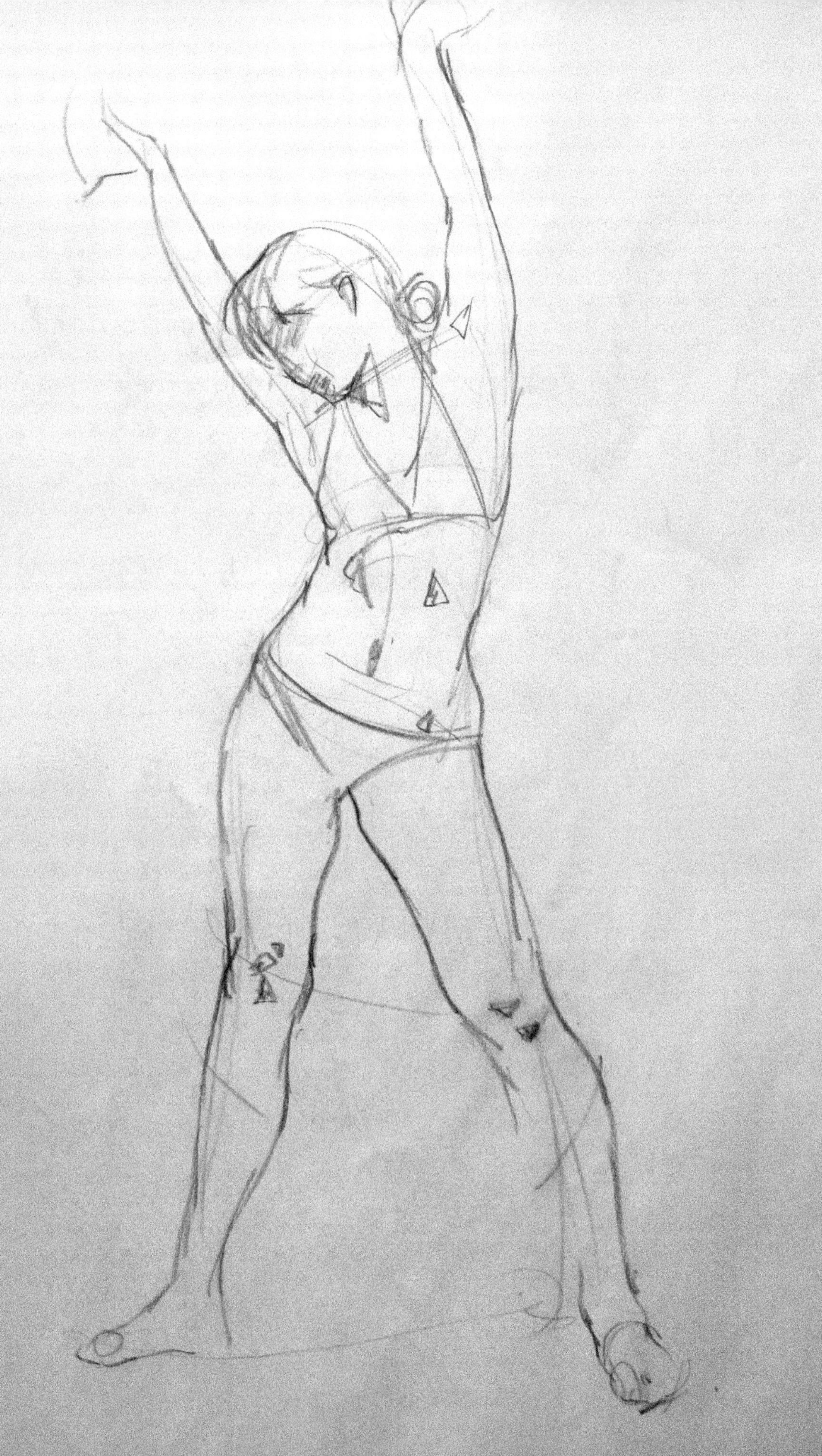

WEIGHT & BALANCE

WEIGHT & BALANCE

Thanks to gravity, everything on earth weighs something. We are all subject to it and are all, therefore, grounded as human beings. Without even thinking about it, we innately balance our weight so as to not tumble over. In drawing, the figure needs to look like he or she is grounded and isn't going to float off into space. It is important to determine how weight is distributed in the figure. In a standing figure, usually one side bears slightly more weight than the other. So, why is it important to identify which side this is? It helps the viewer understand and better feel the pose. If a student can recognize proper weight distribution, their drawings look more believable. Their figures look like living and breathing human beings who aren't going to fall over or float away.

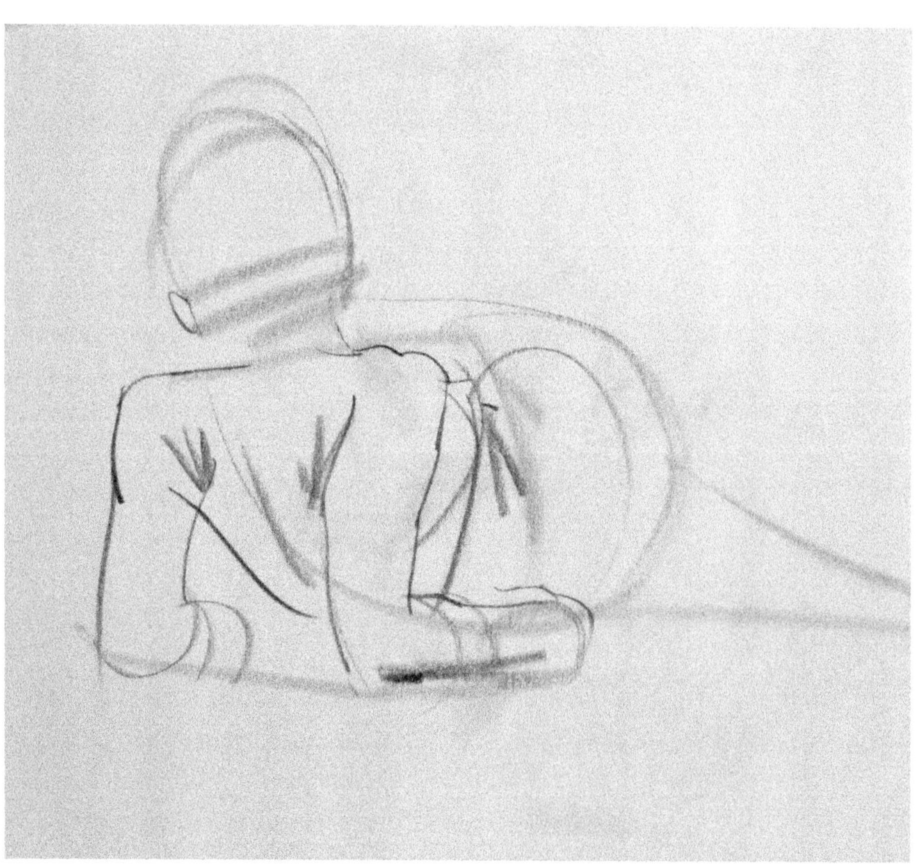

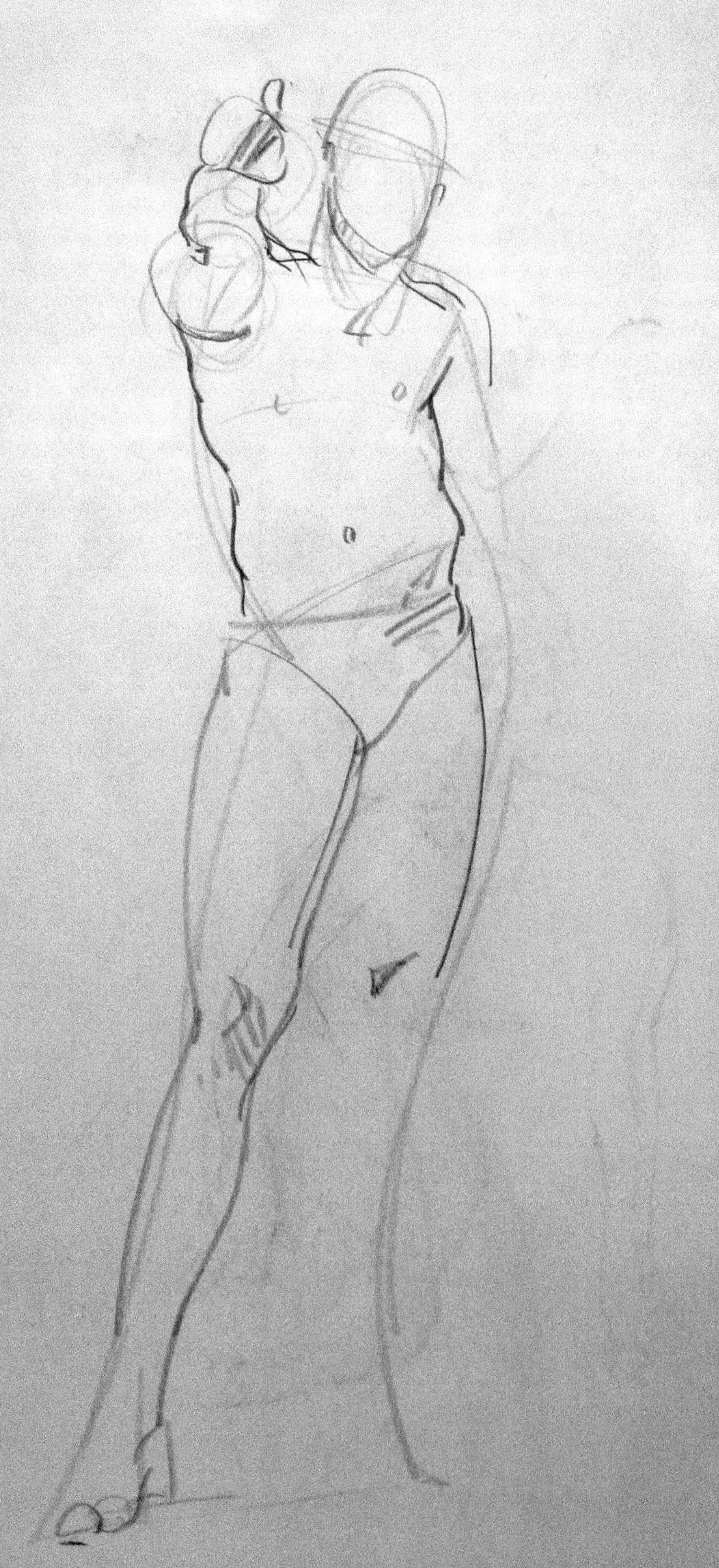

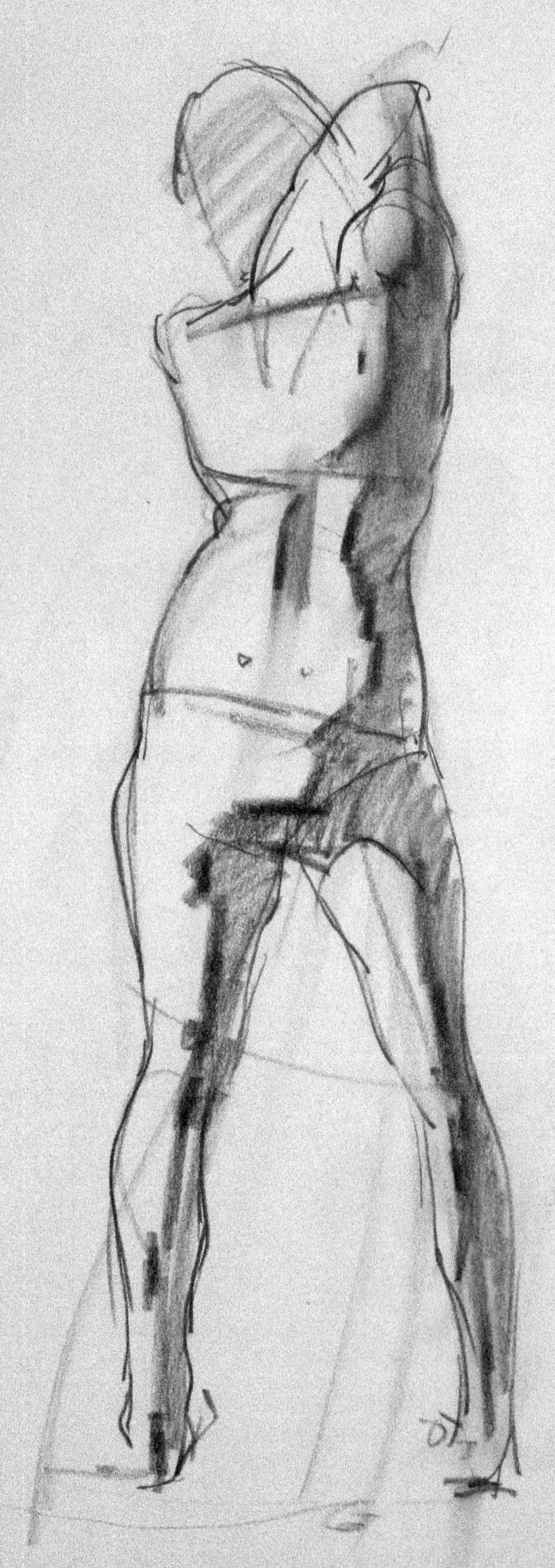

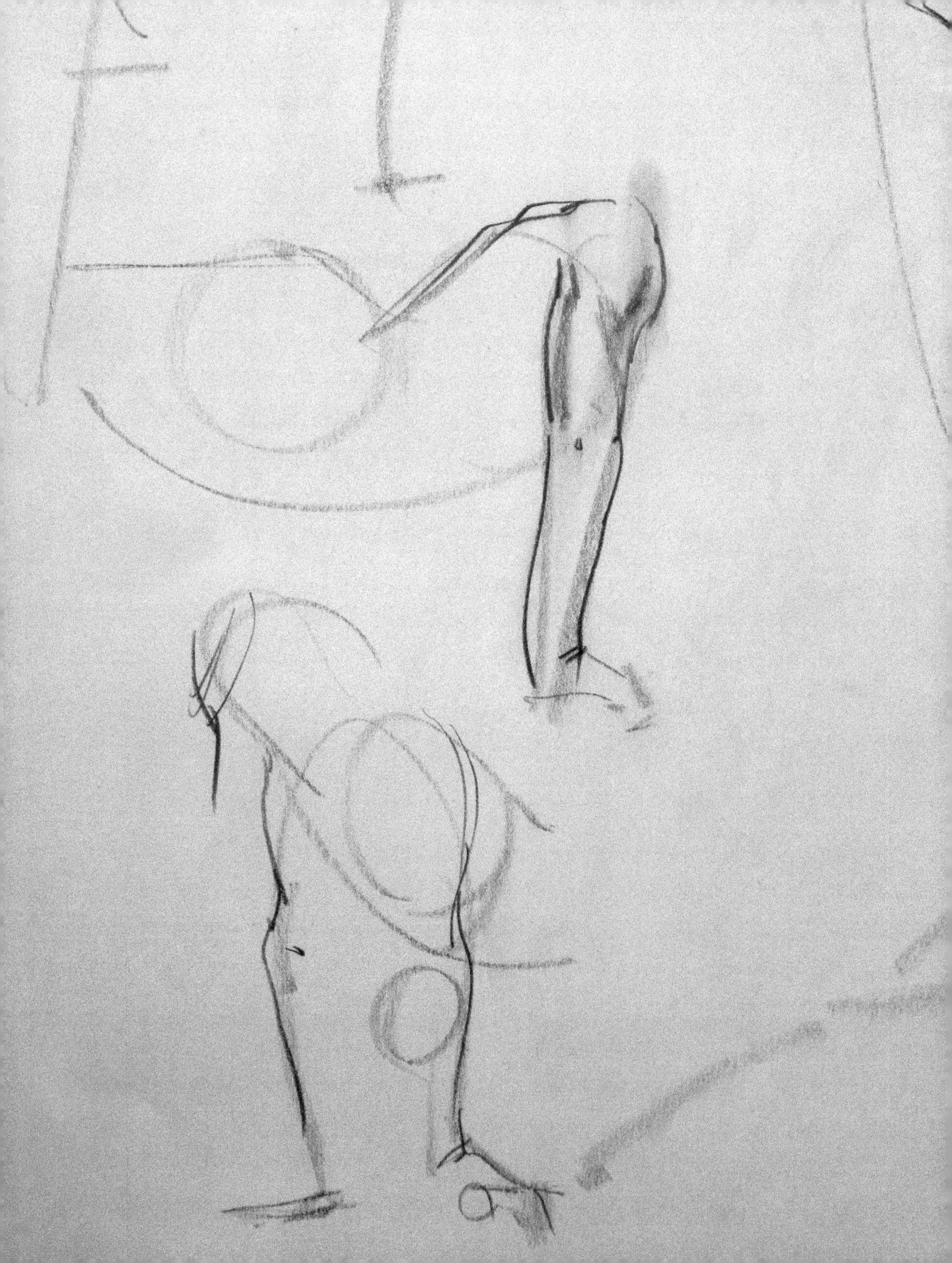

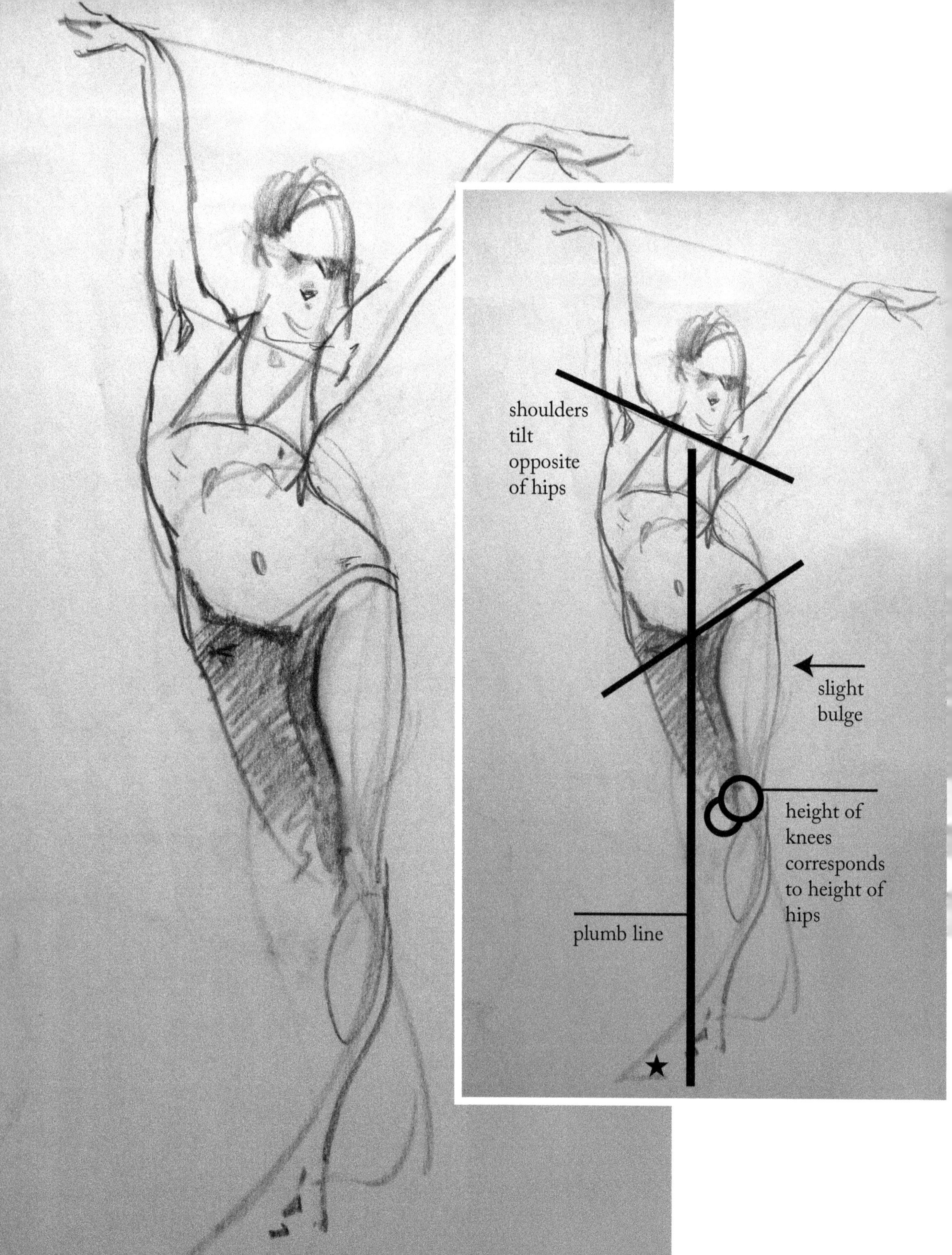

shoulders
tilt
opposite
of hips
slight
bulge
height of
knees
corresponds
to height of
hips
plumb line

INDICATORS OF WEIGHT

There are several ways to identify which side of the body is carrying more weight. The quicker an artist can identify these indicators of weight, the quicker they can assess weight distribution. When time is precious, as it is in gesture drawing, these indicators become extremely useful.

Drop a plumb line (a vertical line used to help with alignment) from the pit of the neck straight downward. This can actually be drawn on the paper, or can be pictured in the mind. Where that plumb line lands tells a lot. The foot that is closer to this plumb line is the one bearing more of the weight. The hip that bears more weight is higher than its counterpart. Like I encourage in the previous section, *exaggerate* this tilt of the hips when drawing it in. In order for the body to stand upright, it often takes a contrapposto stance, or counter-pose, as the shoulders tilt the opposite direction of the hips. The tilt of both the hips and the shoulders act as visual clues. A further indication of weight includes the height of the knees. If one hip is higher (meaning it bears more weight) then the knee on that same leg is going to be higher than the knee on the other leg. This is fairly basic logic, yet it is often forgotten when drawing the model. Bulging muscles also indicate weight. The leg that carries more weight works harder. Notice how the muscles on that leg bulge and contract more than those same muscles on the other leg, which are passive and relaxed in comparison. I often use aggressive and active lines to show more weight, and I use soft, light, and sweeping lines to show less weight and to make this differentiation apparent. When a figure is standing and has a lot of weight on one leg, there is usually a bulge right below the hip (especially in females) on the outside of the upper thigh. This also happens when a model is sitting down and bearing a lot of weight on one arm. The bulge here happens right below the shoulder at the tricep. Additionally, it is important to note that when a figure is standing with a lot of weight on one leg, that leg will curve inwards as it goes down toward the ground. This is the body's way of staying in balance.

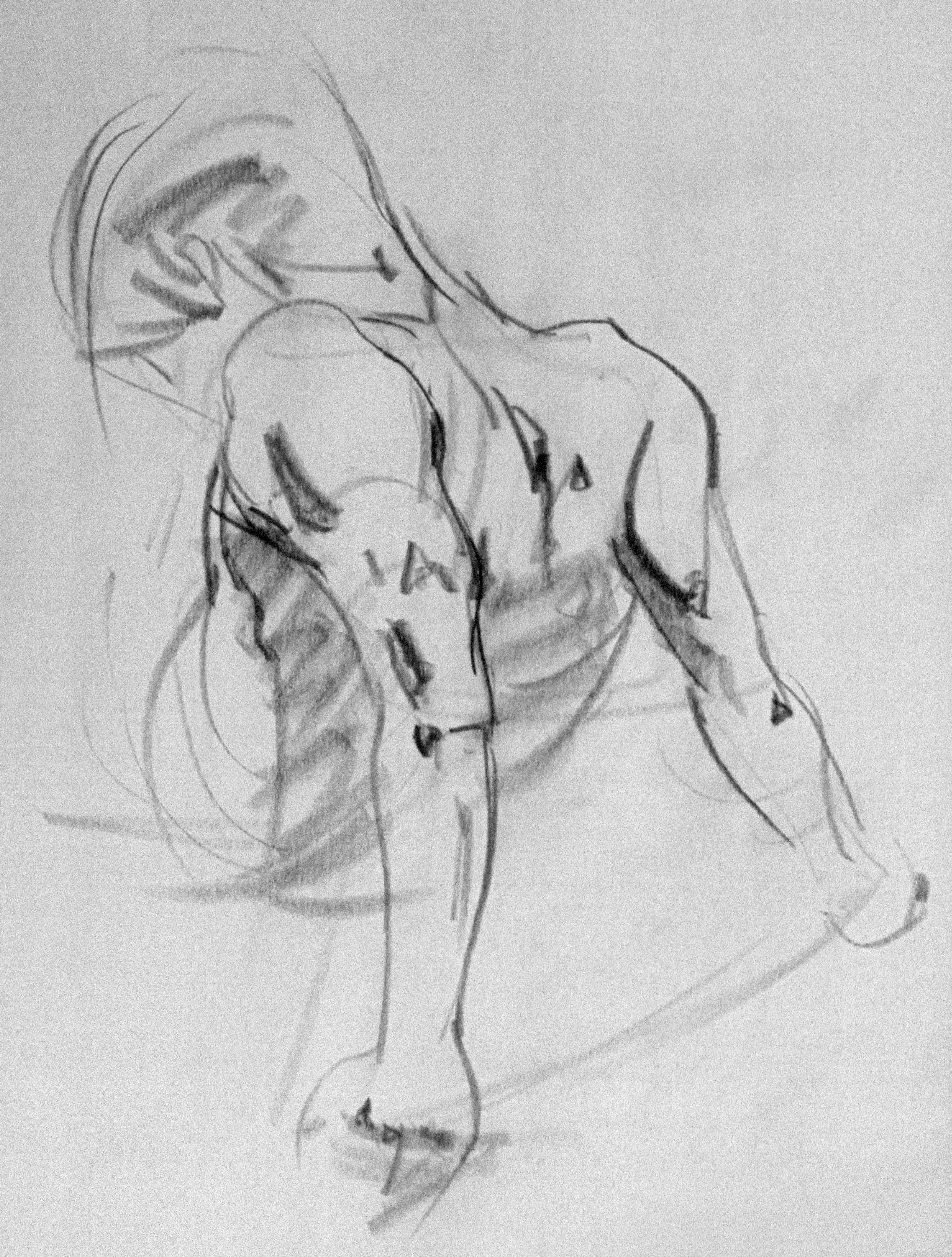

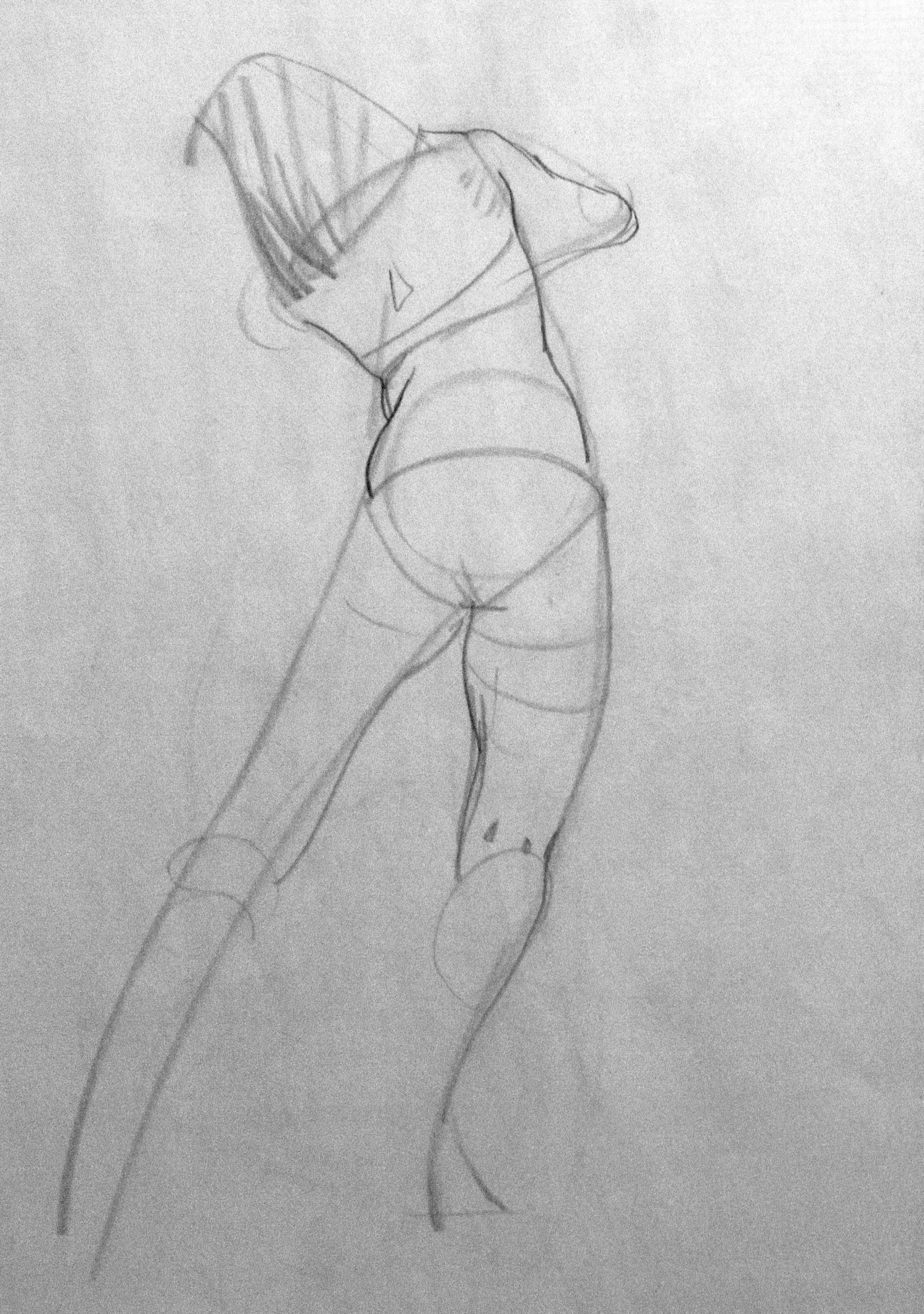

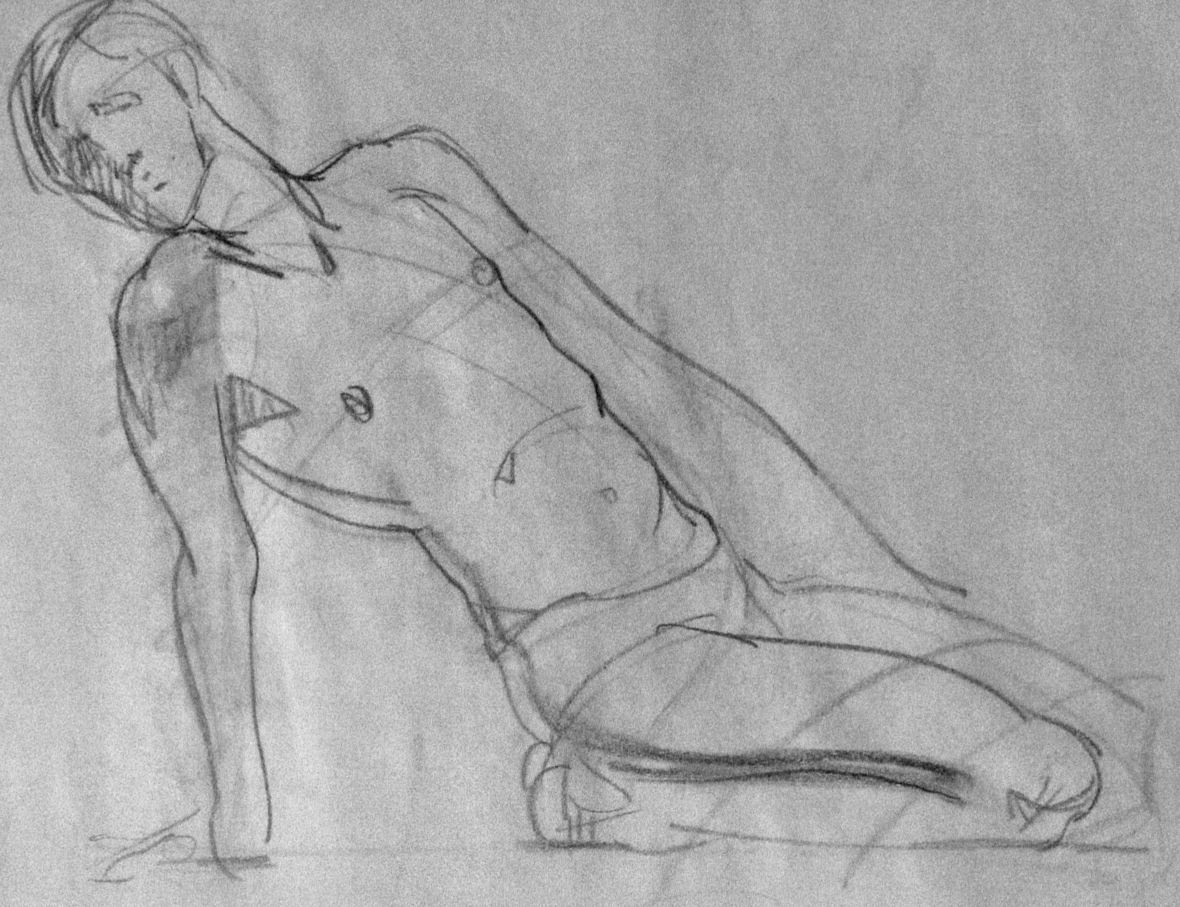

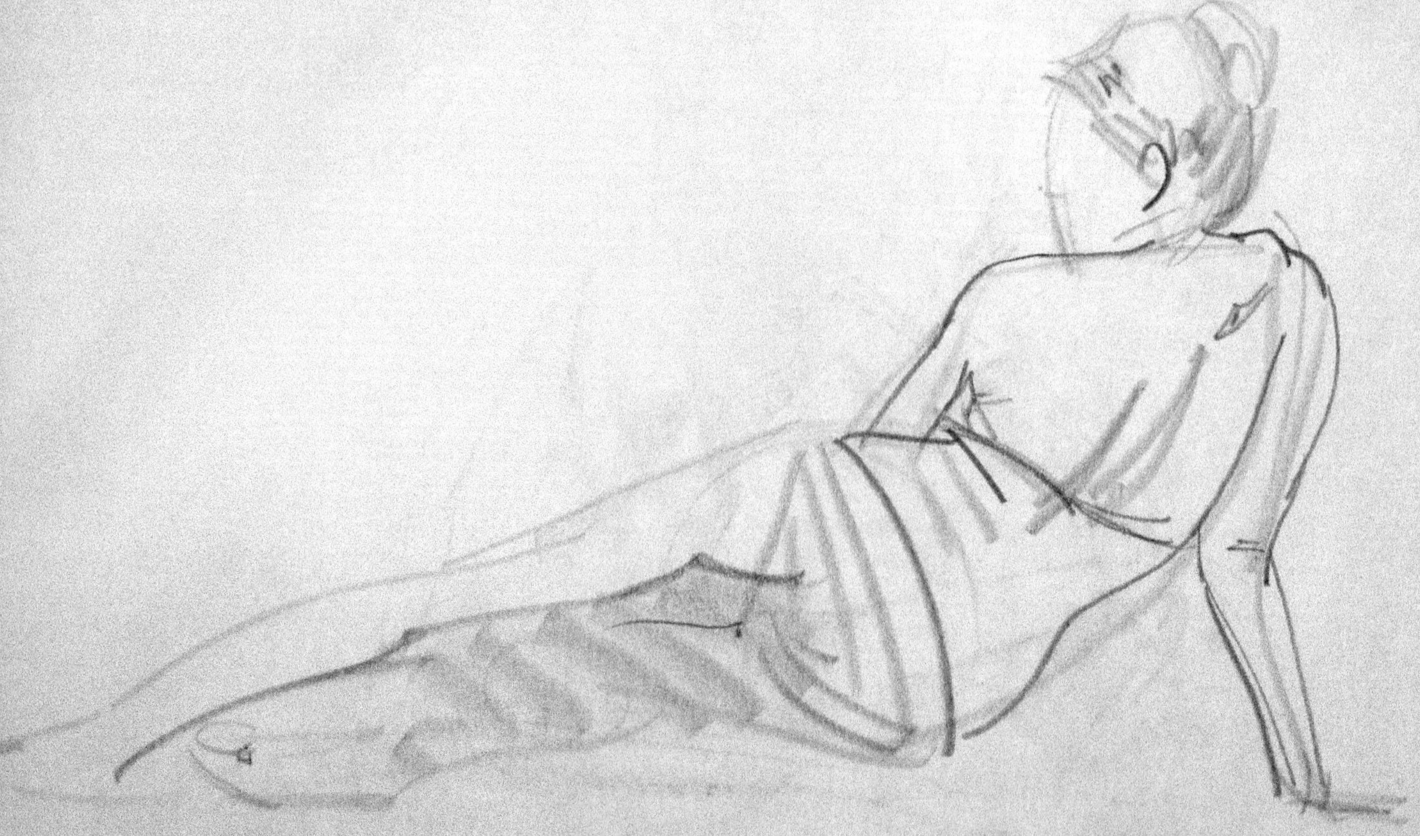

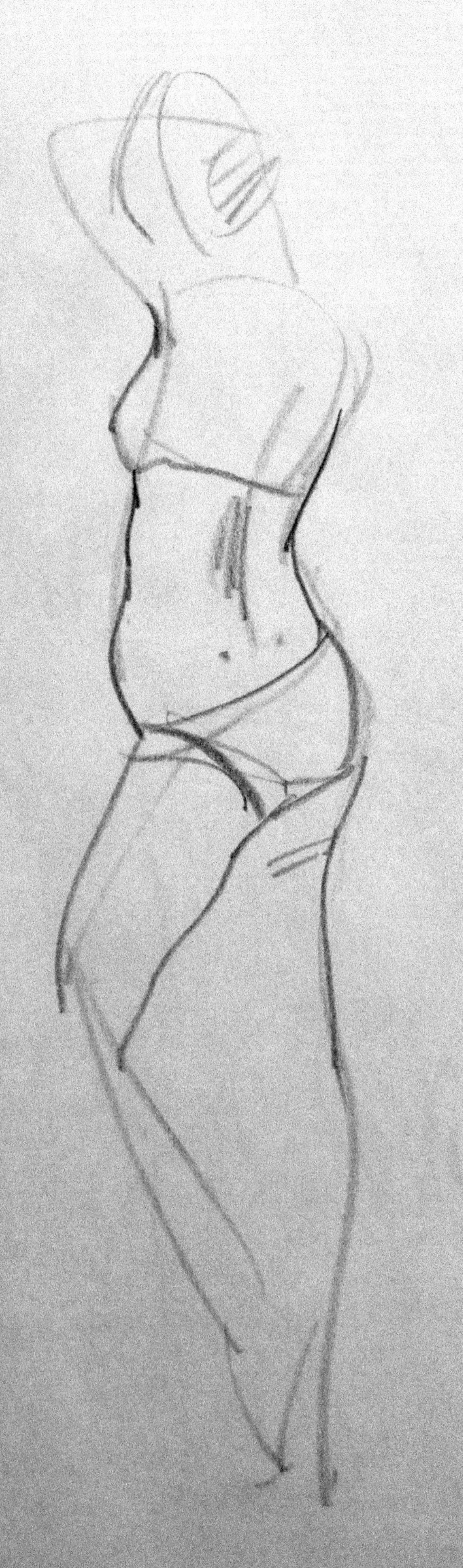

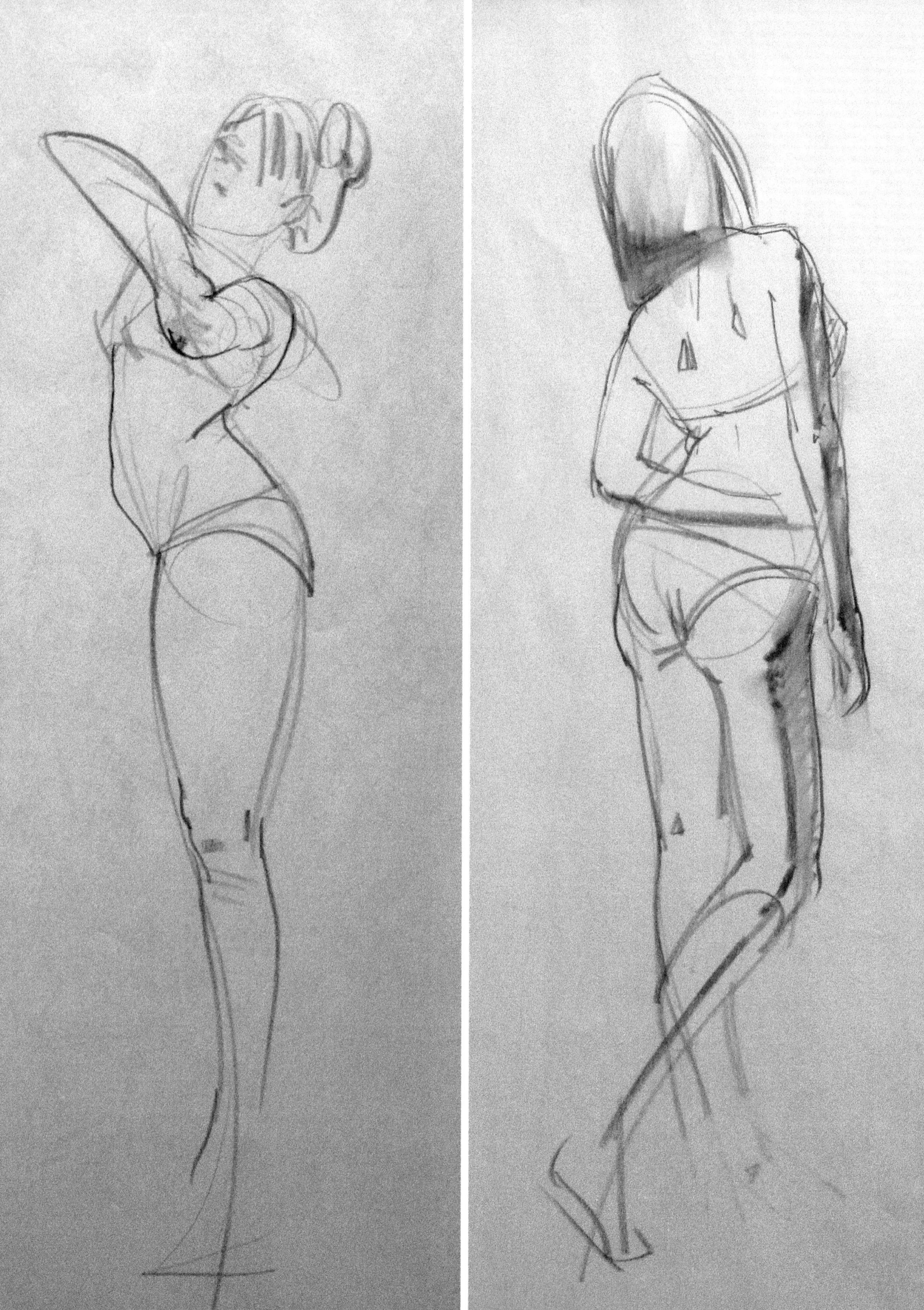

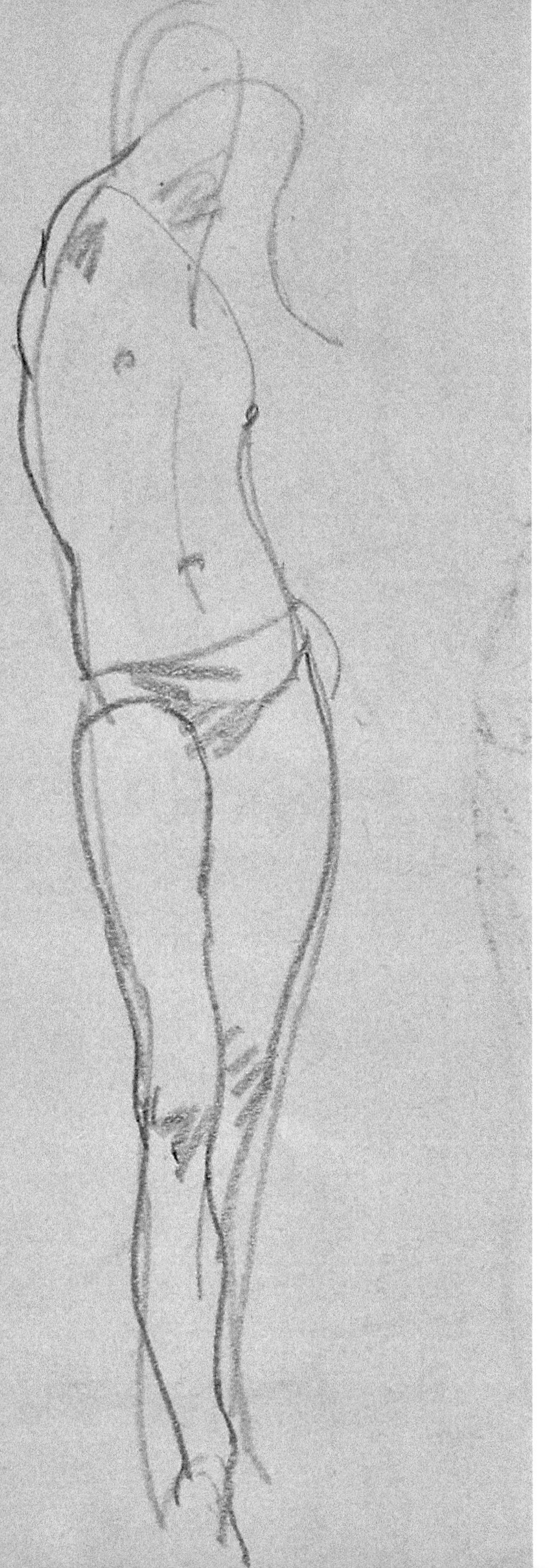

DETECTIVE WORK

Why is it important to pay attention to the weight distribution in each pose? I often ask myself this question, which leads me to a series of answers. If I know which side is bearing more weight, I will know the tilt of the hips. Because I know which hip is higher, I will know which knee is higher and is more active, and I will know where I might accentuate bulging muscles. I will know that the shoulders tilt in the opposite direction of the hips, which will tell me about the bend and stretch of the torso! There are a lot of things I can quickly discover and speedily draw in just by knowing the distribution of weight in a standing figure. In a way, it is sort of like acting as a detective. As soon as just one of these clues is identified, several more can easily be seen. Many of the indicators aren't apparent at first glance though, and watch out for tricky optical illusions. For example, in a certain pose it may appear at first glance that the shoulders are tilting down to the right, but it is clear that the hips are also tilting down to the right. Since it can be decided that the hips are unmistakably tilting down to the right, this would denote that the shoulders should actually be tilting the opposite direction, down to the left. By looking at the shoulders again, sure enough, it is evident that they *are* actually tilting to the left!

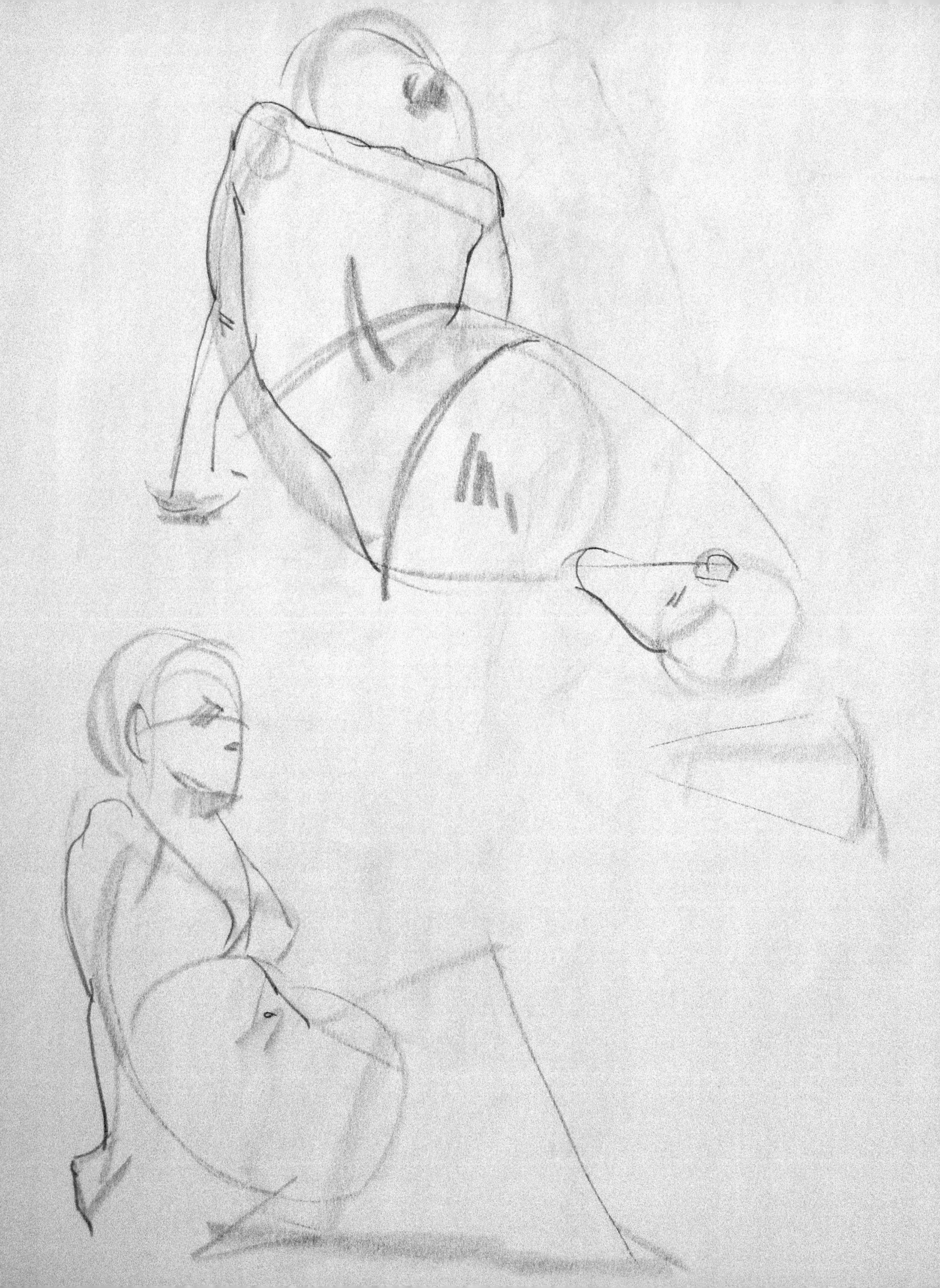

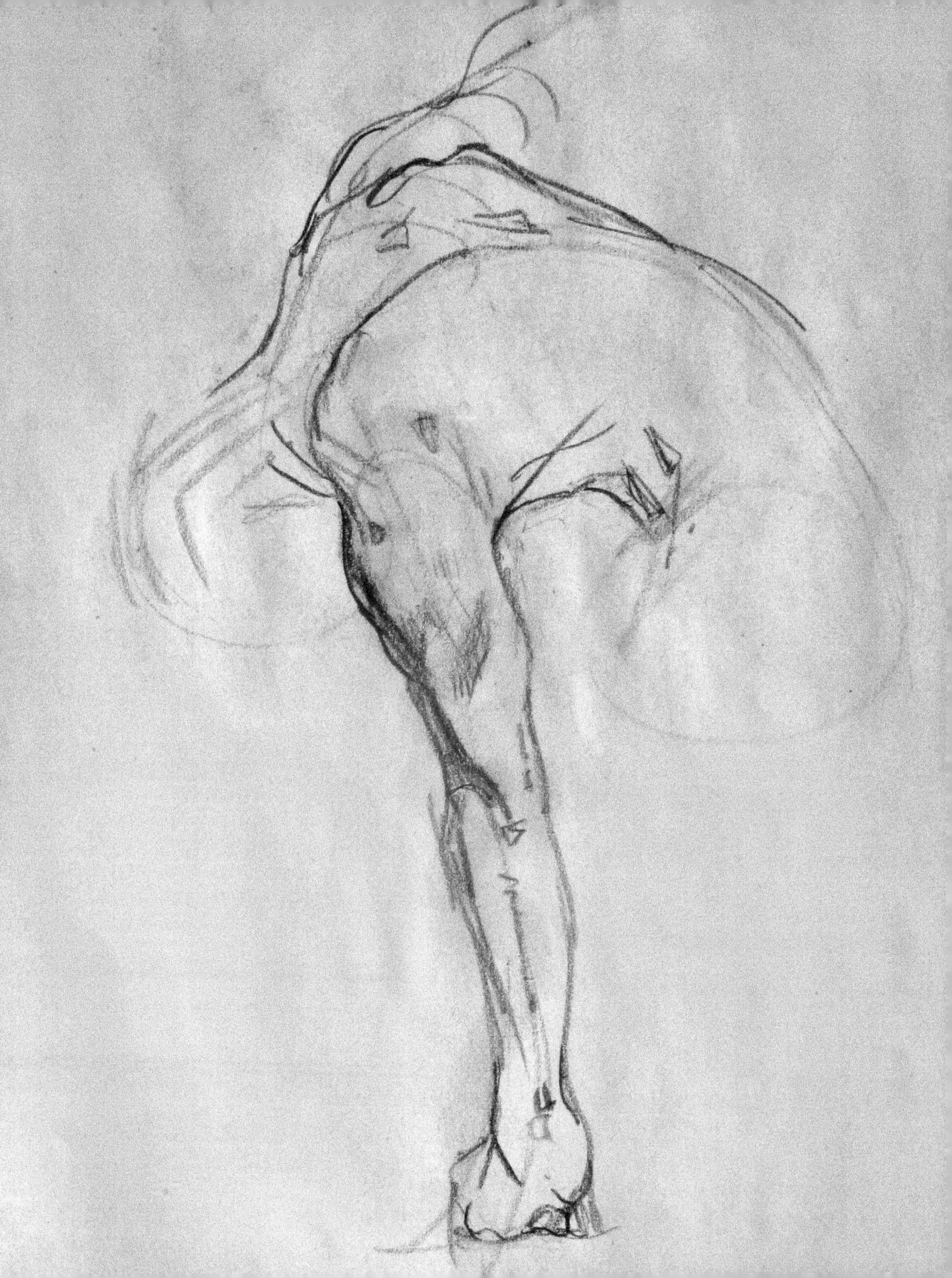

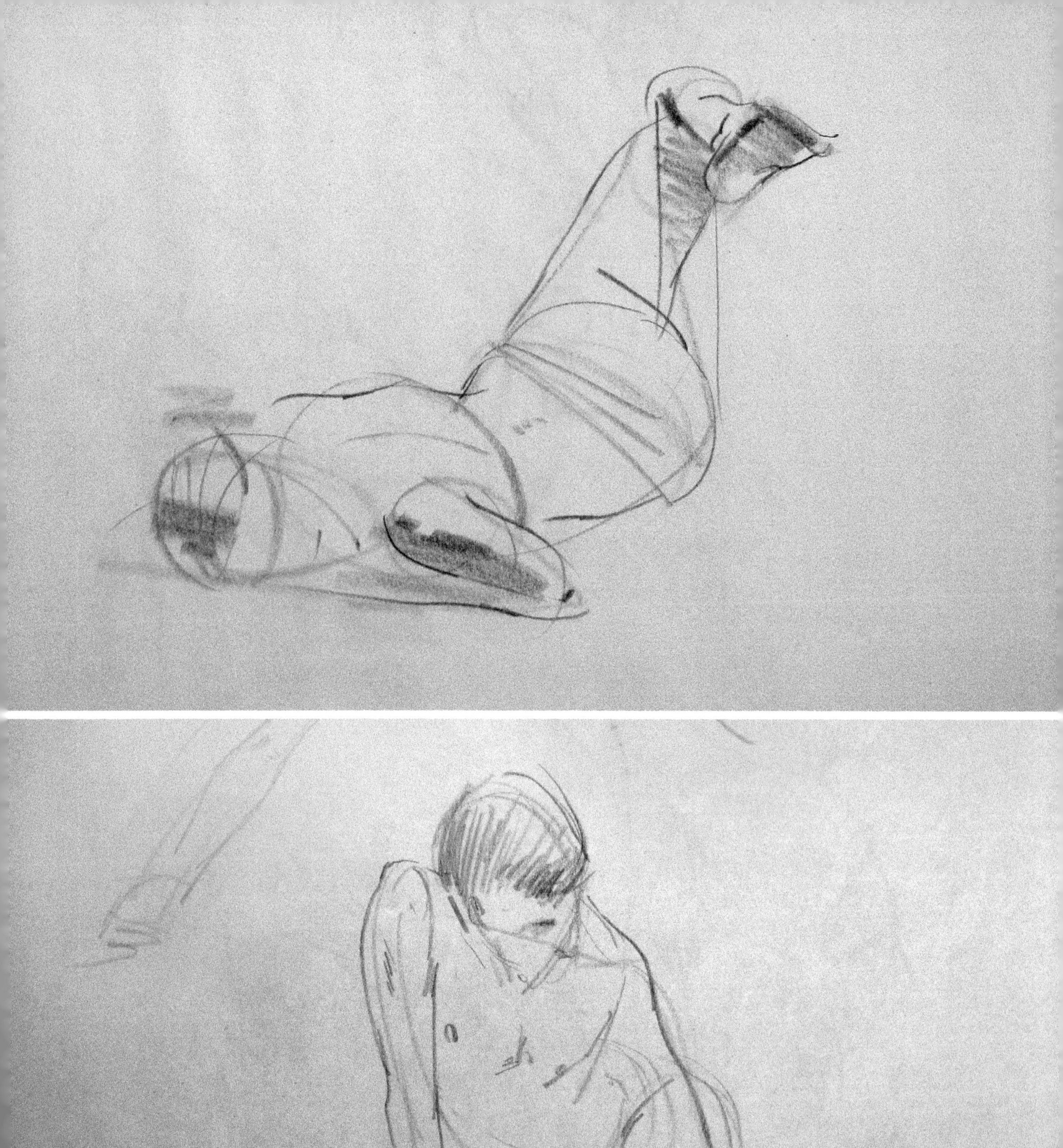

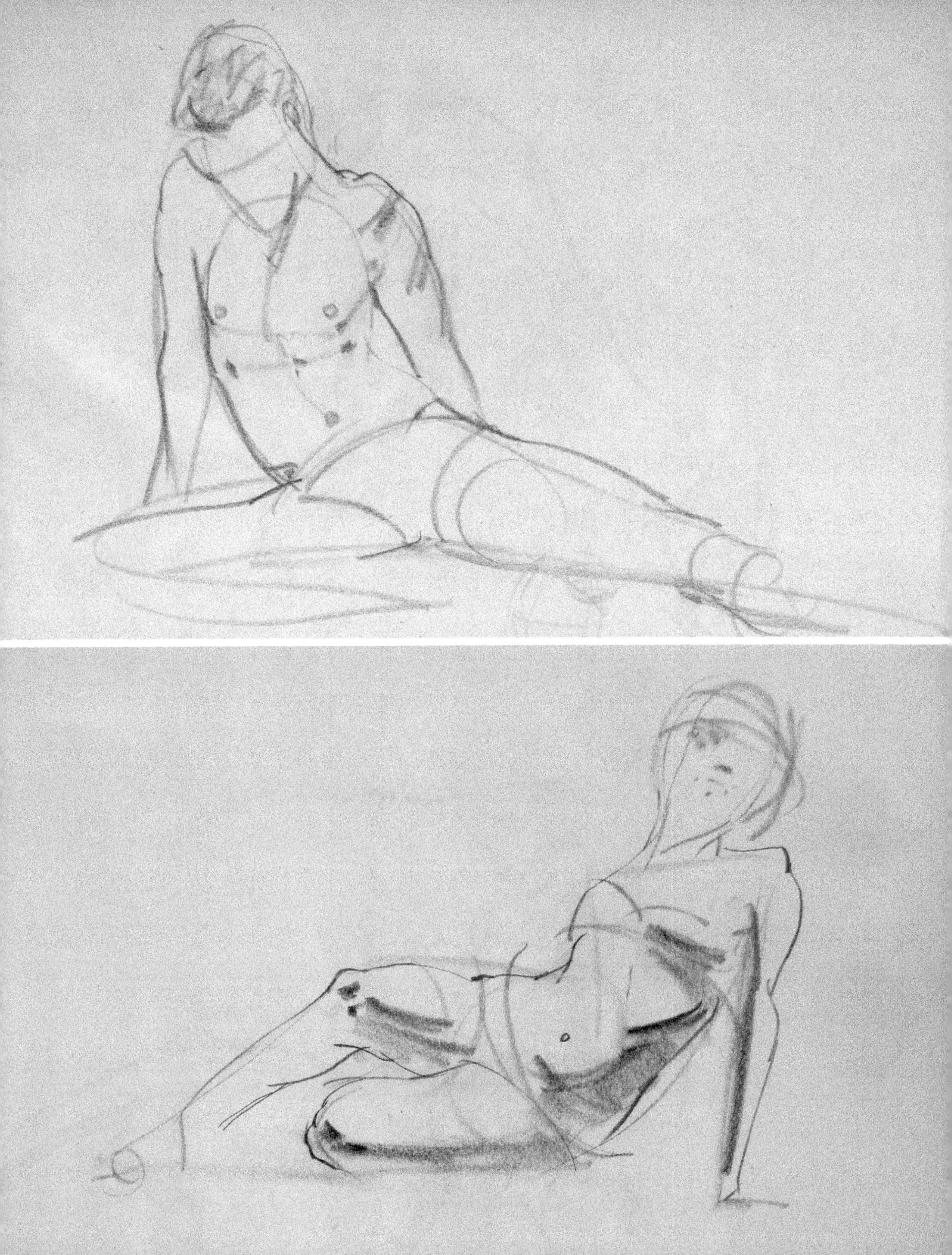

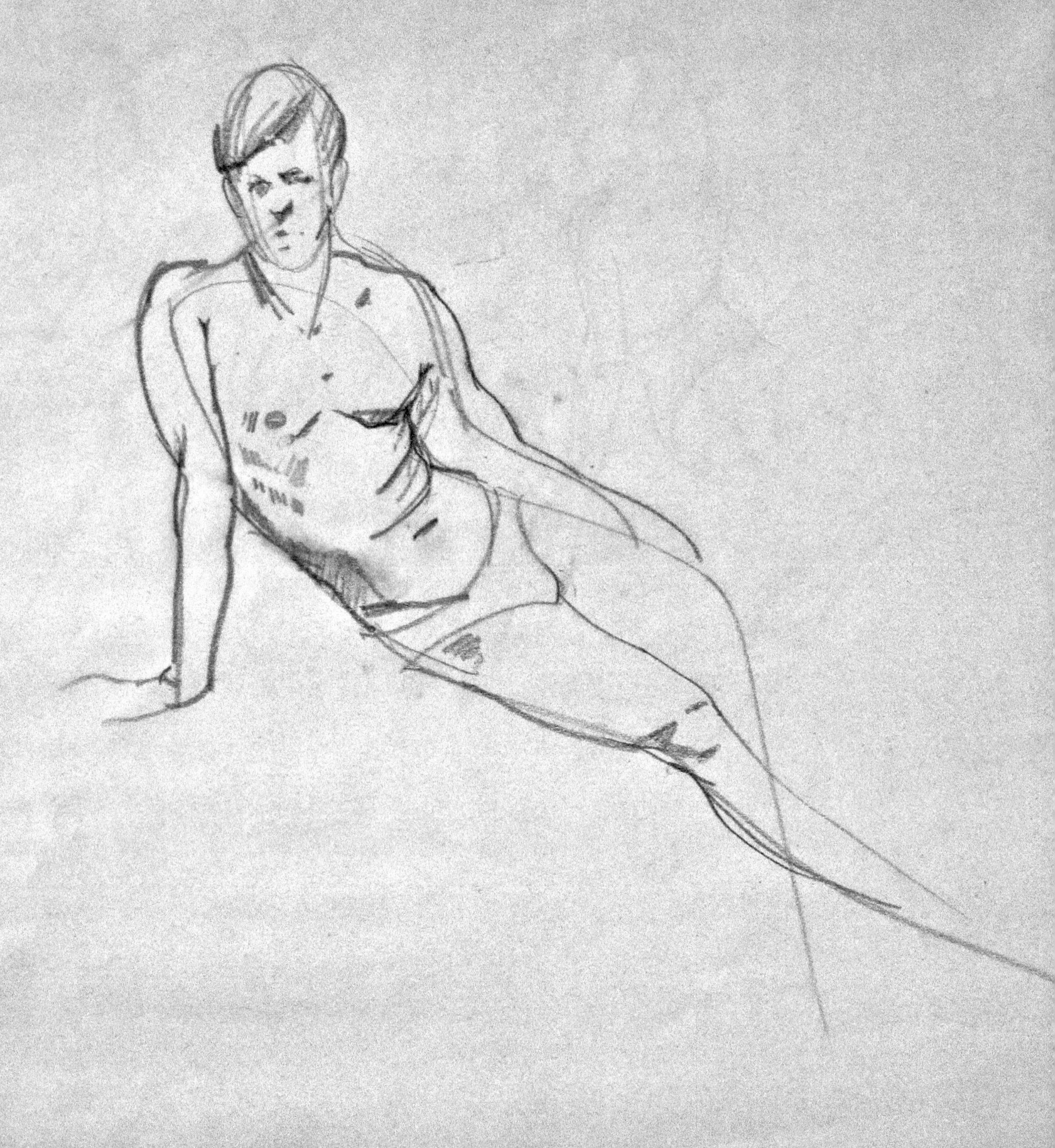

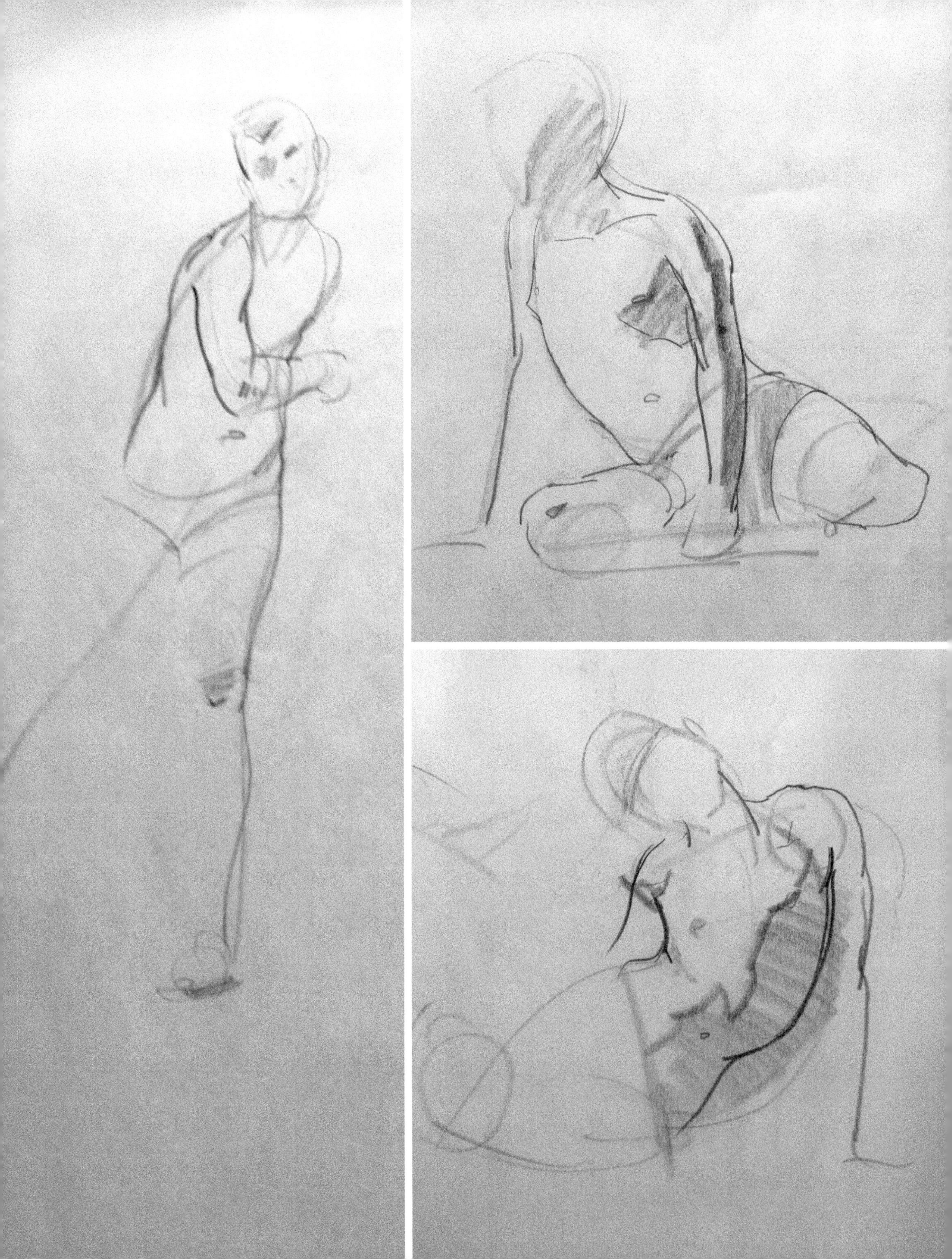

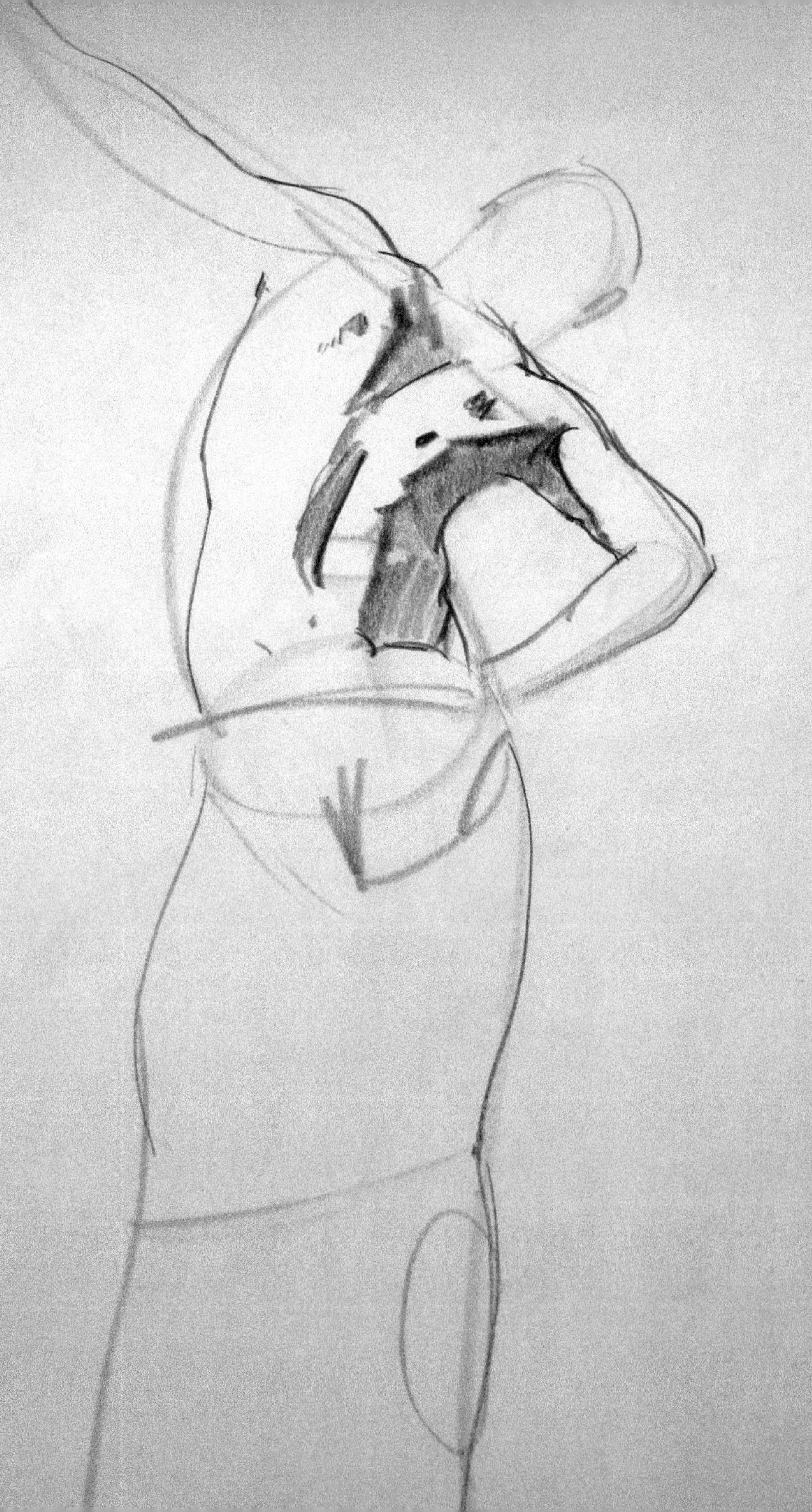

SYMMETRY

SYMMETRY

Symmetry is a simple term with which most everyone is familiar. Simply put, it means that one side mirrors the other. Now, how does this idea of symmetry apply to figure drawing? Symmetry, like weight and balance, helps check the placement of certain landmarks. It gives confidence that the lines and marks are drawn in the right place. Our bodies are symmetrical, meaning that one side mirrors the other (for the most part). We have two eyes, two shoulders, two hipbones, two knees, and so on. Remembering that the figure is symmetrical helps with correct placement of these features.

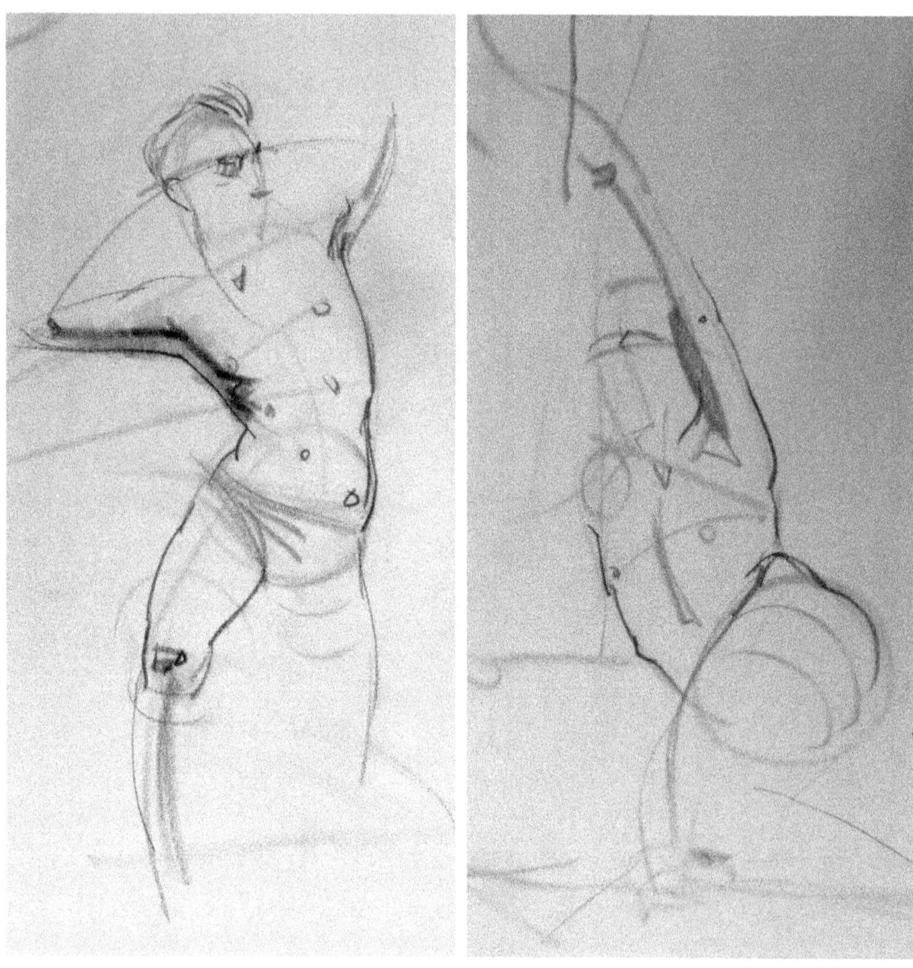

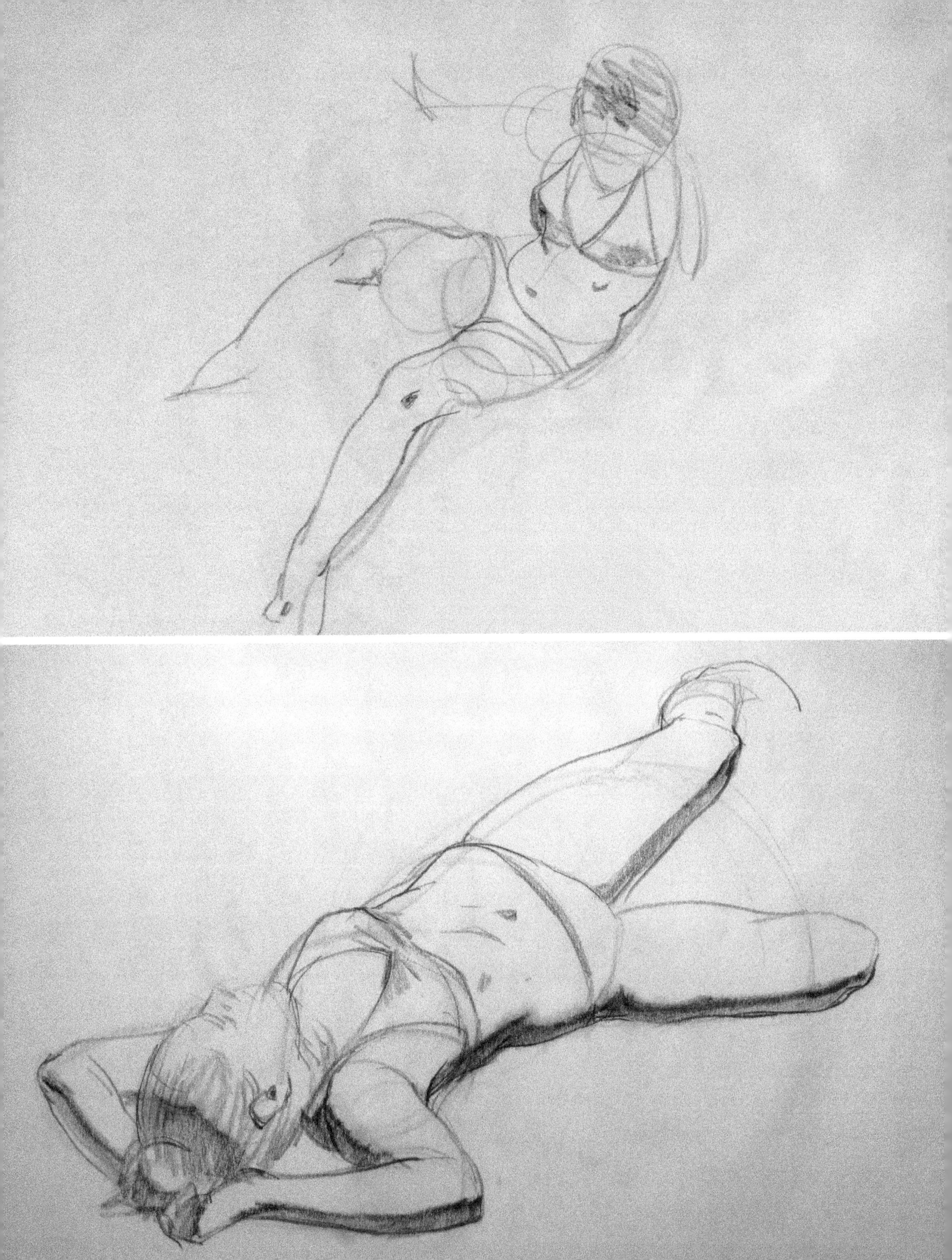

THE LINE OF SYMMETRY

The line of symmetry (also referred to as the line of axis, medial line, or midline) is where one side folds in half and mirrors the other. Think about it as if a long strip of masking tape was placed vertically down the center of the model. That would be the line of symmetry. From the front, it runs down through the center in the following sequence: the forehead, nose, pit of the neck, sternum, navel, and pelvis. The same could be thought of for the backside, which line is basically the spine. Symmetry helps to be accountable for what happens on both sides of the body. If a muscle on one side of the midline is contracting, what is that same muscle doing on the opposite side? Make sure to represent it and accurately show its action and placement.

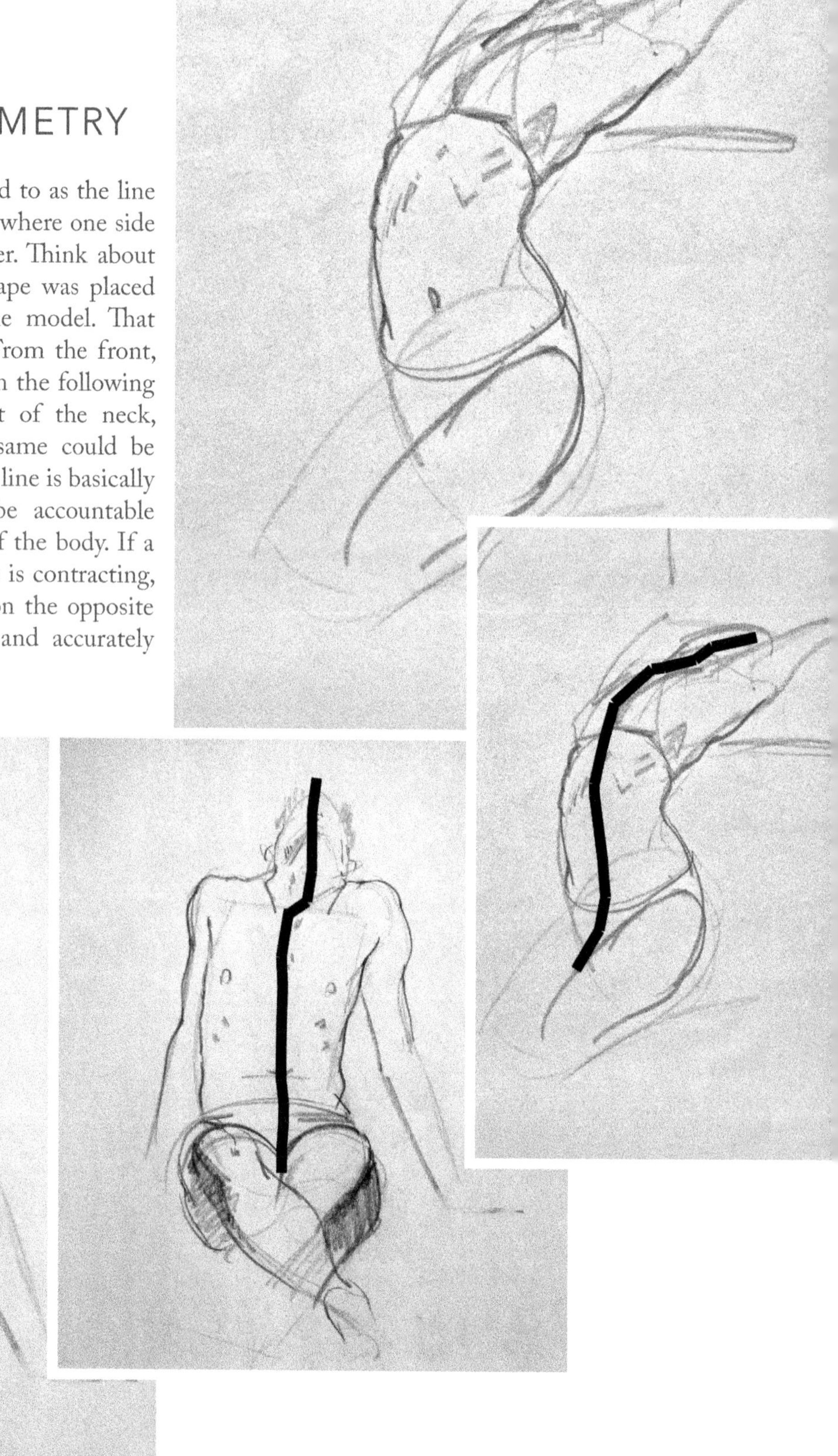

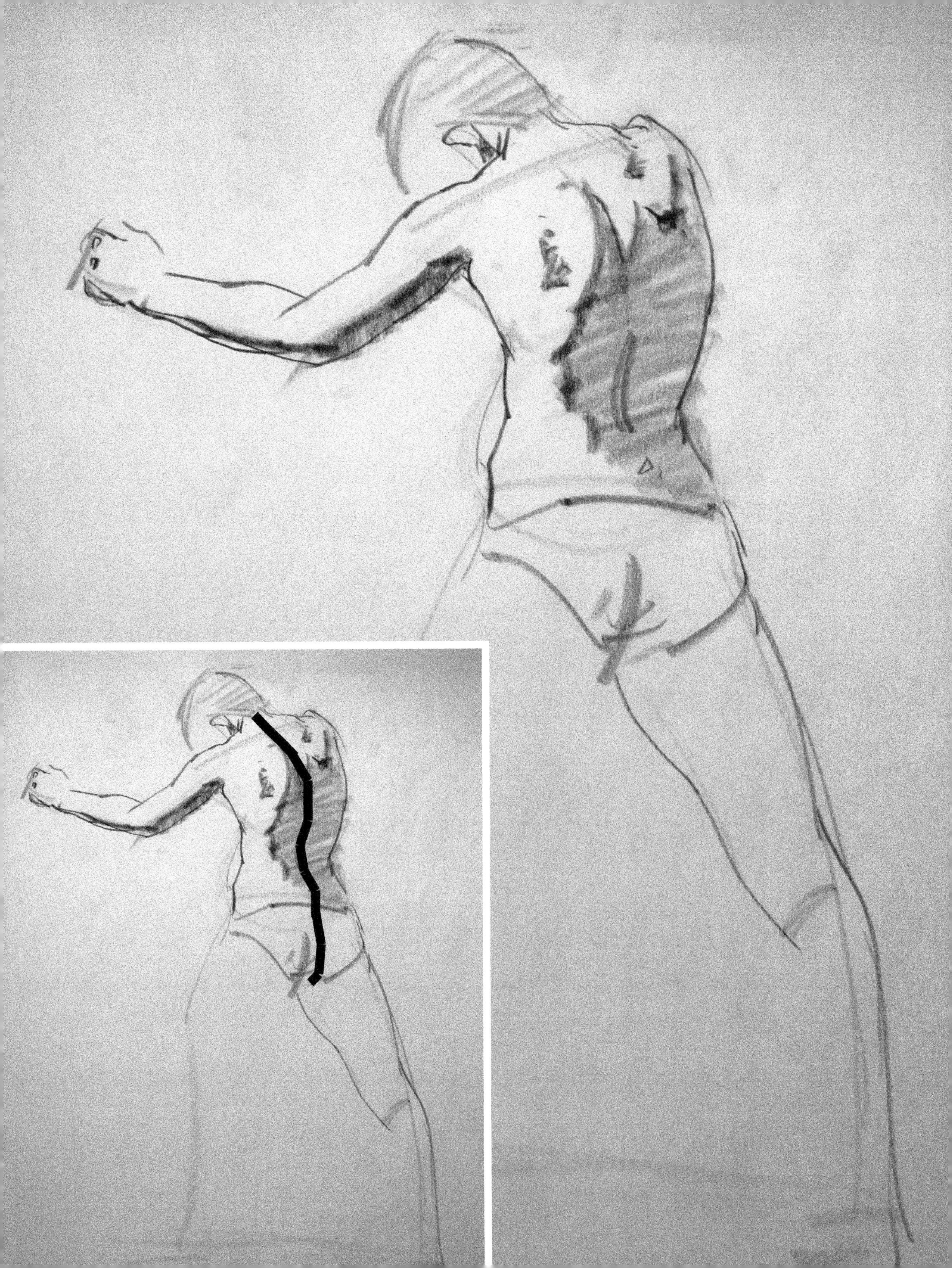

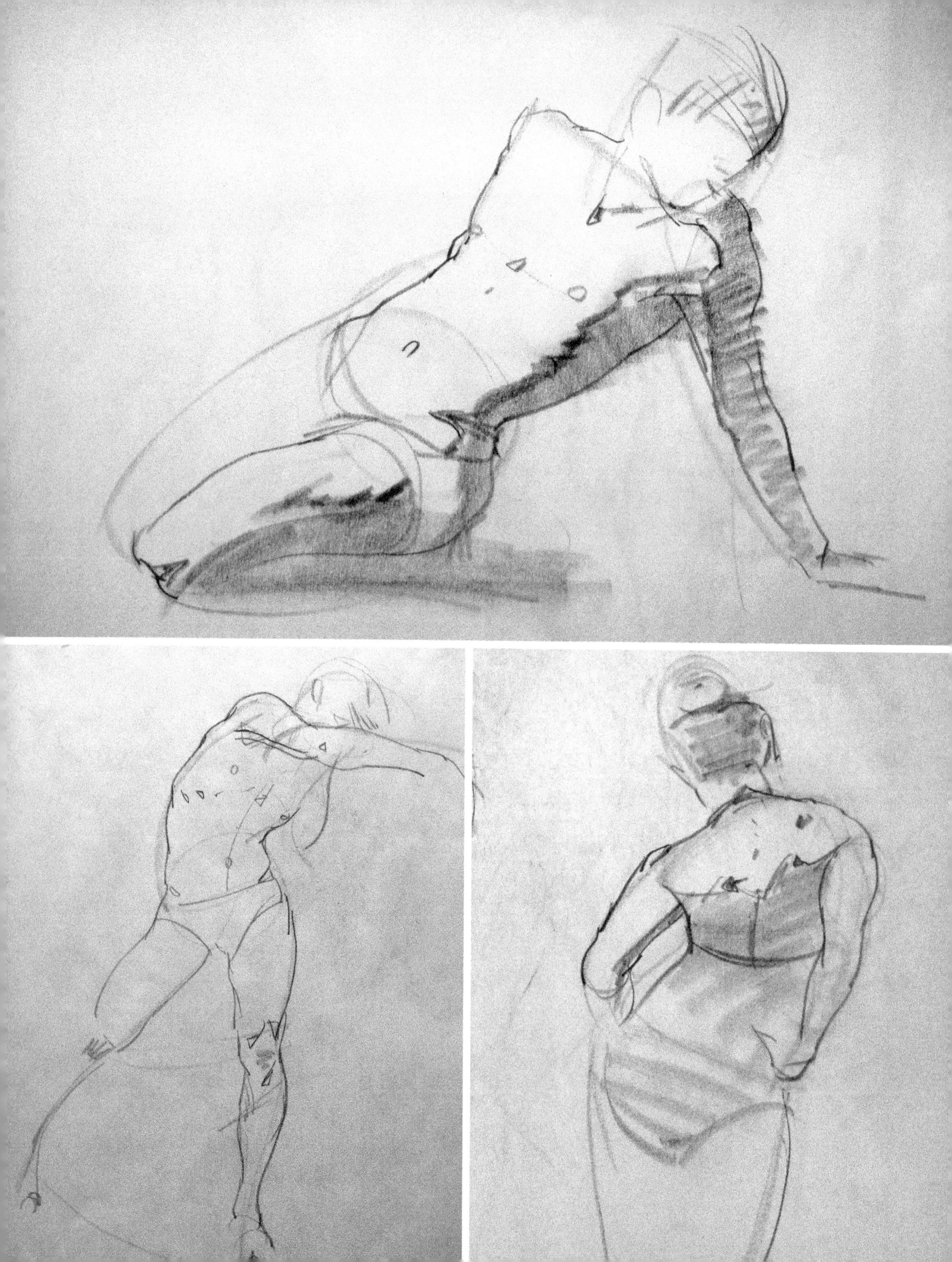

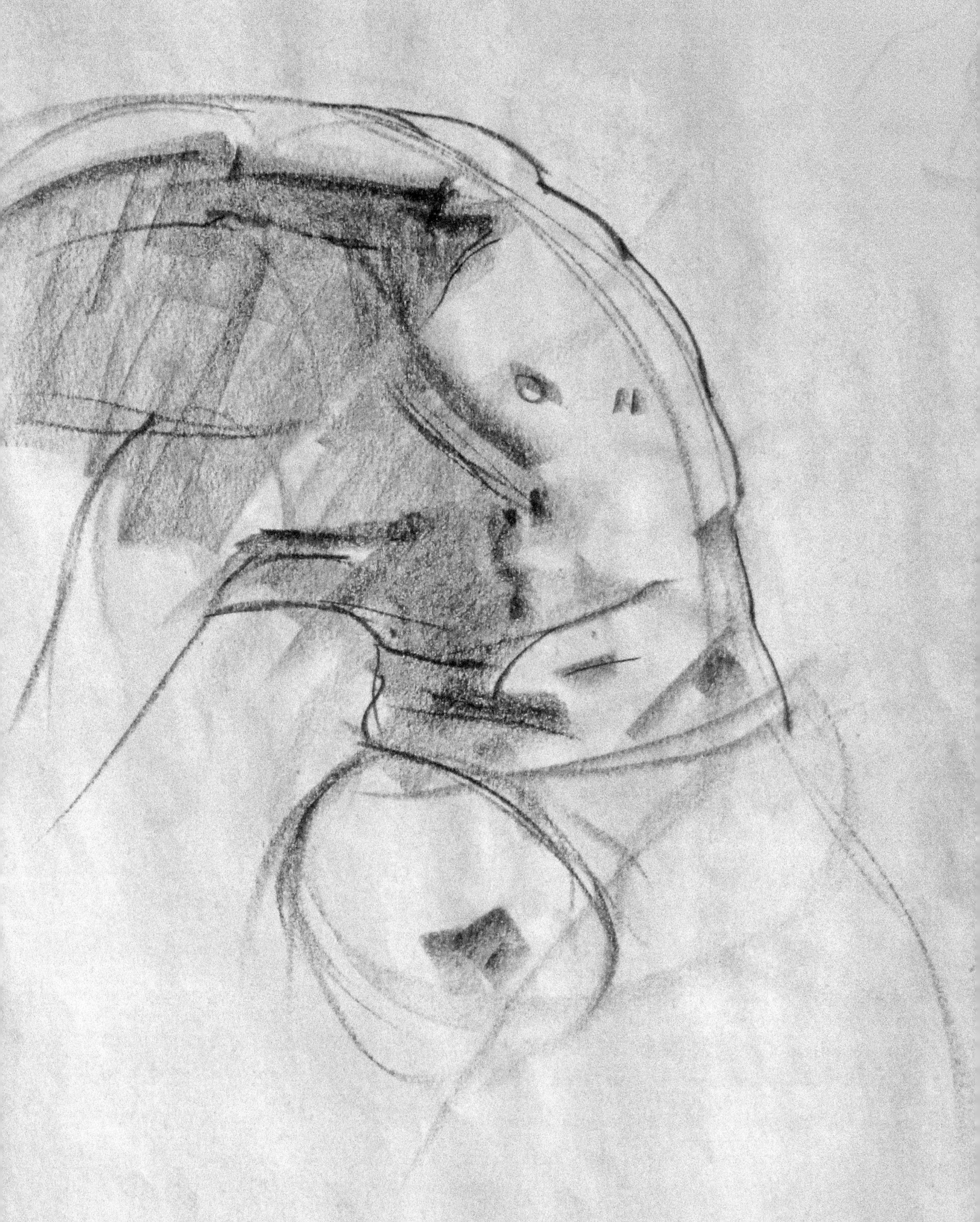

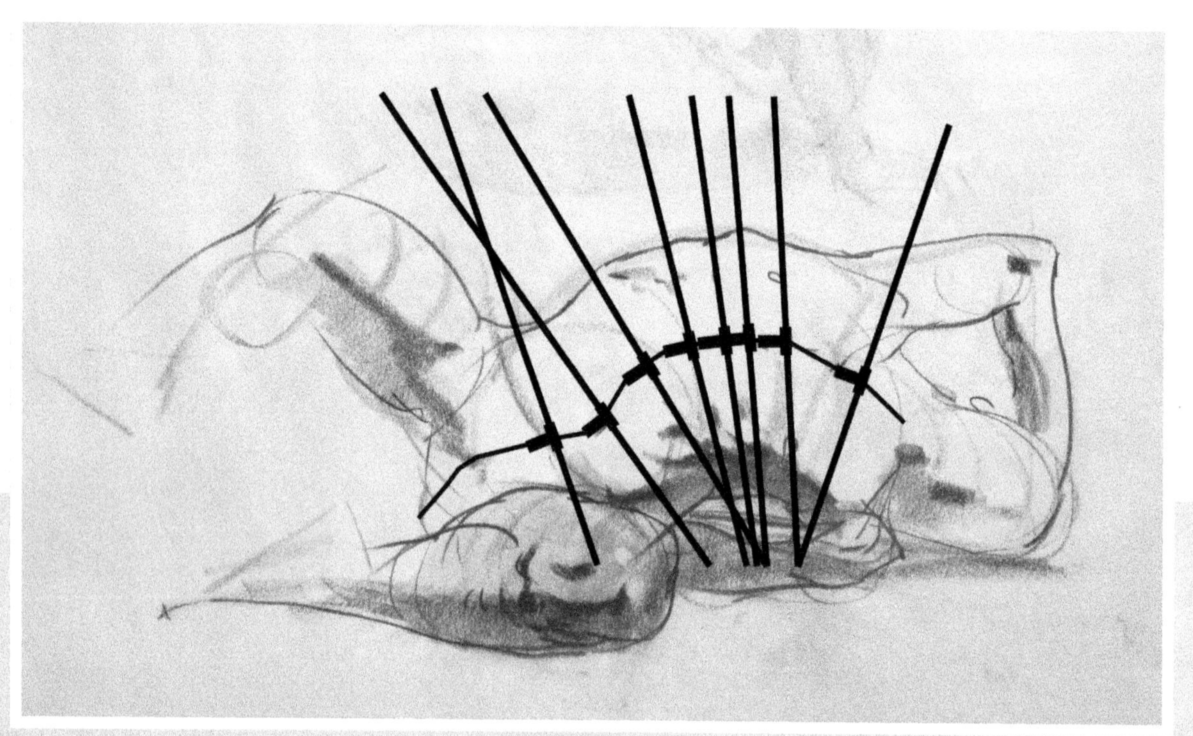

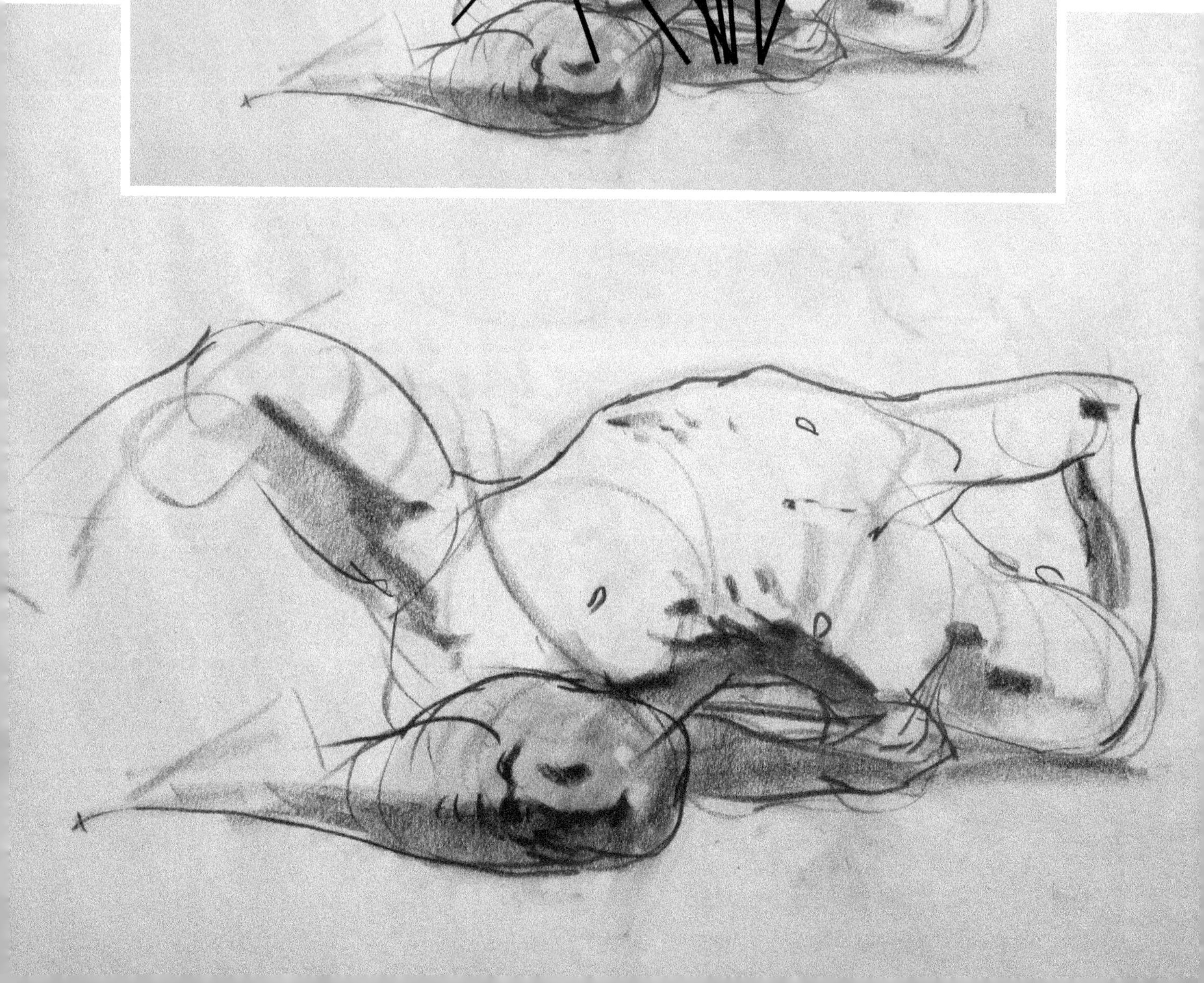

THE T-PRINCIPLE

The T-Principle is also helpful: if a line is drawn to connect symmetrical features on both sides of the midline (e.g., shoulder to shoulder, rib to rib, hip to hip) that connecting line will intersect the midline at a right angle and form a T. This principle holds true no matter what tilt or turn the midline takes.

I find the idea of symmetry to be especially helpful in the stomach/abdominal area and also in the back. These regions are often intimidating because so much is happening under the skin, but yet it is difficult to recognize exactly what. The T-Principle and the idea of symmetry will make sense of the chaos. For instance, a prominent rib may be identified poking out on one side of the abdomen. By paying attention to the tilt of the midline and utilizing the T-Principle to align the jutting rib perpendicularly to and through the axis, it will reveal the precise location of the twin rib on the opposite side. Understanding the law of symmetry gives greater confidence to make deliberate marks. It will also help stabilize the figure and establish greater continuity in your drawings.

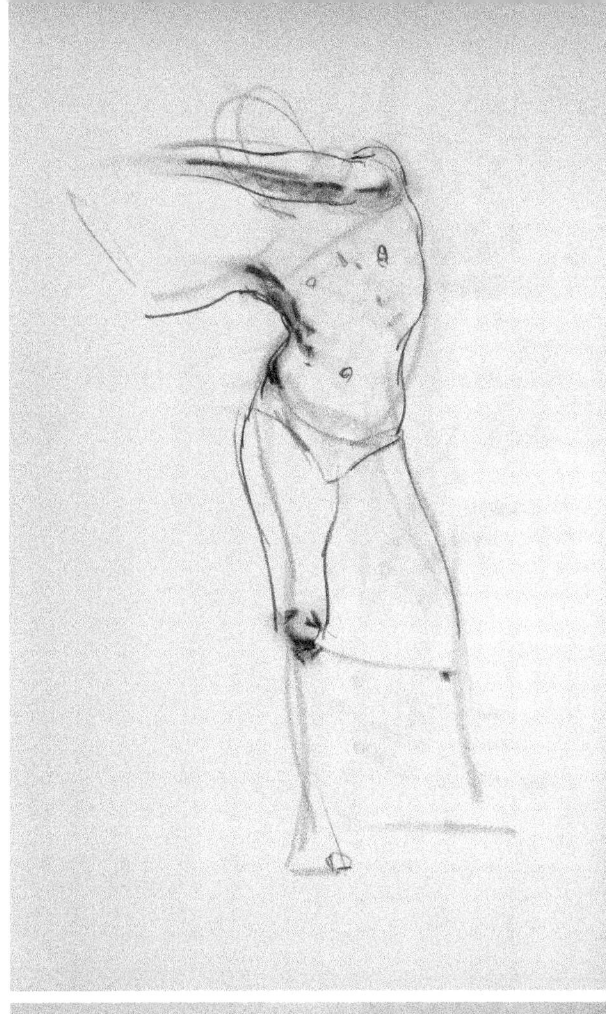

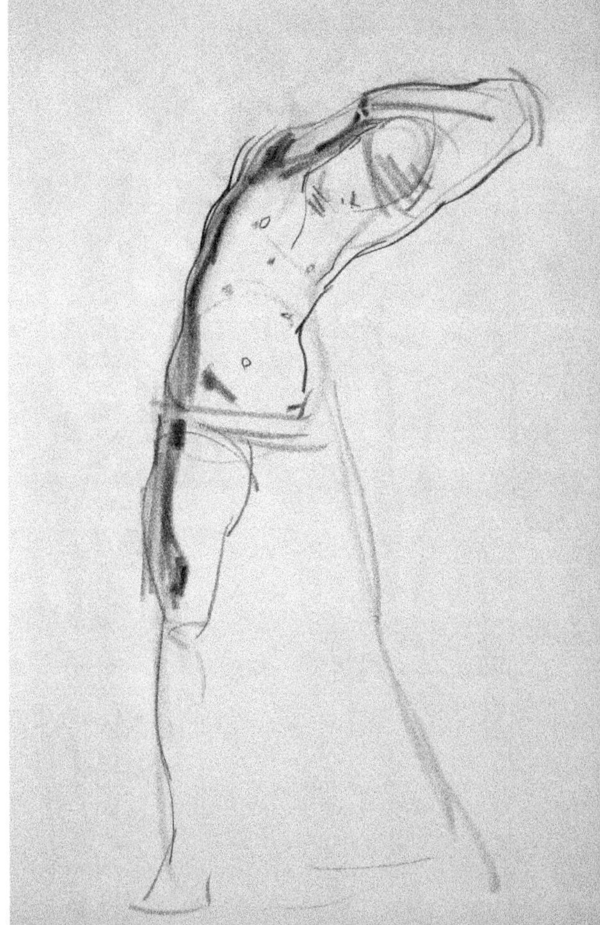

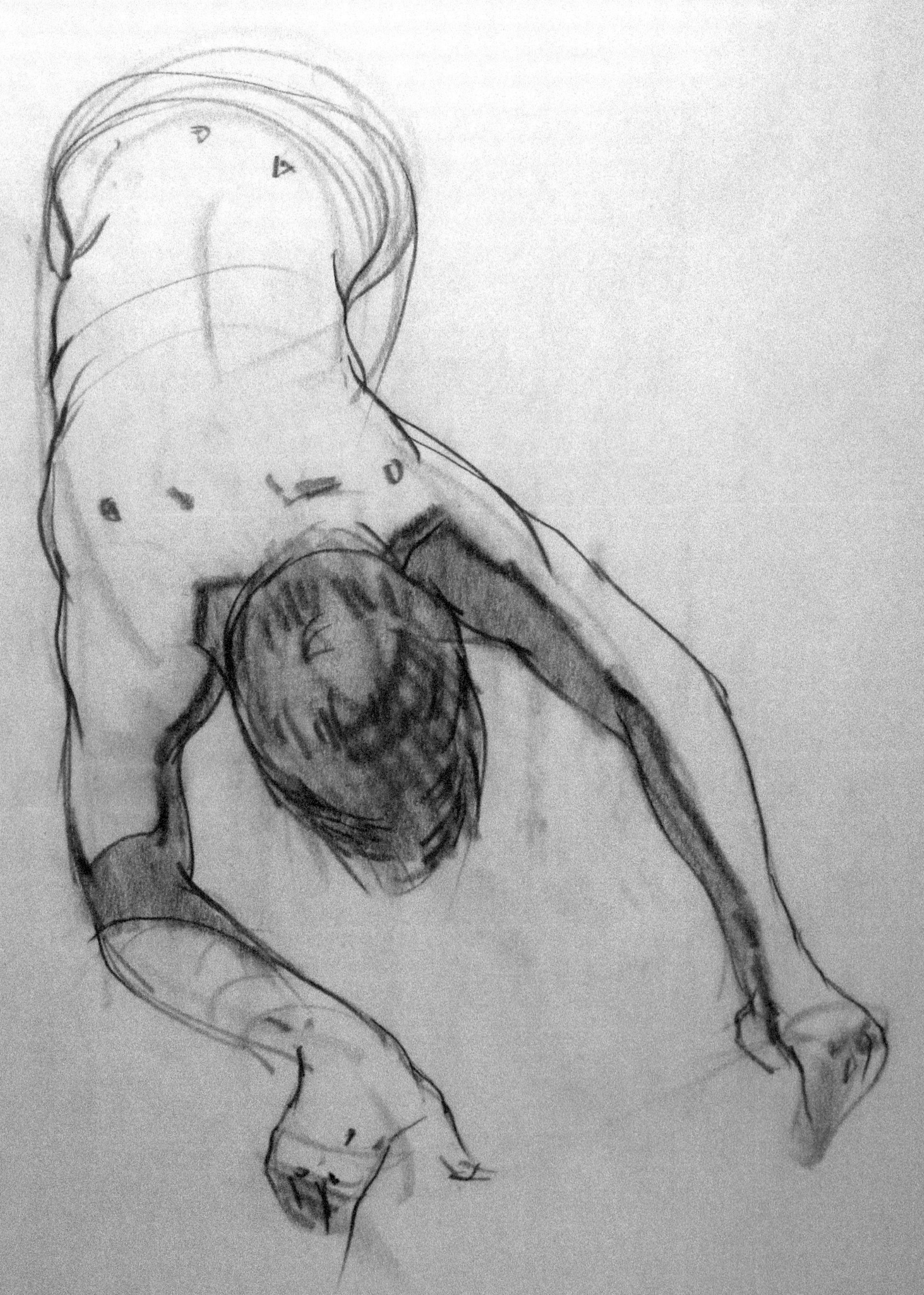

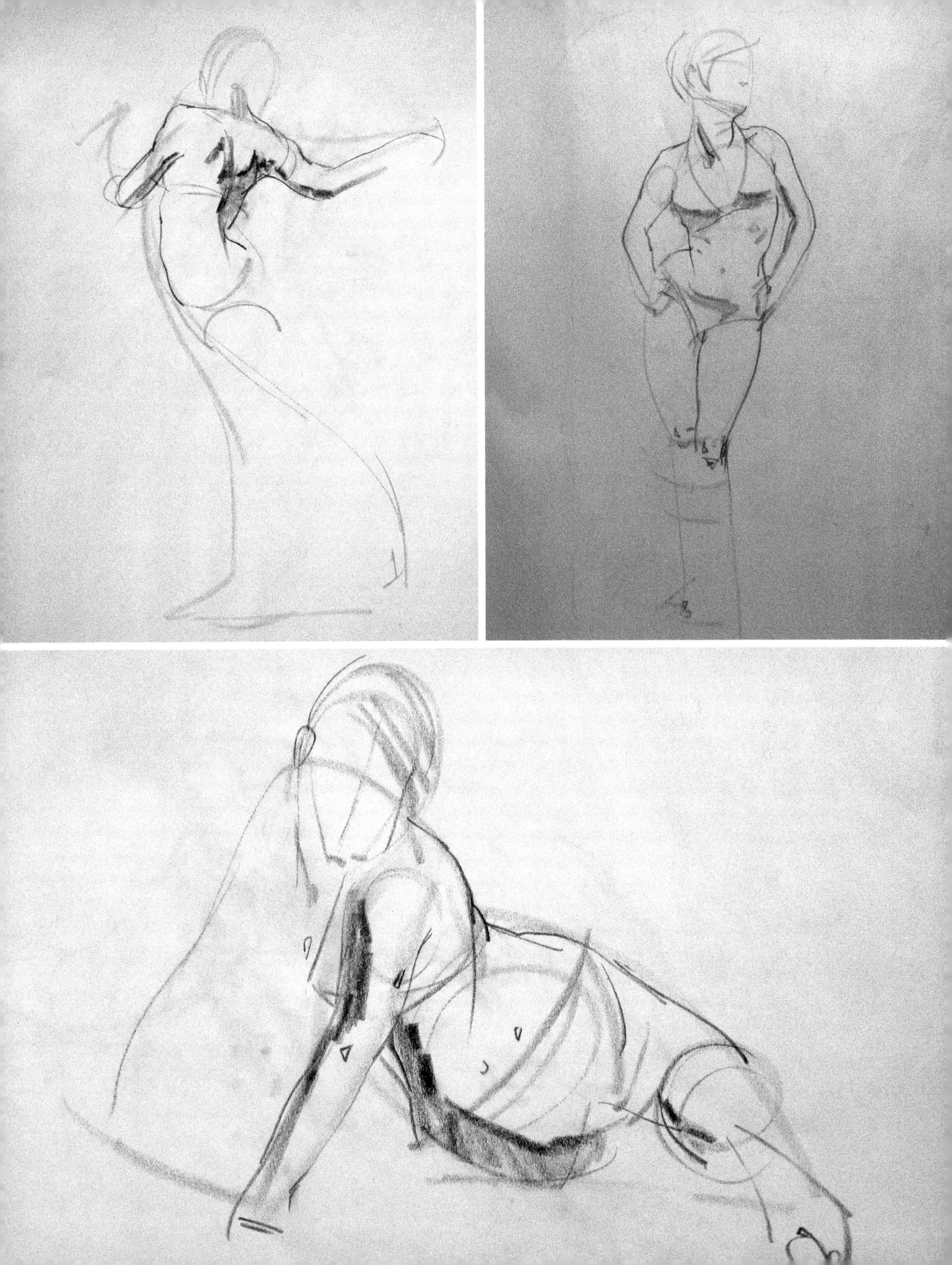

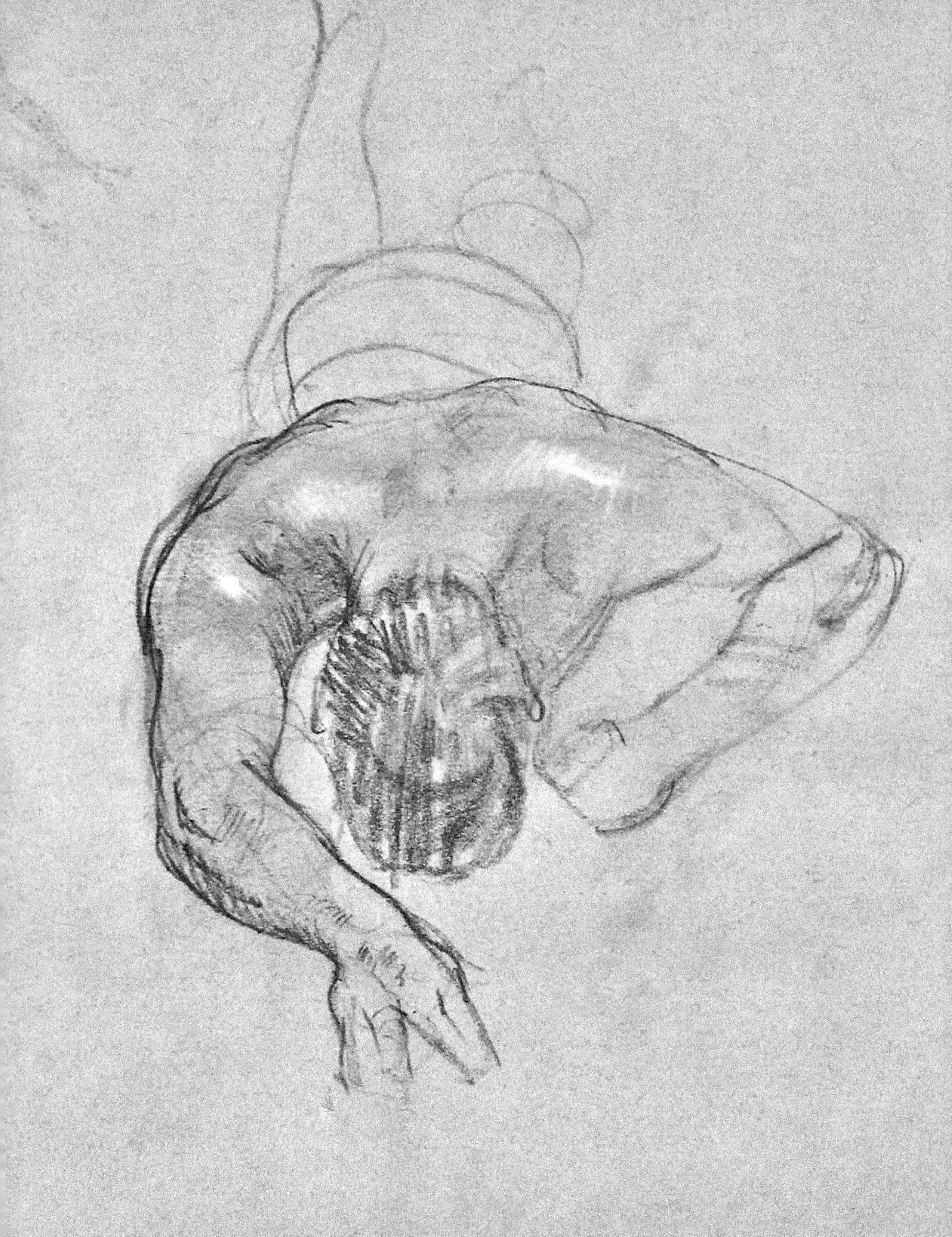

FORESHORTENING

FORESHORTENING

Foreshortening is one of my favorite topics to discuss in class. It is rather intimidating to most students in the beginning, but it is actually pretty simple once understood. Foreshortening is anytime something comes out or moves backward and away. Students often initially think of foreshortening in exaggerated ways. An extreme example would be like the model pointing his or her finger directly at the artist. While, yes, this is most definitely an example of foreshortening, it is absolutely not the only type of it. Foreshortening happens in not so obvious ways as well. In fact, foreshortening is everywhere. Anytime one part of the figure is positioned slightly closer to the artist than another part, it is considered foreshortened. So, how is this illusion created without making the foreshortened form just look short or weird?

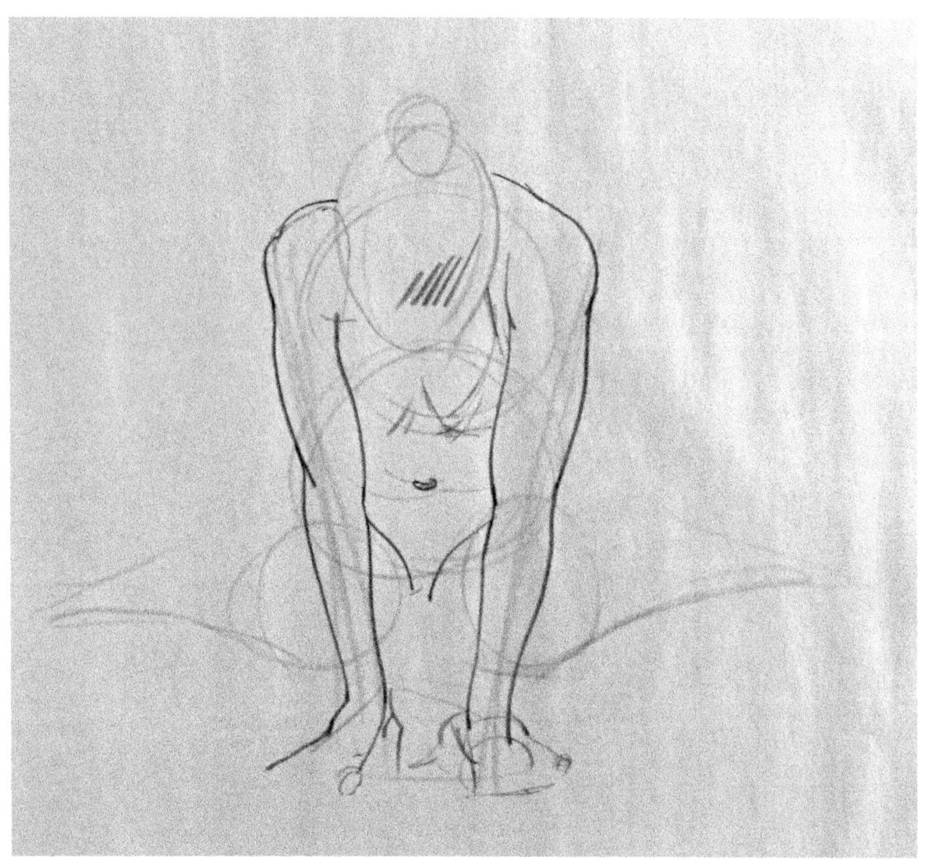

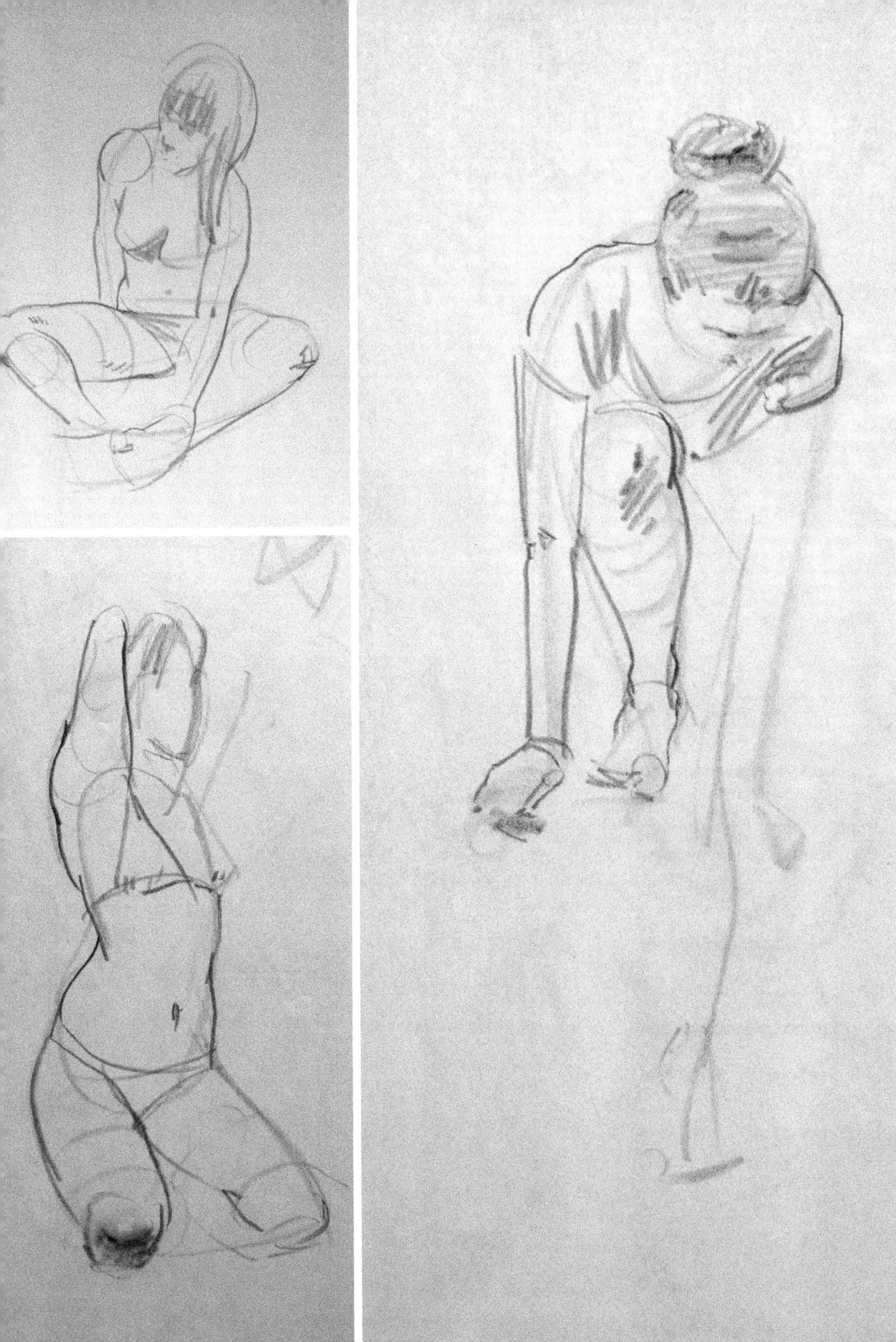

FORESHORTENING STRATEGIES

It is important to remember that information *on* the form will follow the form no matter what perspective it takes. Think of a can of soda pop. Imagine that this can has stripes running horizontally across it. When tipped backward, notice the can's stripes and how they go around and around. They follow the contour of the can. In a pose where the upper leg is going back in space and the foot is coming forward, I will often include a few light wrapping lines around the leg (just like the stripes on the pop can). This helps the viewer's eye travel around and around the leg as it goes backward, instead of zipping on back by following its shortened outline. Another way to pull off the illusion is to pay close attention to overlapping lines. As forms move forward or backward in space, they overlap each other. Make sure it is clear which forms overlap which, and which way the overlaps occur. Lastly, as something moves back in space it will get smaller.

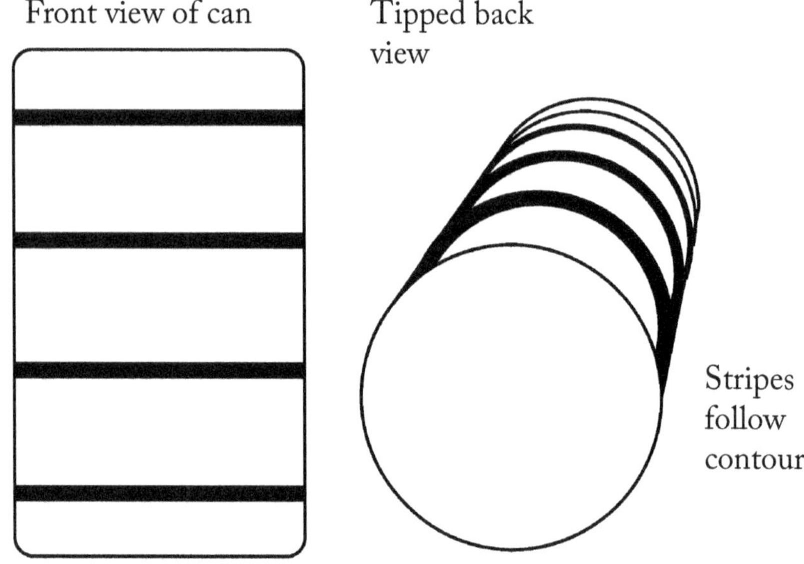

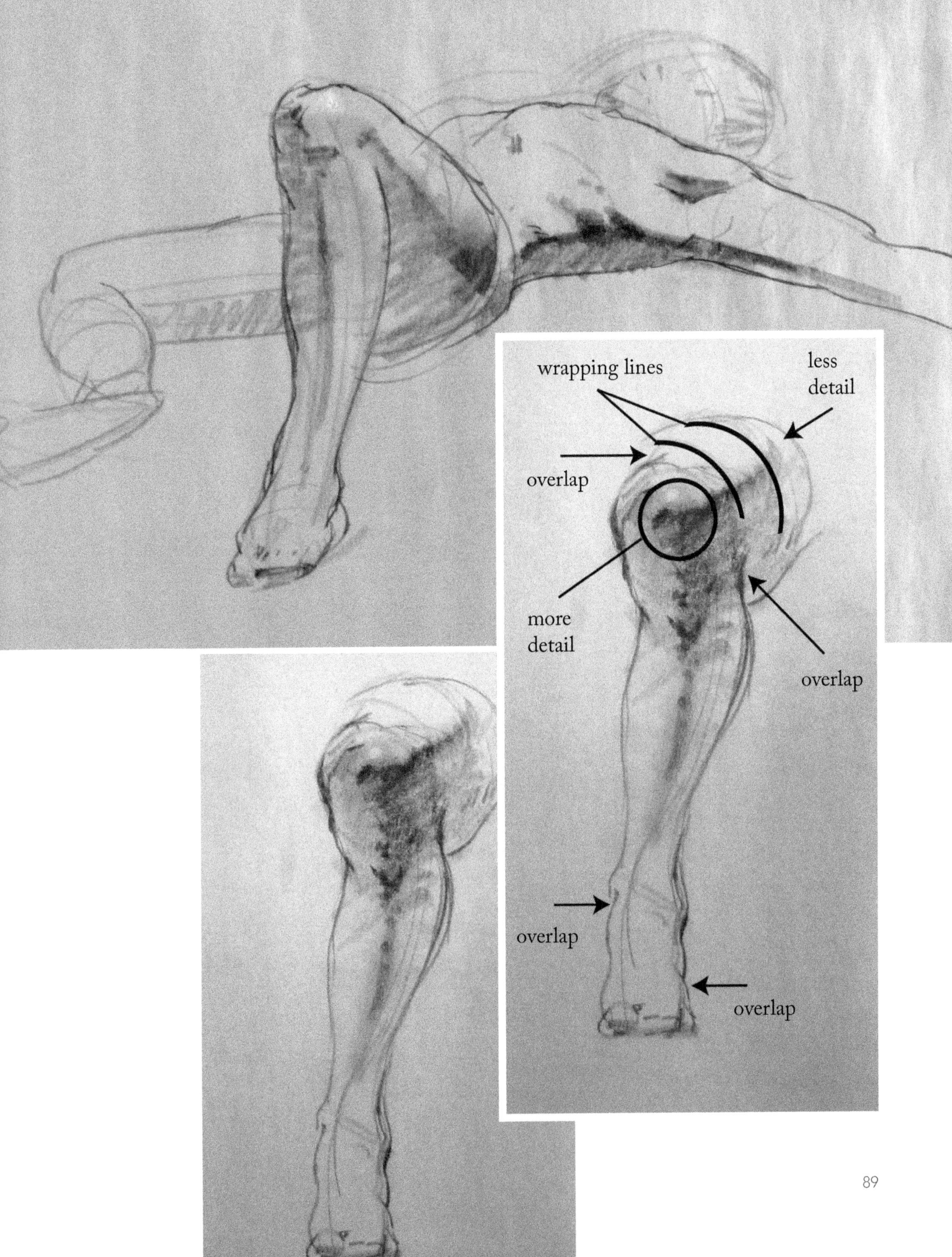

wrapping lines
less detail
overlap
more detail
overlap
overlap
overlap

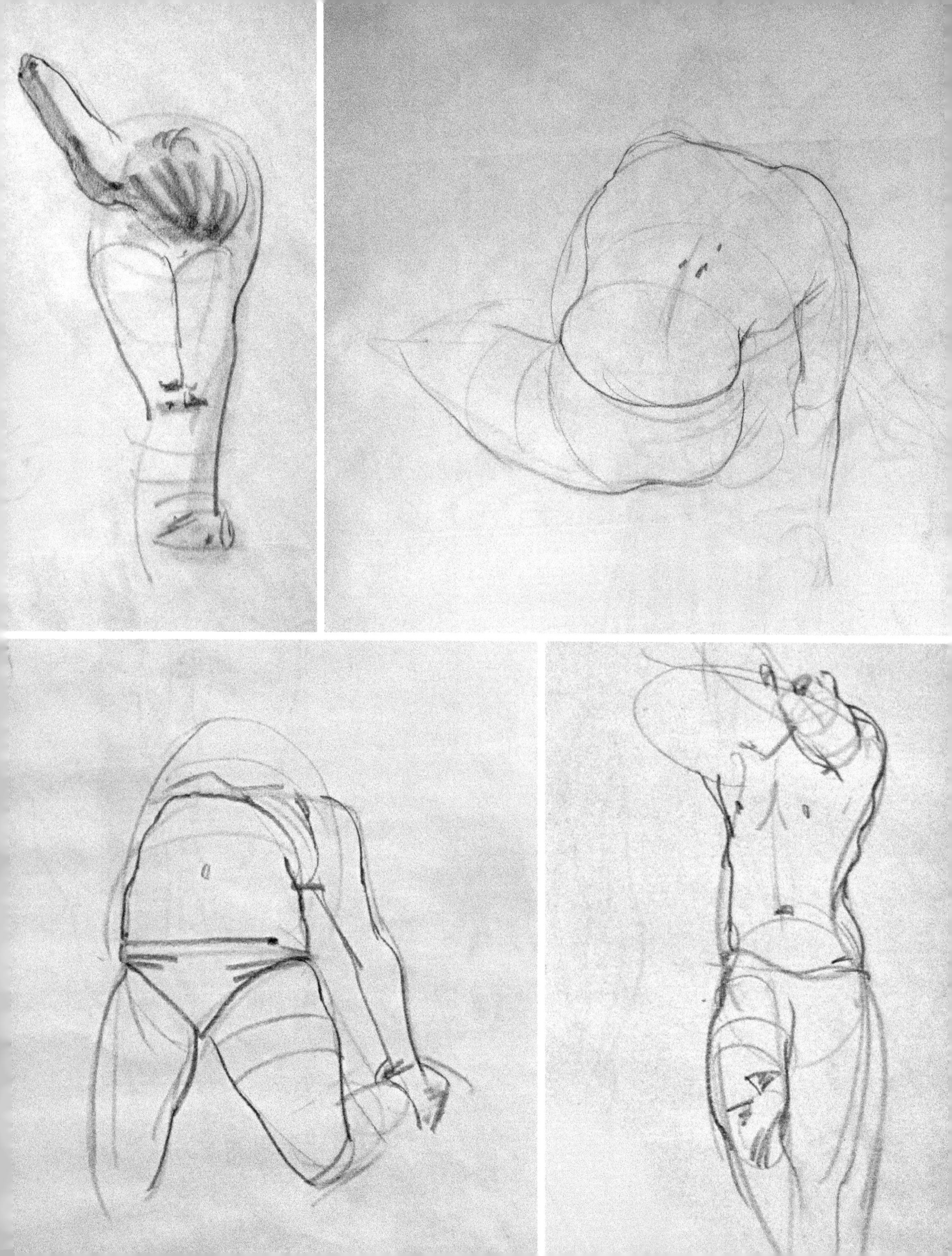

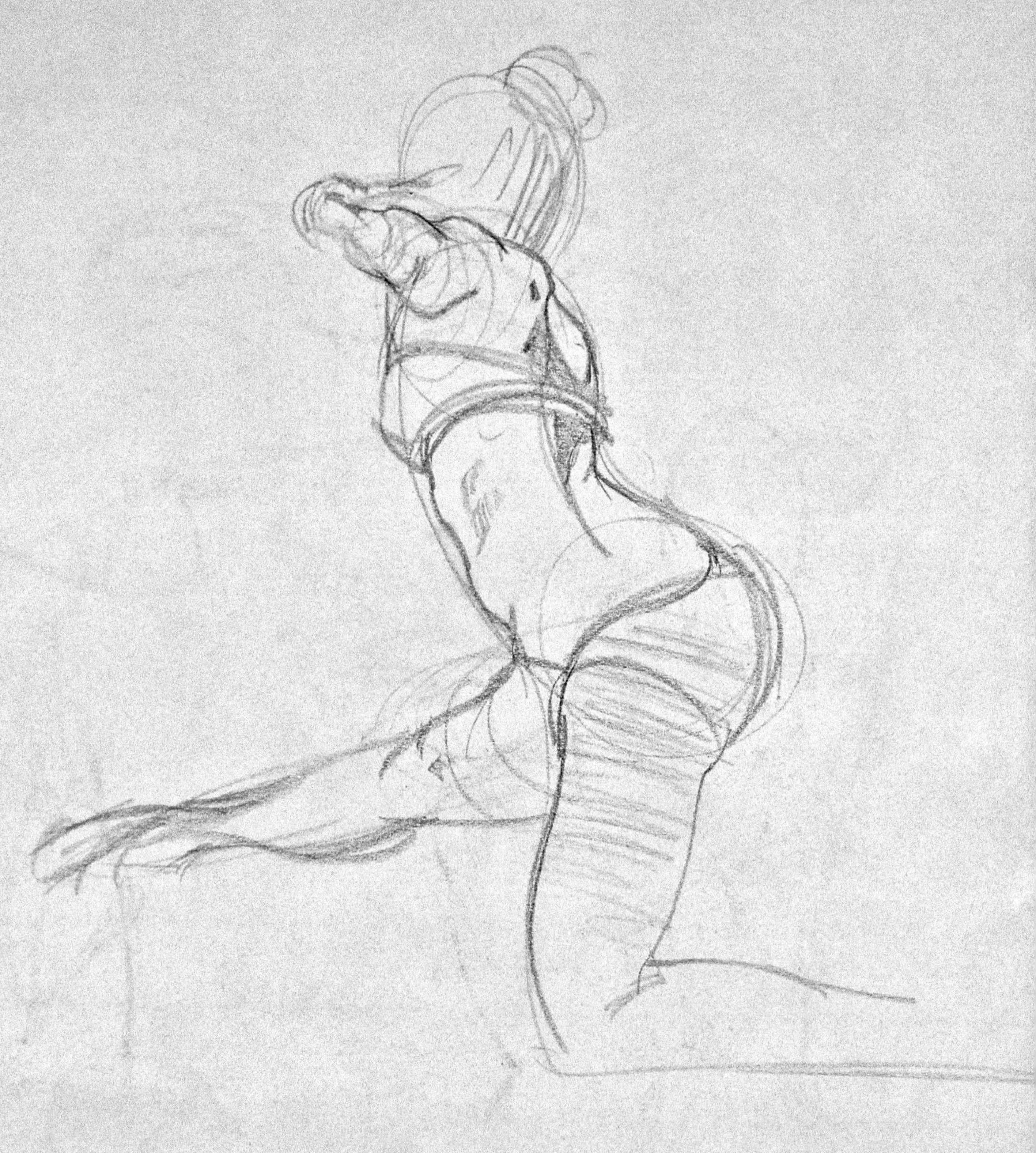

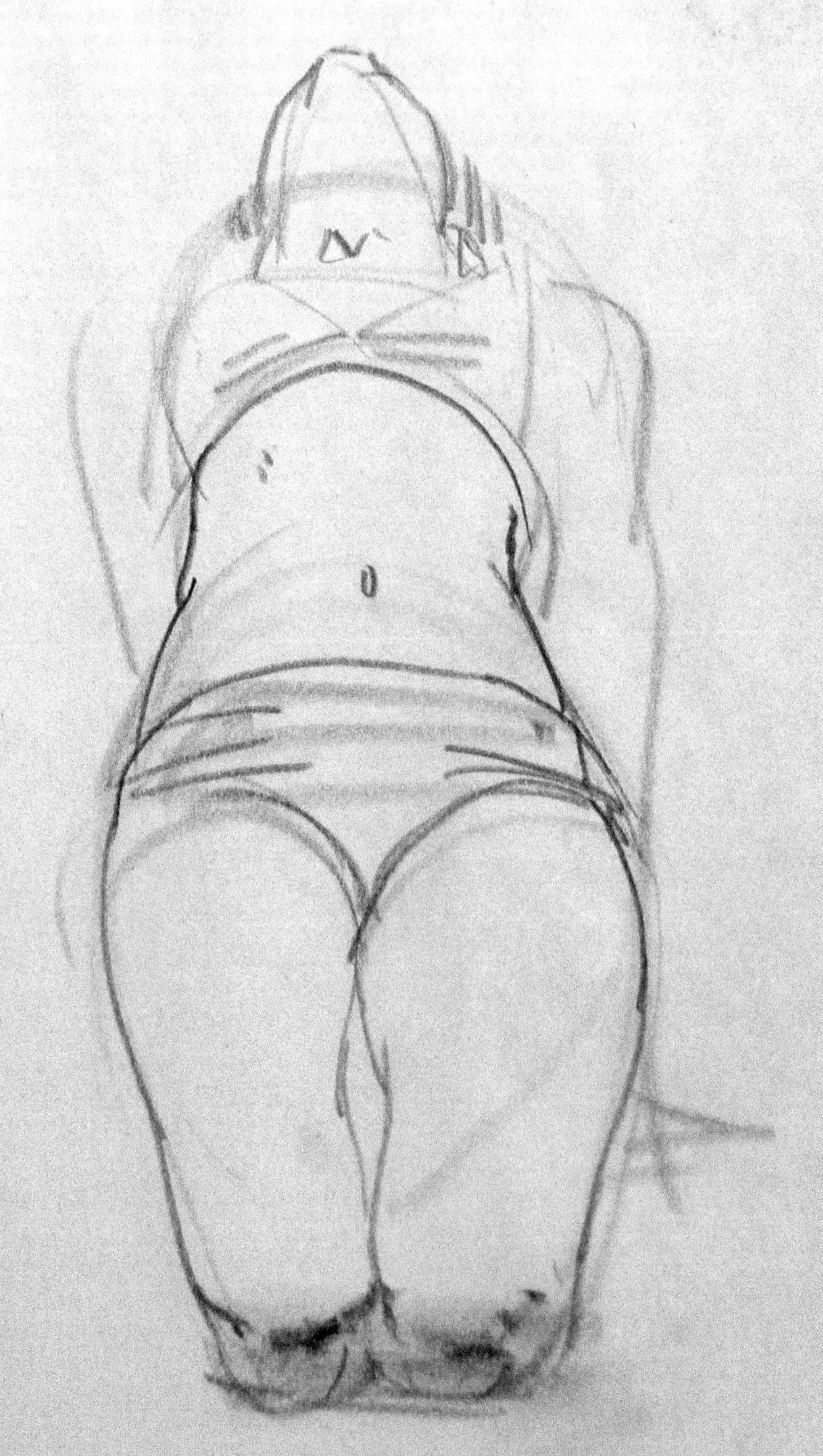

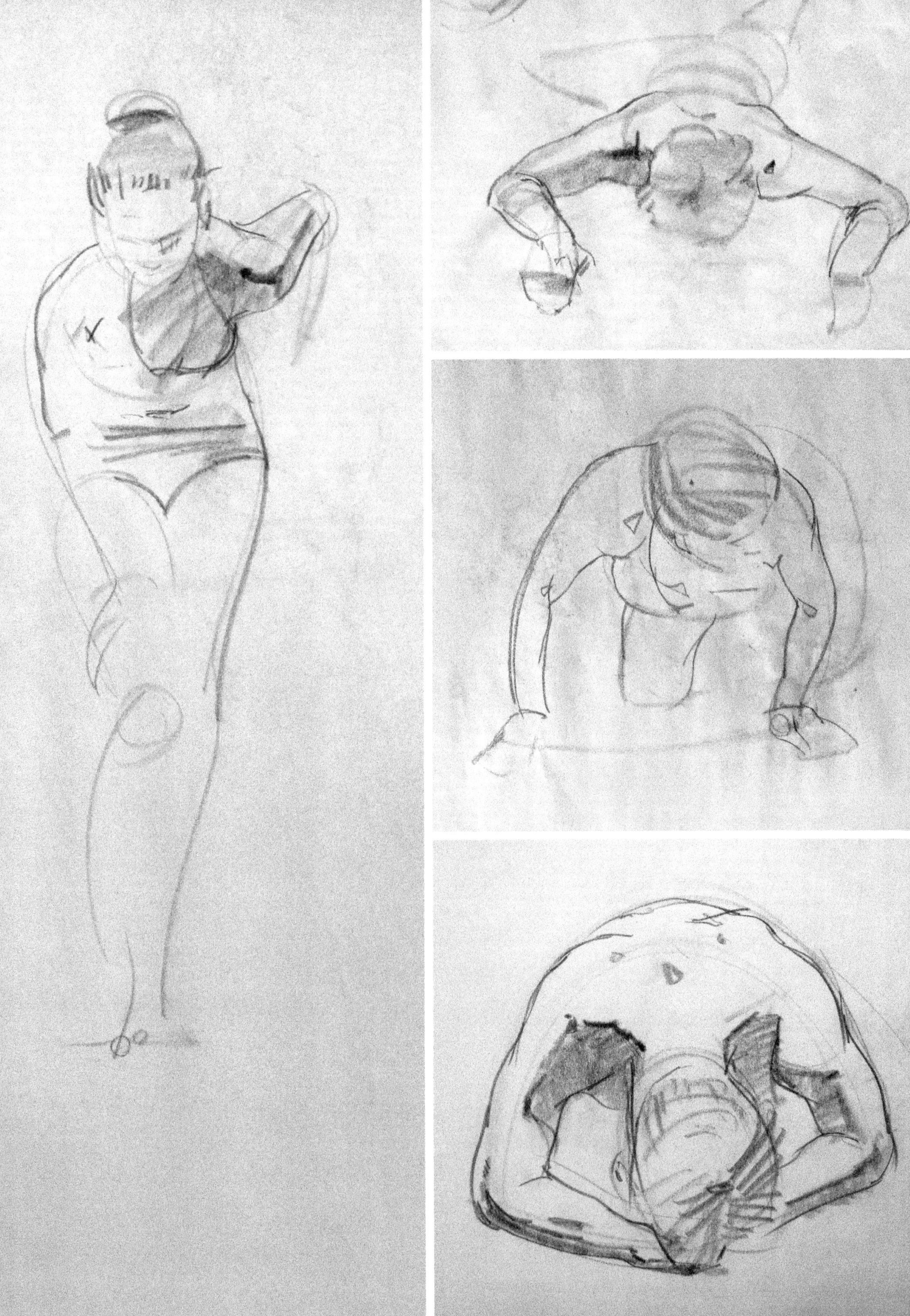

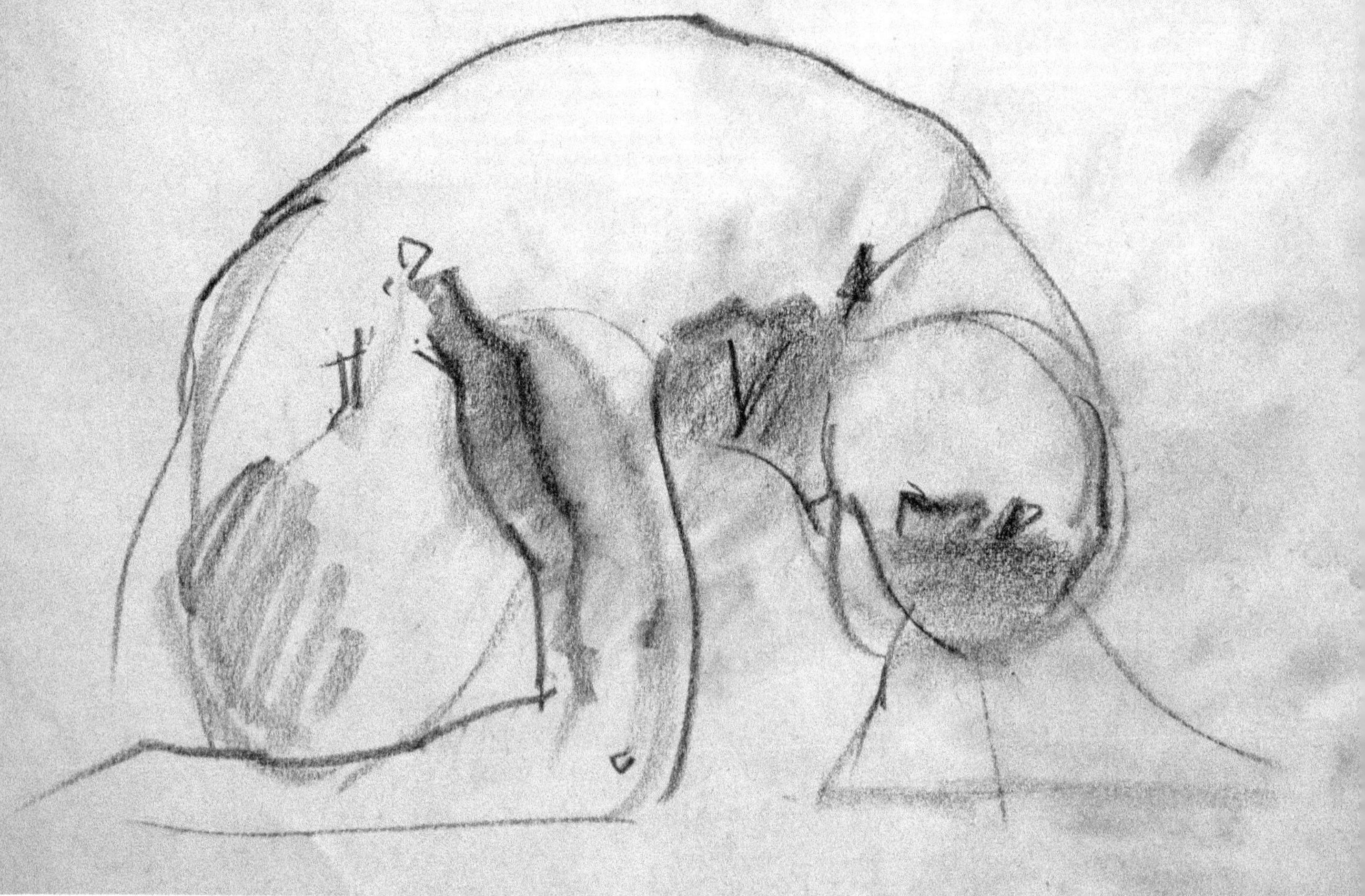

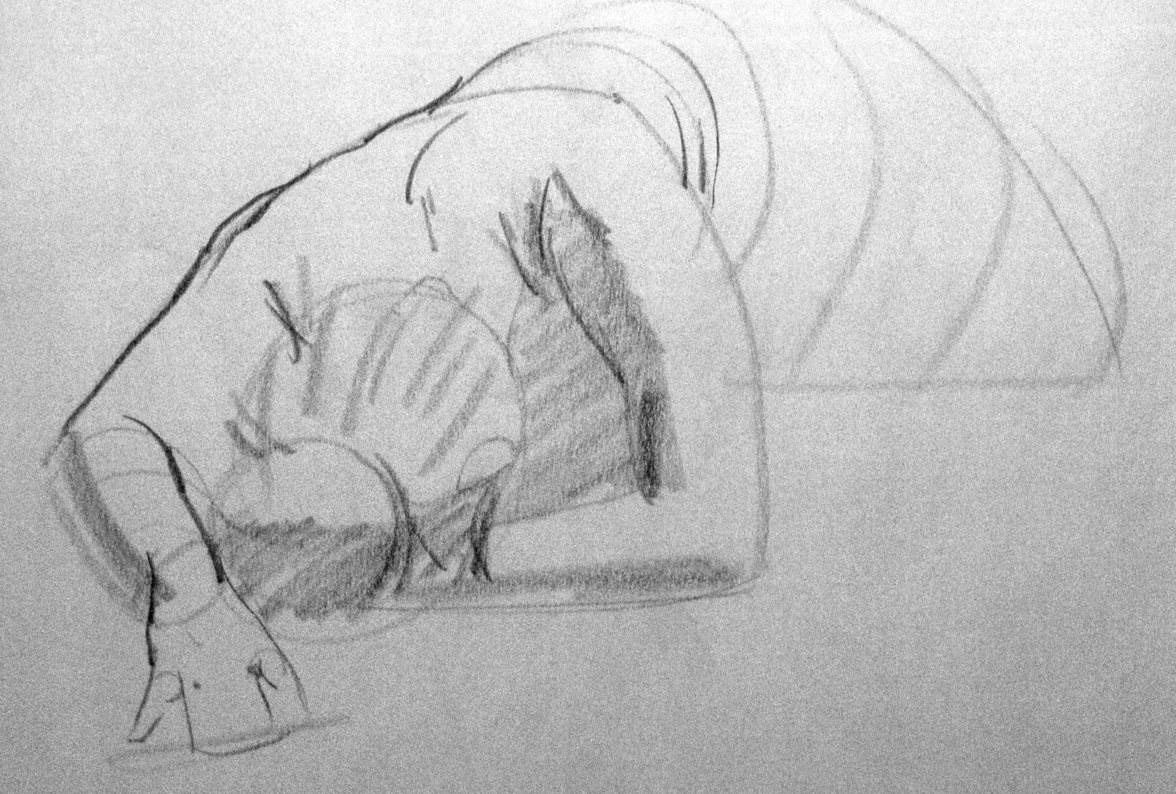

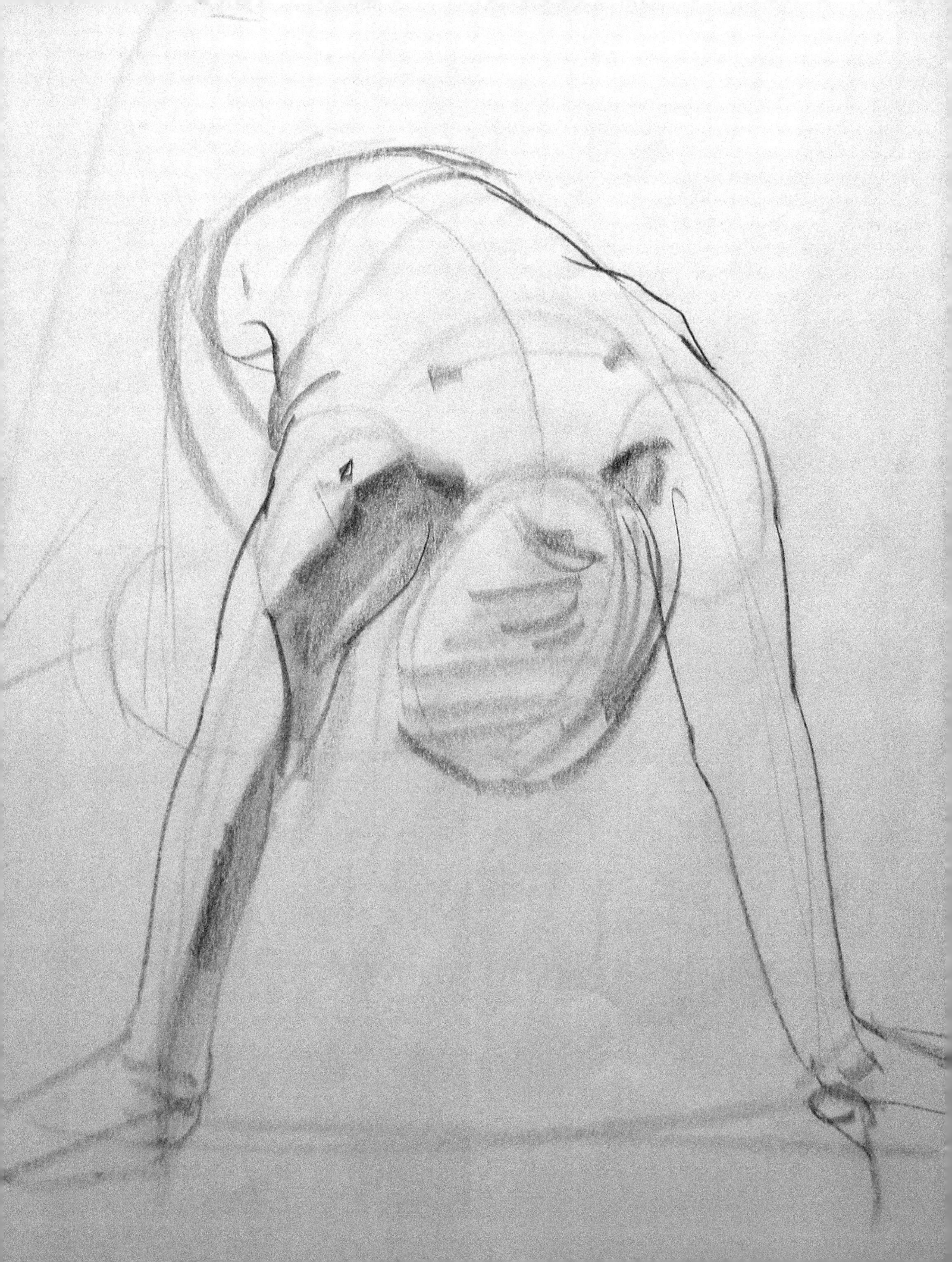

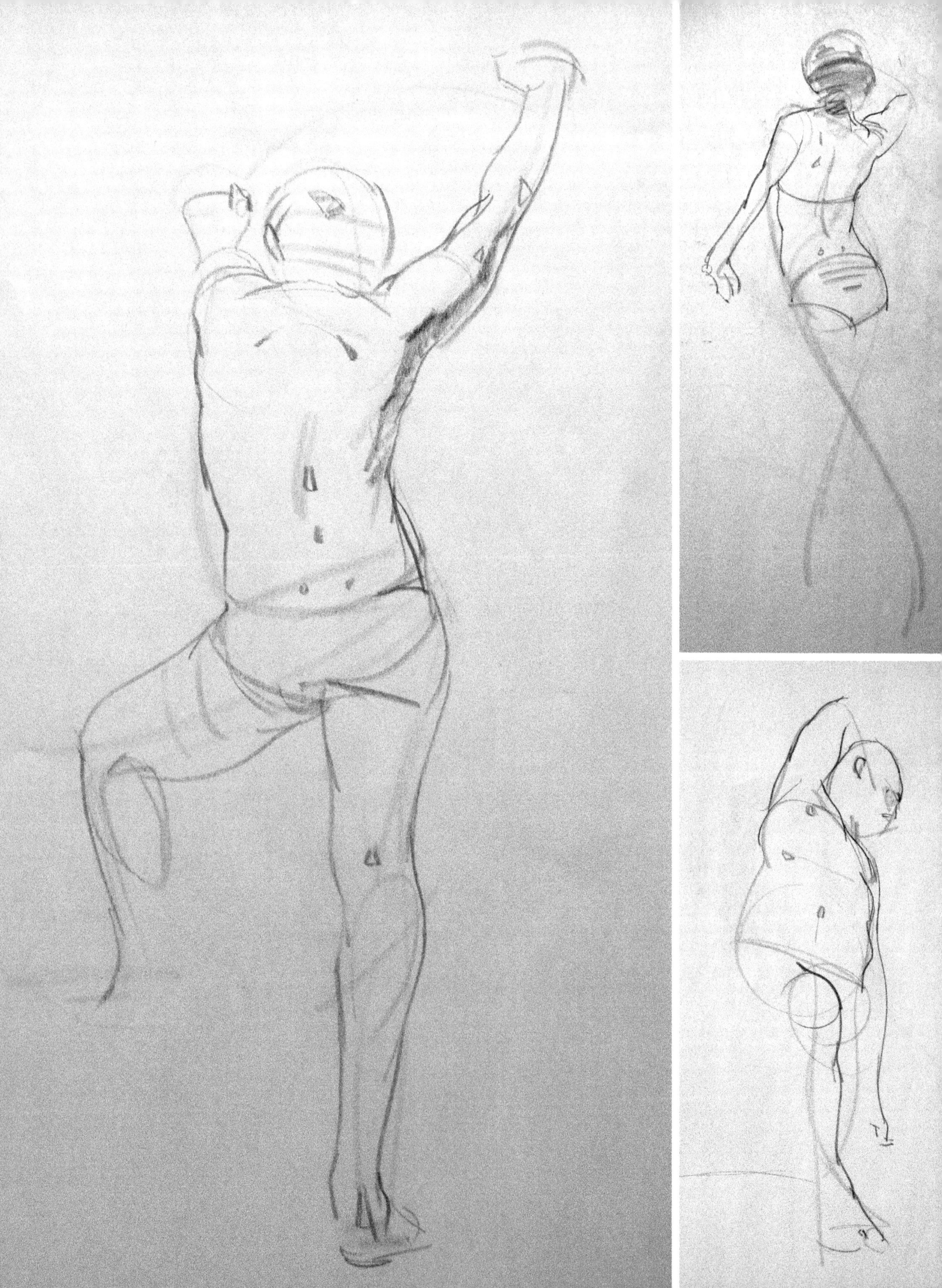

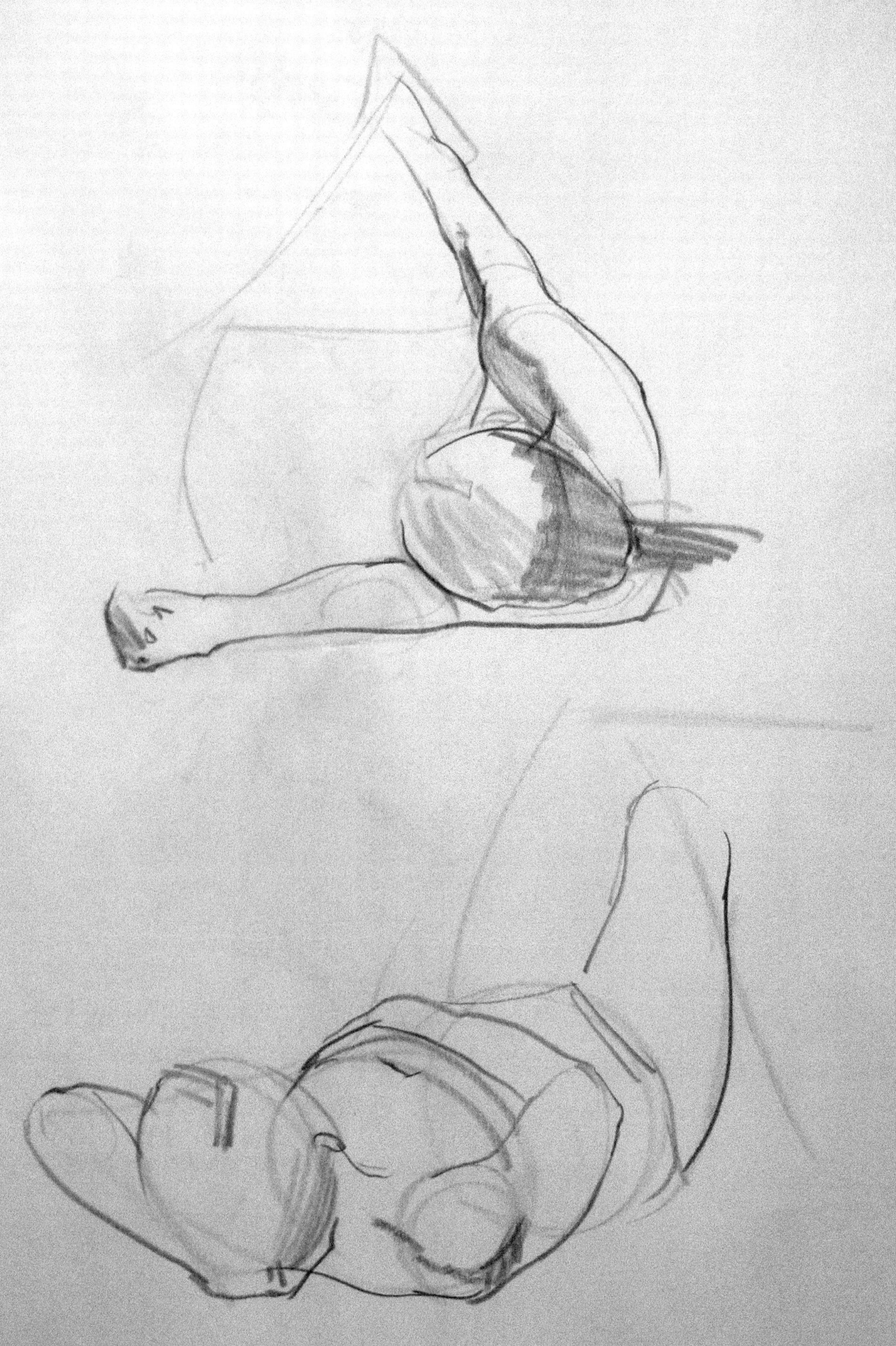

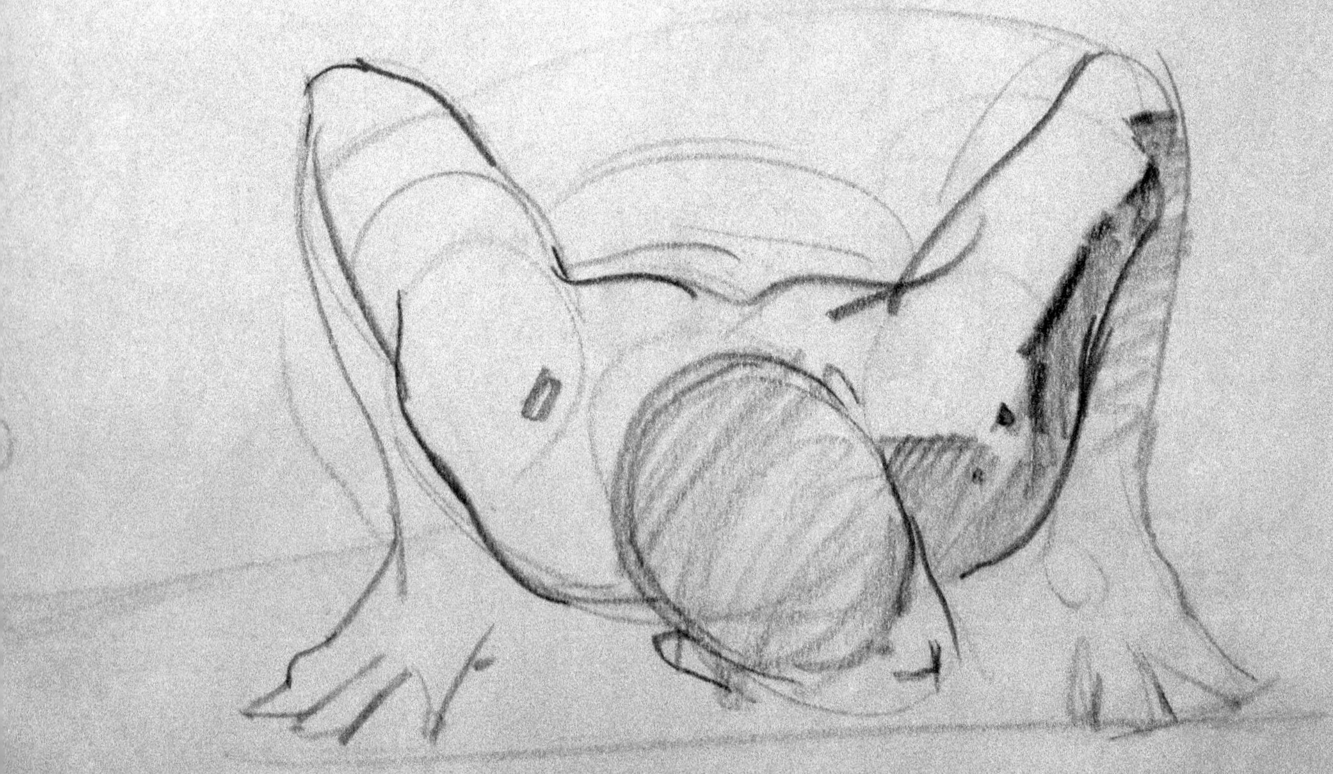

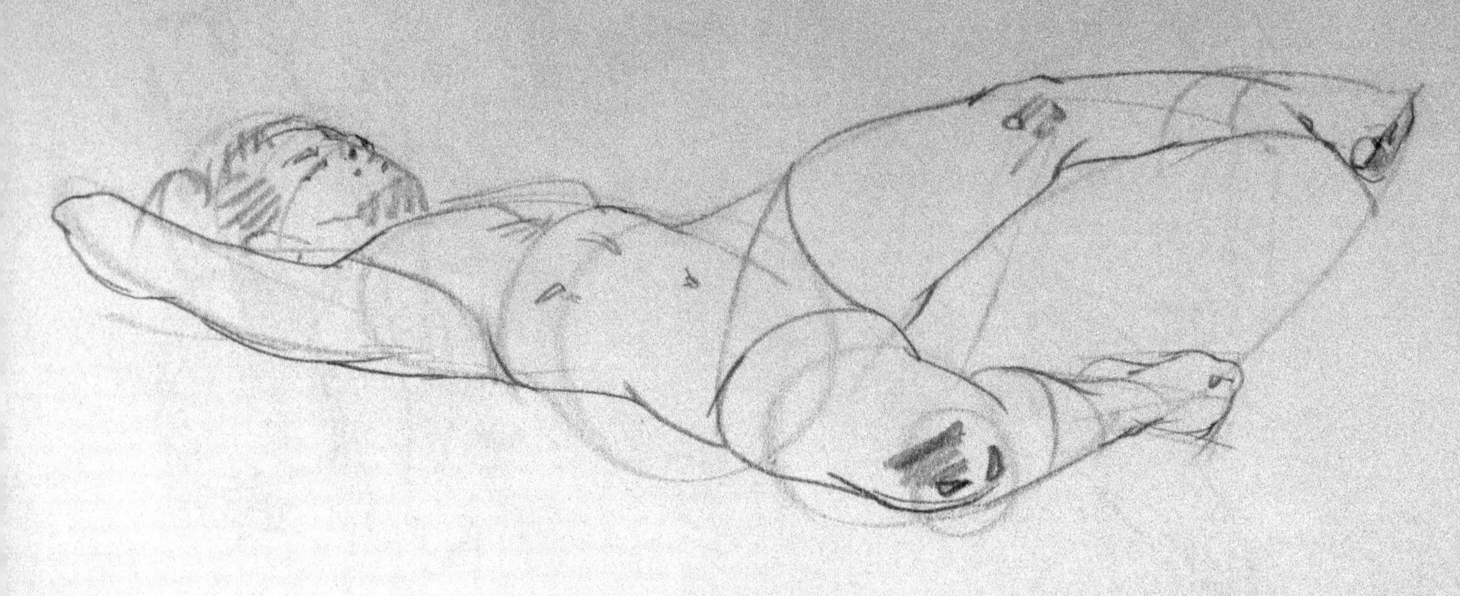

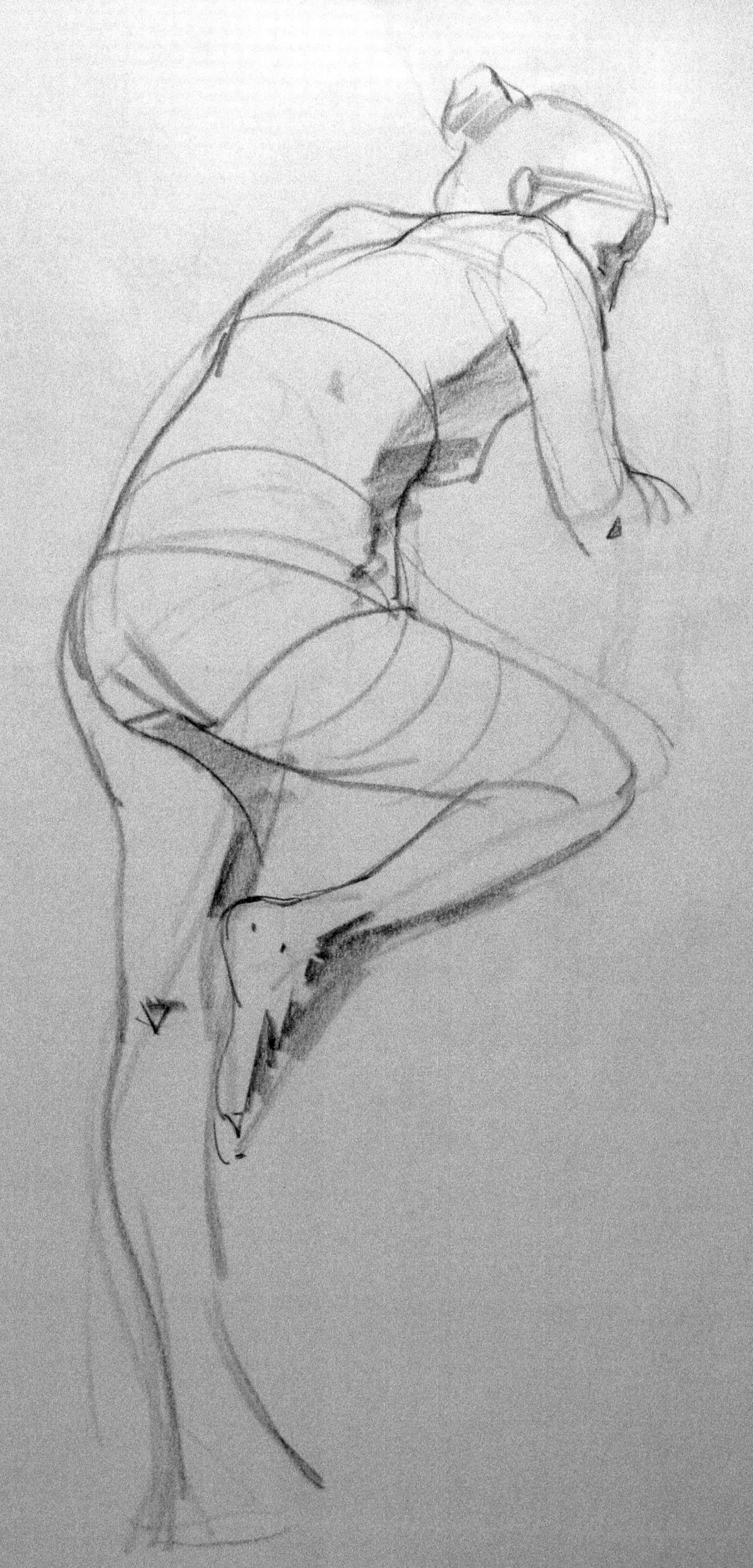

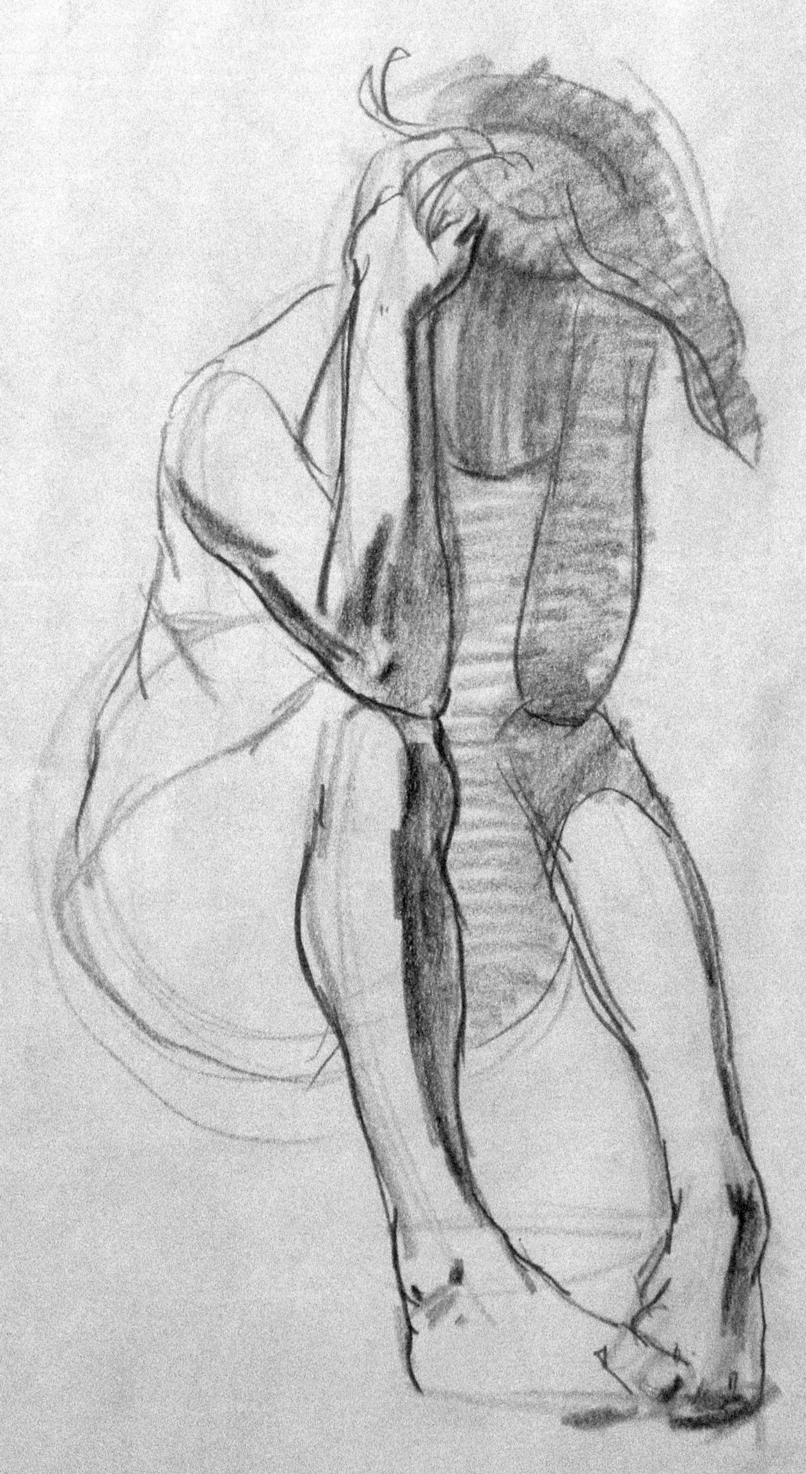

NEAR/FAR

While attempting foreshortening, I would recommend to keep the Near/Far principle in mind. It is something I like to cover alongside foreshortening because they both deal with controlling how to make things go backward or come forward. The artist has the opportunity to give the drawing some kind of direction. That can be done by controlling the eye path, rhythm, or pace, for example. To do this, incorporate the Near/Far principle and emphasize that objects that are near will have *more*. More of what, it is commonly asked? More of *everything*. That is up to you. For instance, it would be smart to give nearer forms more contrast, detail, and/or value. Nearer forms should typically get more attention. Forms that move back in space or are farther back in the distance, on the other hand, should have *less* detail and value, and require *less* attention. The term used in landscape painting for this same idea is called atmospheric perspective. The further the eye gazes out into the distance, the duller and hazier objects become. Air is responsible for this. The same thing happens in figure drawing but in a much narrower field of view.

For example, a seated model may be leaning forward with her elbows on her knees and head in her hands (see image on opposite page). In order to make it appear as though the knees, elbows, forearms, hands, and head are coming forward, Near/Far principles and the idea of atmospheric perspective are used to purposefully give these forms more contrast, darker contours, detailed anatomy, etc. Less detail and less time would then be spent, in comparison, on receding forms, such as the abdomen, hips, and upper legs. This will cause the viewer's eye to focus on the advancing forms, instead of lingering on the less important ones in the distance.

In summary, as things go back in the distance, they contain less and less. Be careful not to make receding forms as dark in value as advancing forms. More advances and less recedes.

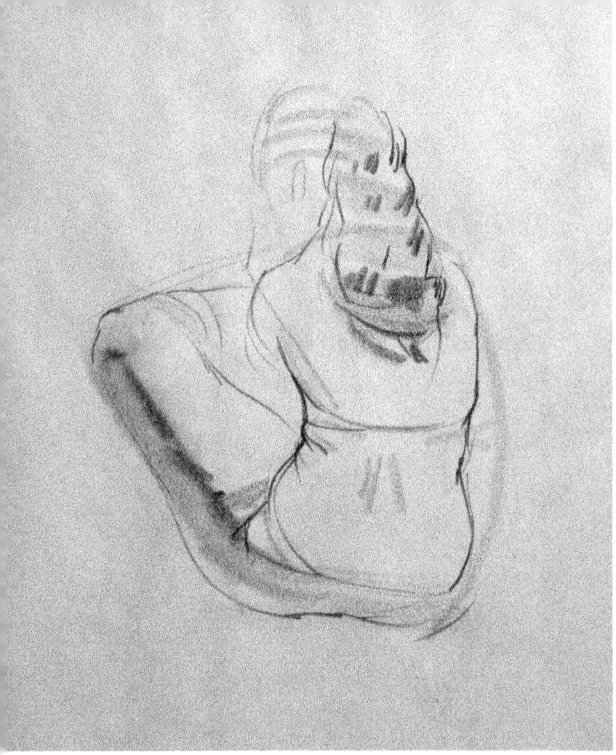

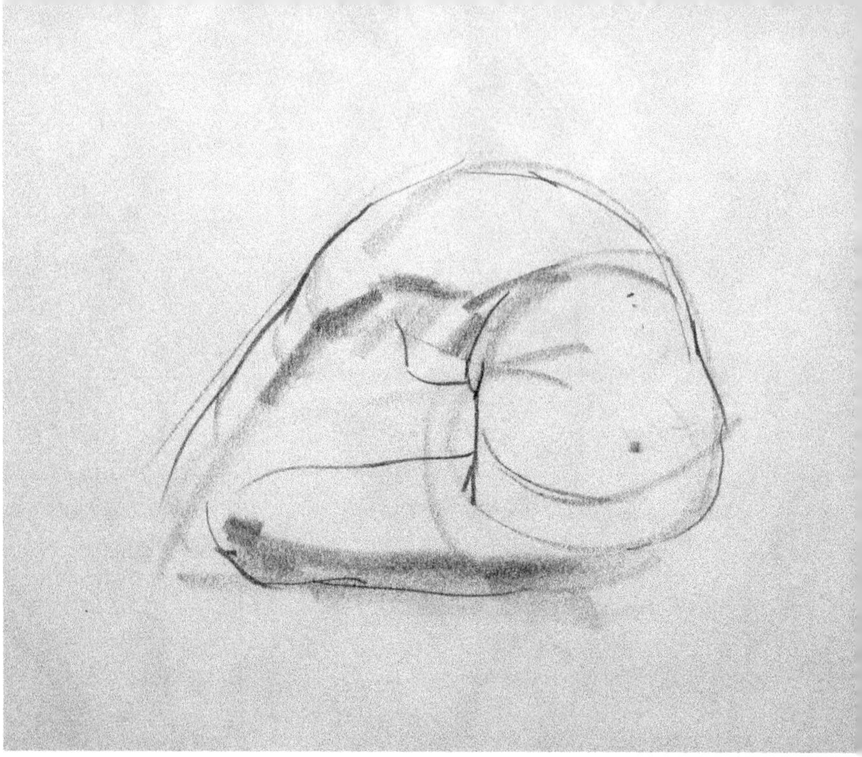

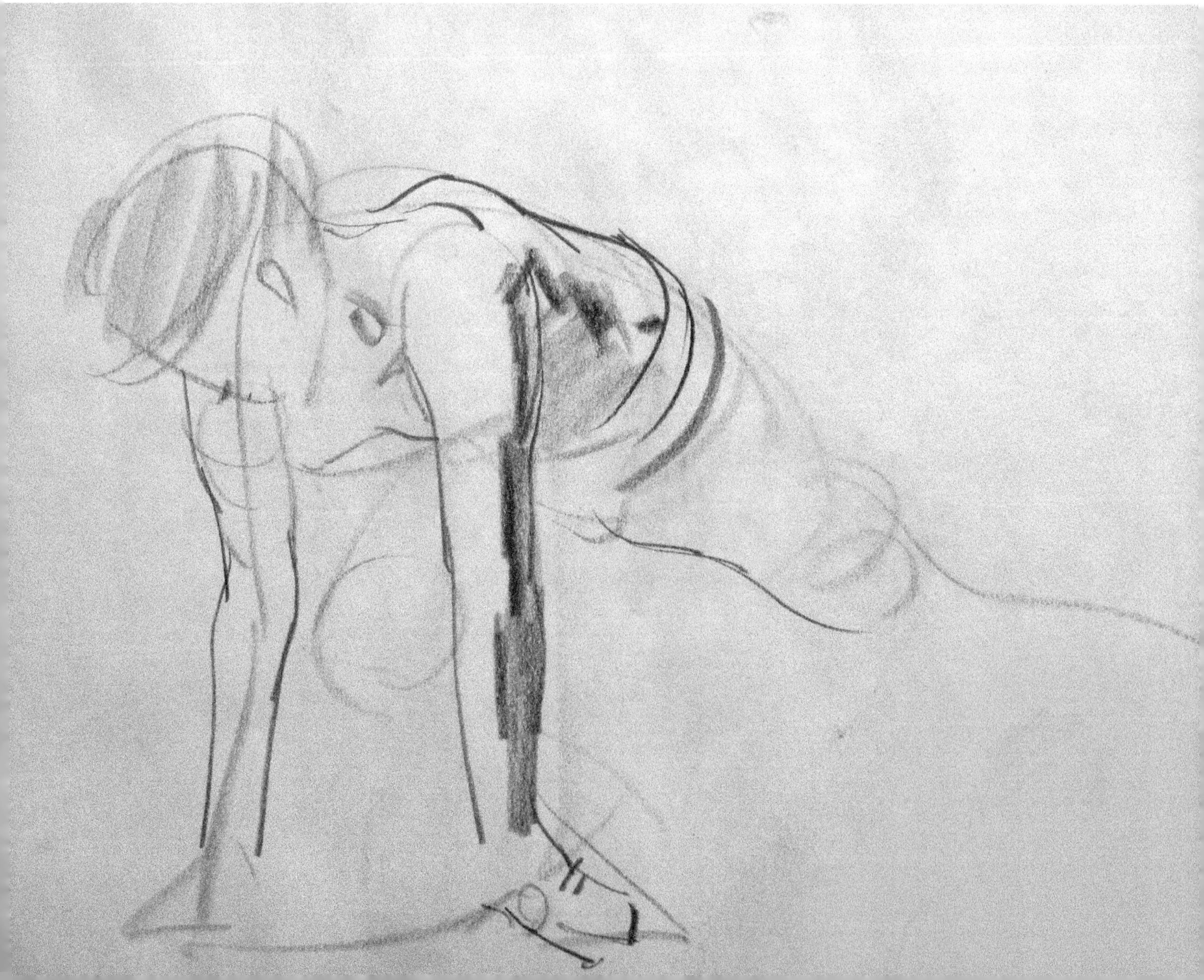

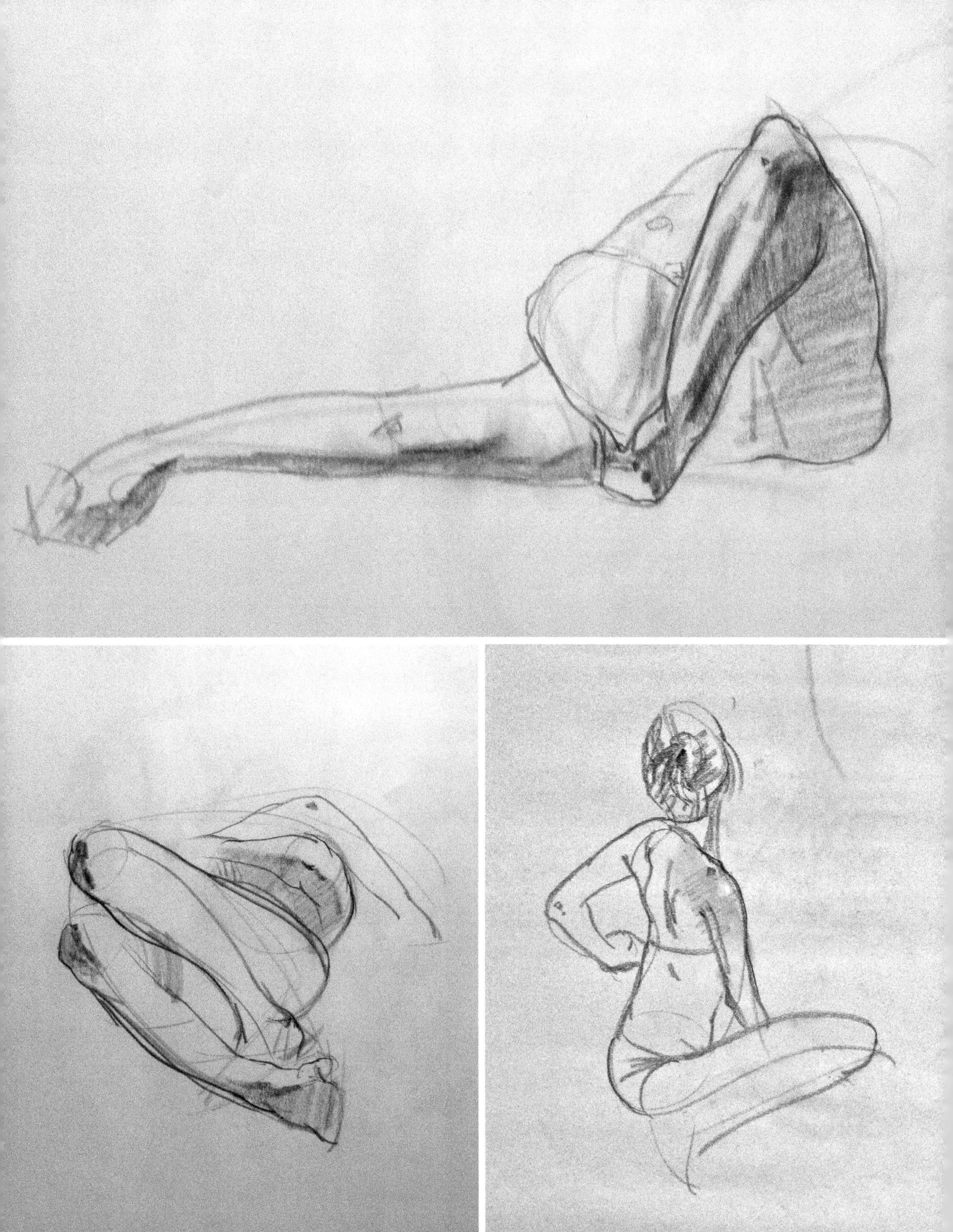

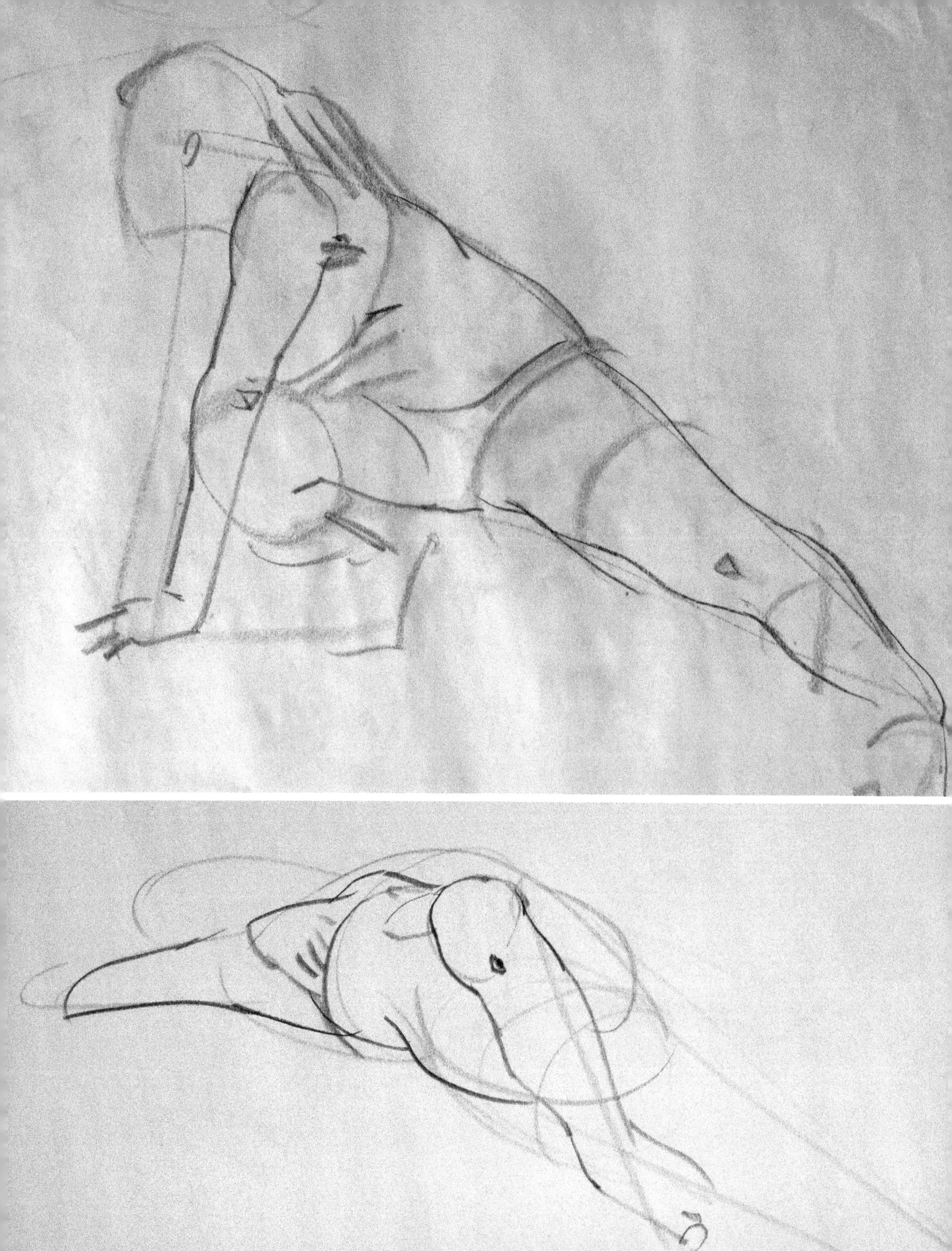

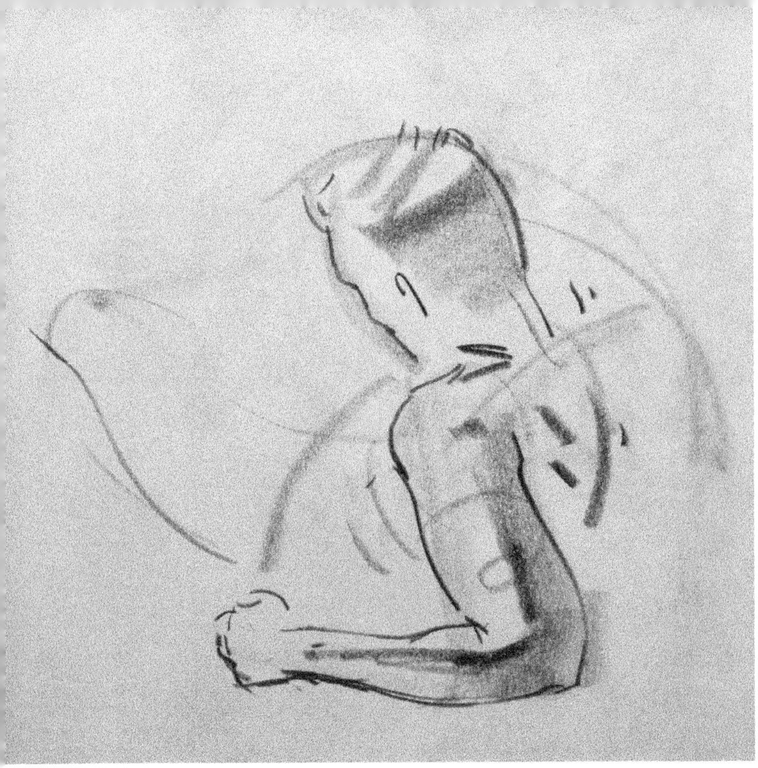

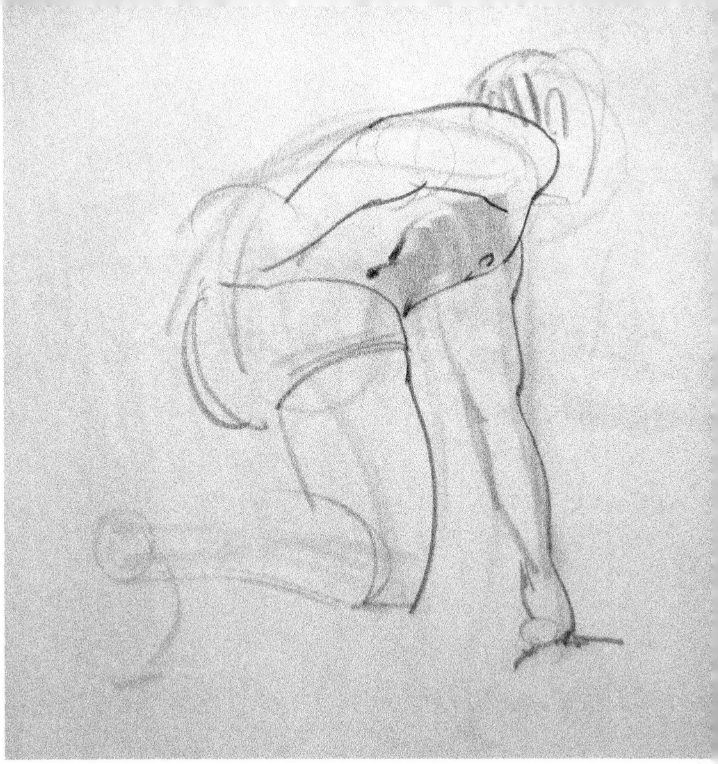

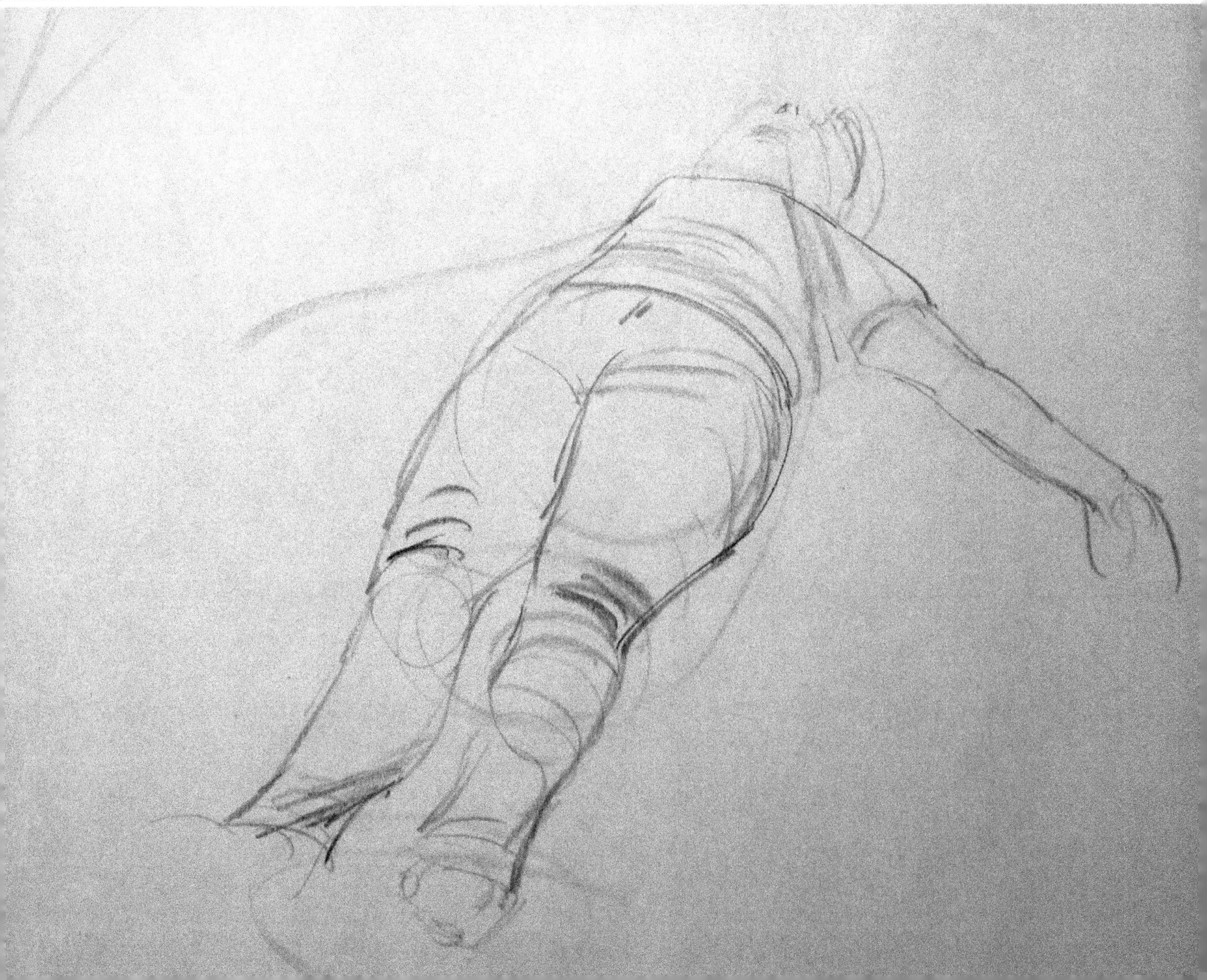

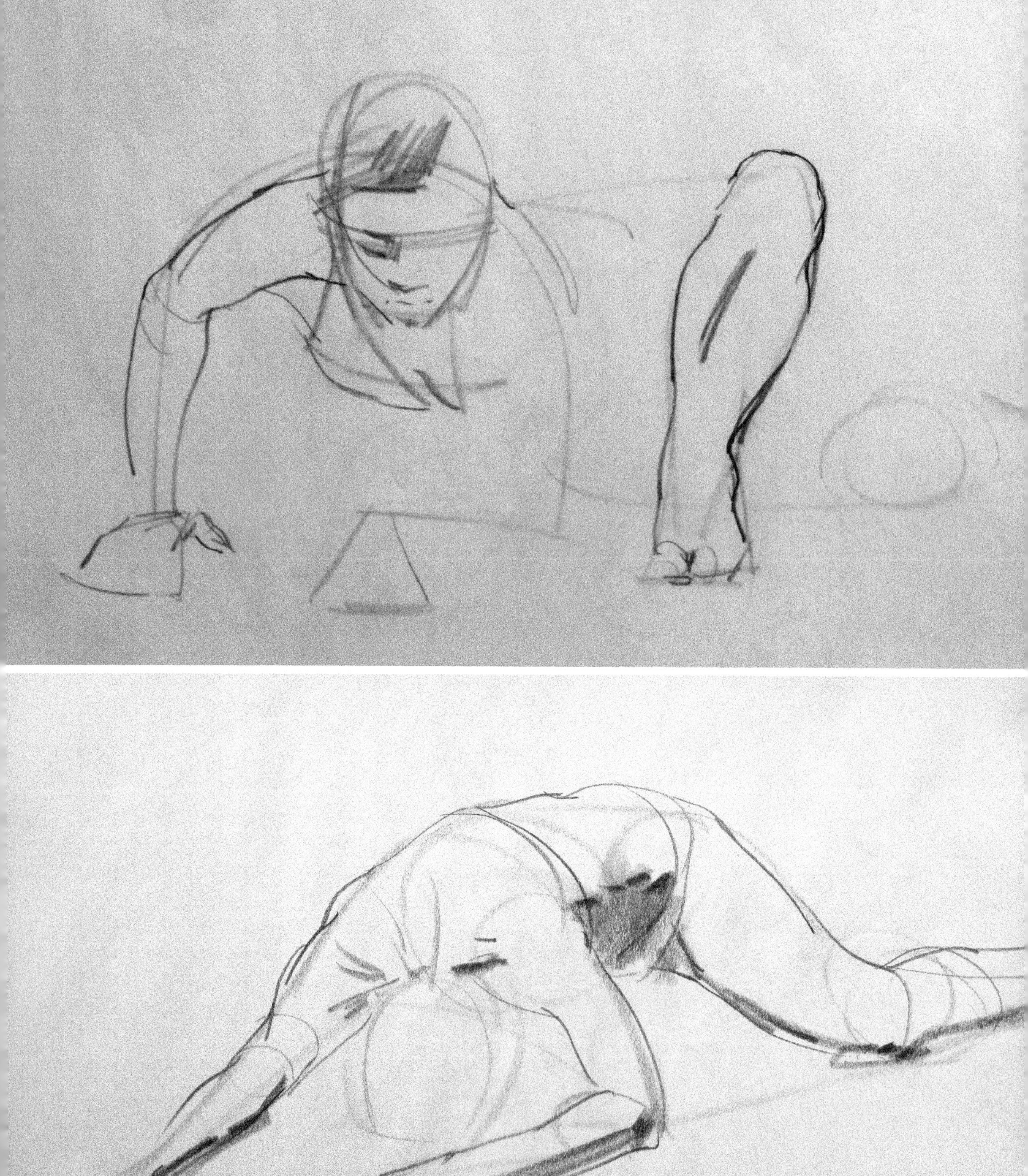

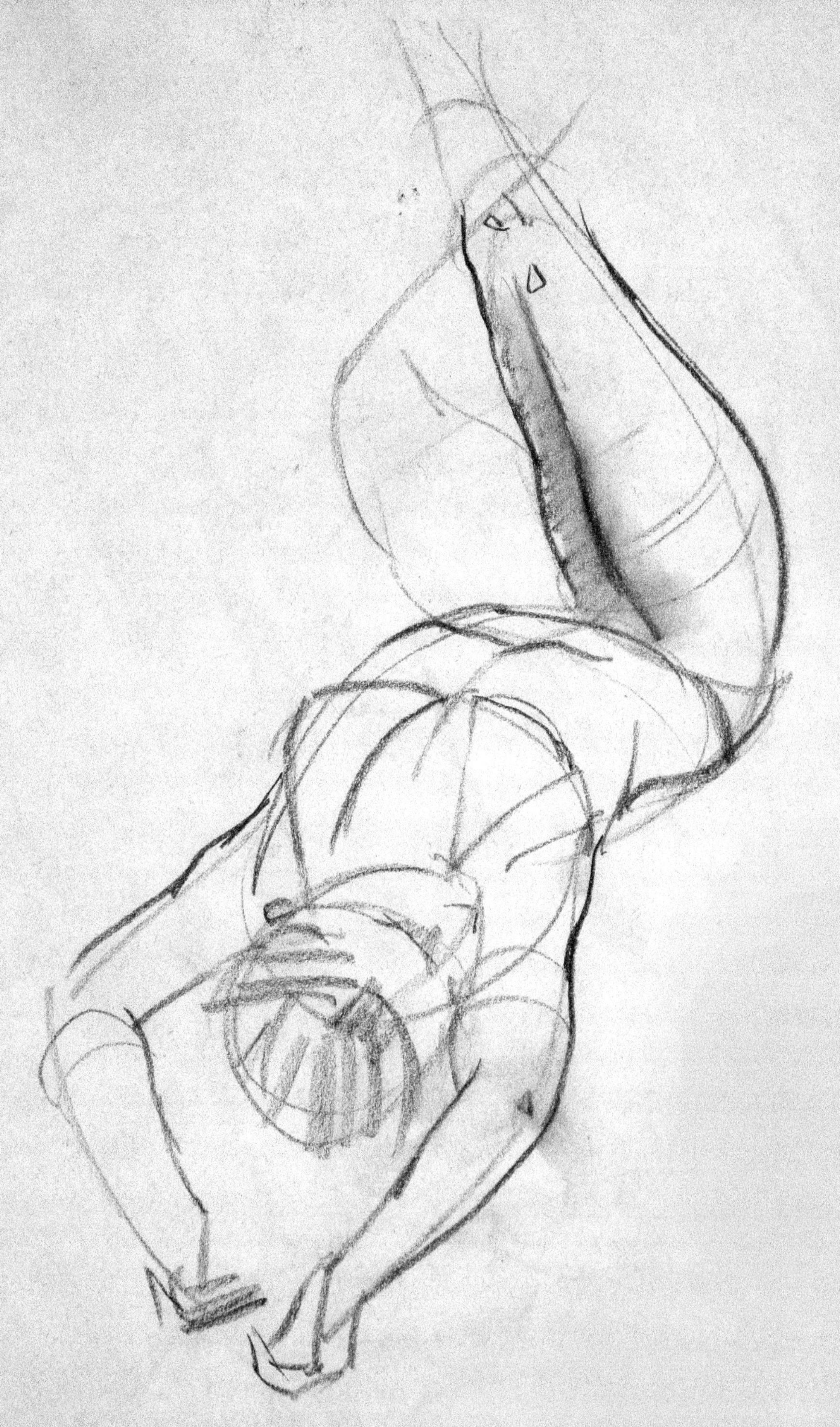

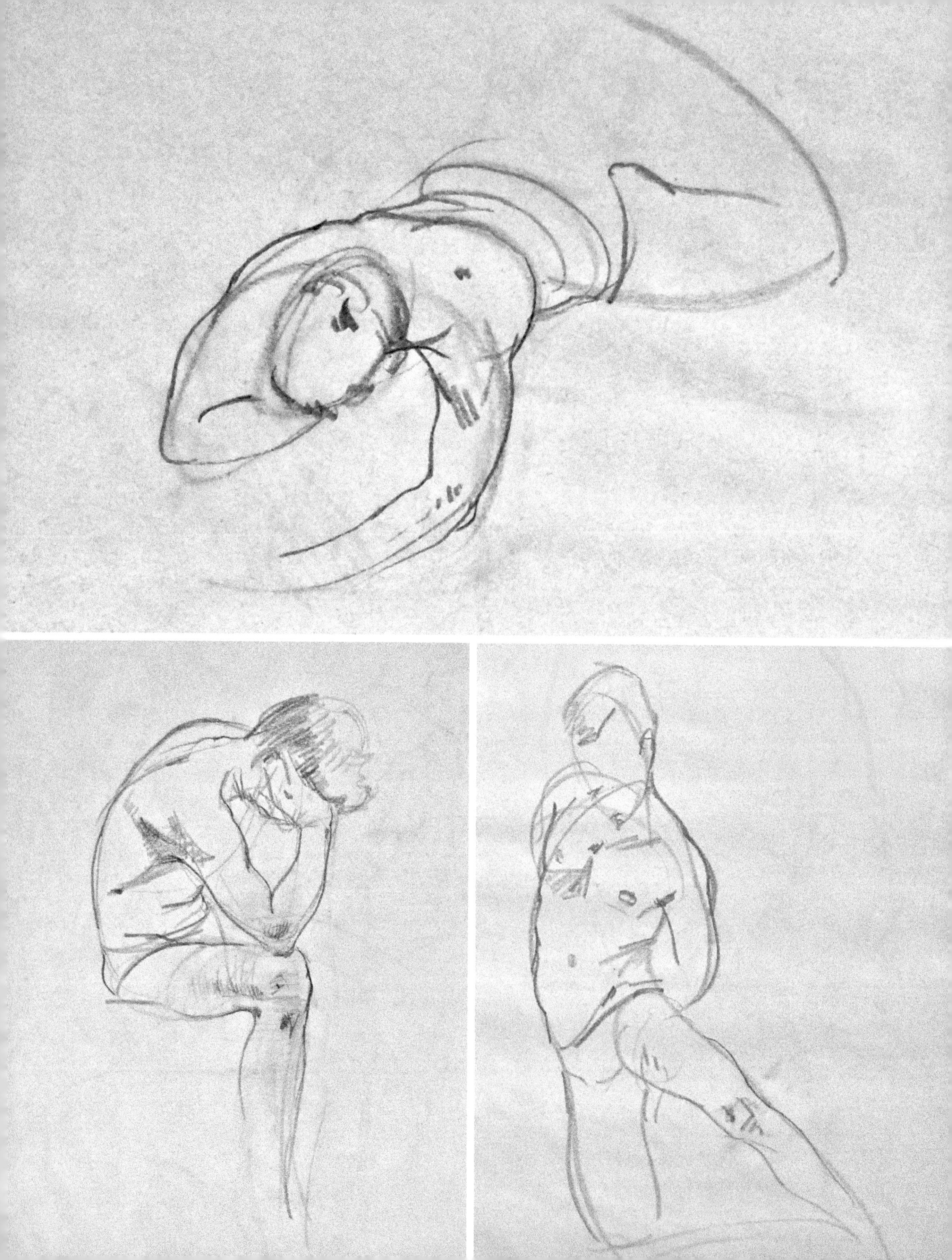

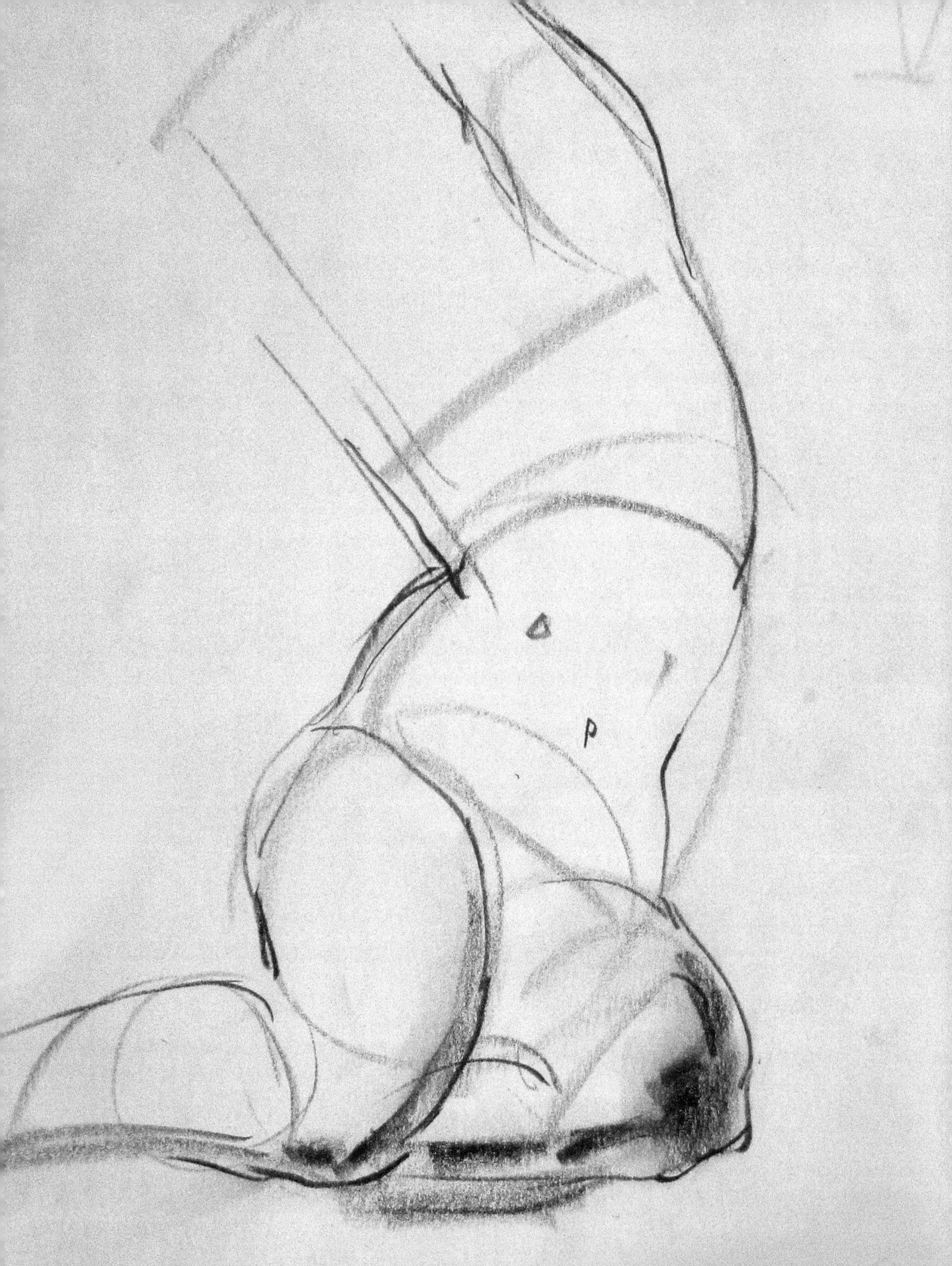

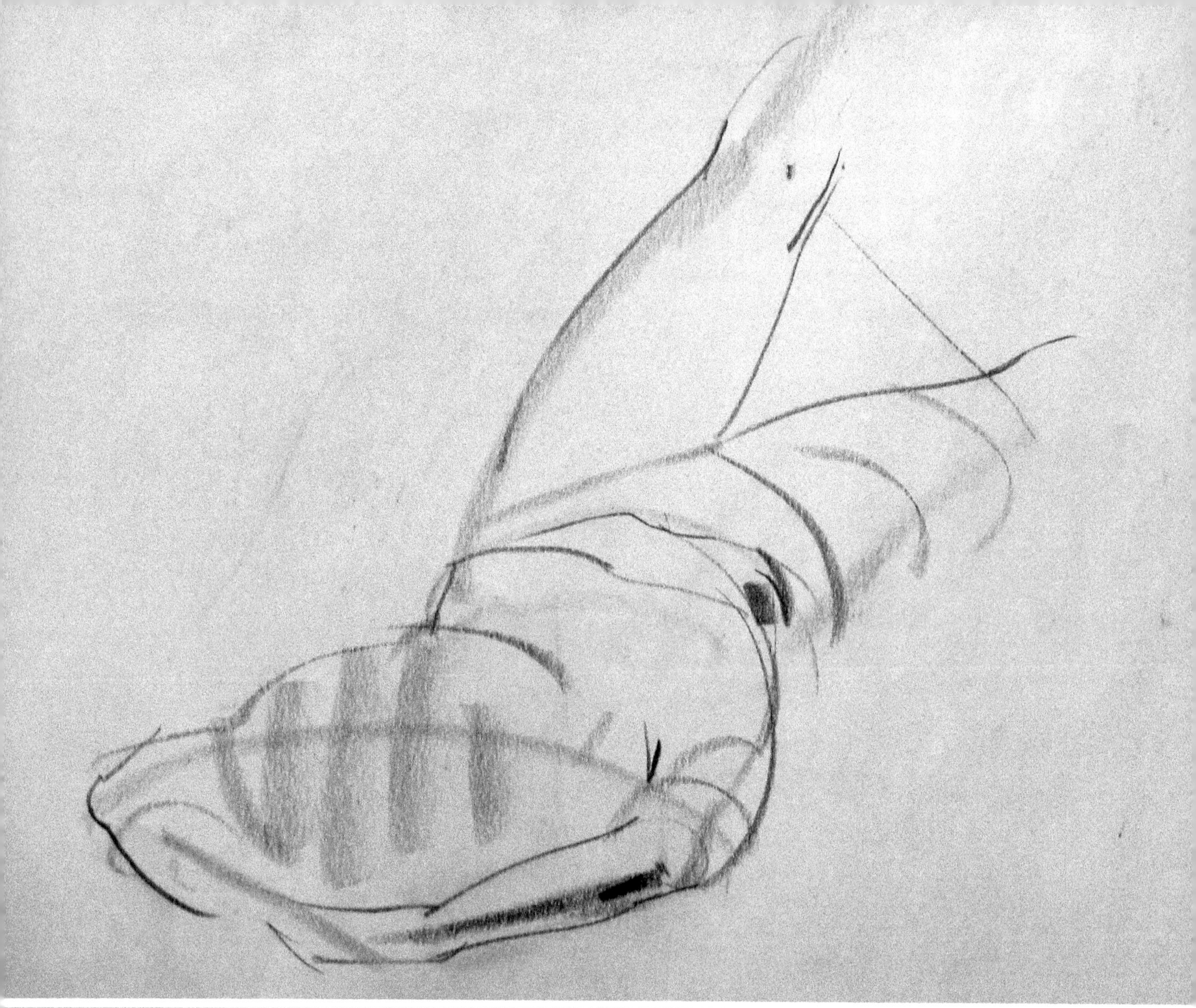

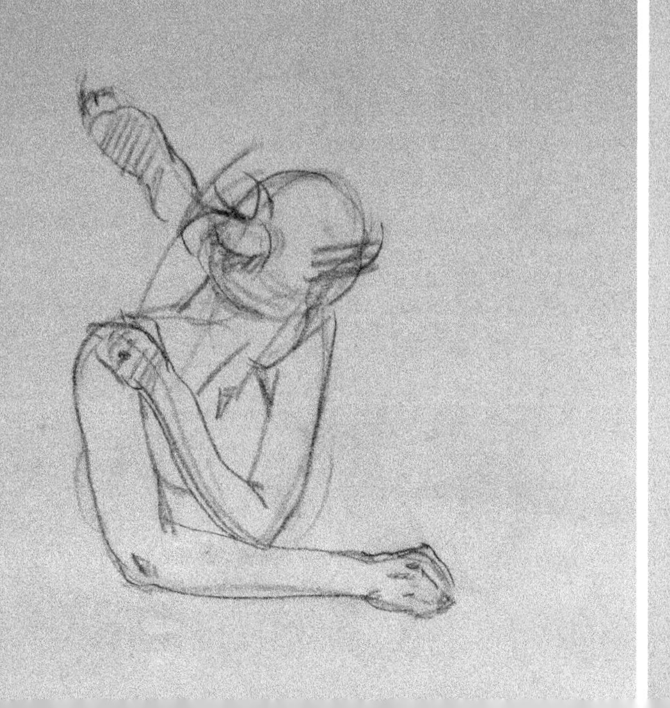

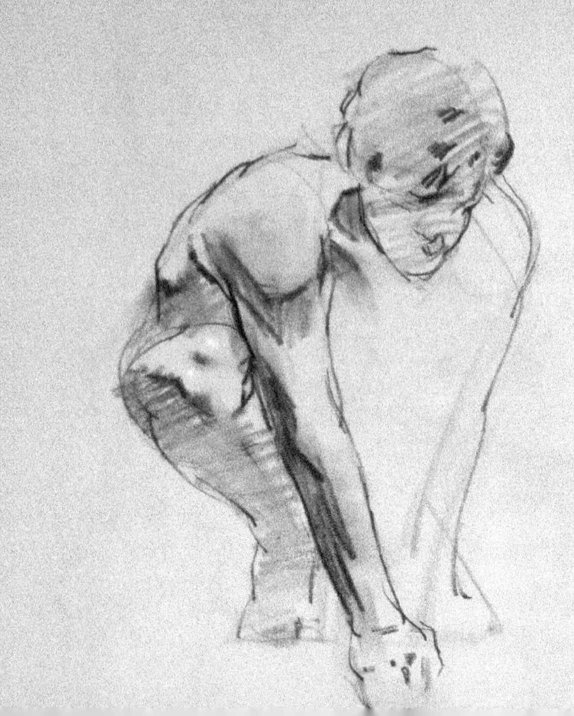

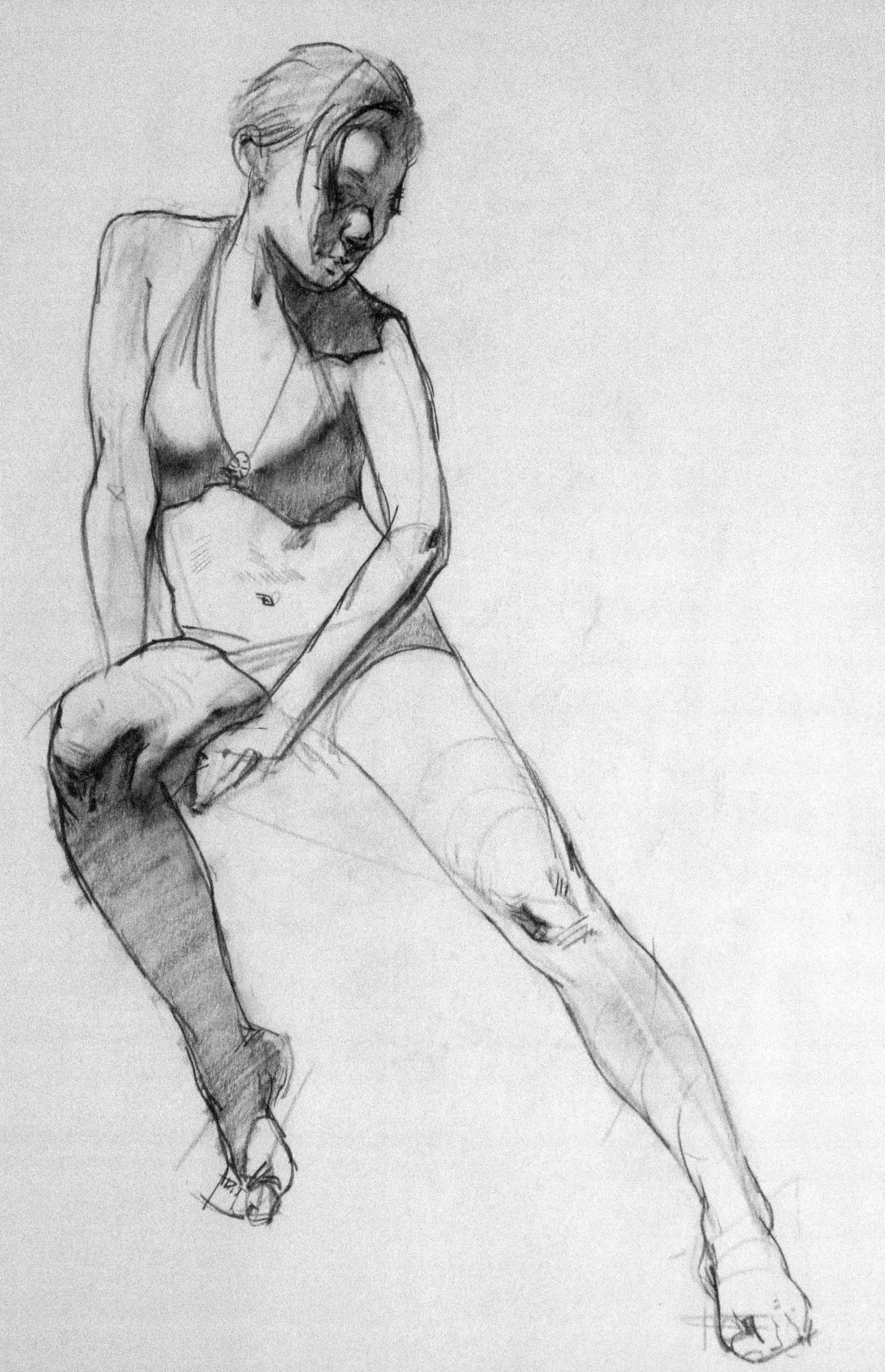

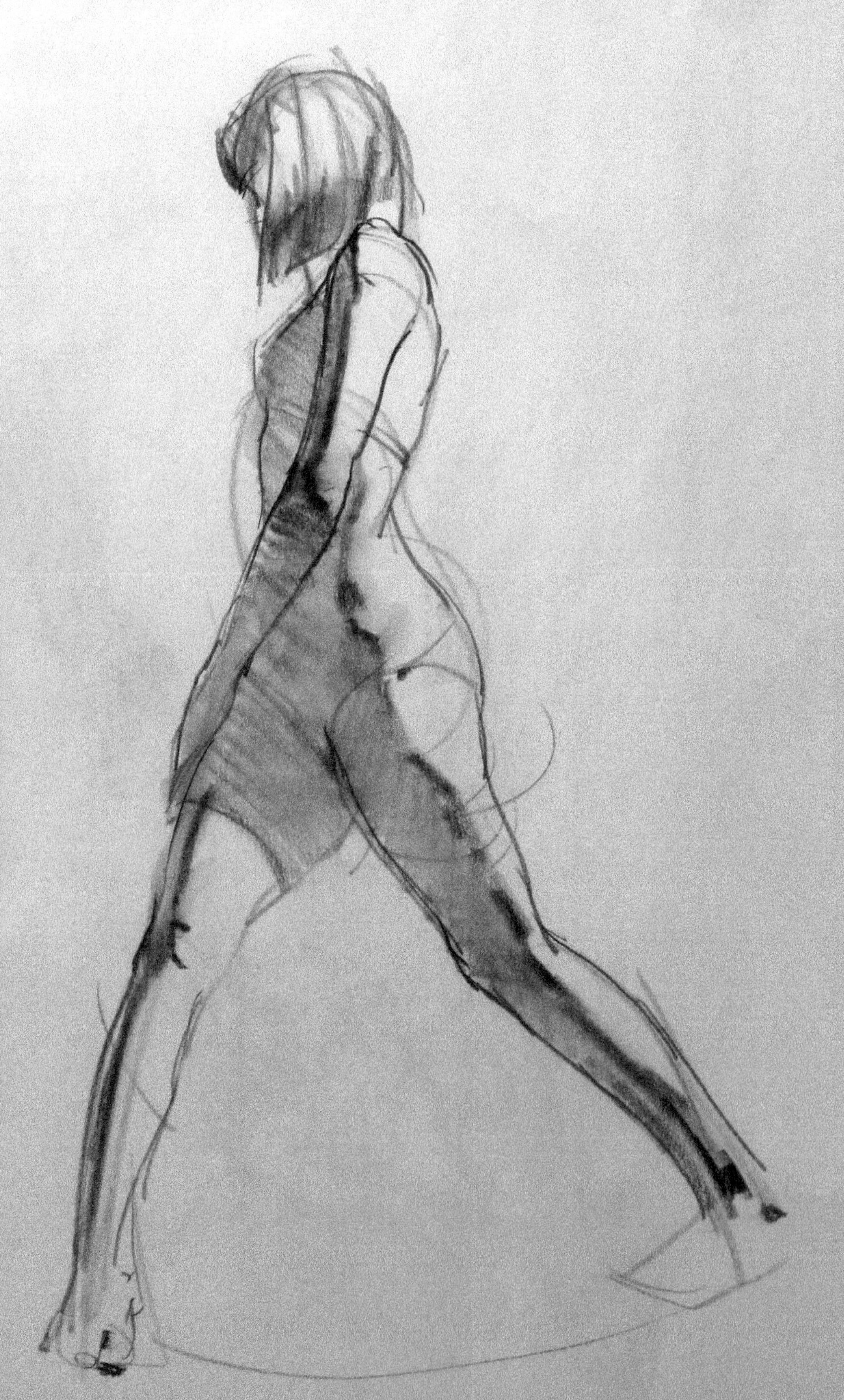

LIGHT & SHADOW

LIGHT & SHADOW

When you incorporate light and shadow into a drawing, the figure really begins to come to life. It adds dimension and makes your figures look real. A common misconception is that a perfectly outlined drawing is needed before adding light and shadow. Yes, it is a good idea to start with a basic gesture before getting too involved in light and shadow; however, try to add the light and shadow as soon as possible. Large flat shapes (shadows) actually help to get accuracy in a drawing. Comparing these large masses is useful in pinpointing lengths and distances.

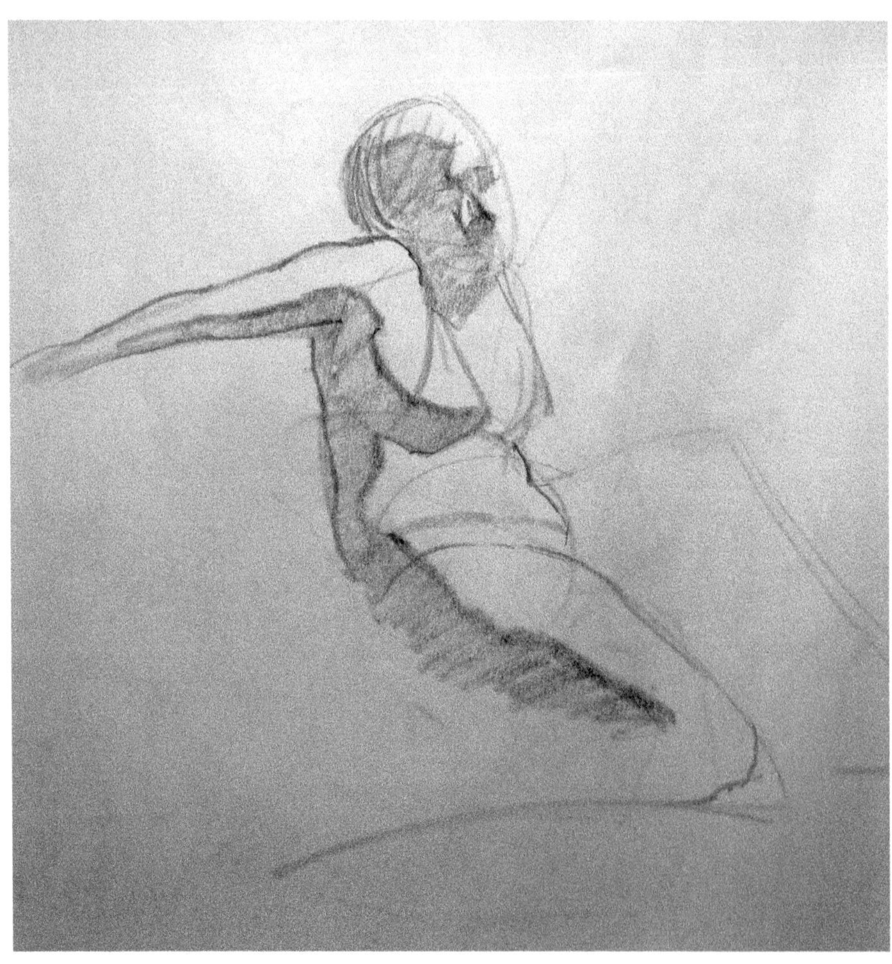

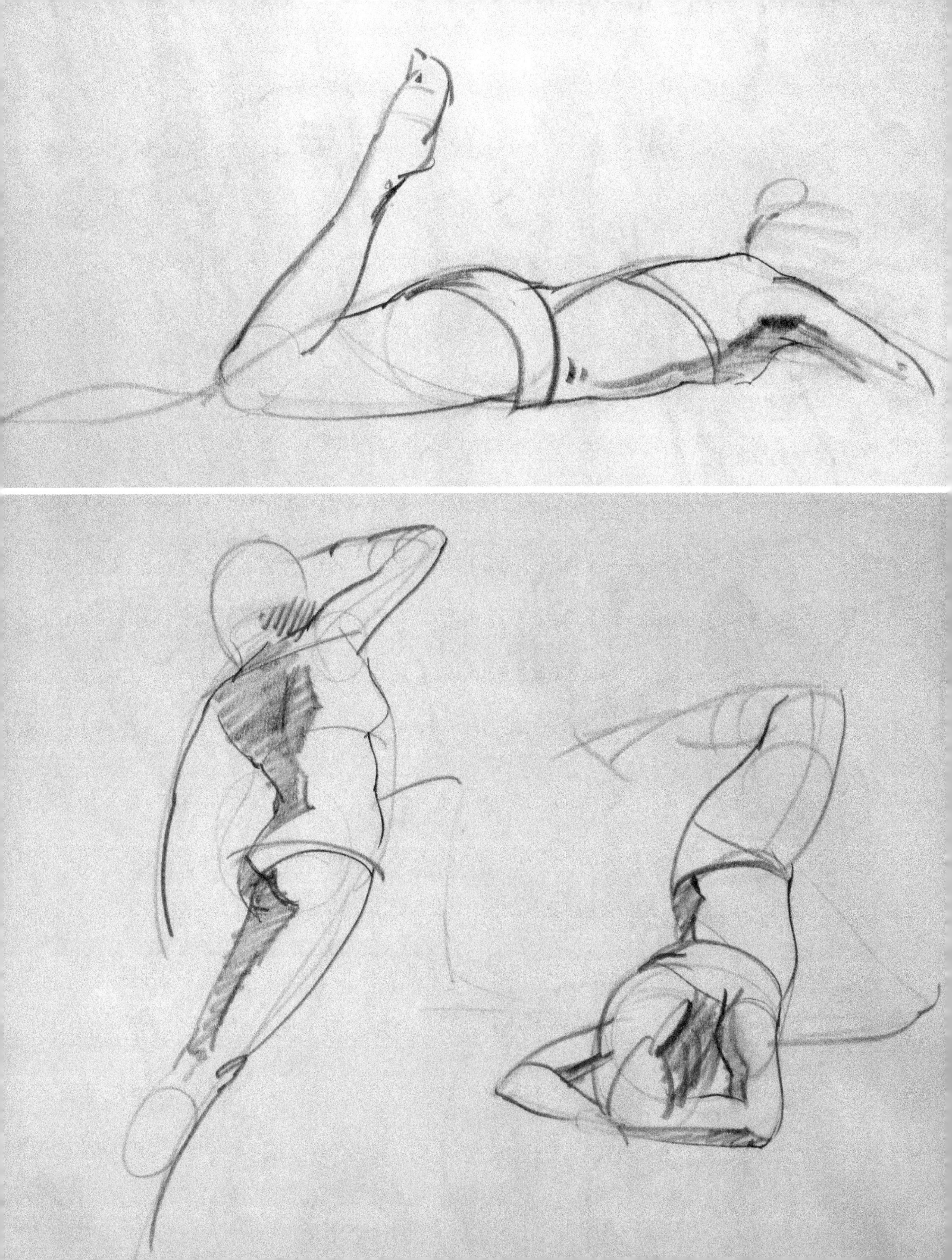

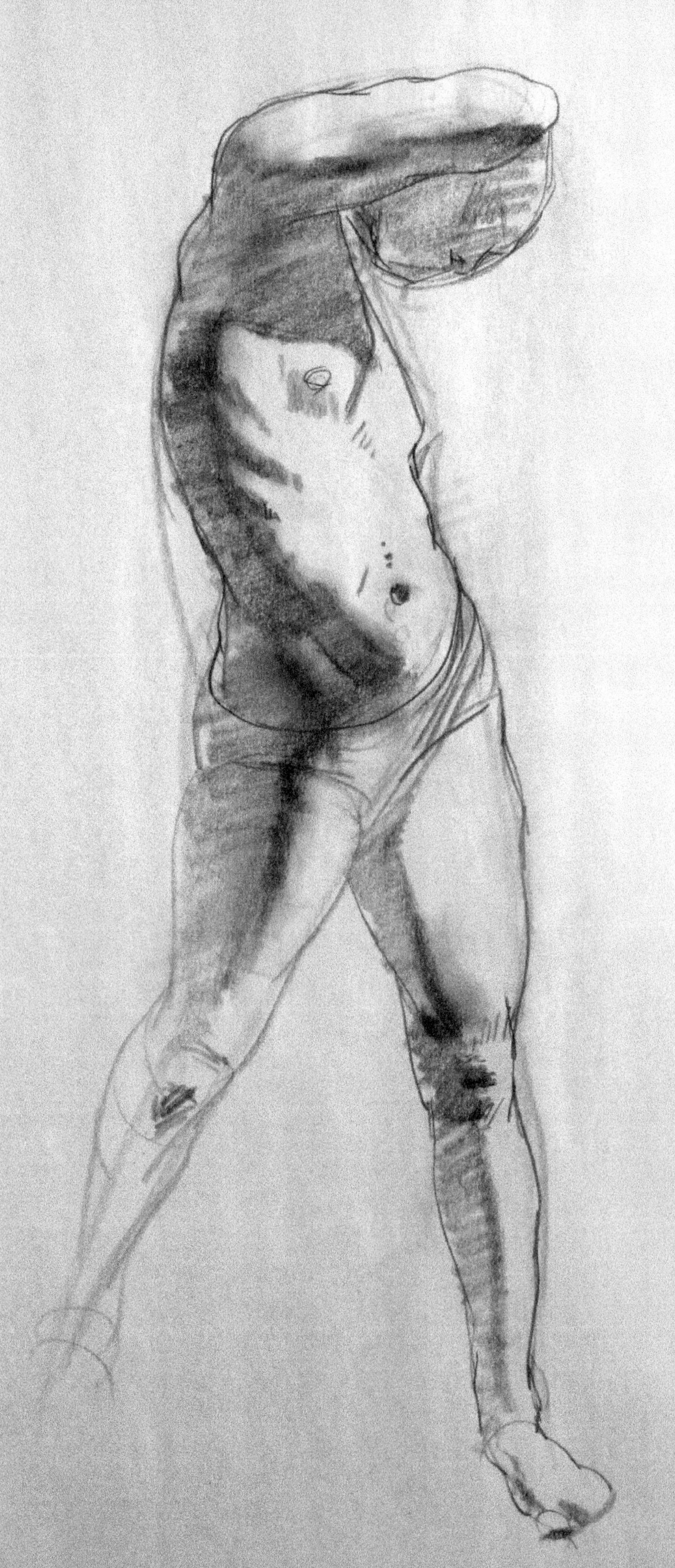

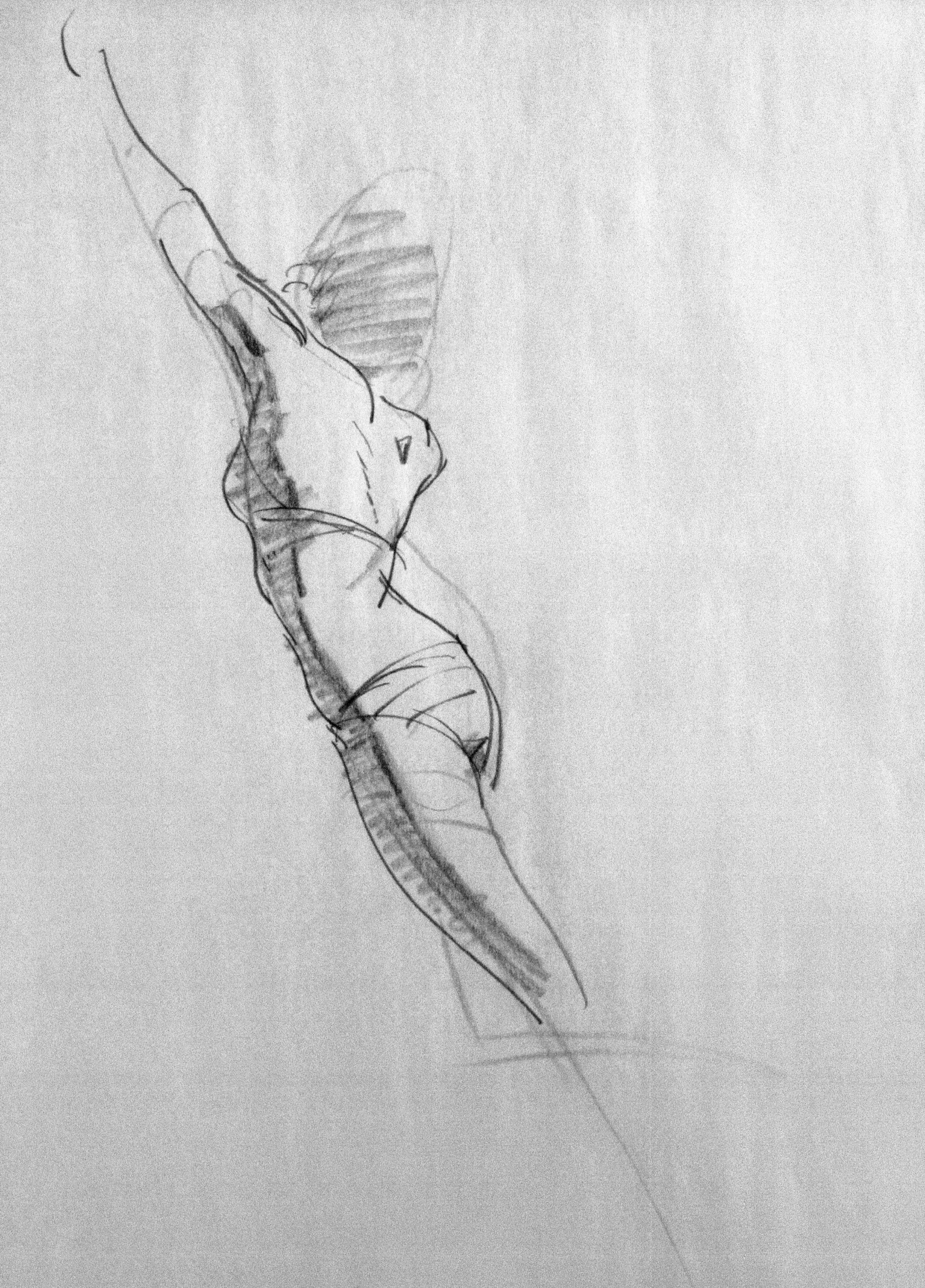

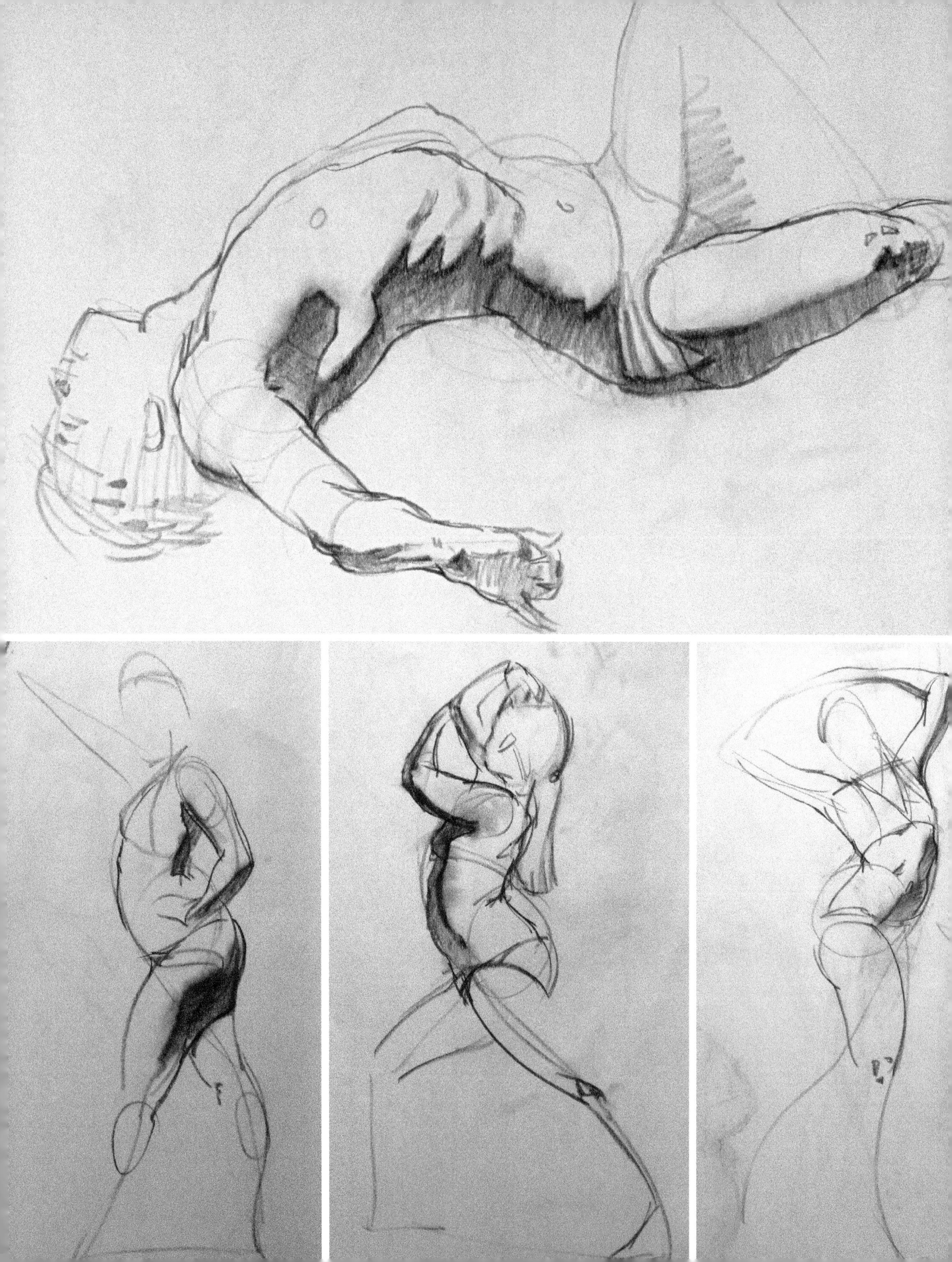

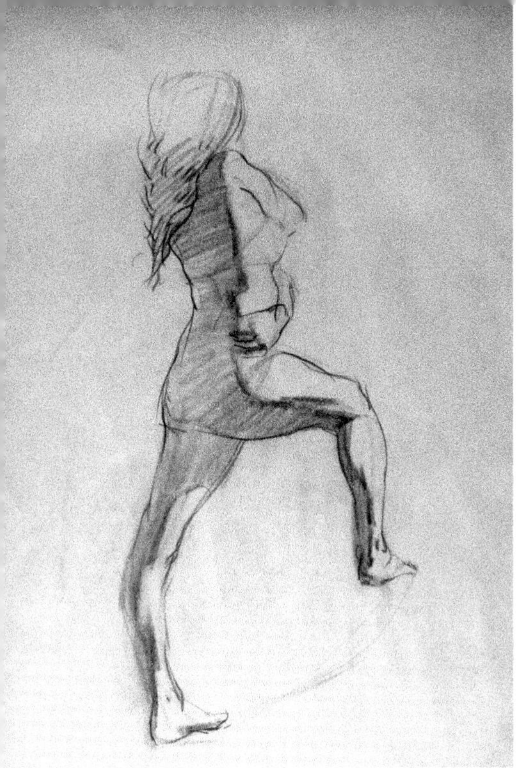

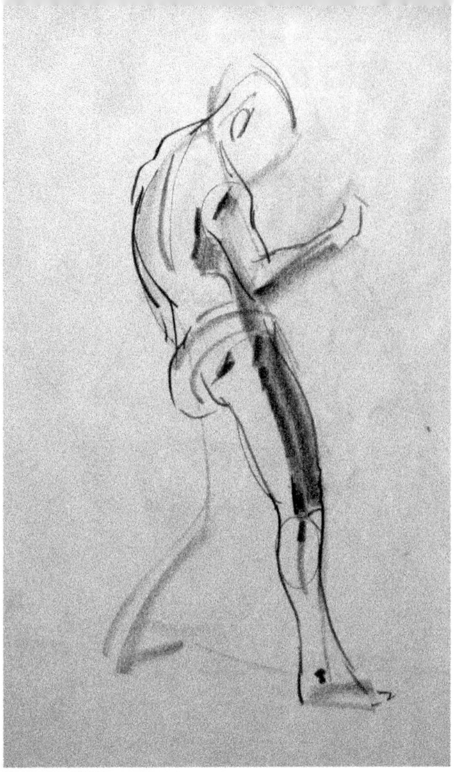

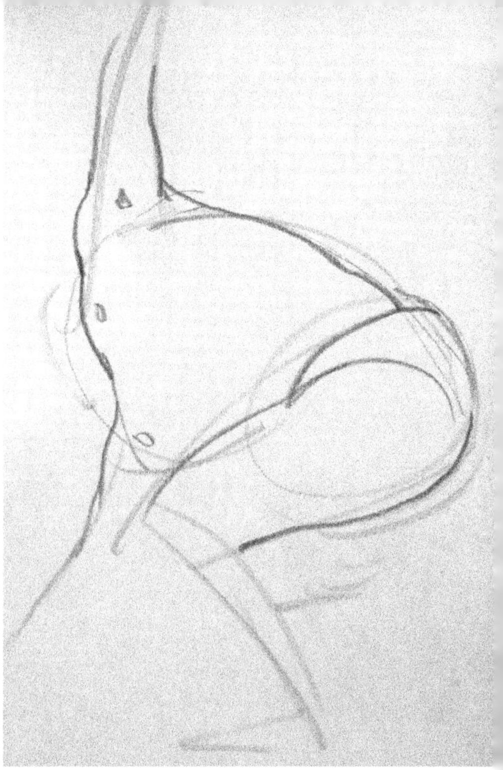

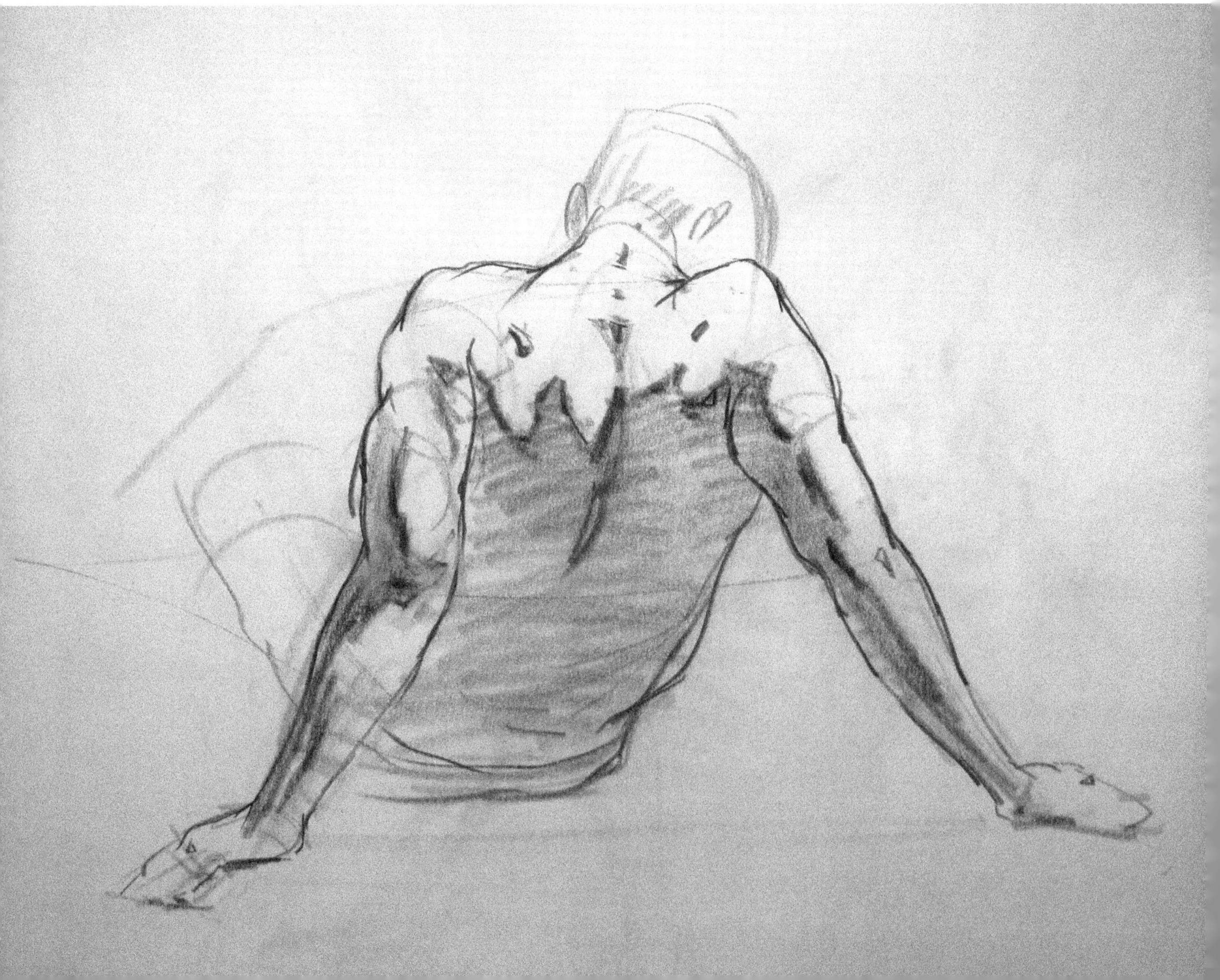

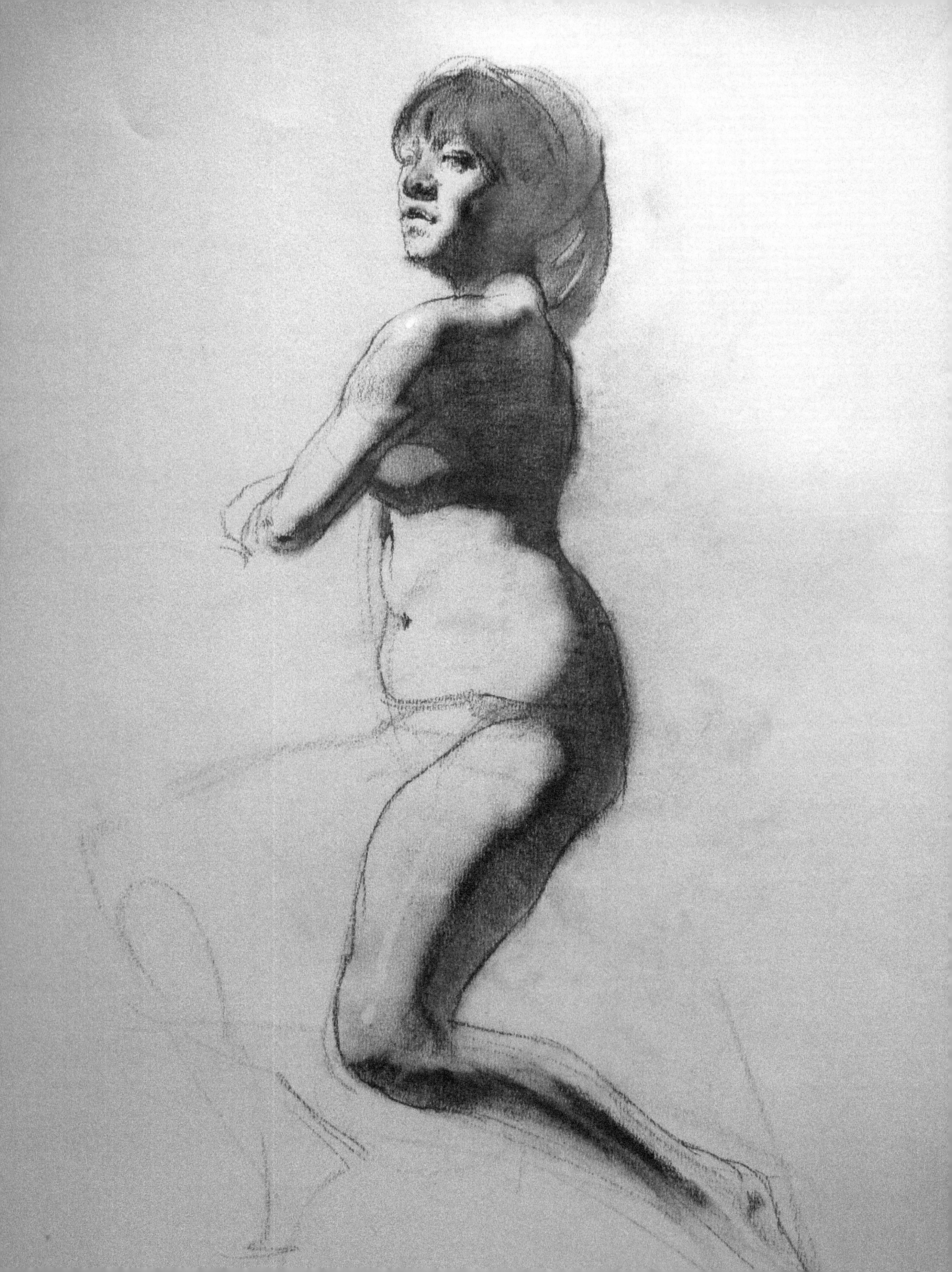

FLAT SHAPES

Shadows are simply flat shapes. They lack light. Wherever there is shadow, there cannot be light. They do not mix. Make shadows flat by smearing them or by using the broad side of the conté or charcoal to fill in its entire shape. Even if information in the shadow can be seen when looking at the model, simplify it or even choose to leave it out entirely. Remember editing? This is where a lot of editing takes place. The light side of a drawing is typically where the information should be. The shadows help to describe what is happening in the light. Shadows with too much information in them dement the form. A flat shape is stabilizing. It is a tricky concept to understand because in real life the eye sees information in the shadows. On a two-dimensional surface, however, the eye needs the shadow side to appear flat and even in order for the drawing to *appear* three-dimensional.

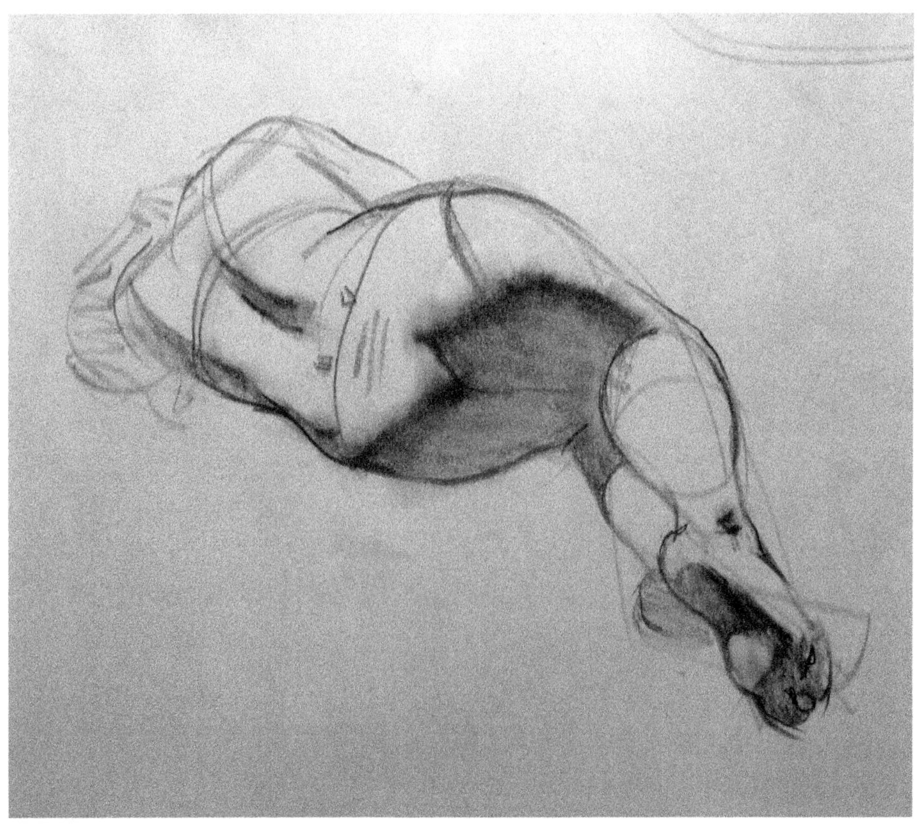

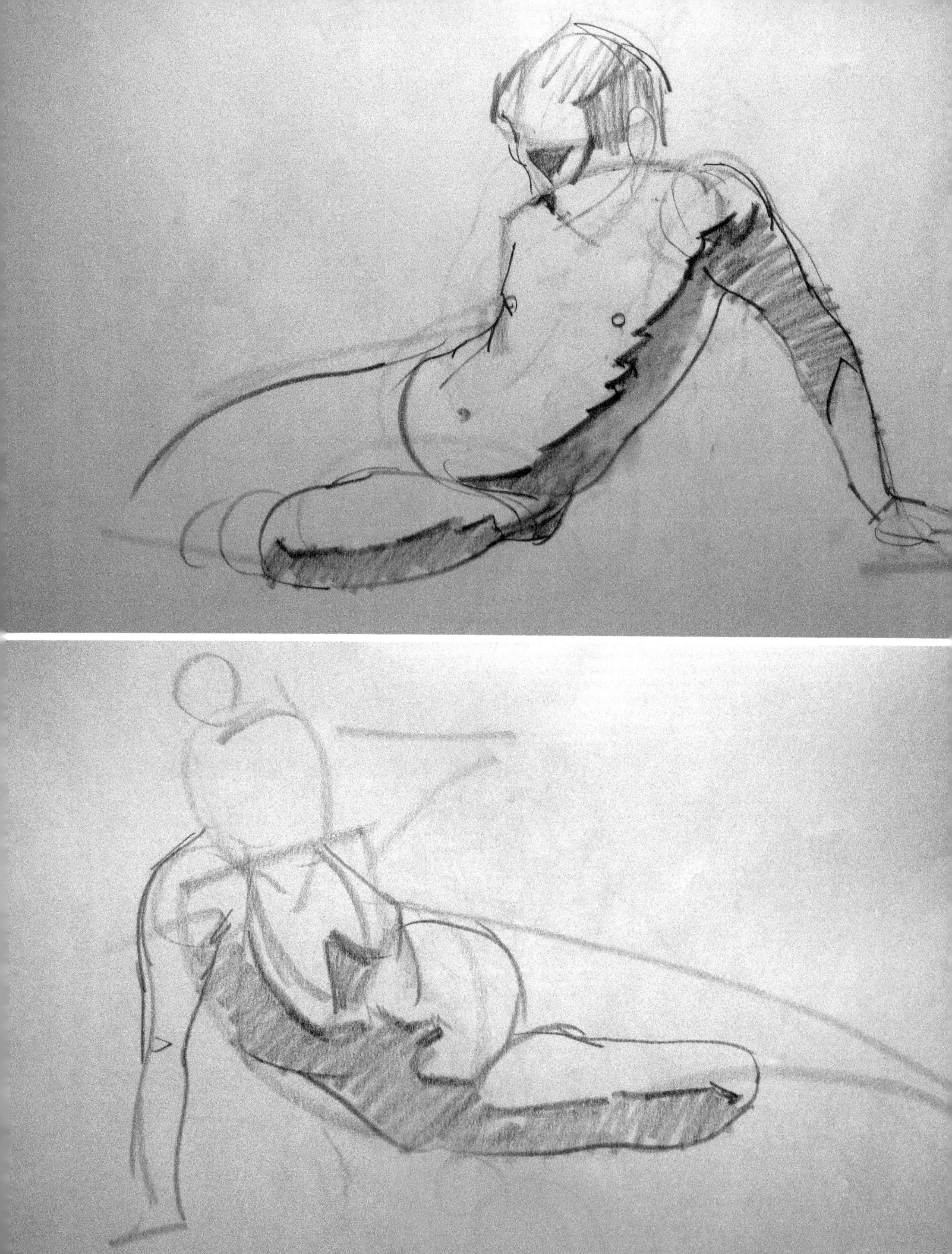

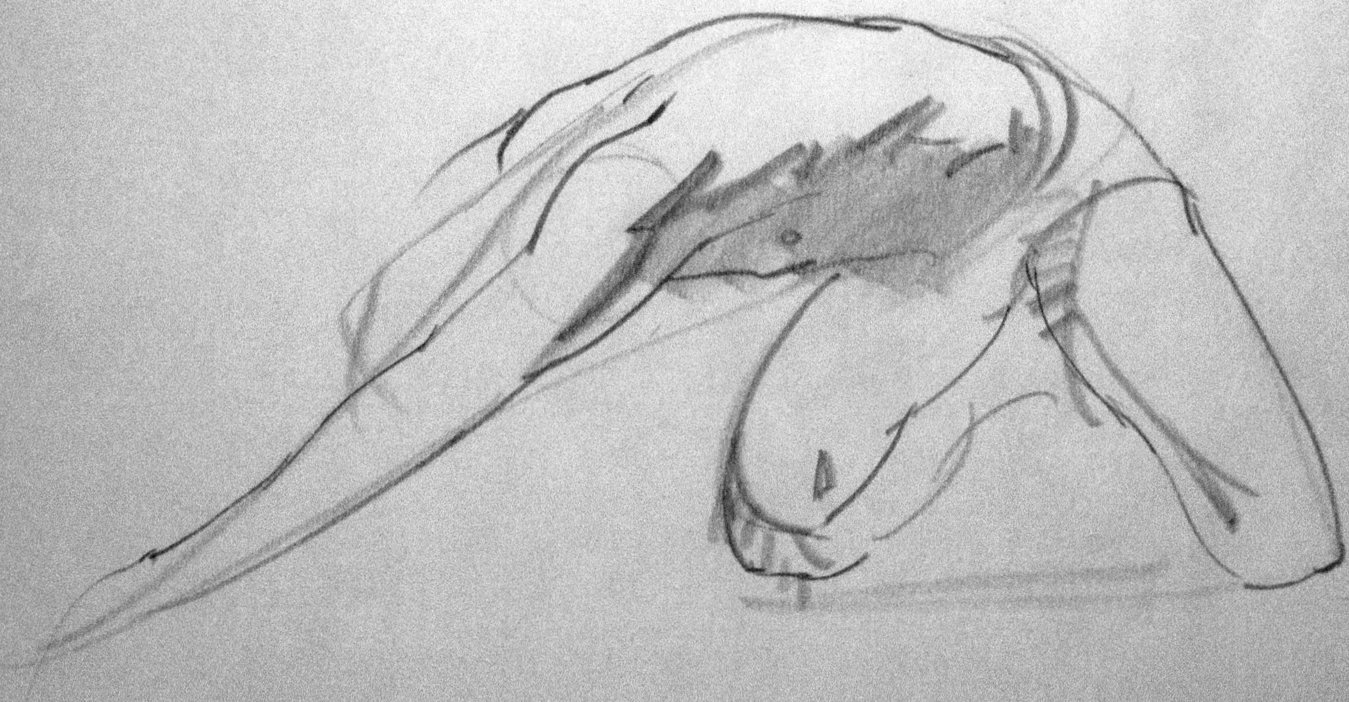

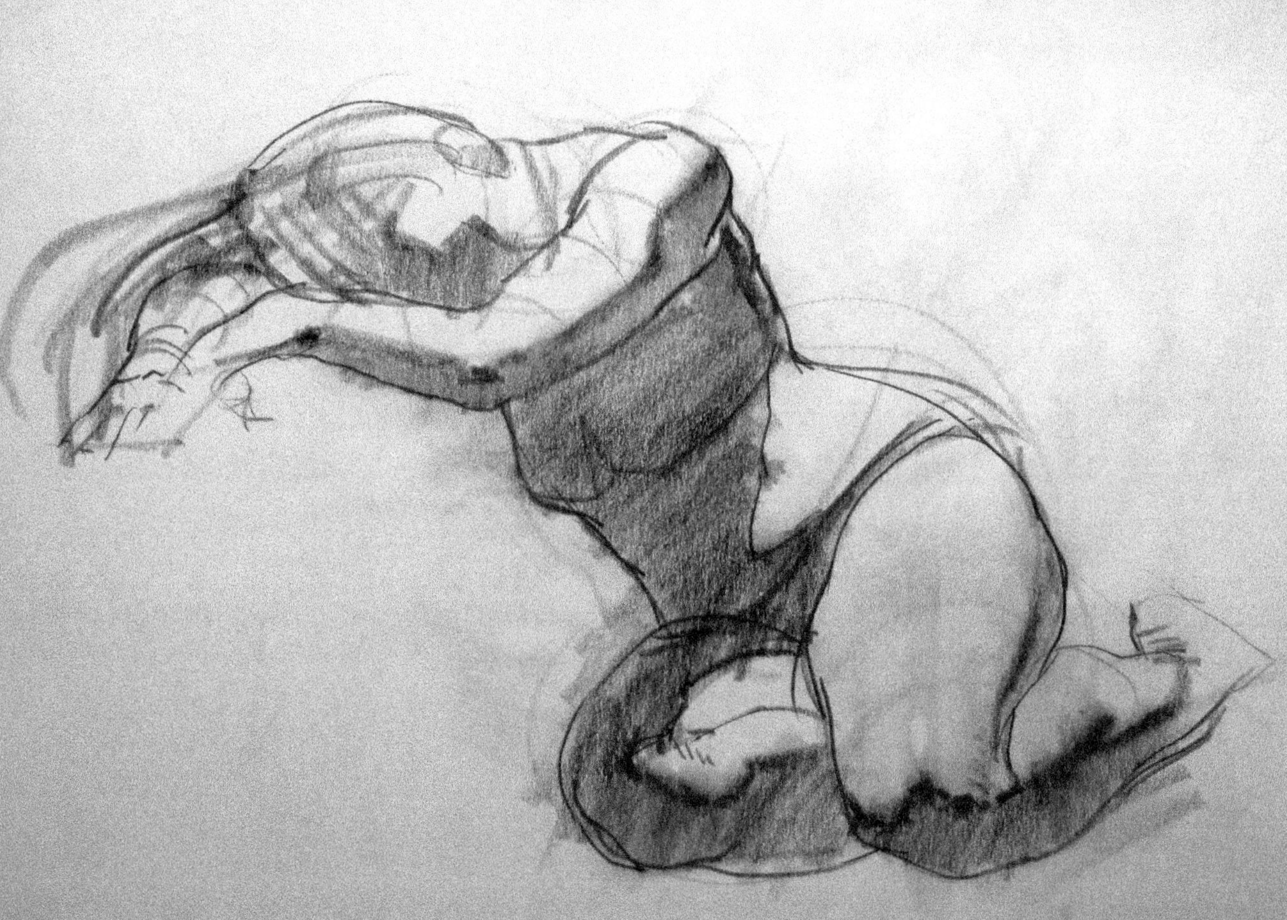

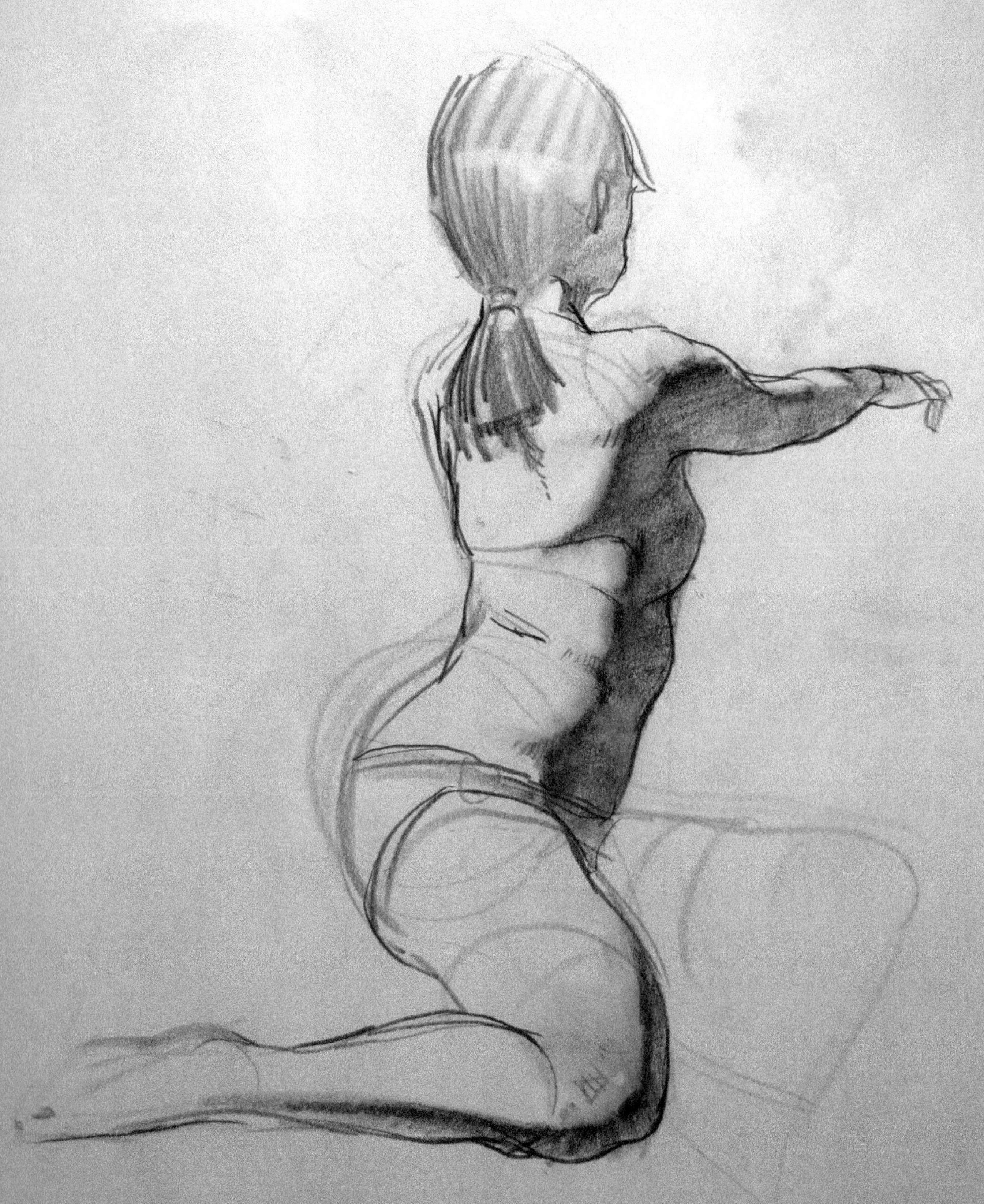

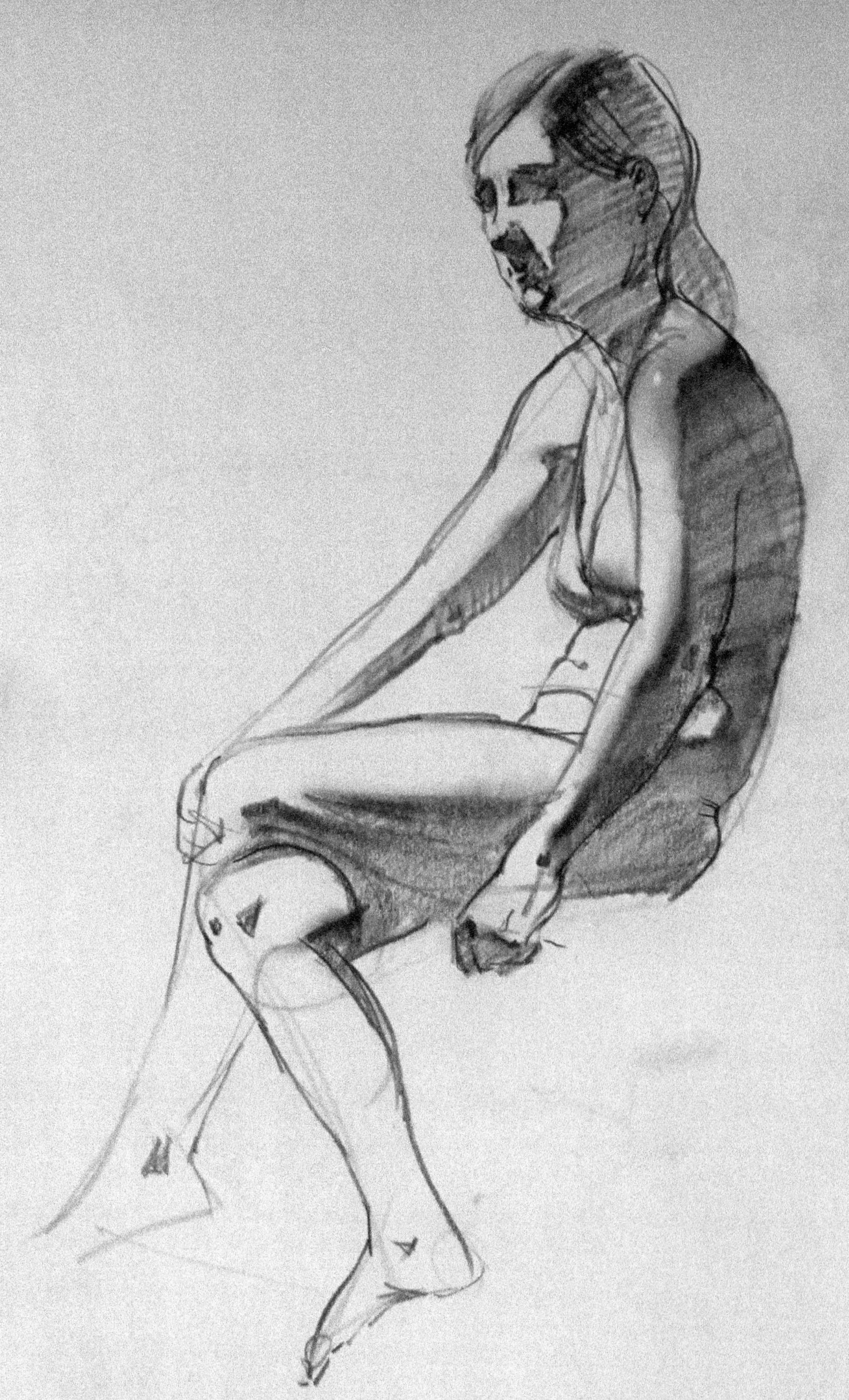

EDGES

One of the most important parts of a shadow is its edge (the transitional boundary that separates the light side from the dark side). The edge of a shadow tells a lot about the form upon which it rests. Hard edges indicate cast shadows and soft edges indicate form shadows. What is the difference between the two types of shadows?

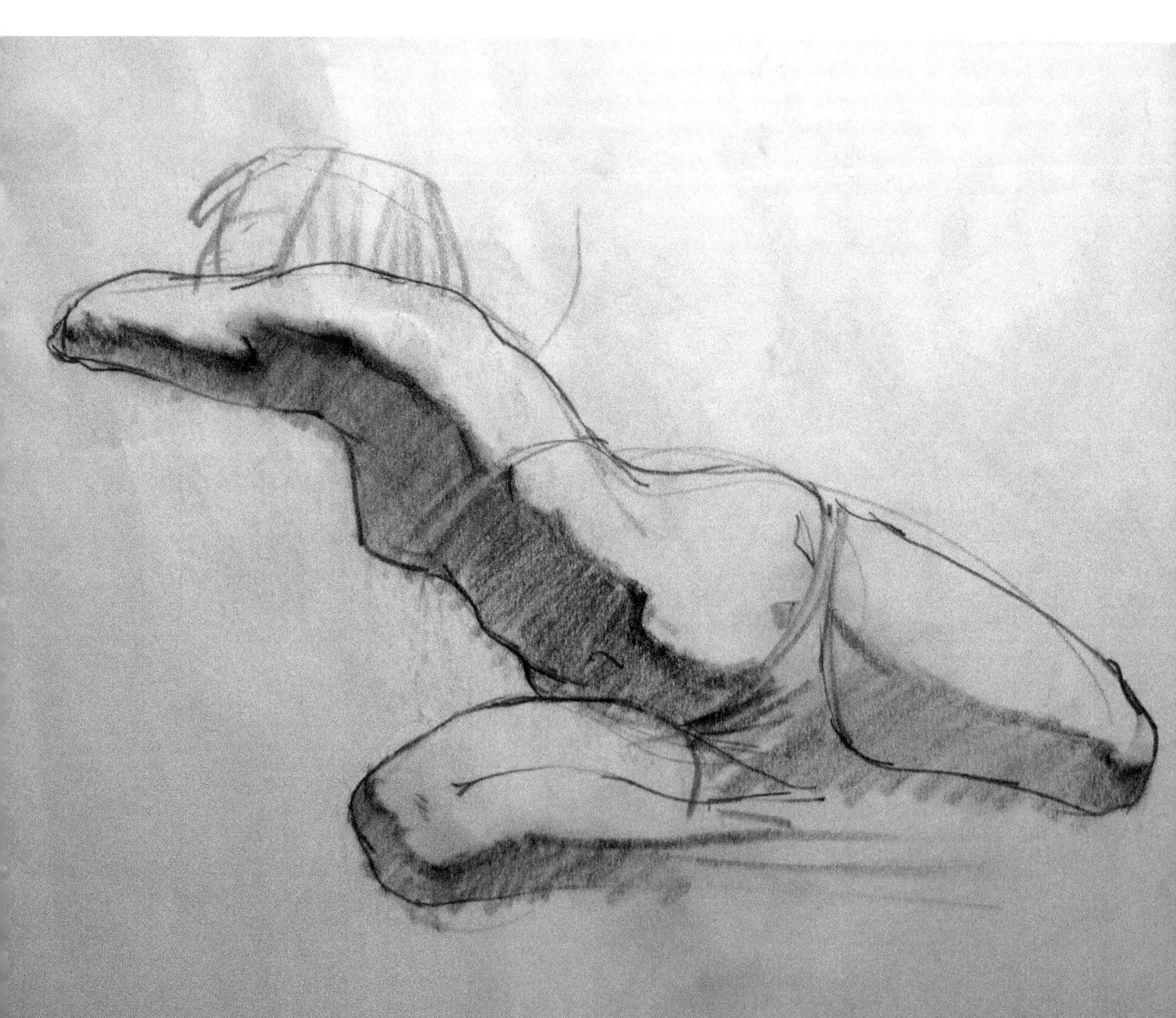

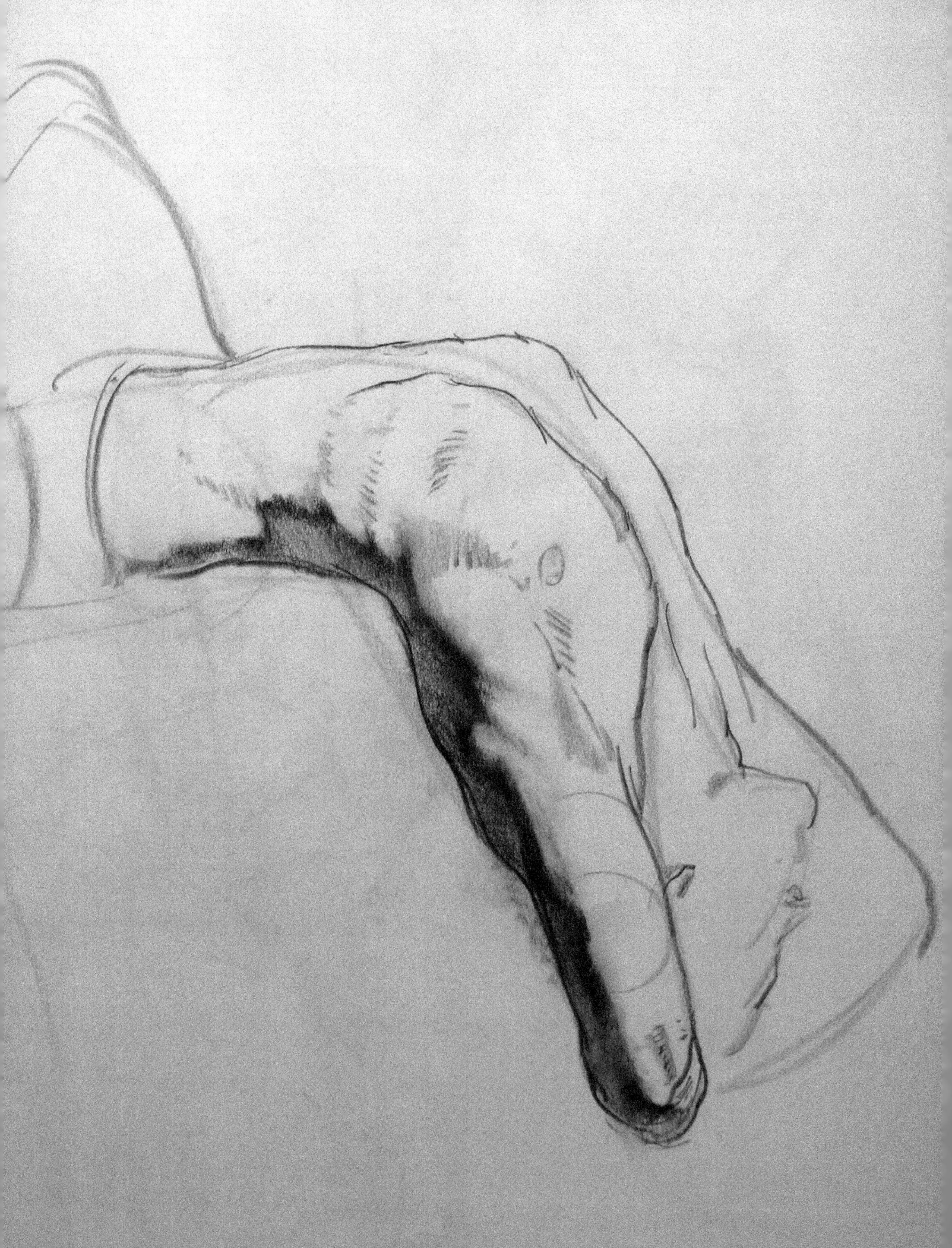

CAST SHADOWS

A cast shadow appears when one form blocks another form from receiving light. When the light source is coming from above the model, a typical cast shadow, for example, can usually be found under the nose. Its edges will be hard. The nose blocks the upper lip from receiving light, and a shadow with crisp edges would be found there.

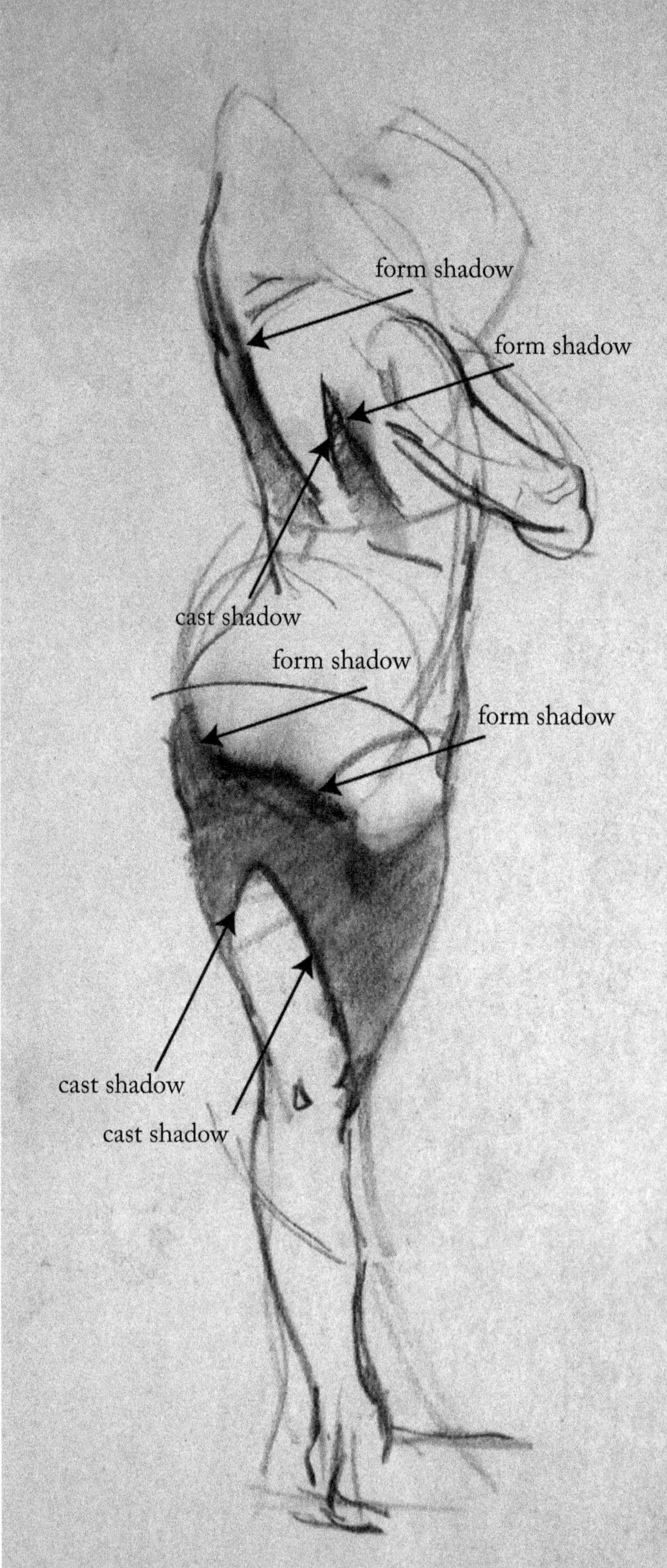

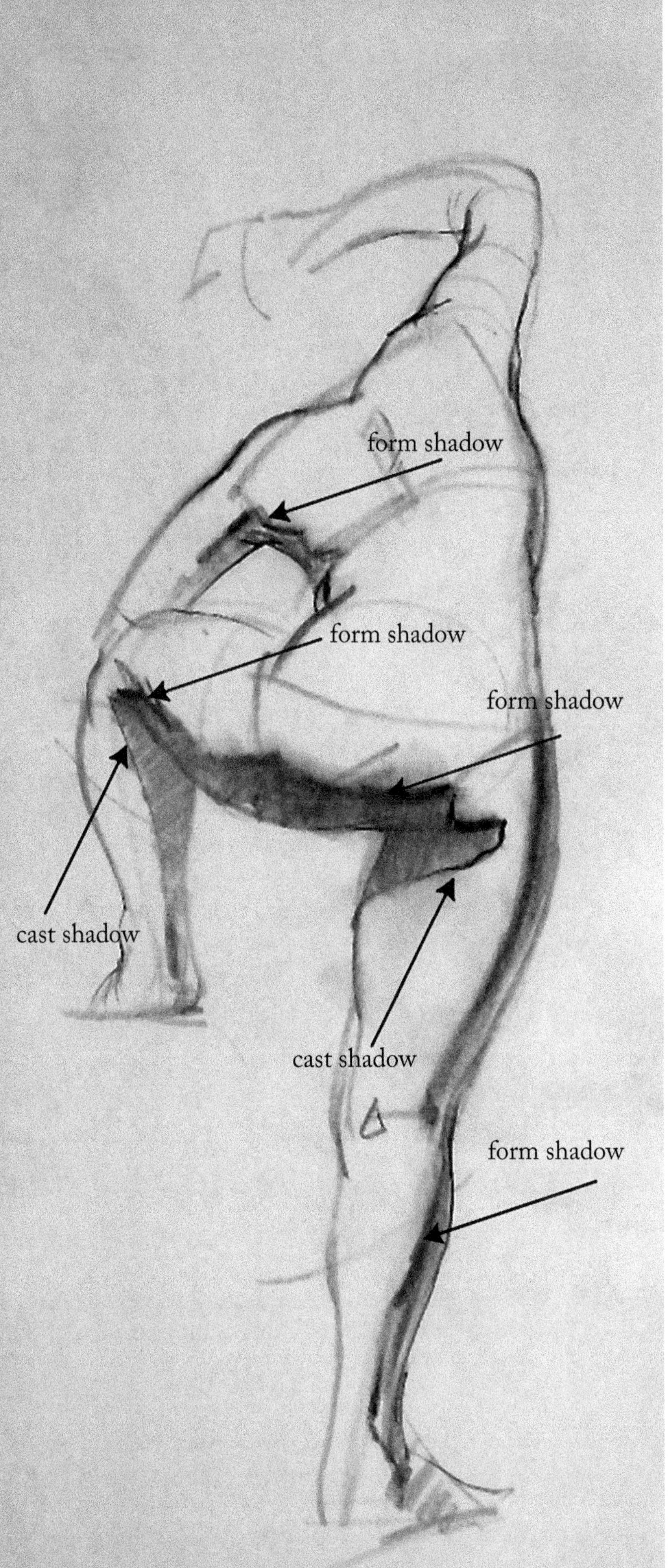

FORM SHADOWS

A form shadow occurs when a form turns away and no longer receives light. Although a gradual turn takes place, it is the transitional edge of the shadow that needs most of the attention. It will be soft. This is called the penumbra, and it is slightly darker than the rest of the shadow.

Whether constructing cast shadows or form shadows, make sure they are bold and confident shapes. Weak shadow shapes are difficult to read. Shadows that lack uniformity end up looking like dirt on the skin instead of like shadows.

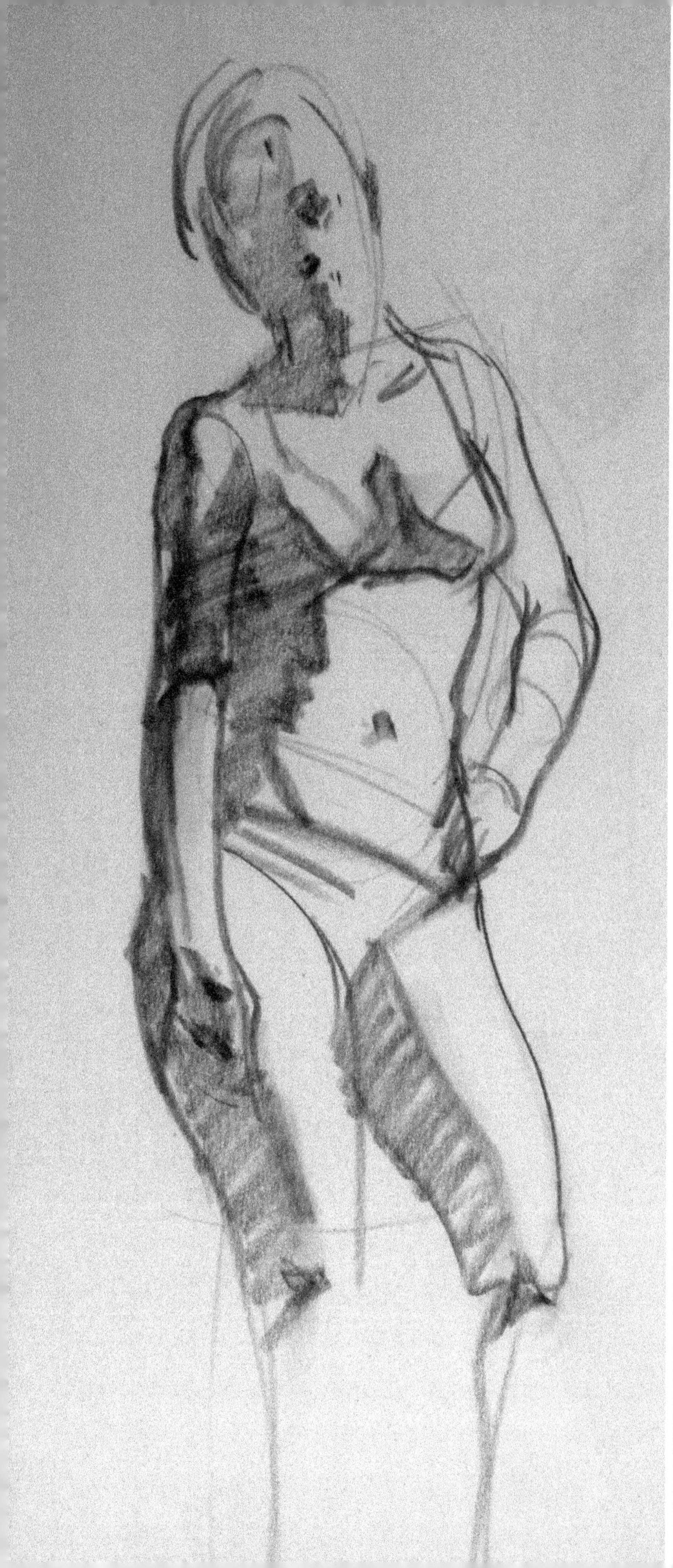

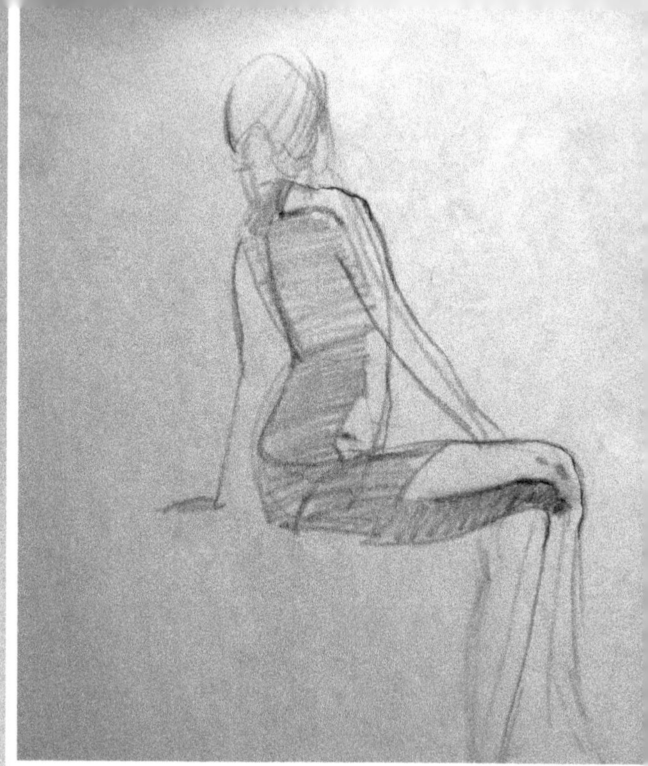
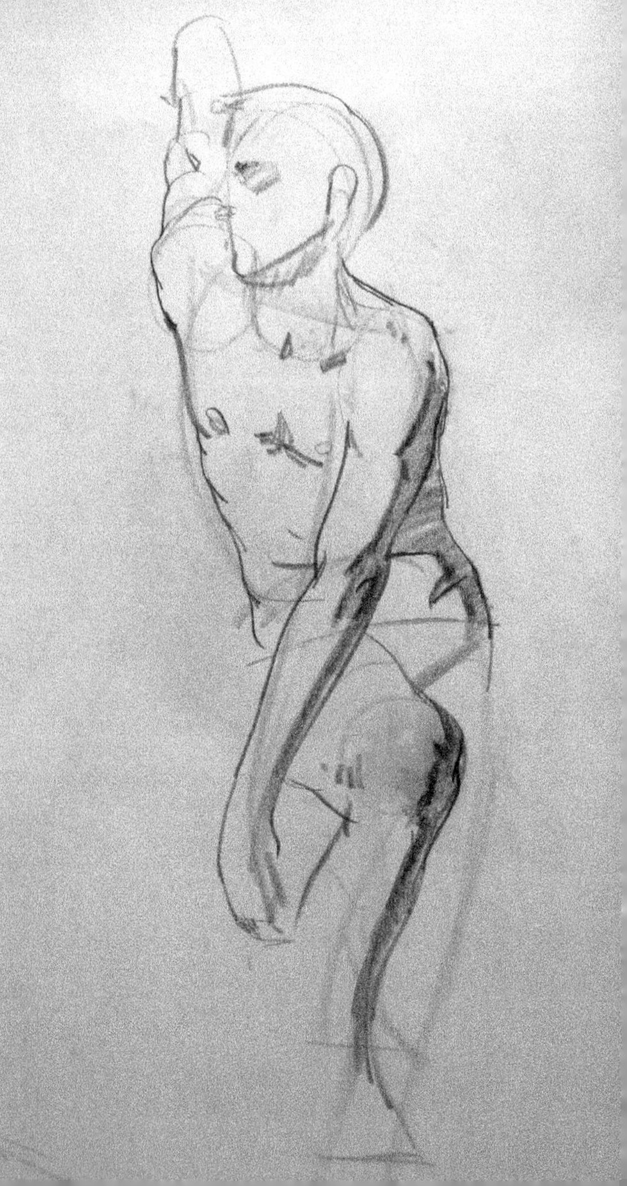

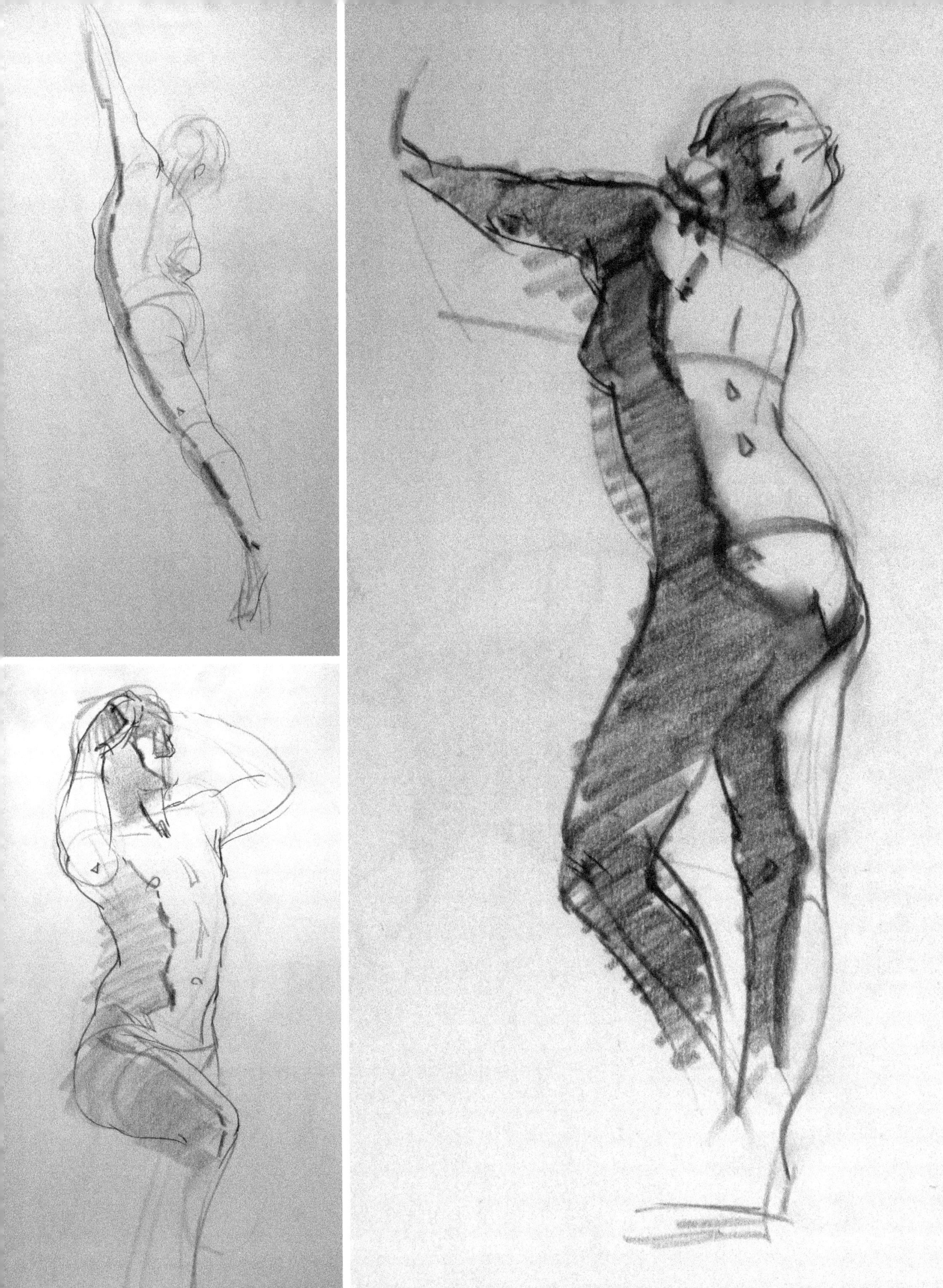

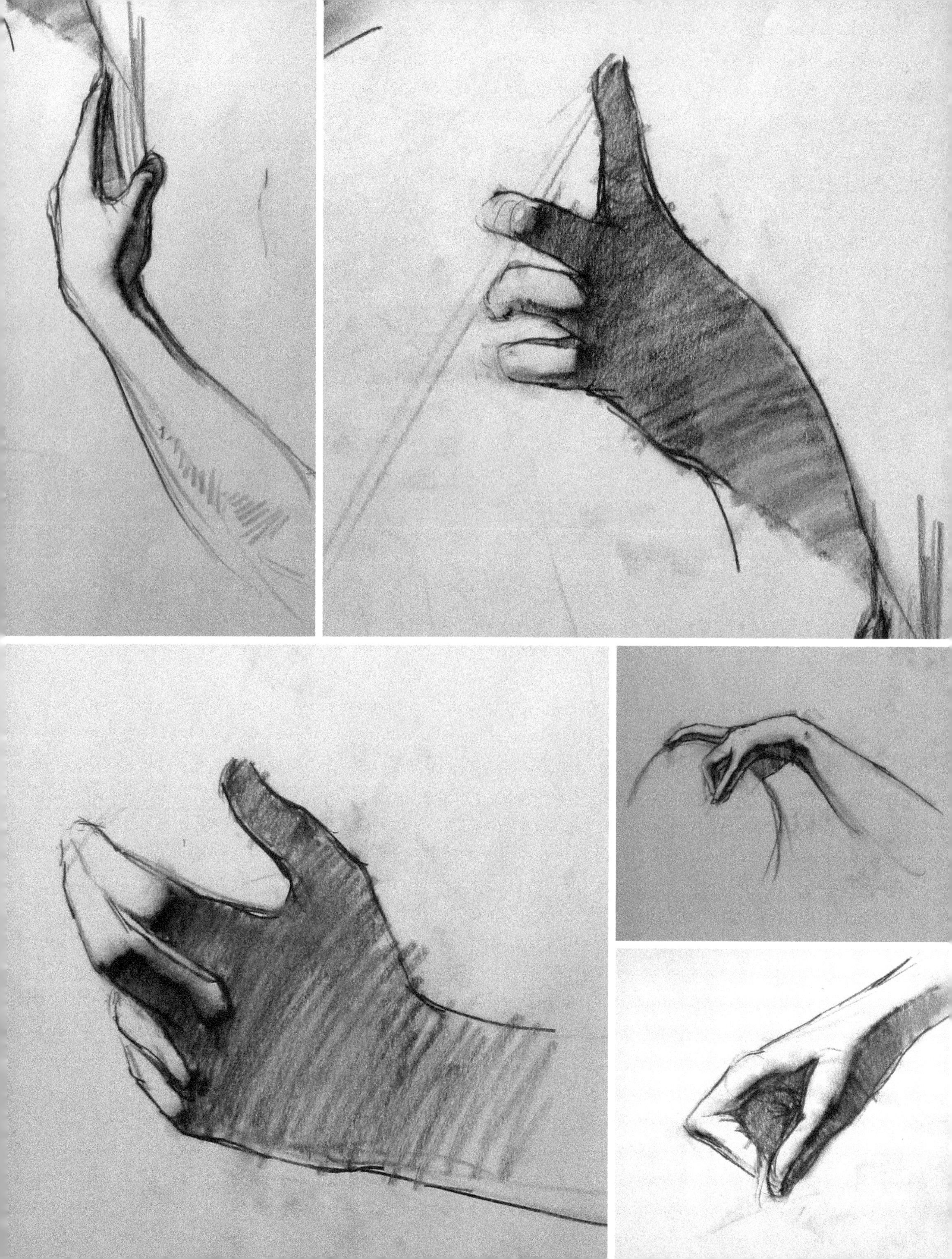

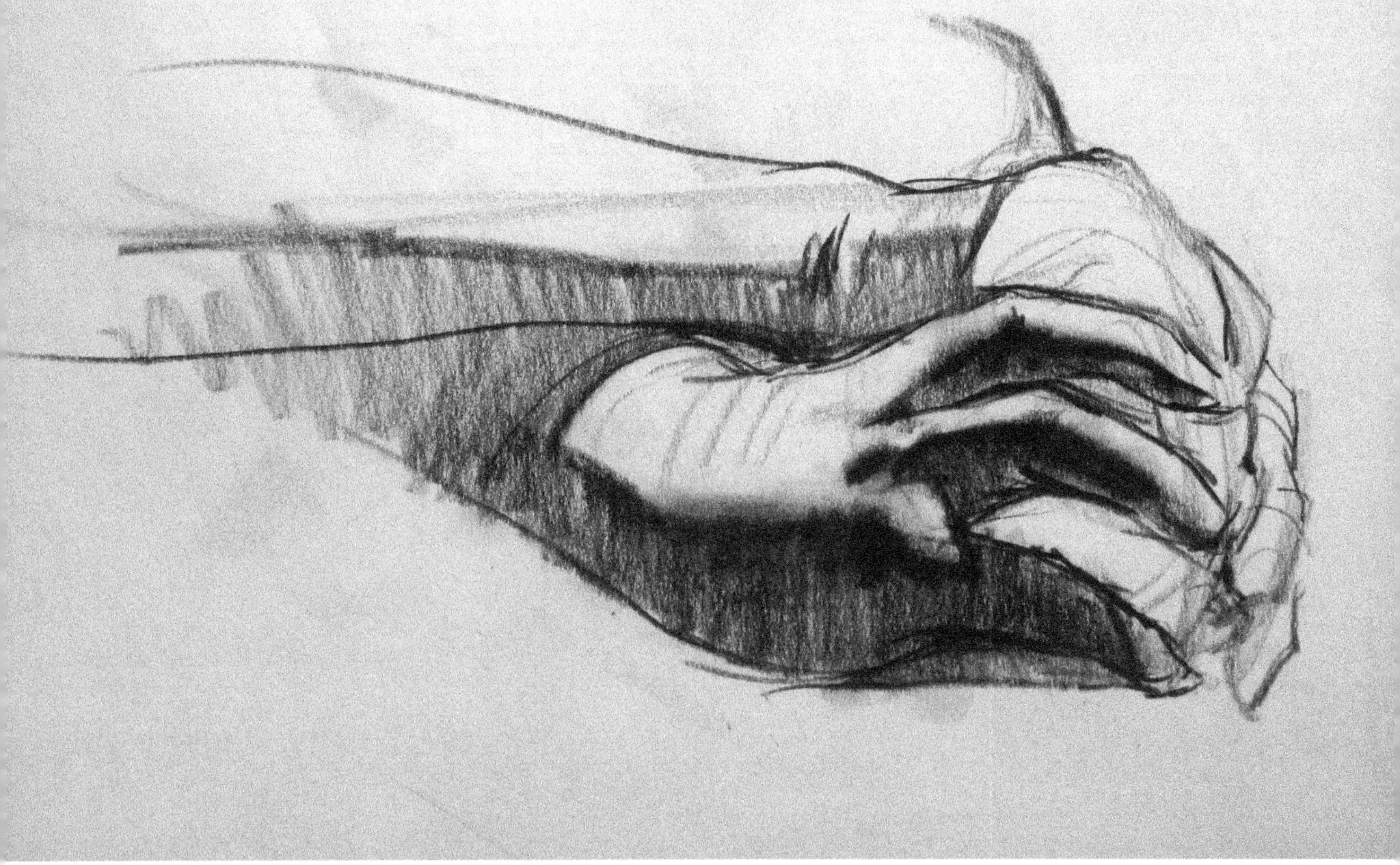

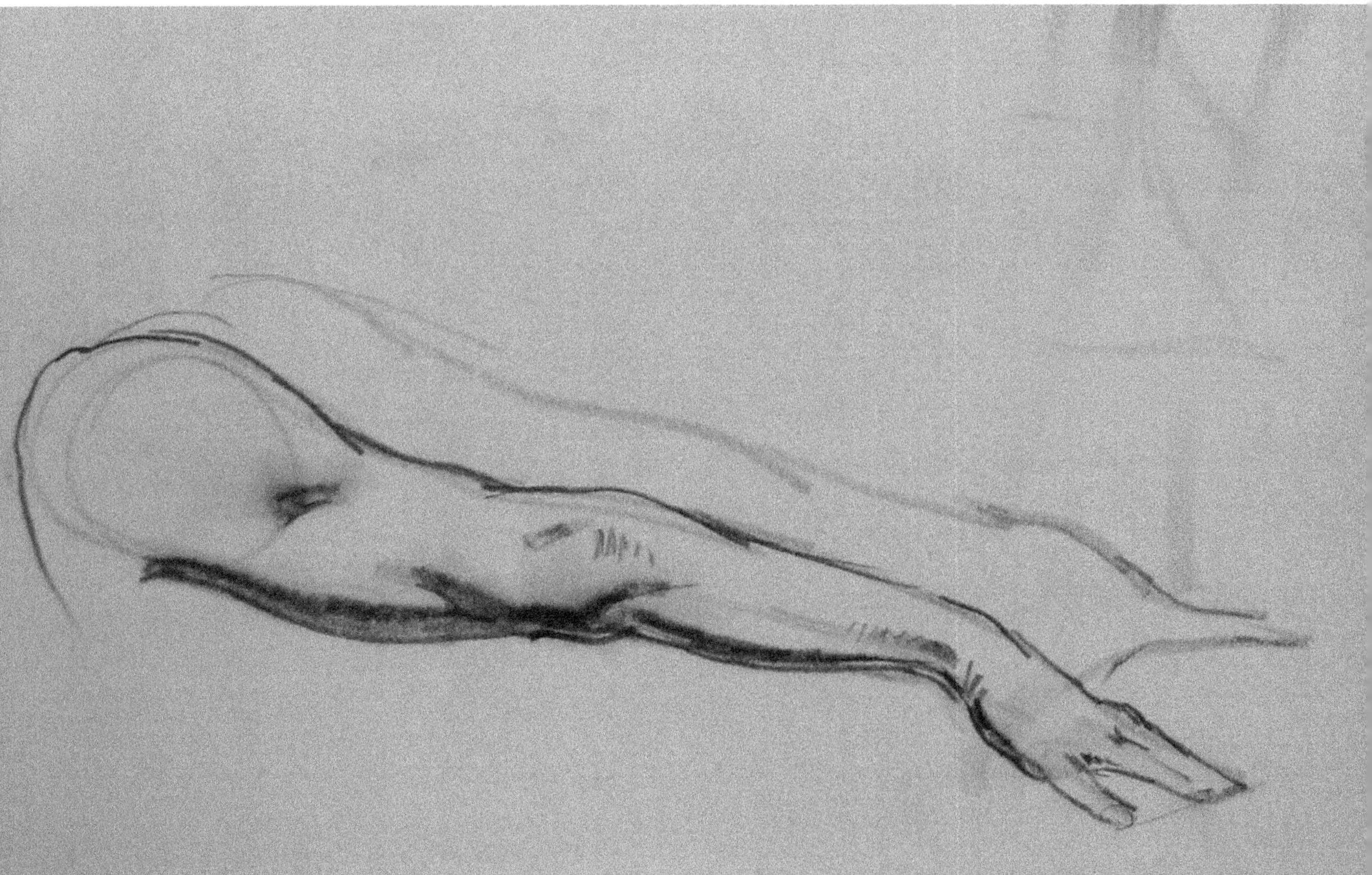

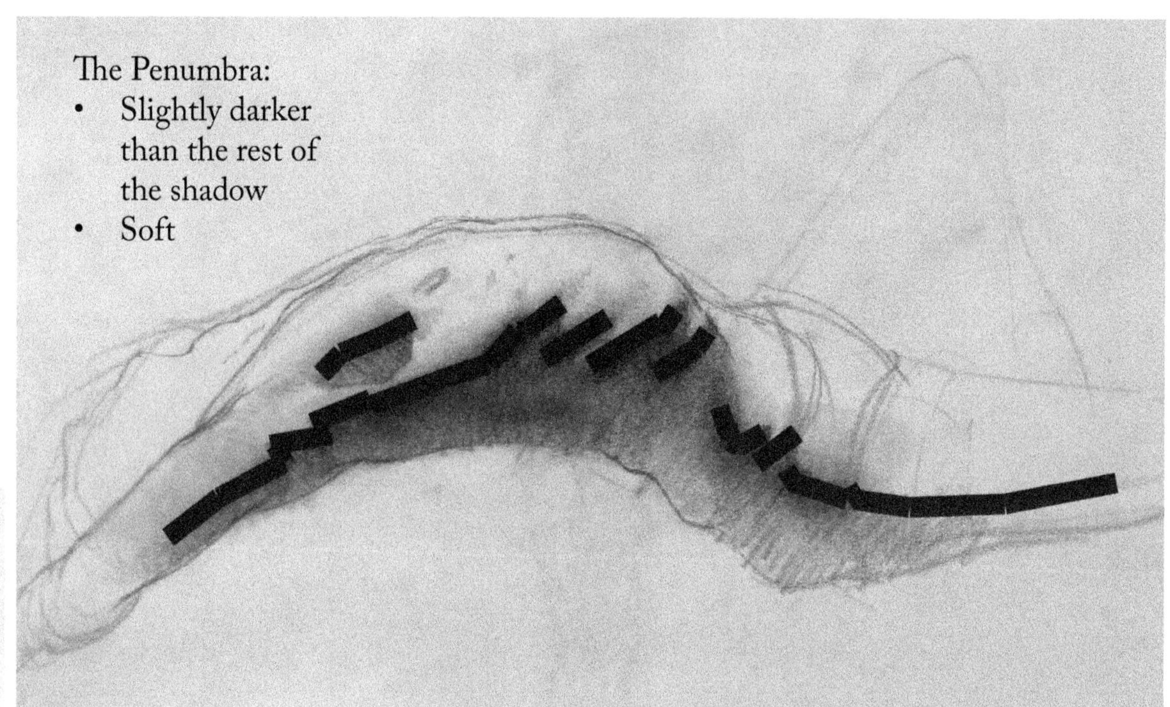

The Penumbra:
• Slightly darker
  than the rest of
  the shadow
• Soft

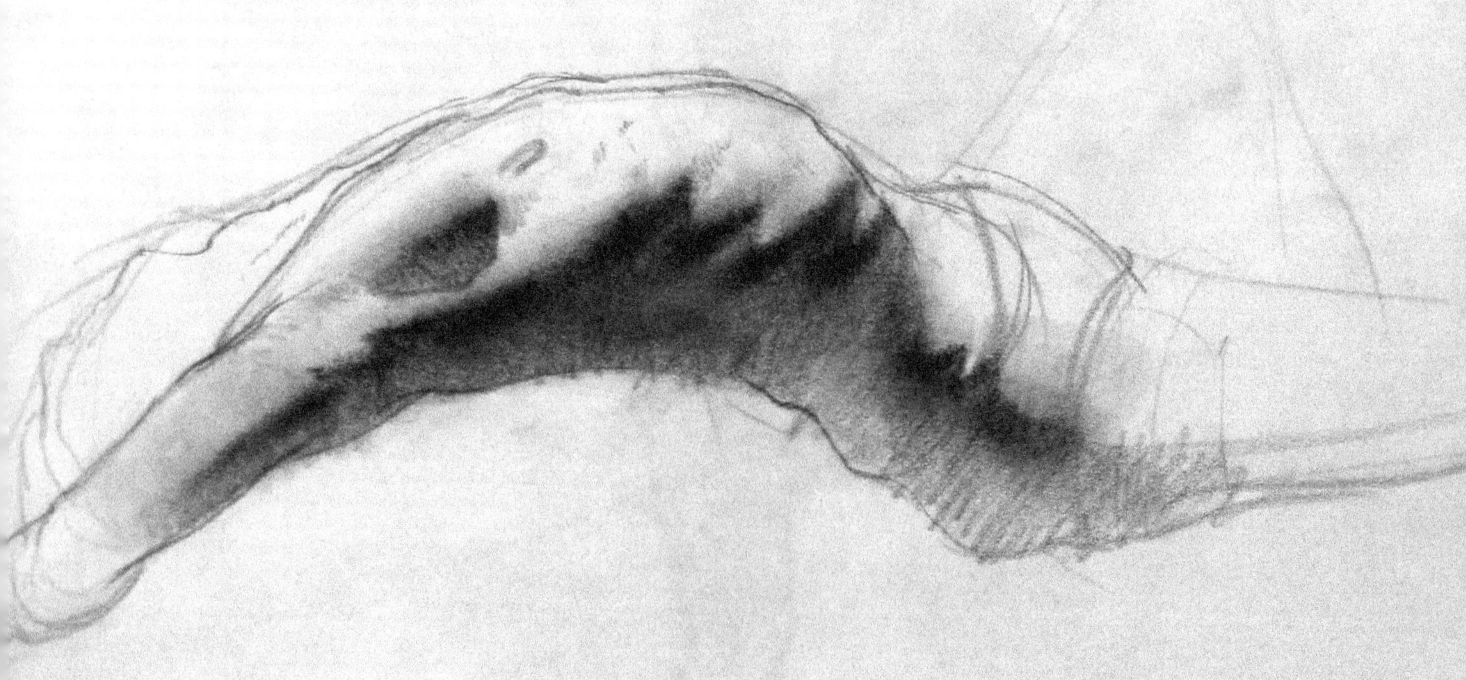

THE PENUMBRA

As mentioned before, the penumbra (also known as the "core" or "terminator edge") is the dark form shadow edge that essentially connects the light side to the dark side. The reason it is slightly darker than the rest of the shadow is because as the form turns, light from somewhere in the room (whether it is reflected or ambient) bounces back into the shadow, making the penumbra *appear* darker. Now remember, as previously stated, light and dark do not mix. This is still true. This bouncing or secondary light does happen in the shadow, however, since it is so inferior and minute in comparison to the primary light source, it is still considered to be dark. Nothing in the shadow side will ever be as light as anything in the light side.

This same principle also holds true in the reverse sequence: Nothing in the light side will ever be as dark as anything in the shadow side. In quick drawings, there isn't much time to model into the light side anyway; however, it is helpful to remember this principle when half tones are visible. The word "modeling" here refers to the adding of halftones and paying attention to the subtle value changes as various planes in the light side tilt slightly toward or away from the light source.

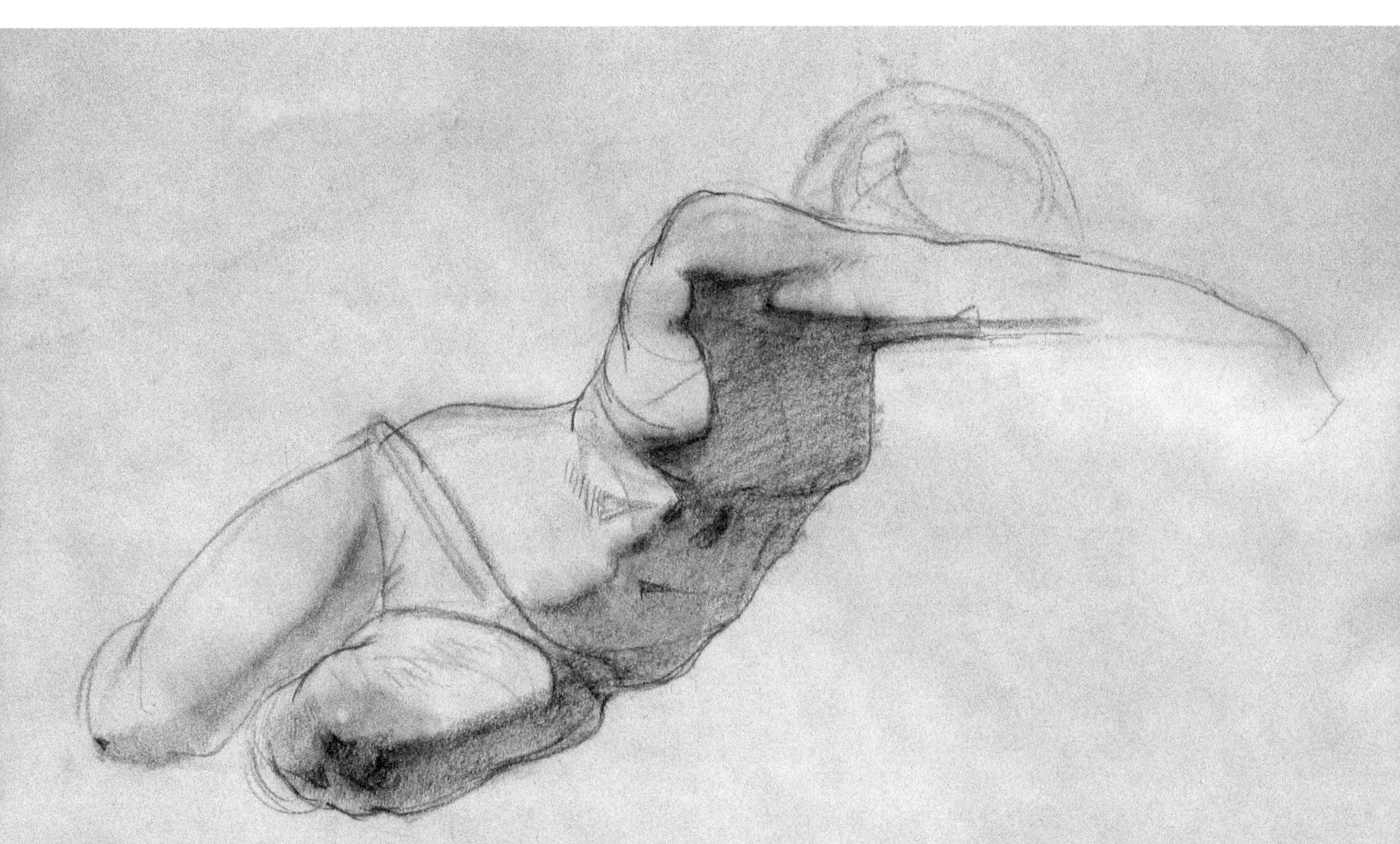

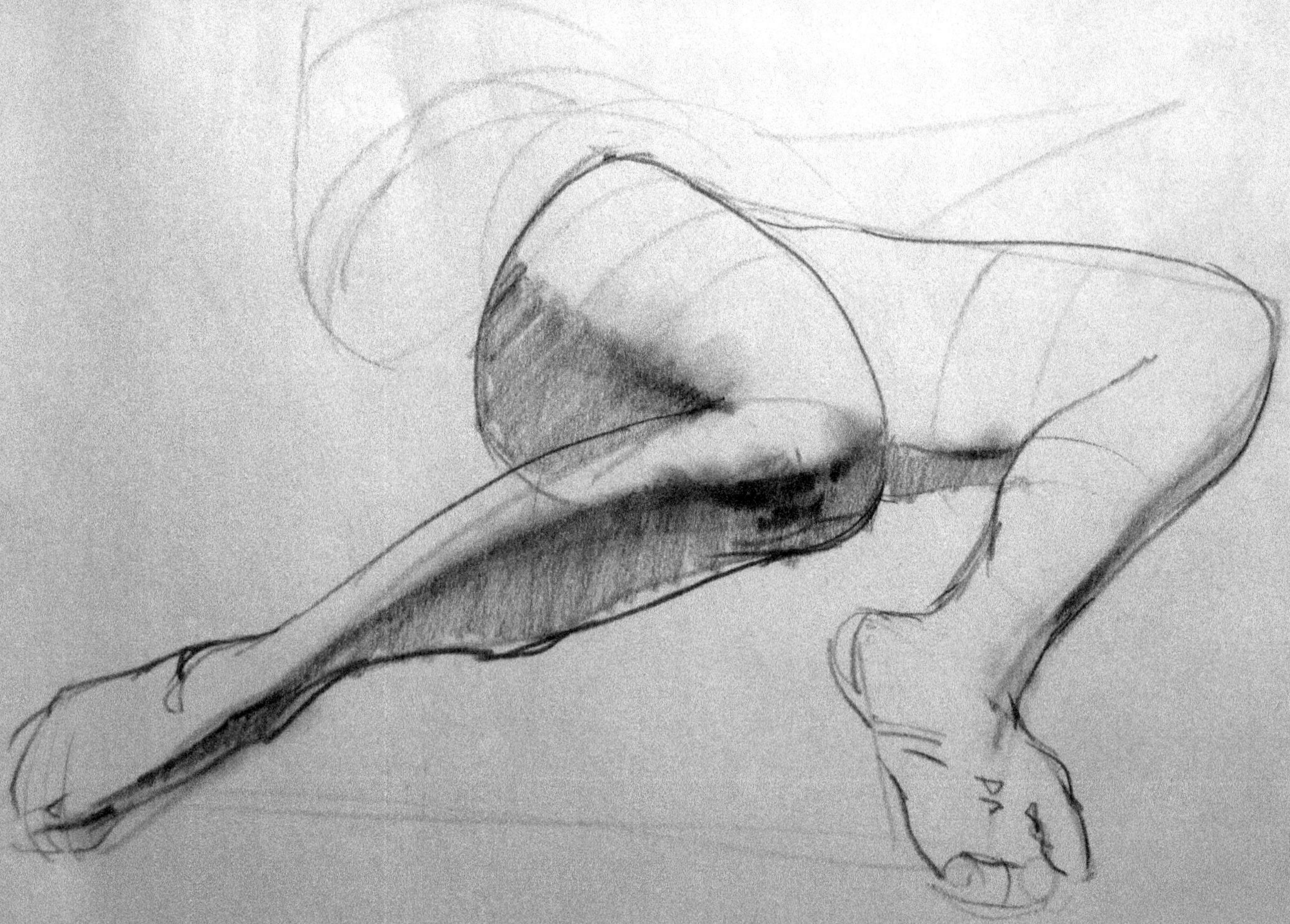

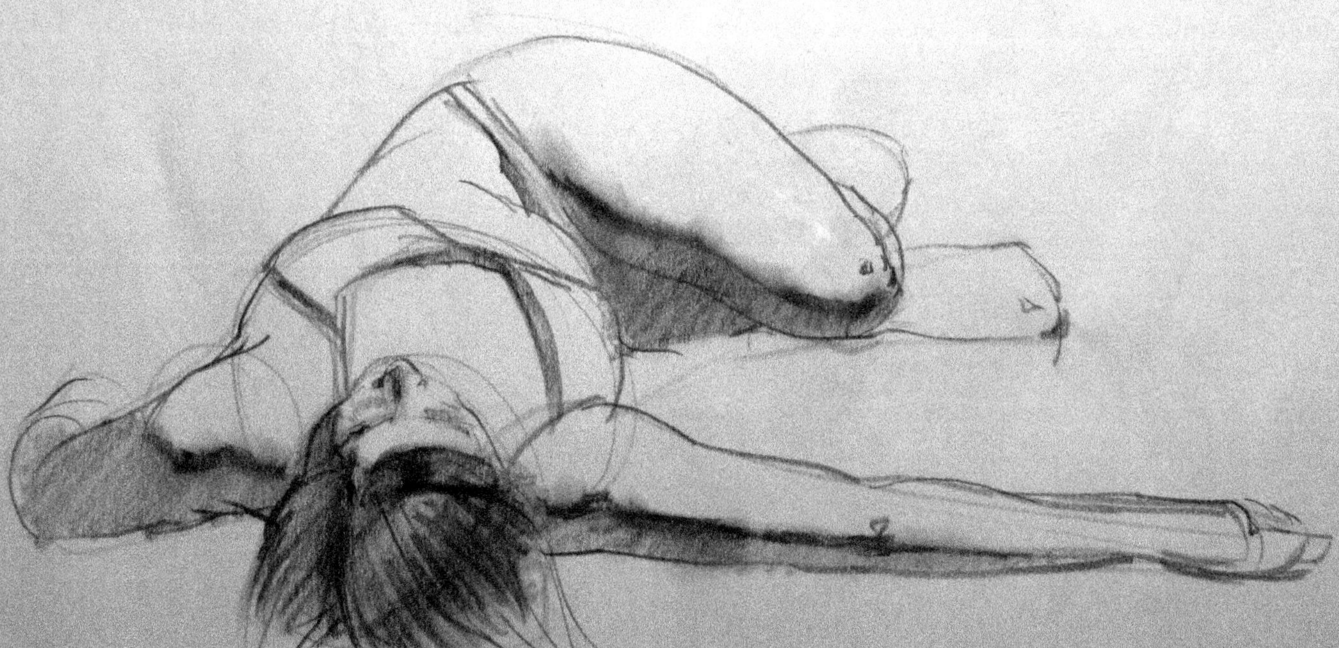

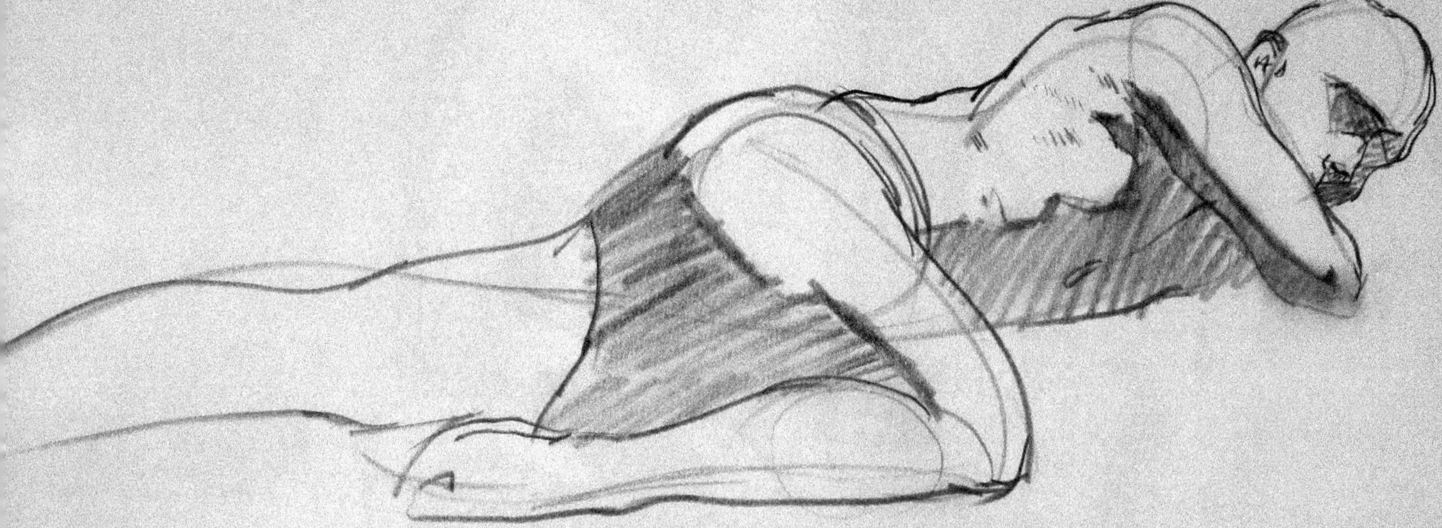

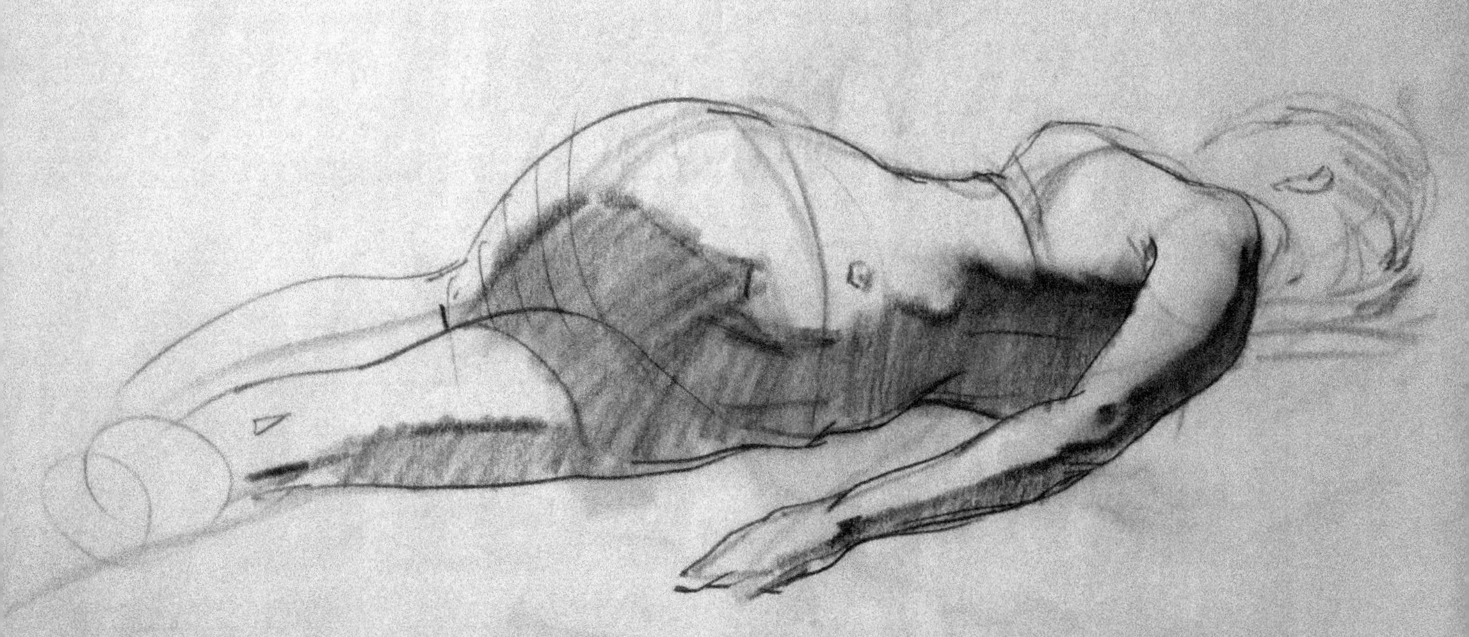

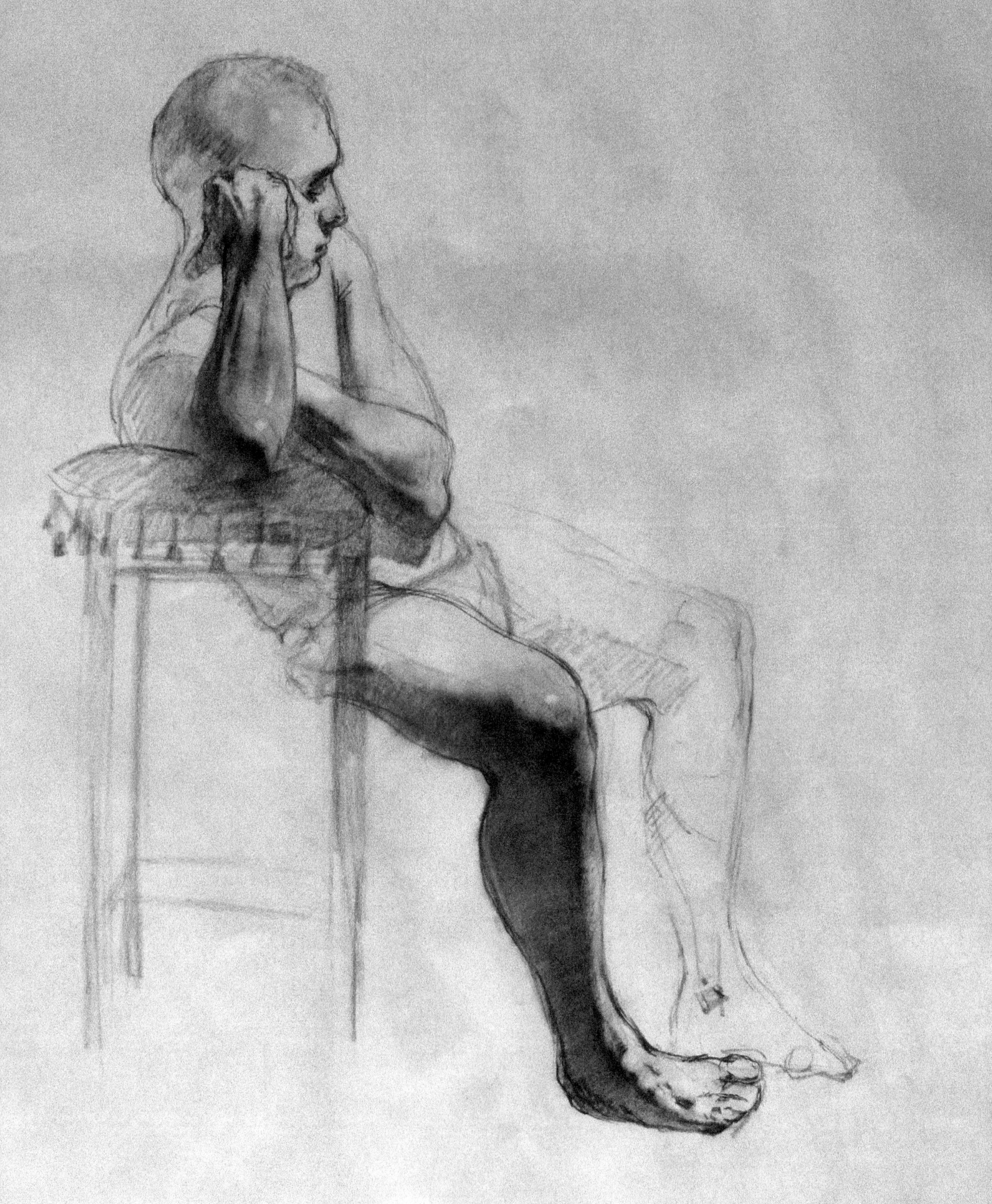

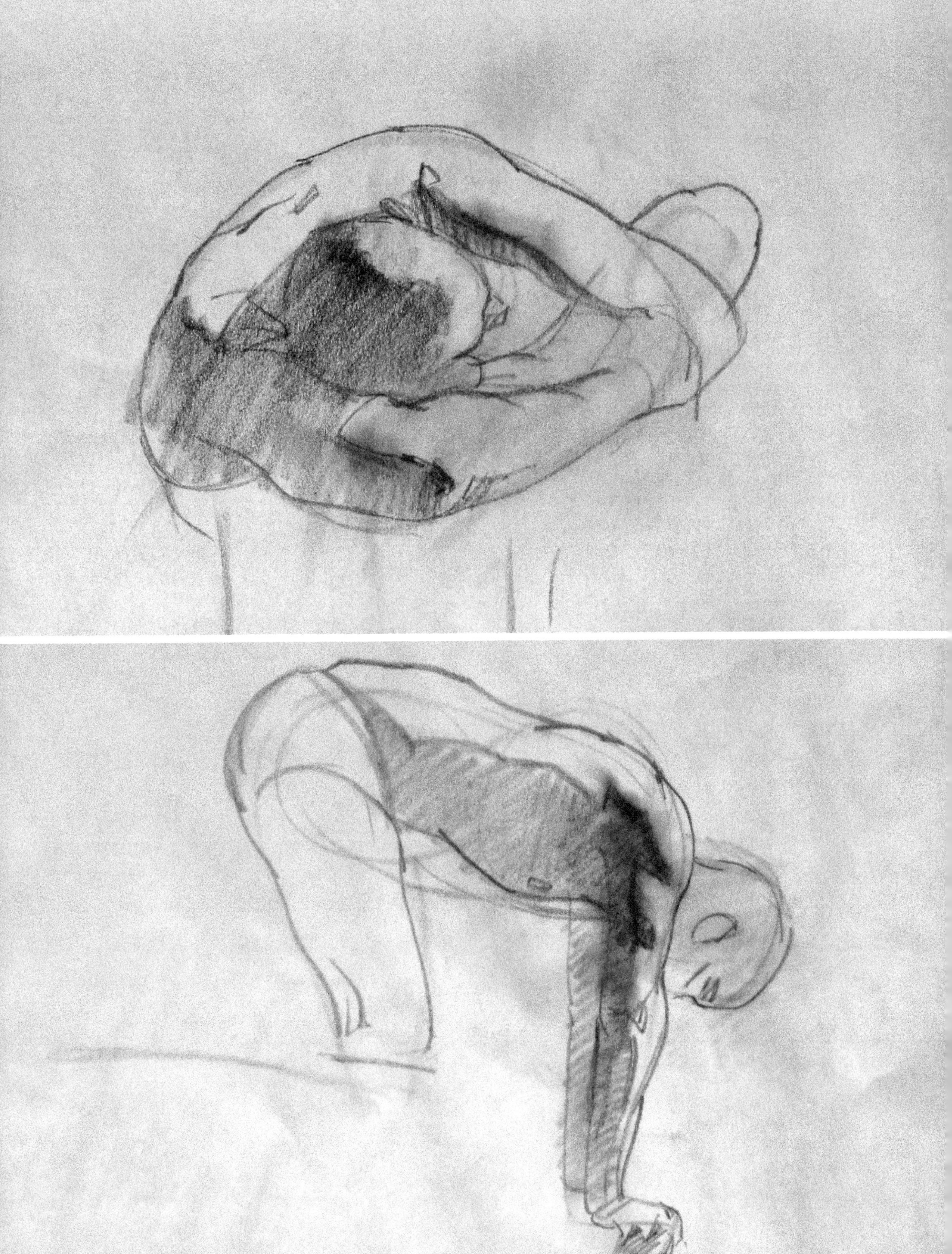

HIGHLIGHTS

If working on newsprint or other off-white paper, consider including a white charcoal pencil or conté stick in your materials. This can be used for adding highlights. A highlight often appears on harder surfaces (e.g., bone or quick-turning forms), and it will be located at the point of the form that is closest in proximity to the light source. Students often get carried away with adding highlights. I caution them to add highlights strategically, sparingly, and only in places wishing to attract attention. If a white charcoal tool is unavailable, the addition of highlights is still possible. Simply give the area a light tone (lightly smear just a bit of charcoal or conté with your finger) and then use a kneaded eraser to pull out the highlight. Just make sure the tone does not upset the overall value pattern of the drawing.

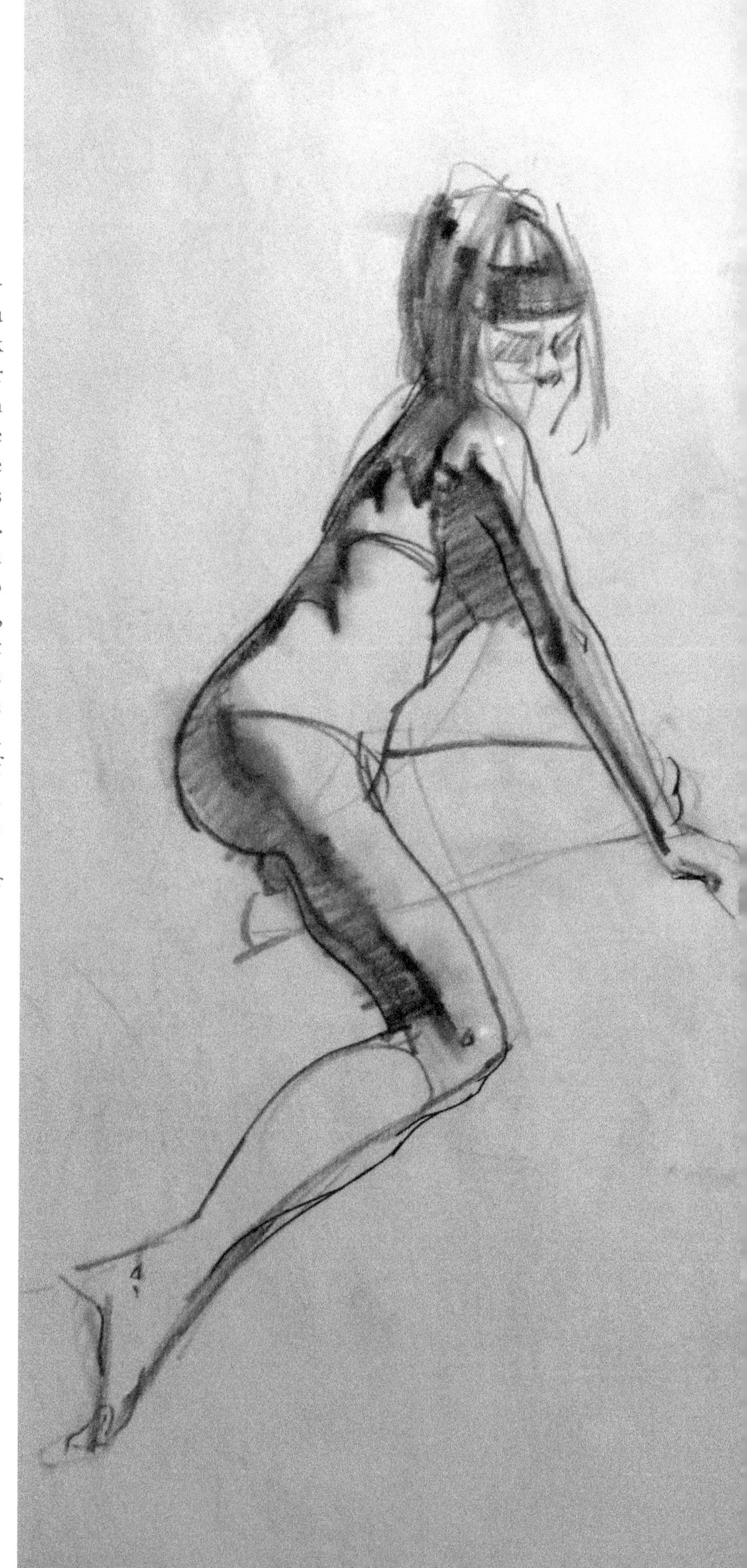

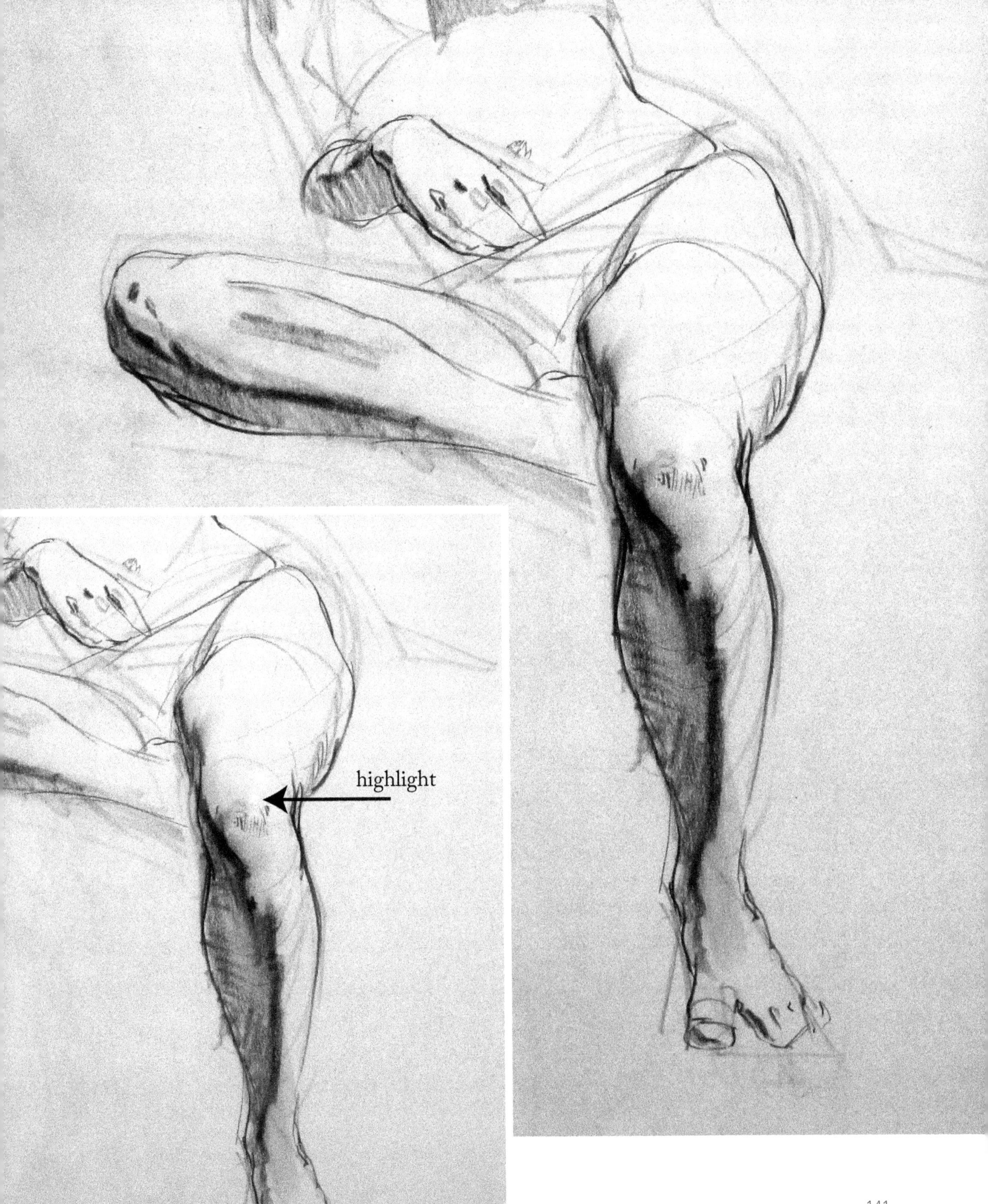
highlight

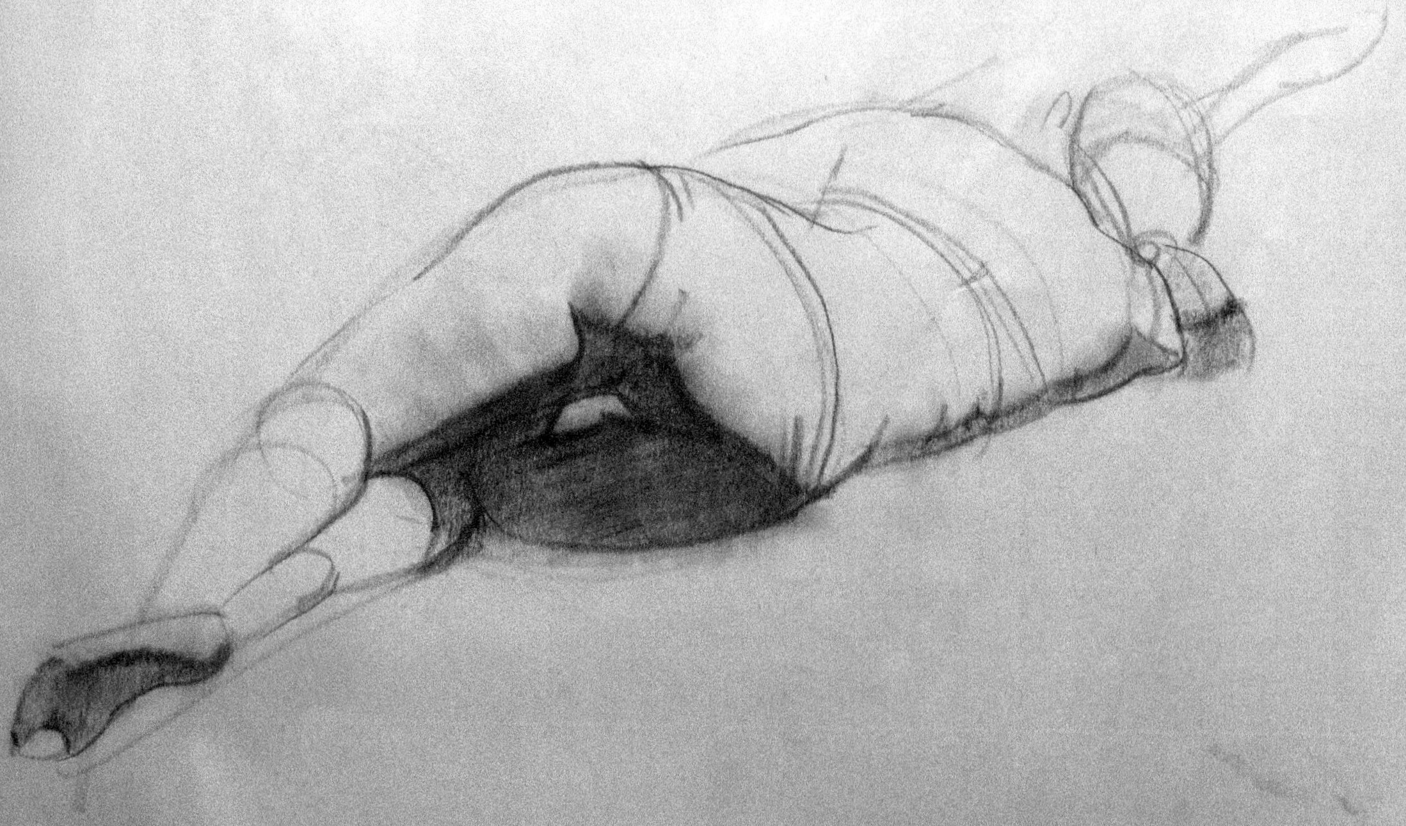

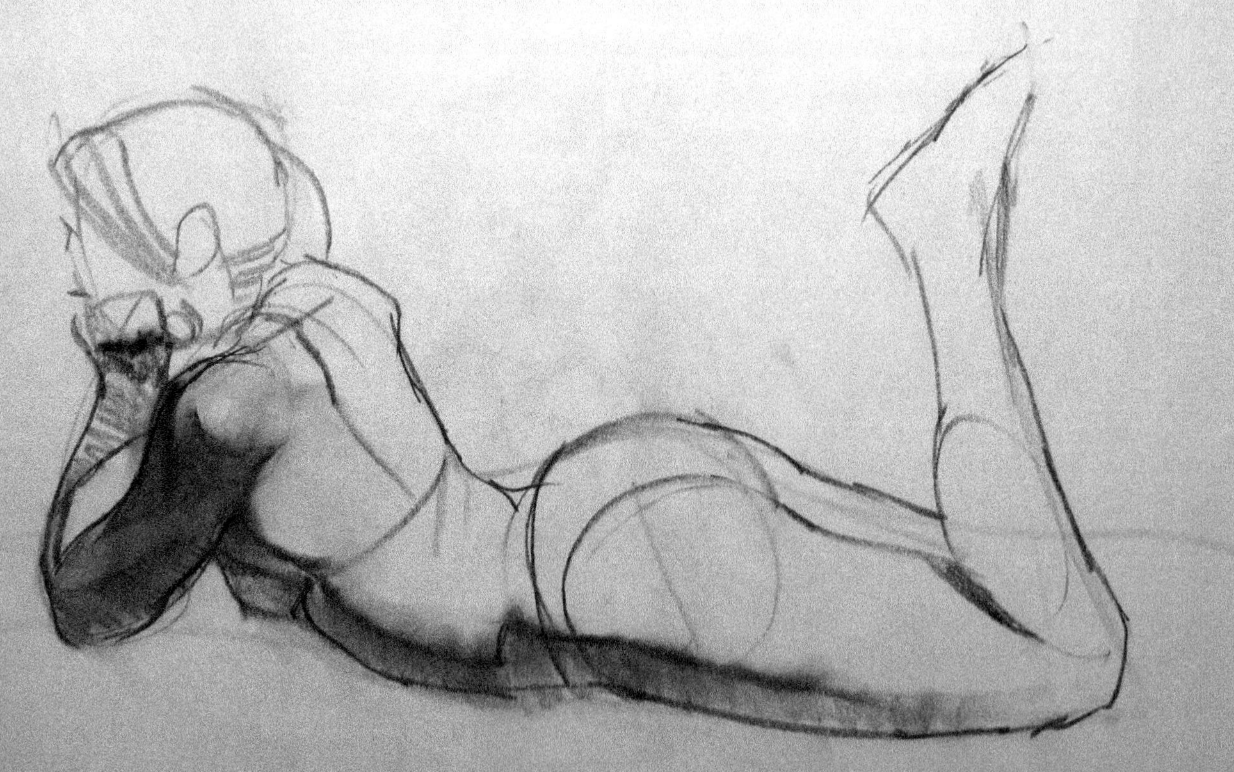

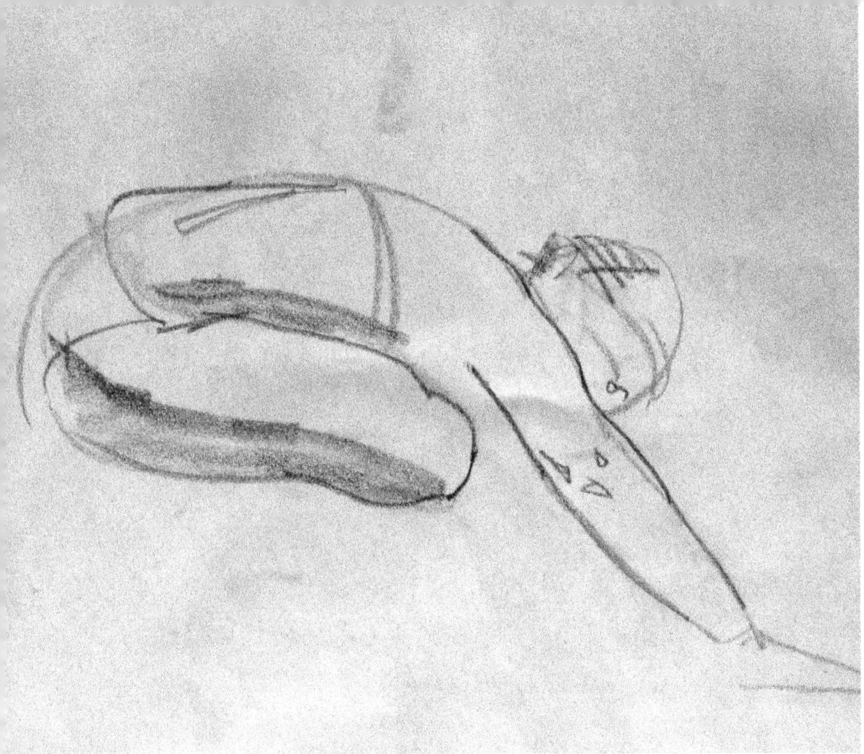

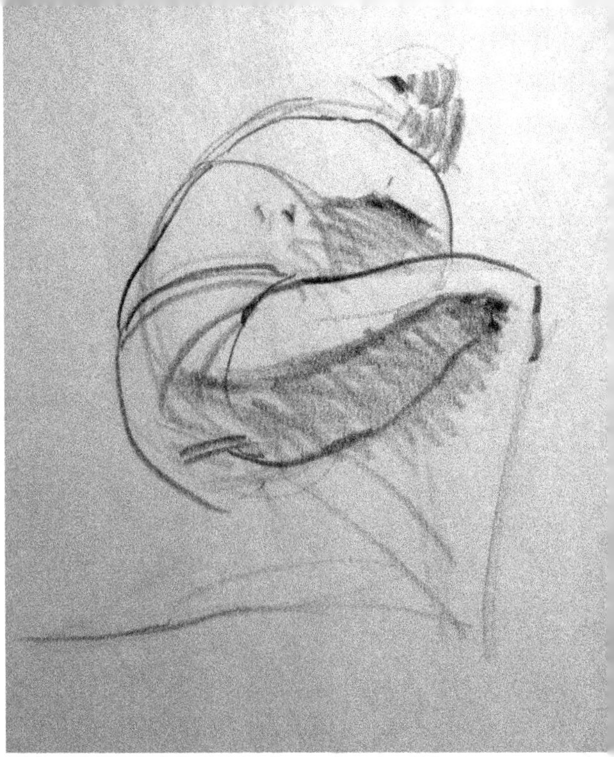

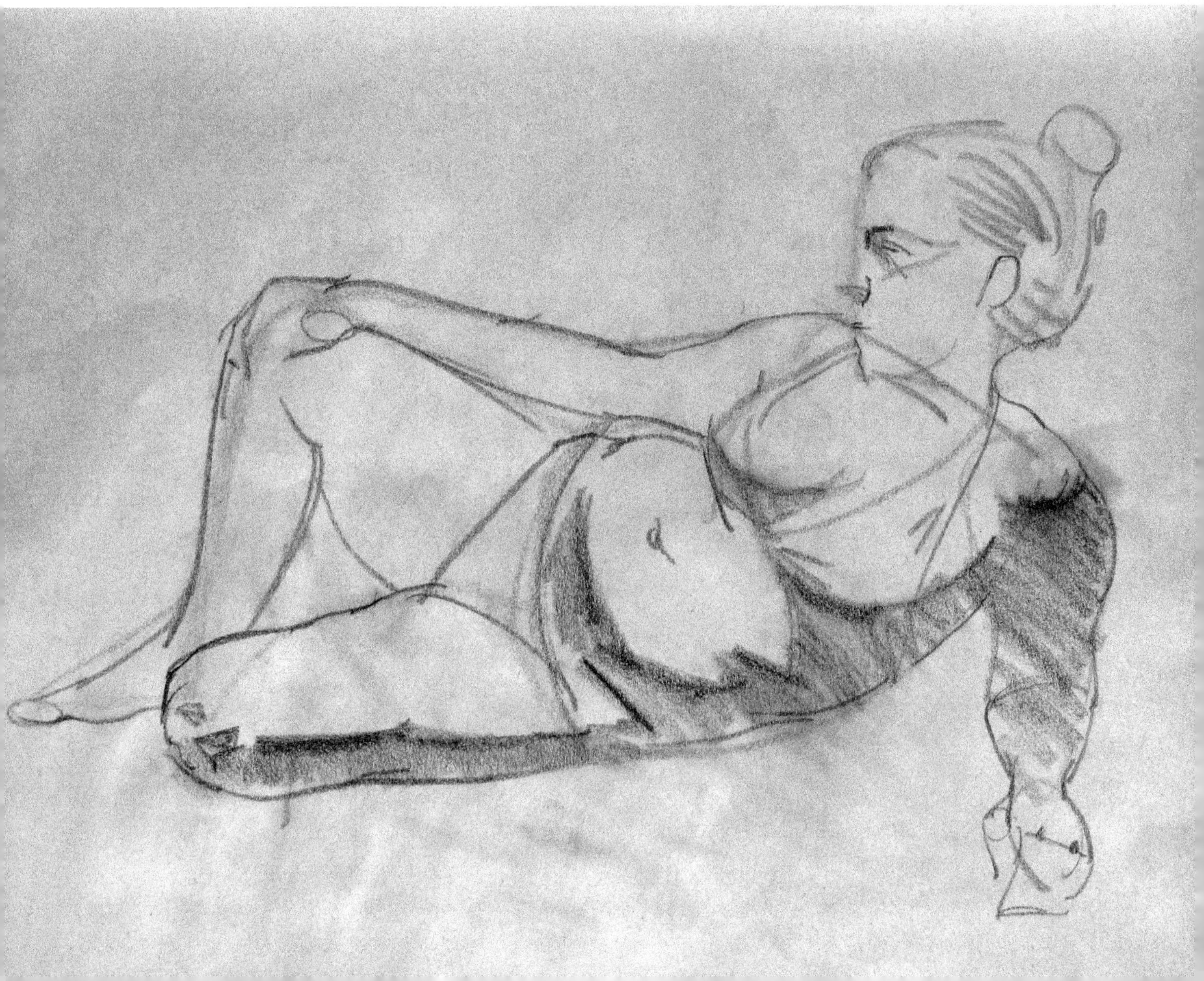

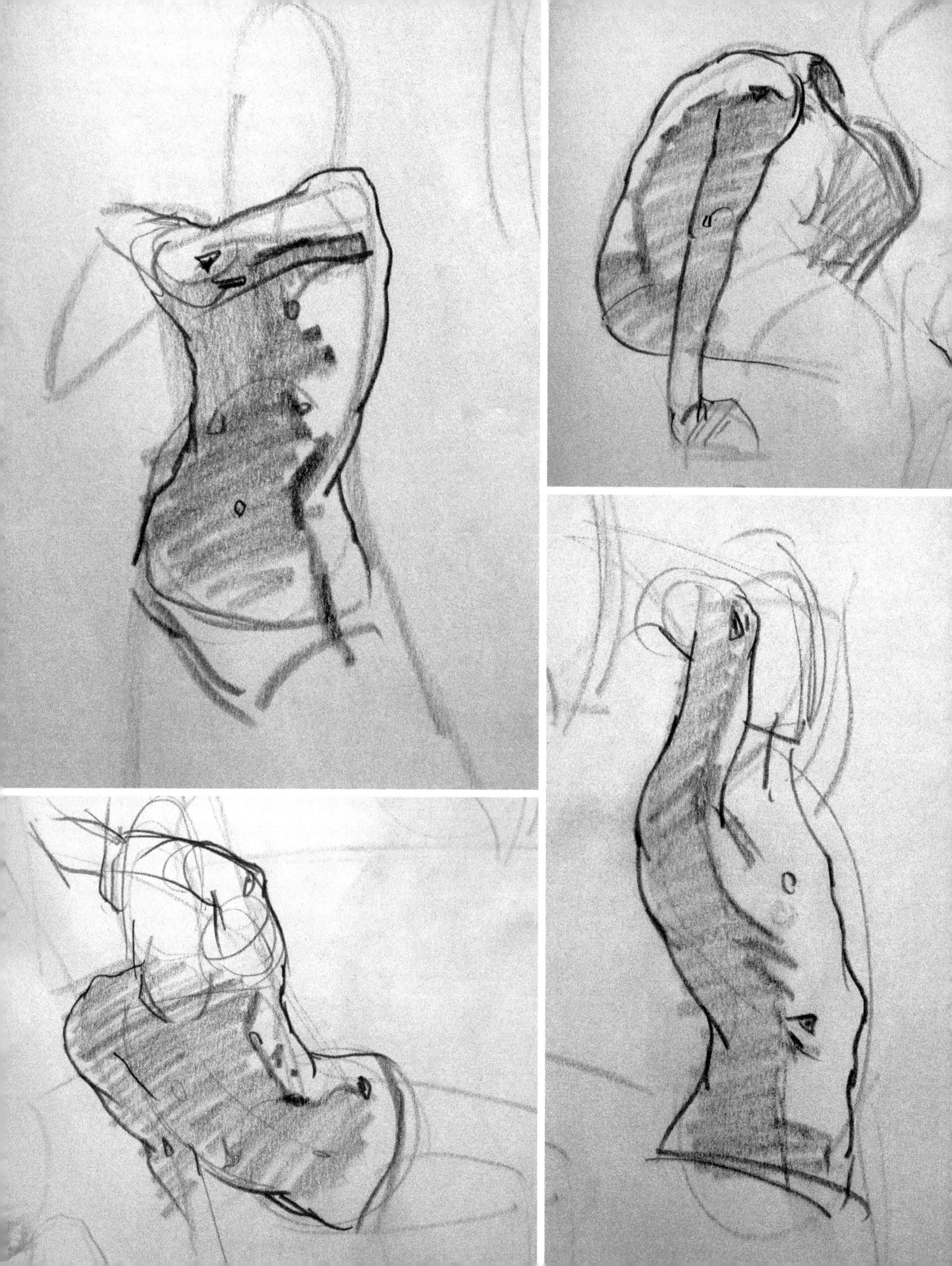

DOWN OR ACROSS THE FORM?

With short poses, I have found that I am most efficient at drawing penumbras quickly when I draw *down* the form instead of *across* the form. This must be done carefully, however, because it is important to make sure these edges (form shadows) are still soft. Students often forget to keep the penumbra soft when choosing to work this way. It can be tricky. It takes getting to know the drawing tool very well, and again, like so many things, this comes with practice. The goal is to be able to make a soft yet bold penumbra with just one pass of the conté.

When adding light and shadow, start with the penumbra, make an outline of the entire shadow, and then simply fill it in. As long as the transitional edge quality is correct (hard or soft), nothing else in the shadow matters much. Have fun here by losing the outer contour of the shadow side completely or flattening it out in some creative way.

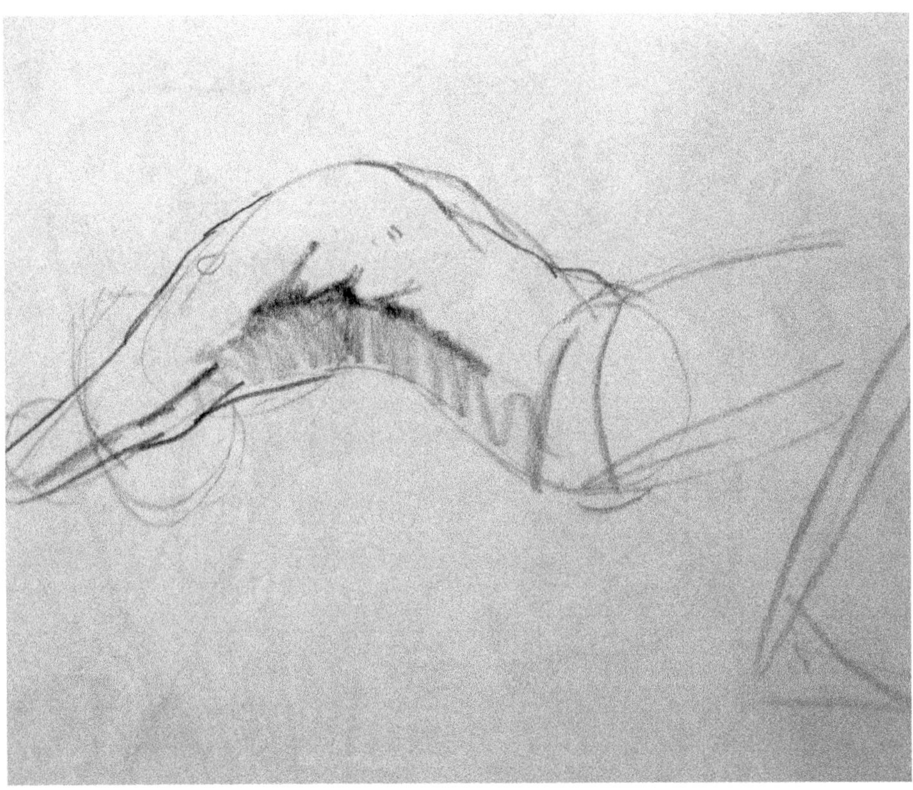

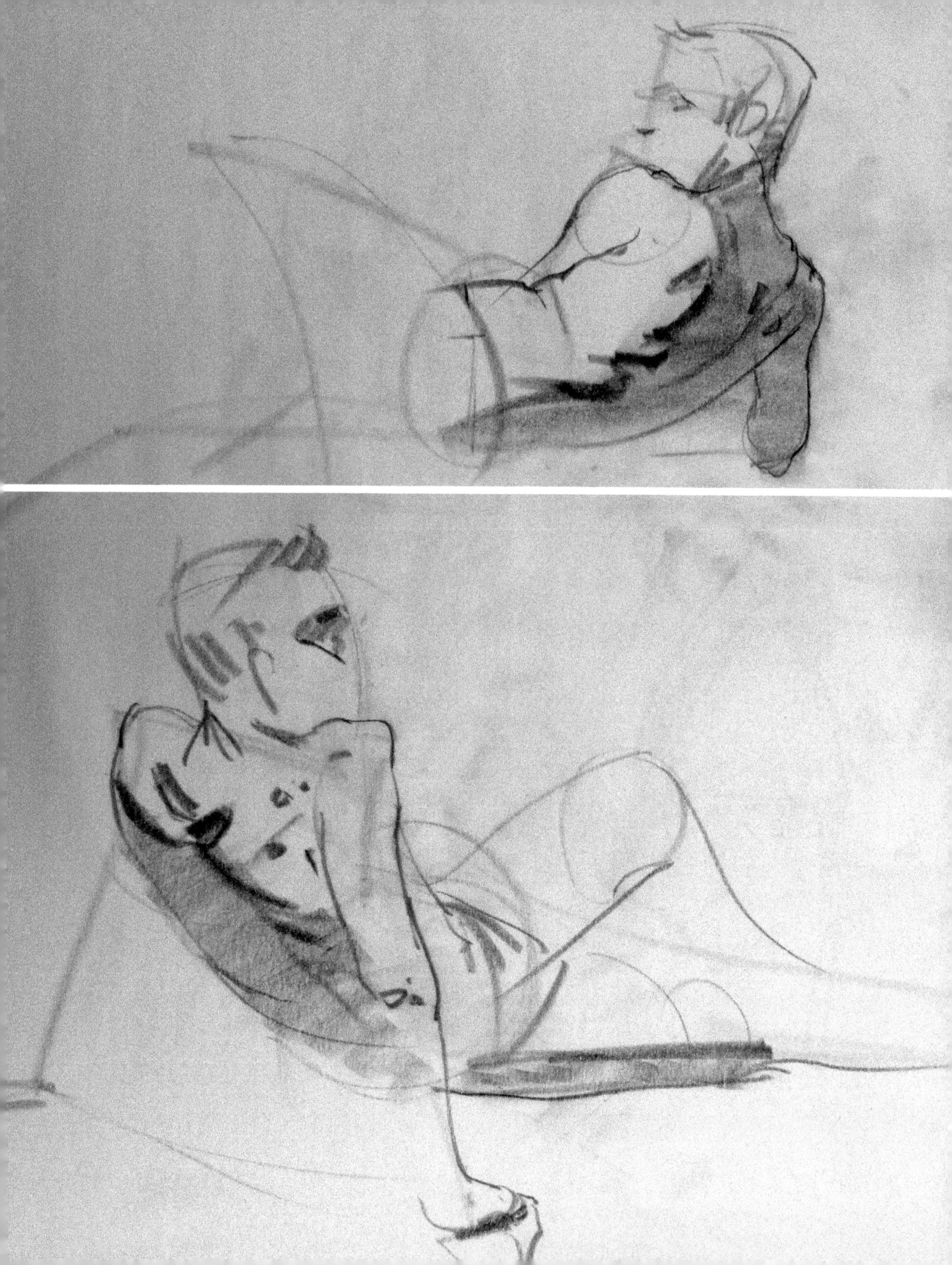

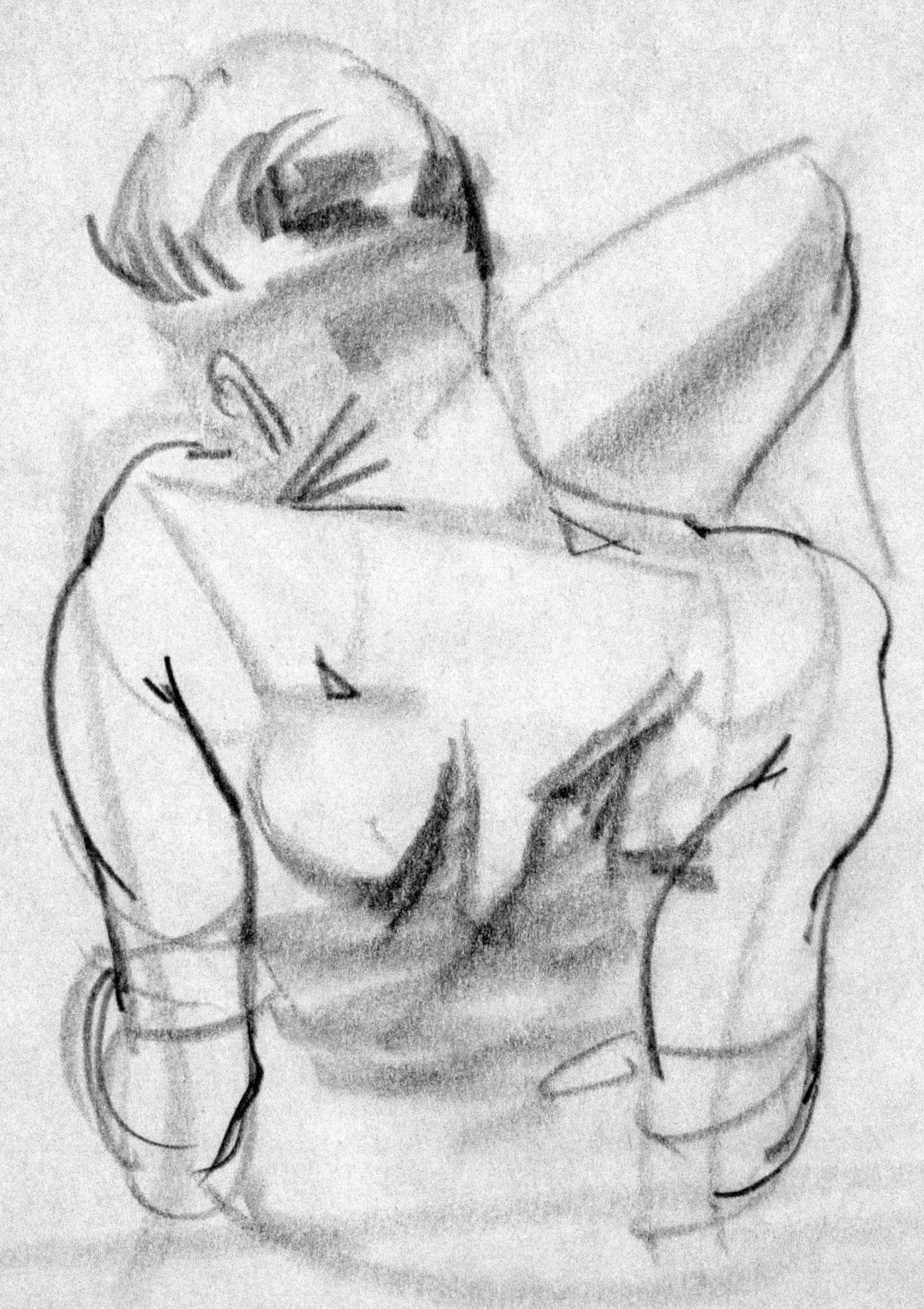

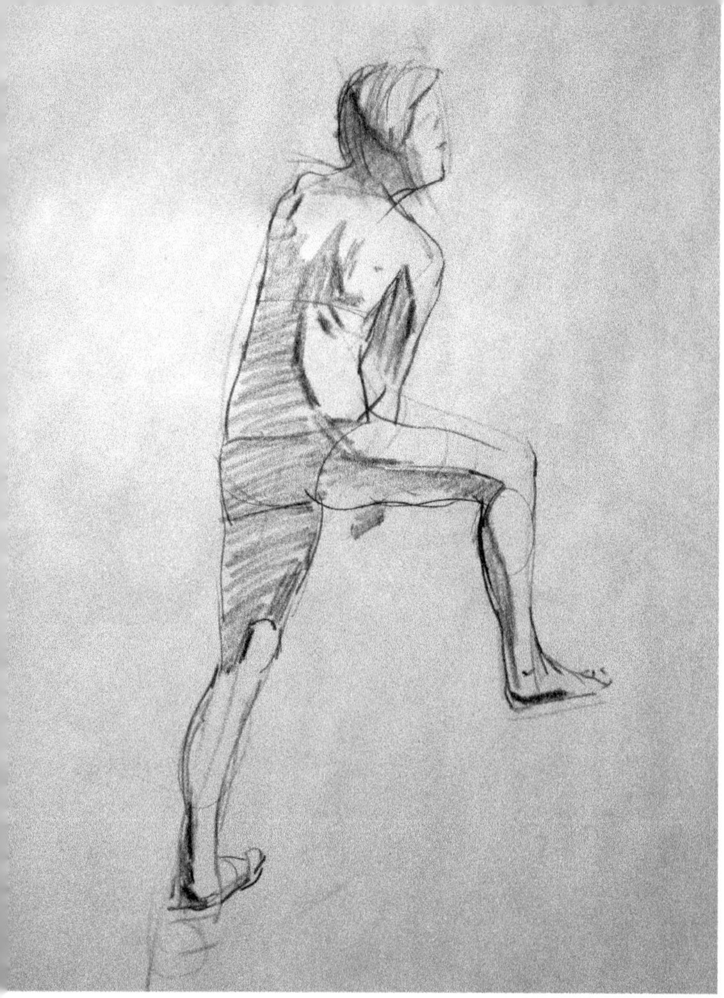

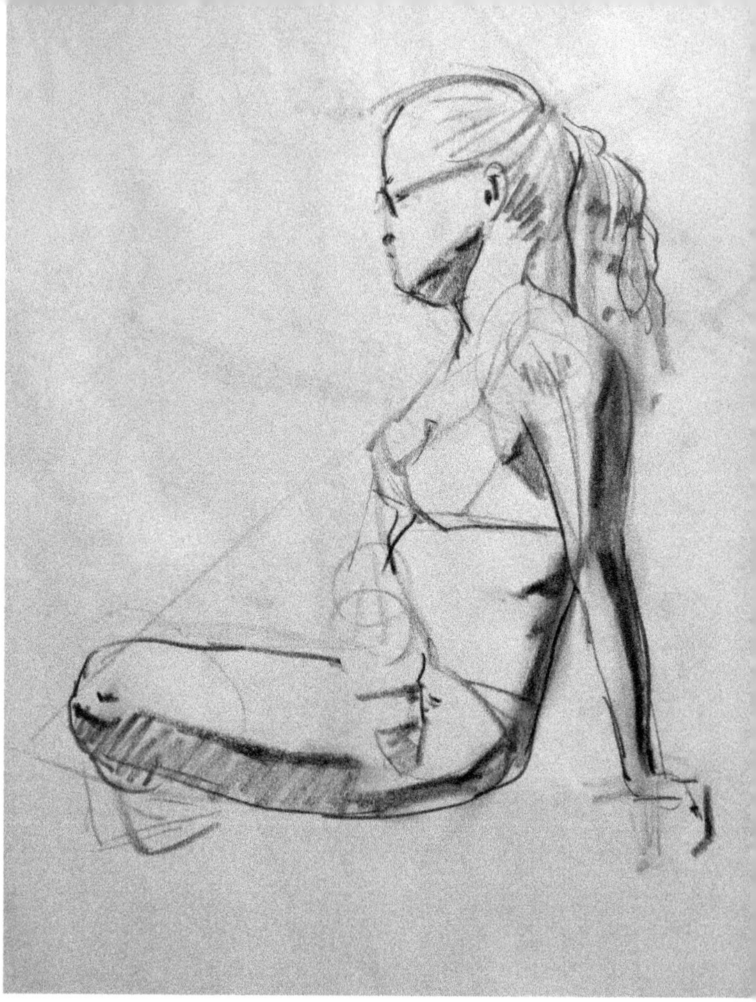

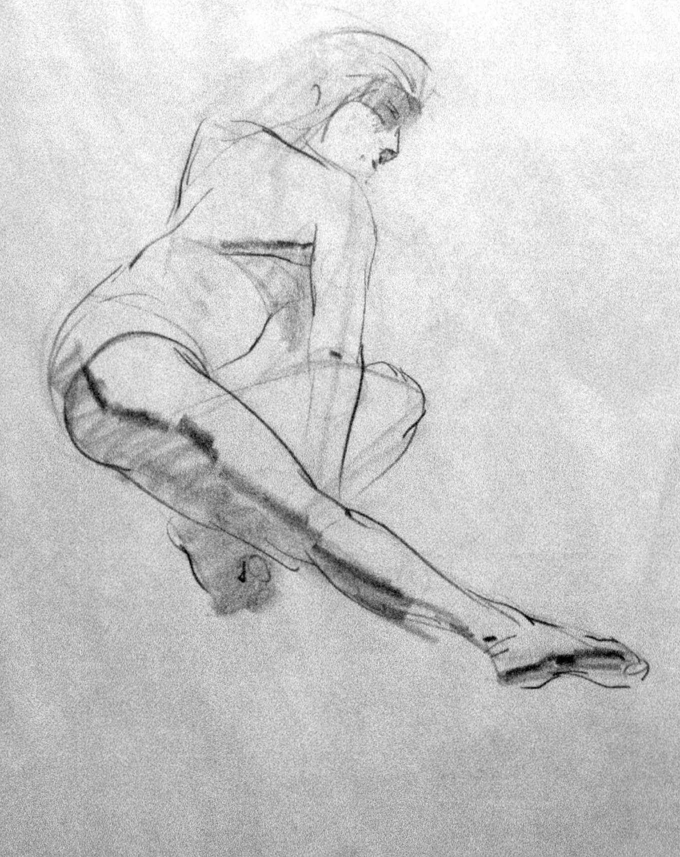
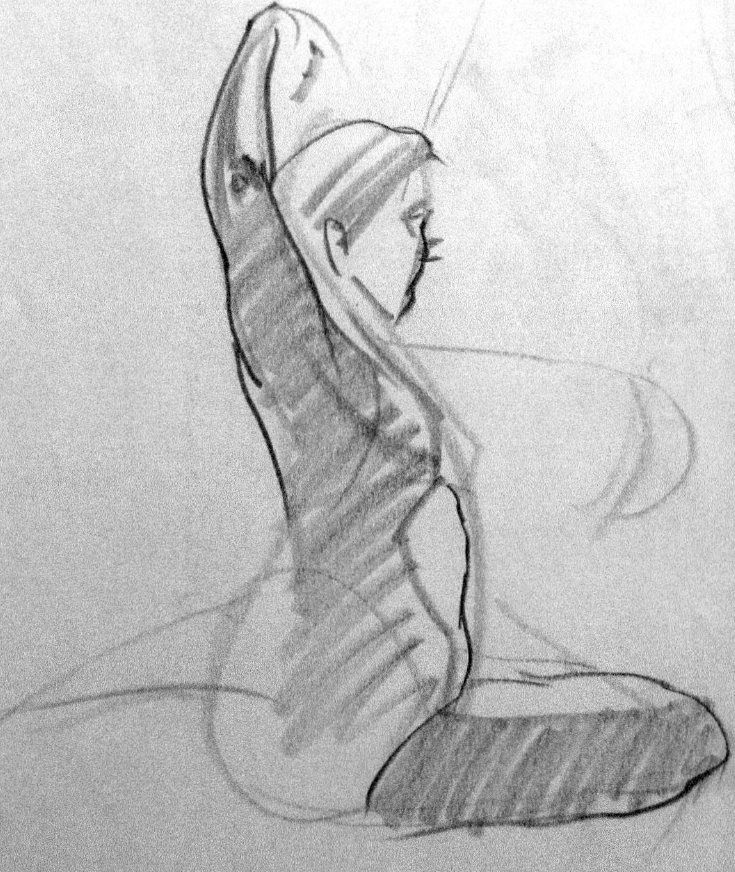

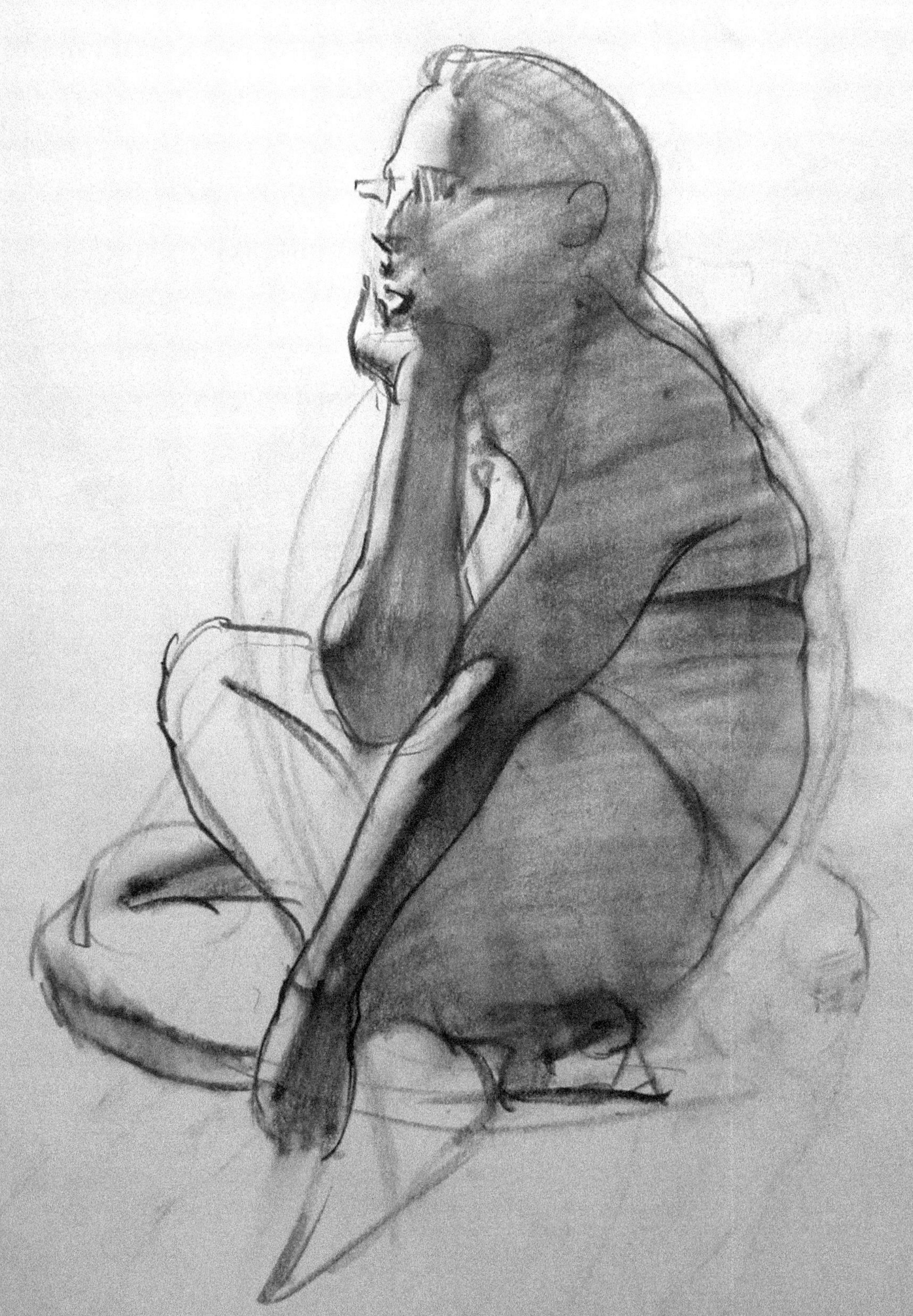

SOFT EDGE SURFACES

One last thing to note when making shadows is to pay attention to the surface on which the shadow is resting. A penumbra on a bone or tendon will appear different than the penumbra on fat or muscle. The penumbra on the upper thigh, for example, will be wide and very soft, because it is on a large, fleshy form. Move down to the knee and see the penumbra take on a different appearance. The knee (bone) turns quickly, so the penumbra here will be thinner and *less* soft. At times the penumbra on hard surfaces, like bone, tendon, or cartilage, may even *appear* to be hard. Although it is tempting in these instances to draw in what looks like a razor sharp edge, refrain from doing so and understand that it is still a form shadow and must have some sense of softness to it. If not, the penumbra will read as a cast shadow and end up looking awkward.

Often a long shadow edge actually consists of multiple penumbras and form shadows. This is because the figure is made up of lots of overlapping forms. Bone is overlapped by tendon, which is overlapped by muscle, which is often overlapped by fat. Try to observe these surface differences. Instead of making one big long penumbra that runs the length of the entire body, notice these overlaps and draw in the correct quality of softness where appropriate.

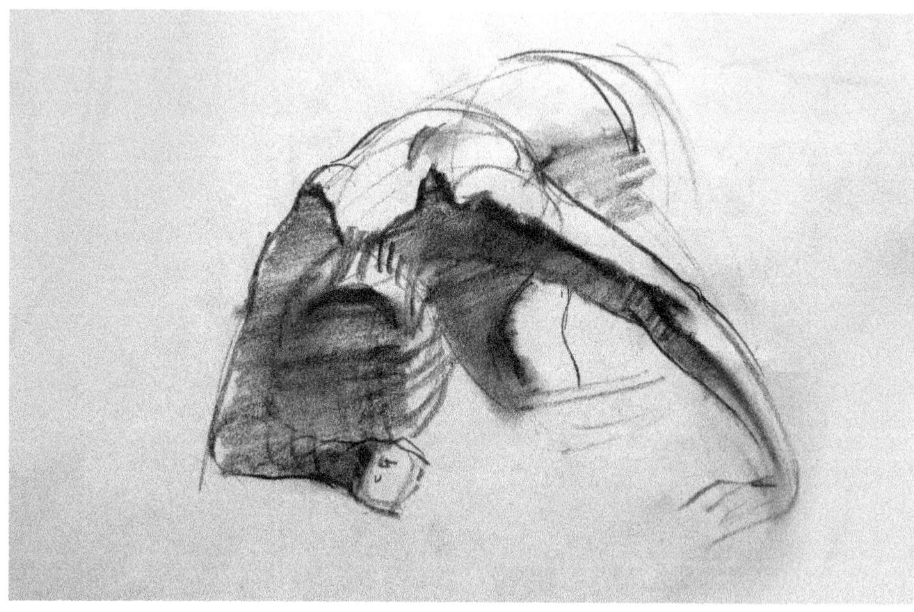

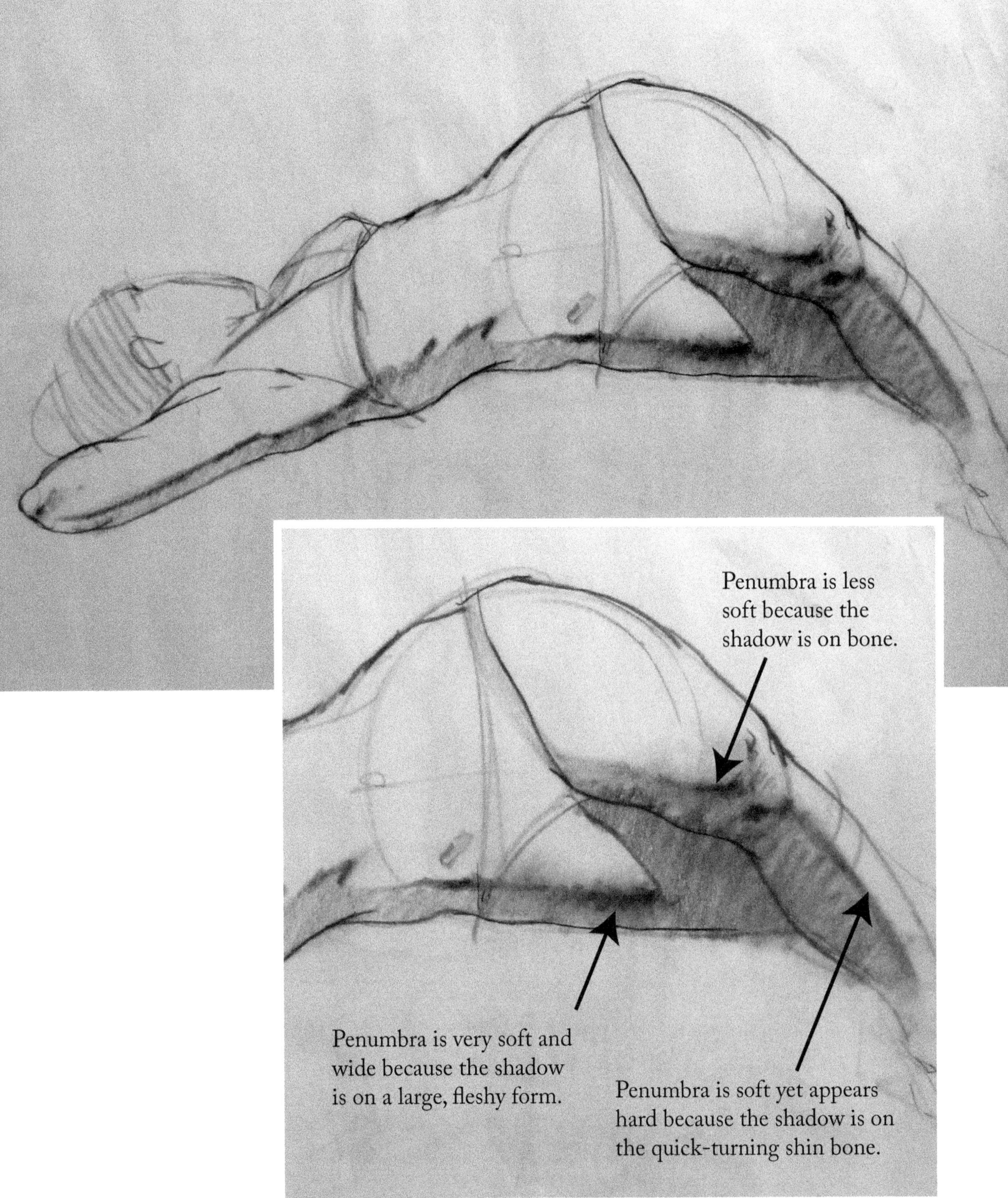

Penumbra is less soft because the shadow is on bone.
Penumbra is very soft and wide because the shadow is on a large, fleshy form.
Penumbra is soft yet appears hard because the shadow is on the quick-turning shin bone.

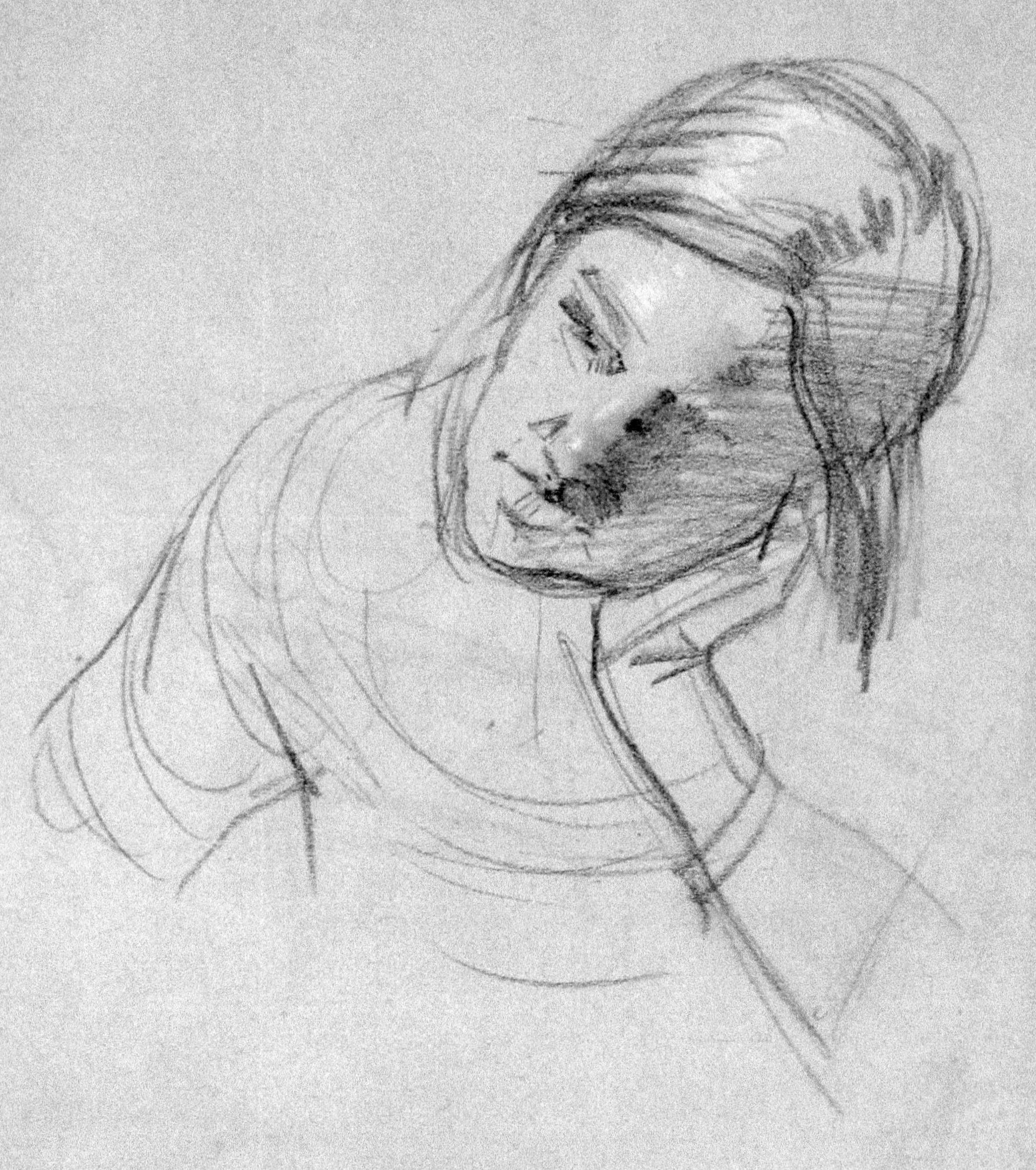

HEADS

HEADS

Although drawing the human head is frightening for a lot of people, it is my favorite branch of figure drawing. In full body gesture drawings, I look at the figure as a whole and usually don't have much time for the details of the head and face. When my intent is to do a *head* gesture, however, I focus on the head as a whole, allowing me time for detailed work on the facial features. The head drawings in this section were done in less than twenty minutes. Most of them are in the five- to ten-minute range. Some head drawings, shown on pages 178 and 179 of the chapter, are exceptions and took about two twenty-minute sessions to complete.

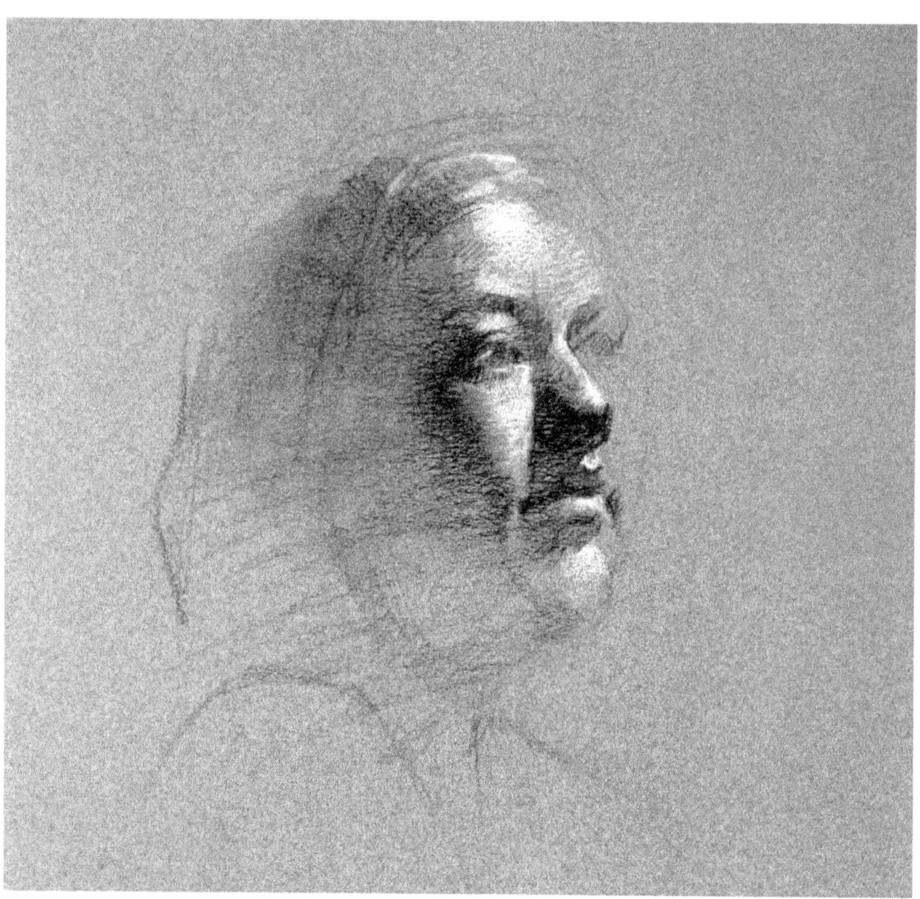

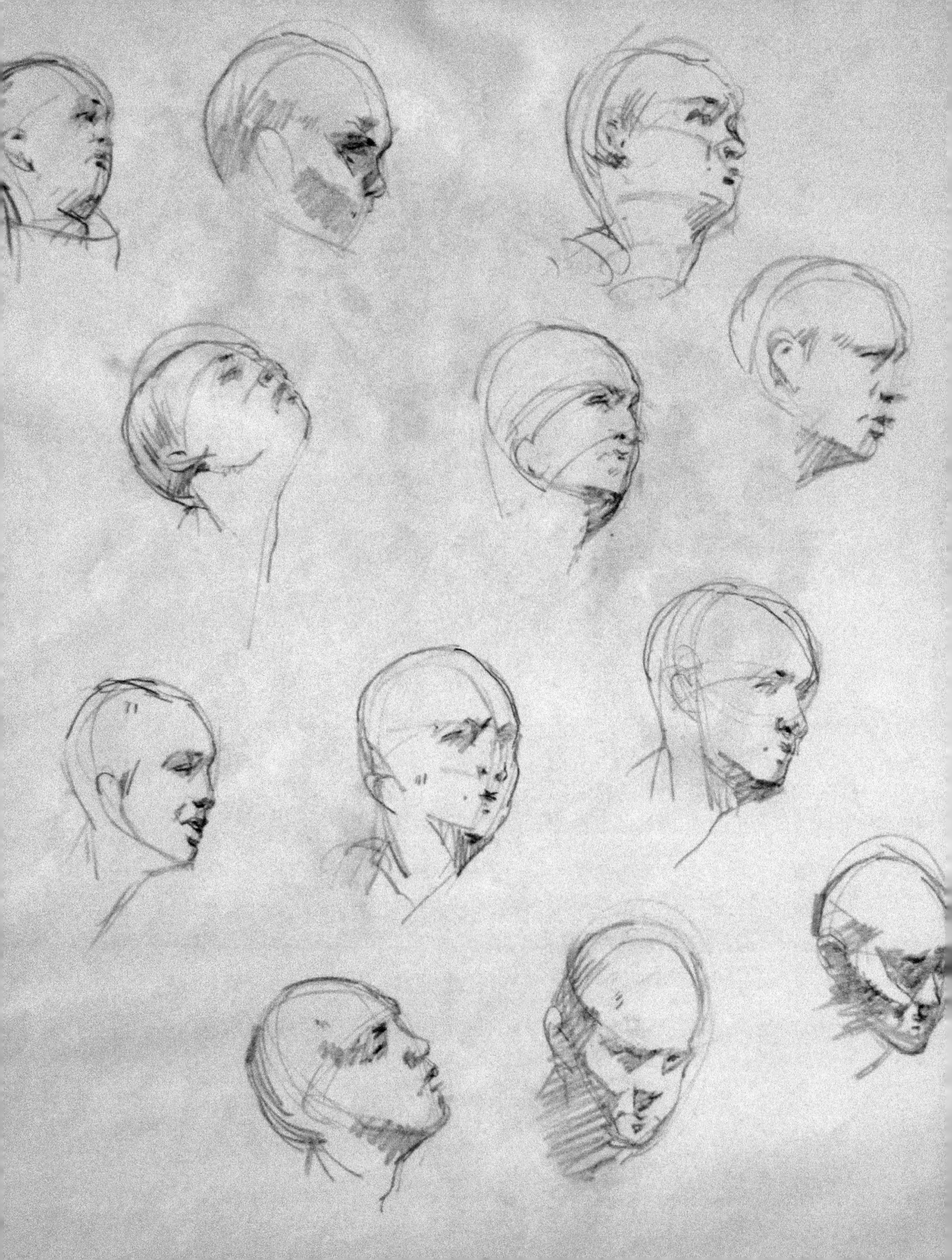

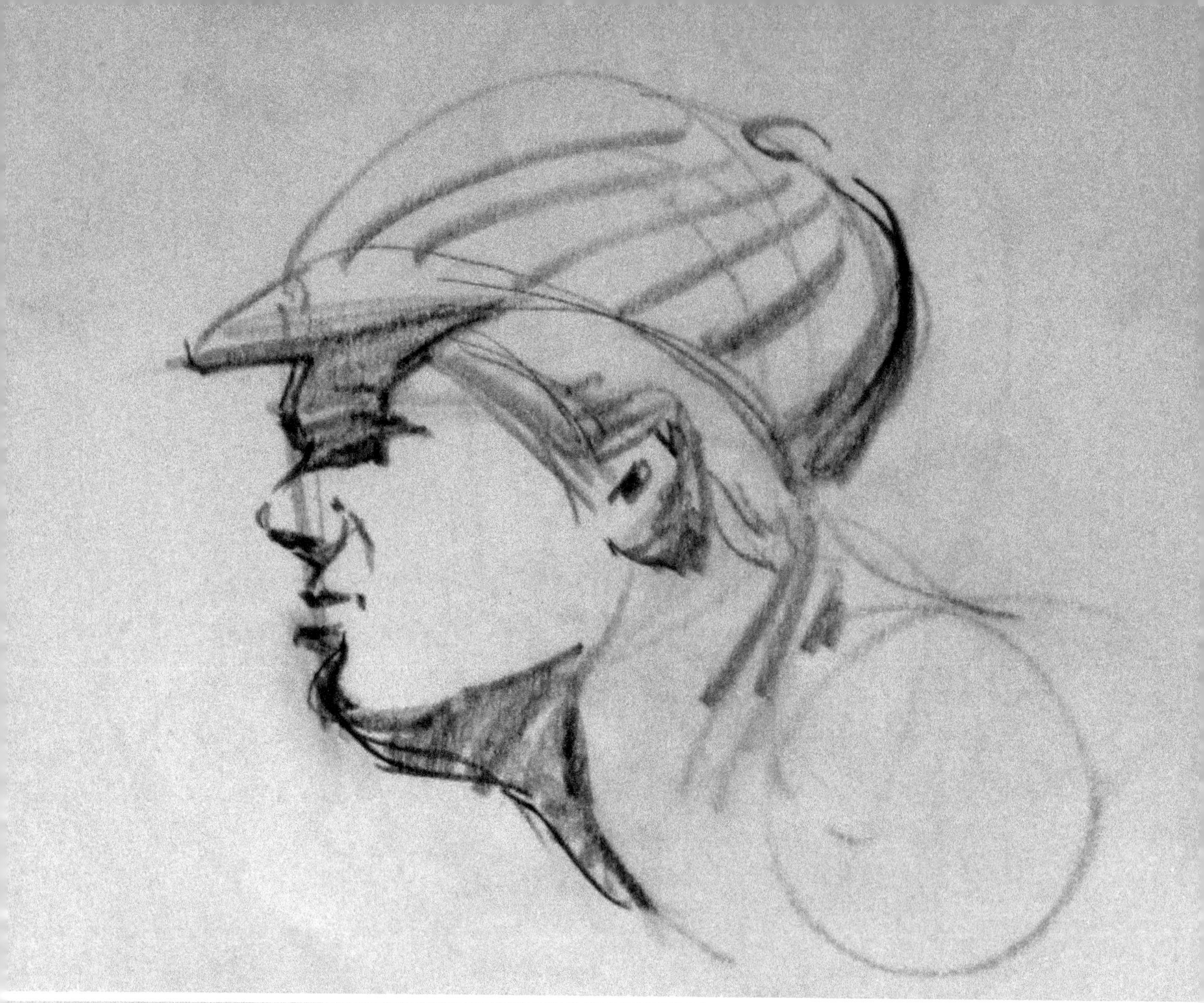

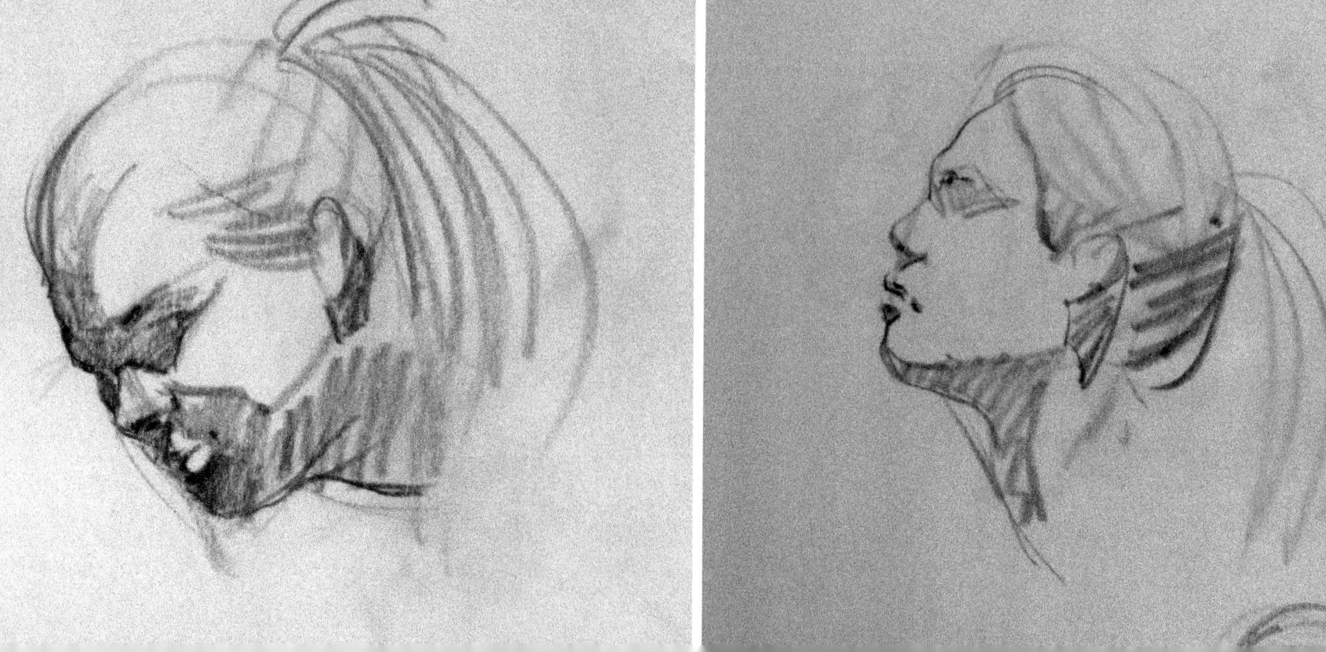

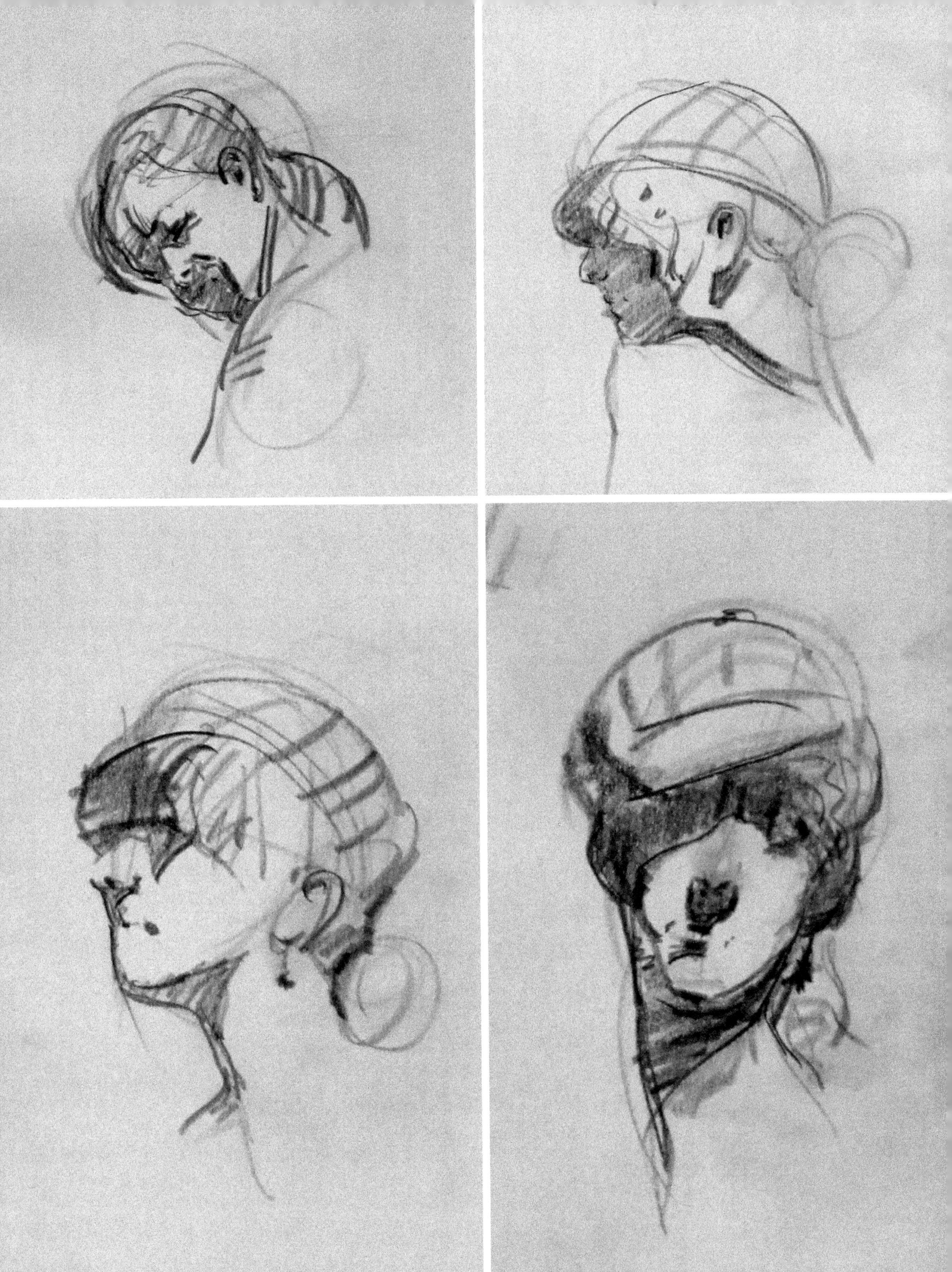

SHADOW SHAPES

Light and shadow principles are very important to utilize while doing head gestures. Likeness is most likely achieved when the drawing has accurate shadow shapes. Beginners often have preconceived ideas about what a head and its facial features look like. For example, they think the eye is almond shaped with eyelashes extending out. Yes, symbolically an eye looks like this, although when students draw it this way, it looks like it was drawn by a kindergartener. Perhaps that is too harsh, but it is mostly true, and I can understand why students get frustrated. In order to achieve a representational depiction, they need to forget about what they *think* an eye looks like and pay attention to what they *see* the eye looking like, which will simply be a series of shadow shapes. Then, just make sure the shadow edge qualities are correct (either soft or hard). Knowing the basic proportions of the head beforehand is also helpful.

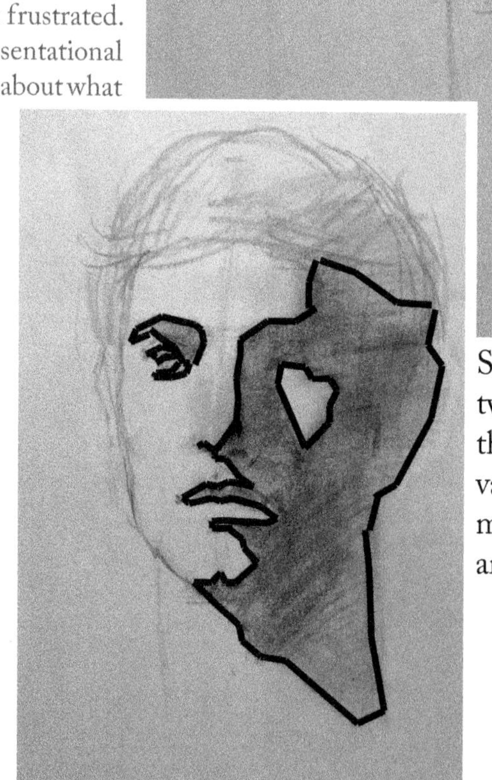

Simplify the values down to two: light and dark. Outline the shapes made by the dark value, fill them in, and then make sure the edge qualities are either soft or hard.

BASIC HEAD PROPORTIONS

The eyes are positioned about halfway from the top of the head to the bottom of the chin. The face itself, from hairline to chin, can be broken up into thirds. They are hairline to eyebrows, eyebrows to bottom of nose, and bottom of nose to chin. It is helpful to have these proportions memorized. Start with these generic guidelines, and then look at the model to see how he or she differs from the standard. If you use both the standard proportions and the changes made by observation of the model, there is a good chance of getting a likeness. I usually include some part of the neck as well because it adds information and a little more drama, especially if there is a slight twist.

Be aware that these standard proportions are for heads that are exactly on the same eye level as the artist. Often the artist will *not* be positioned at exactly the same eye level as the model, in which case, he or she will still use the standard proportions but will also have to remember principles of foreshortening.

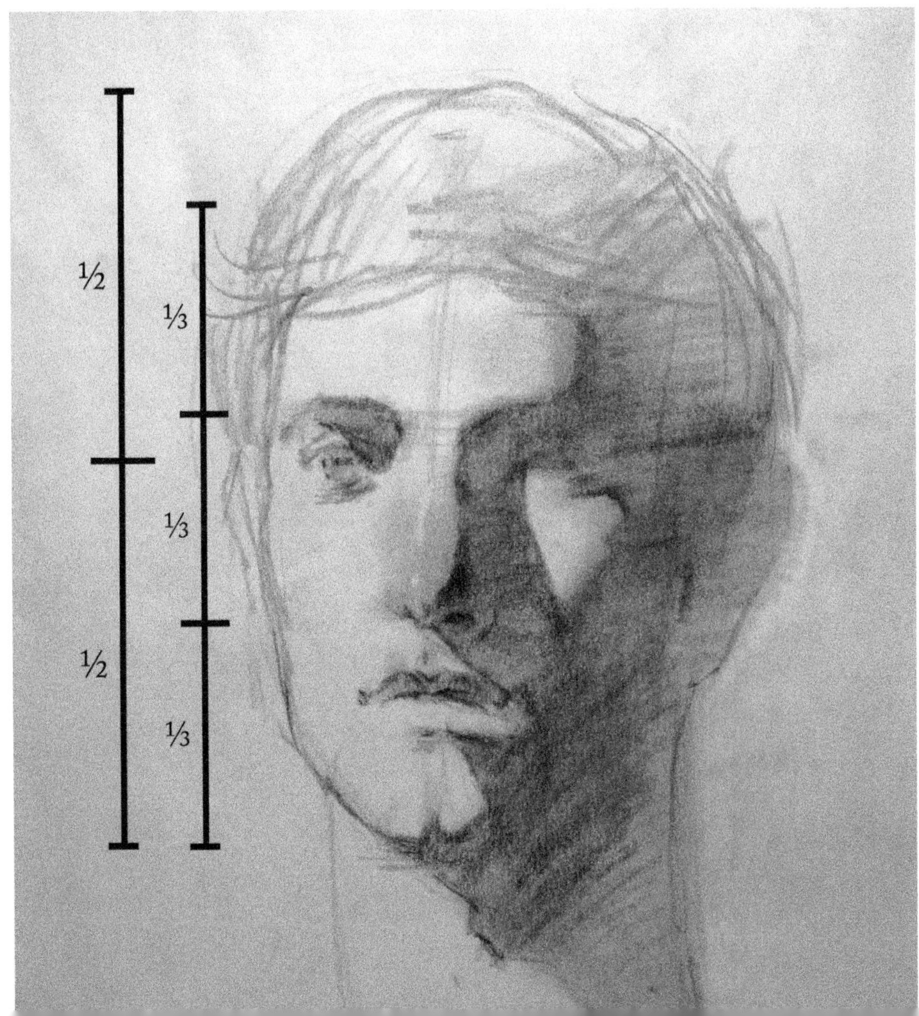

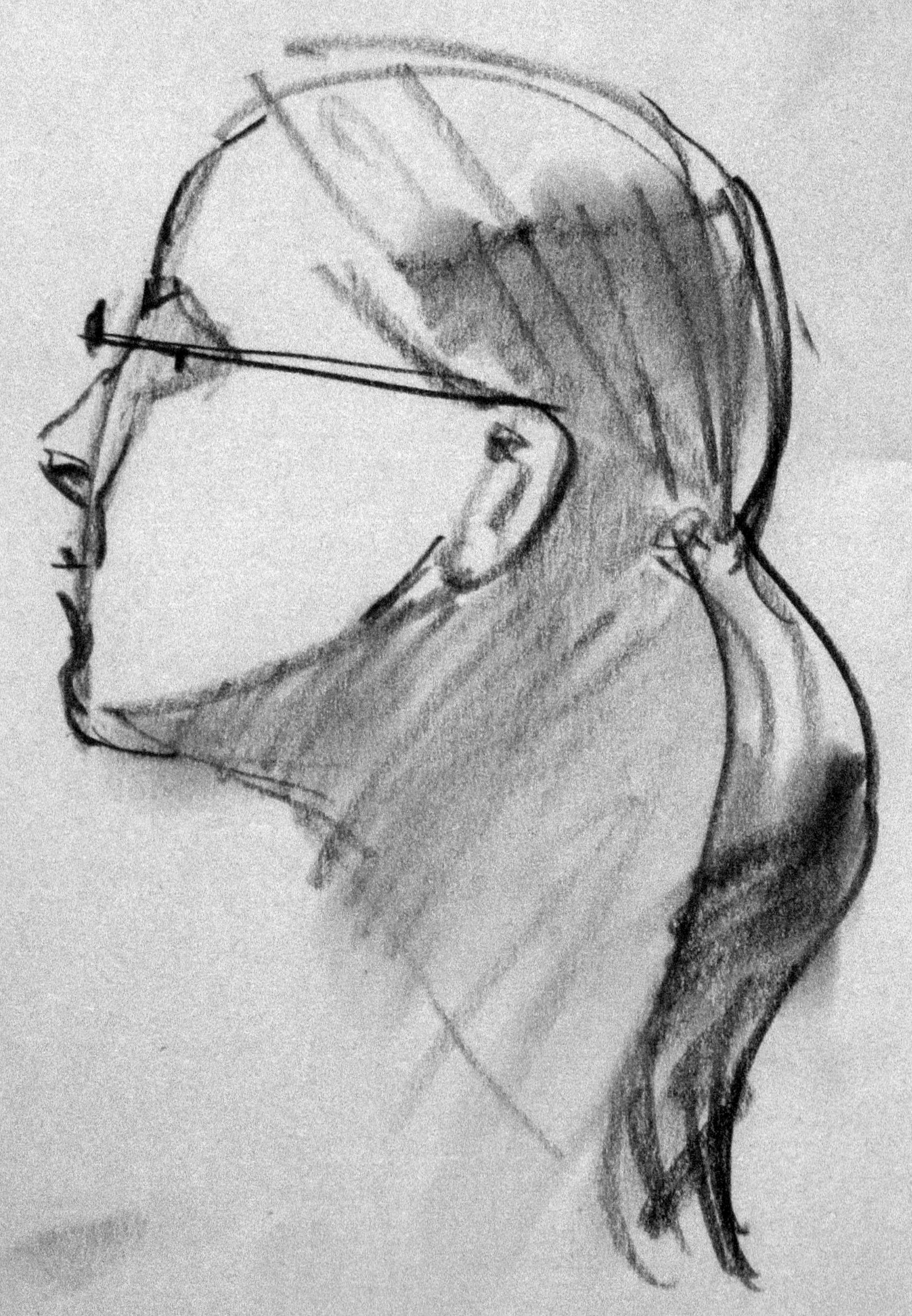

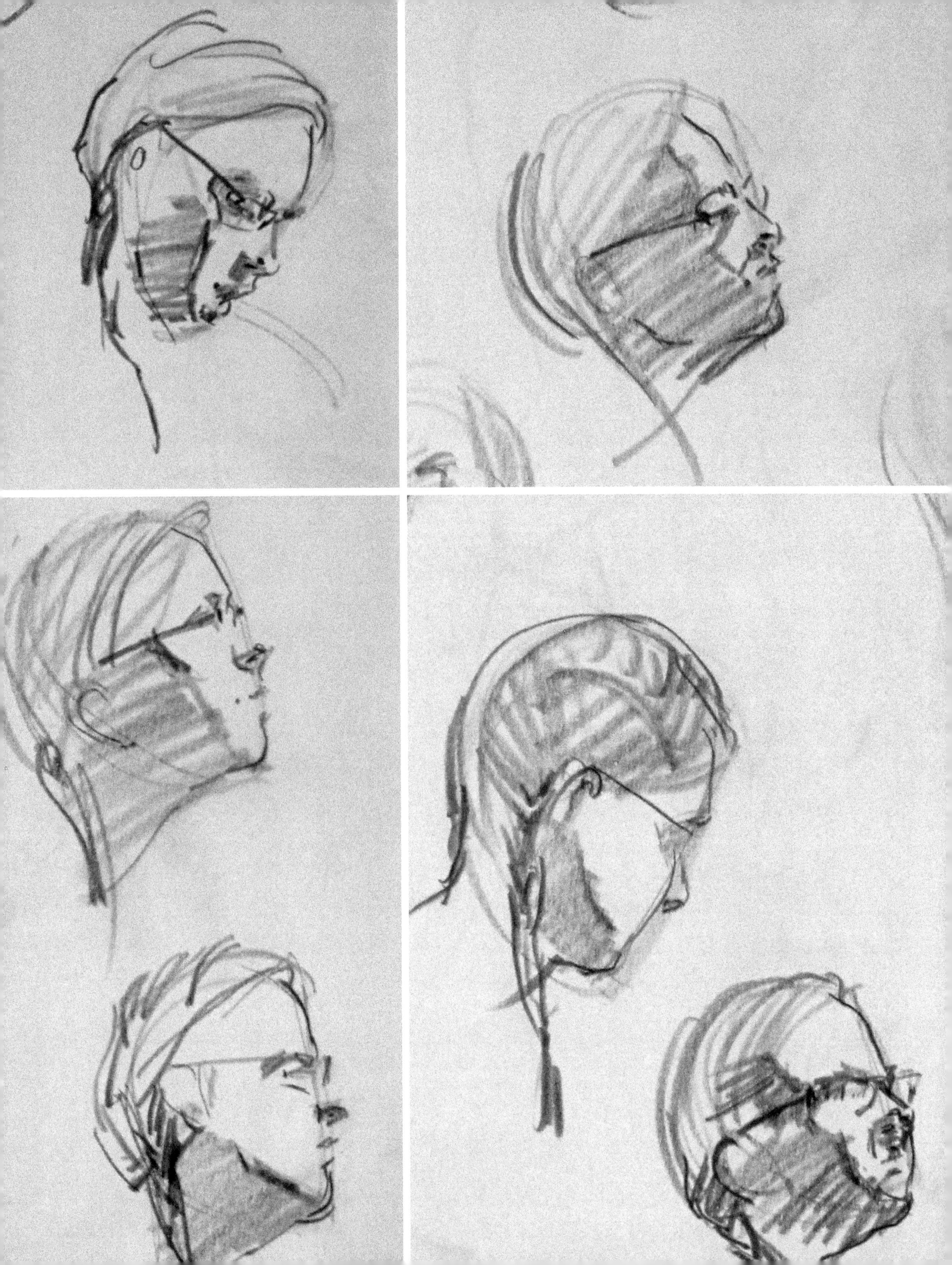

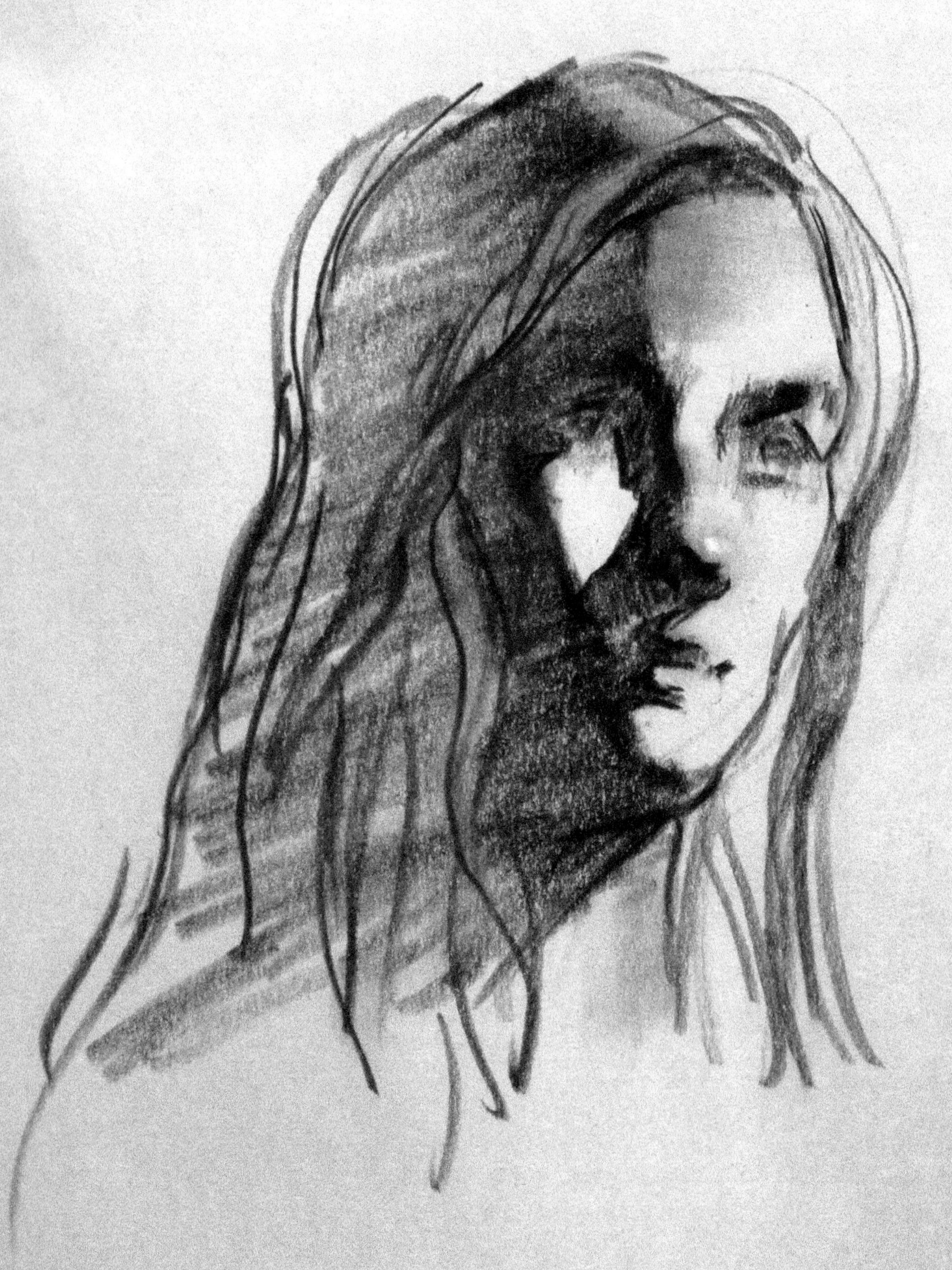

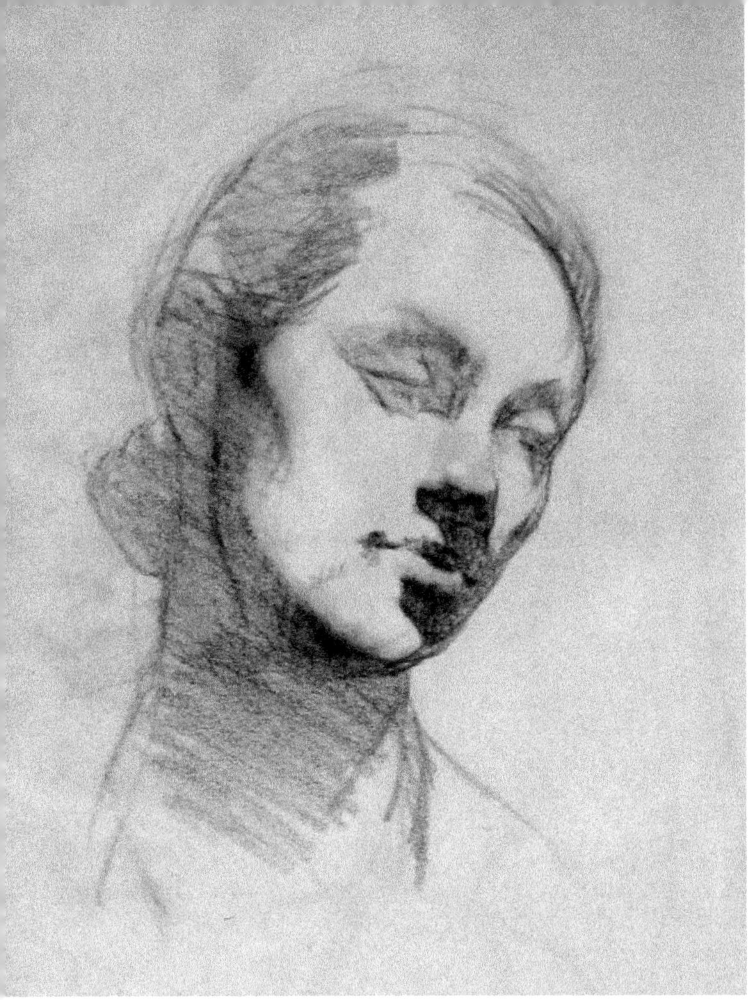

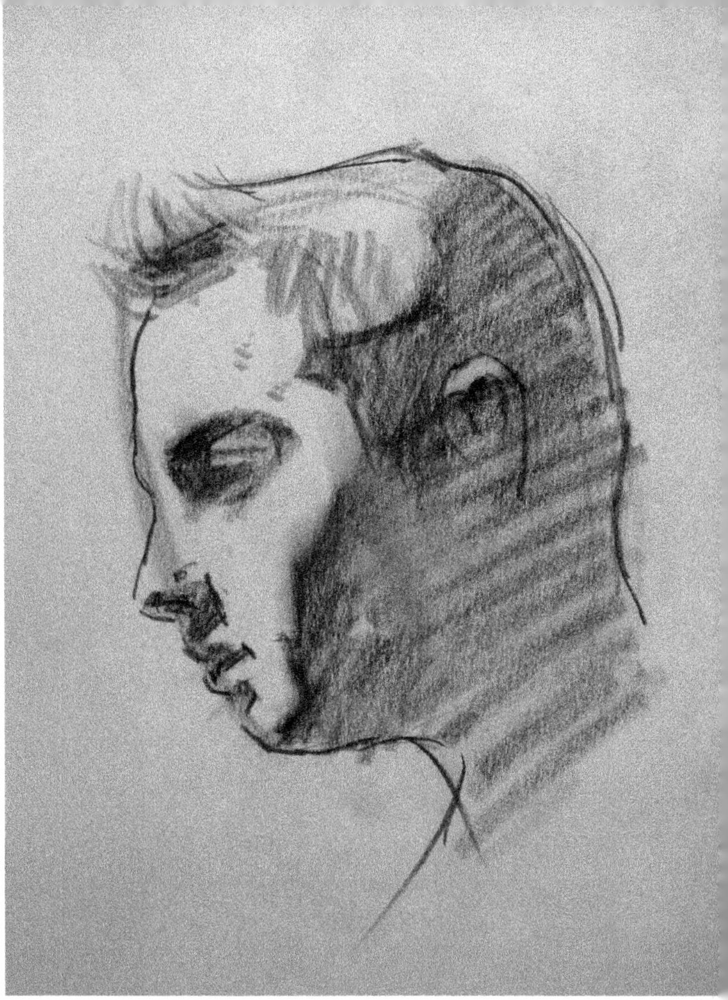

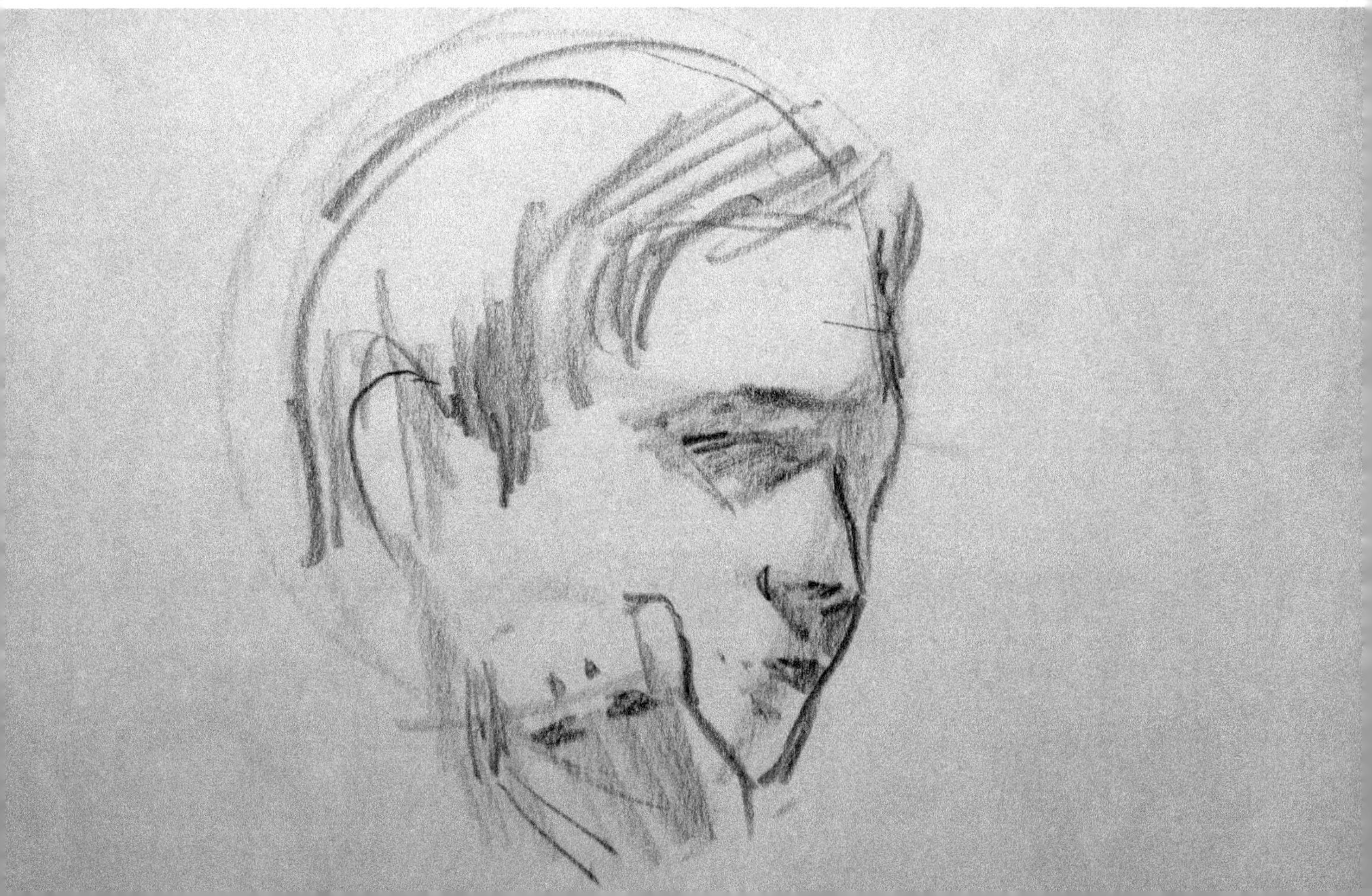

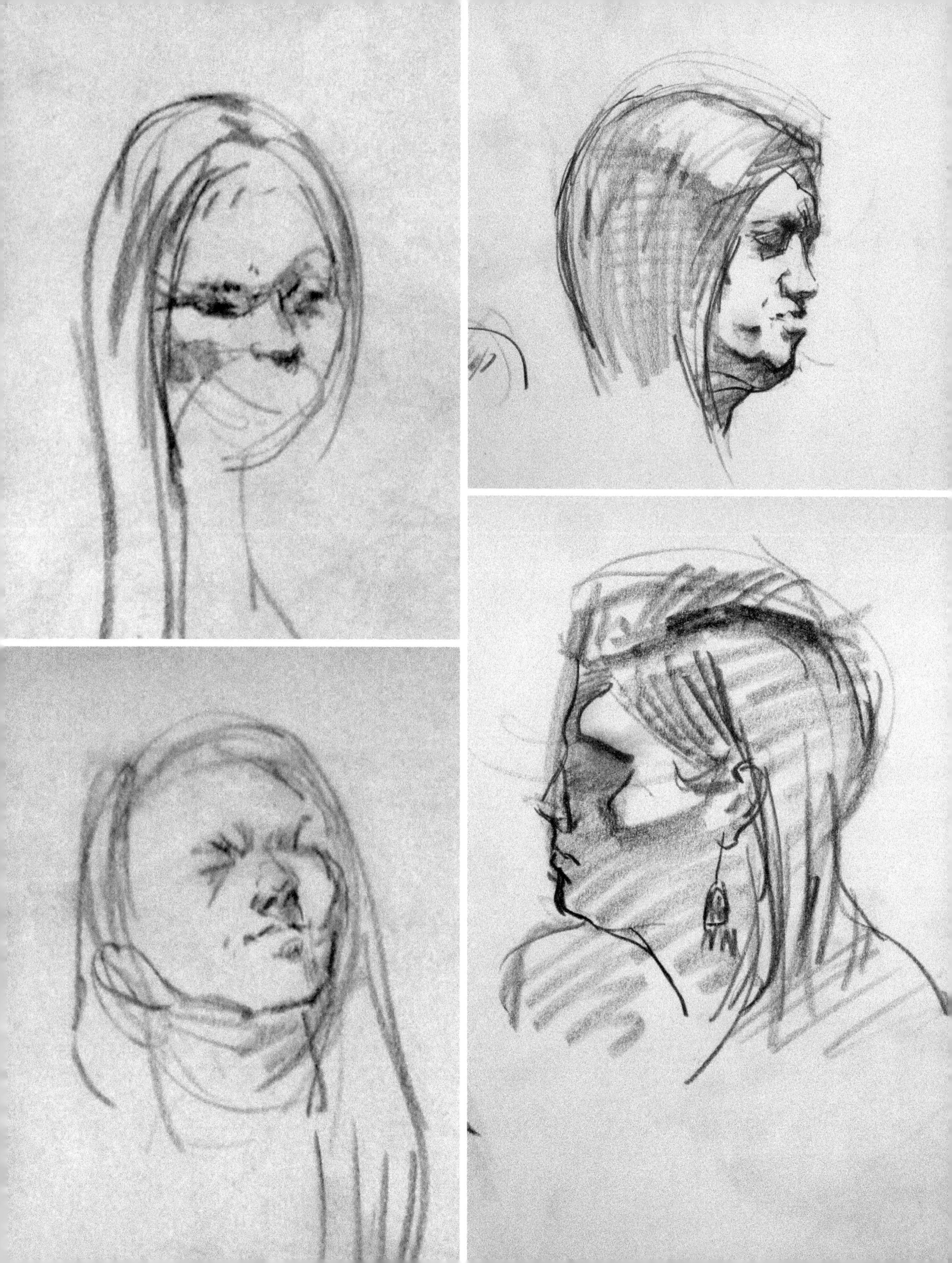

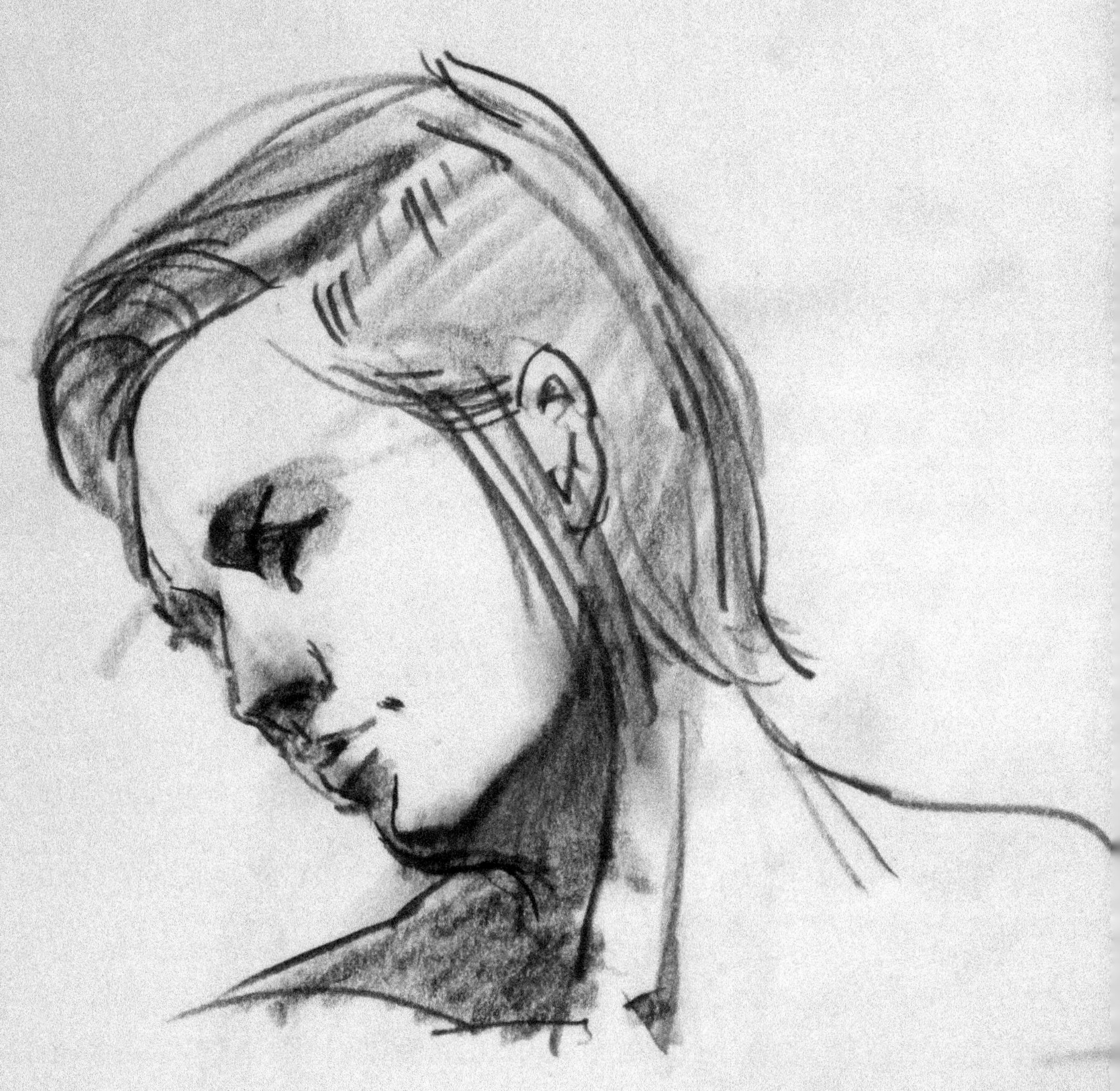

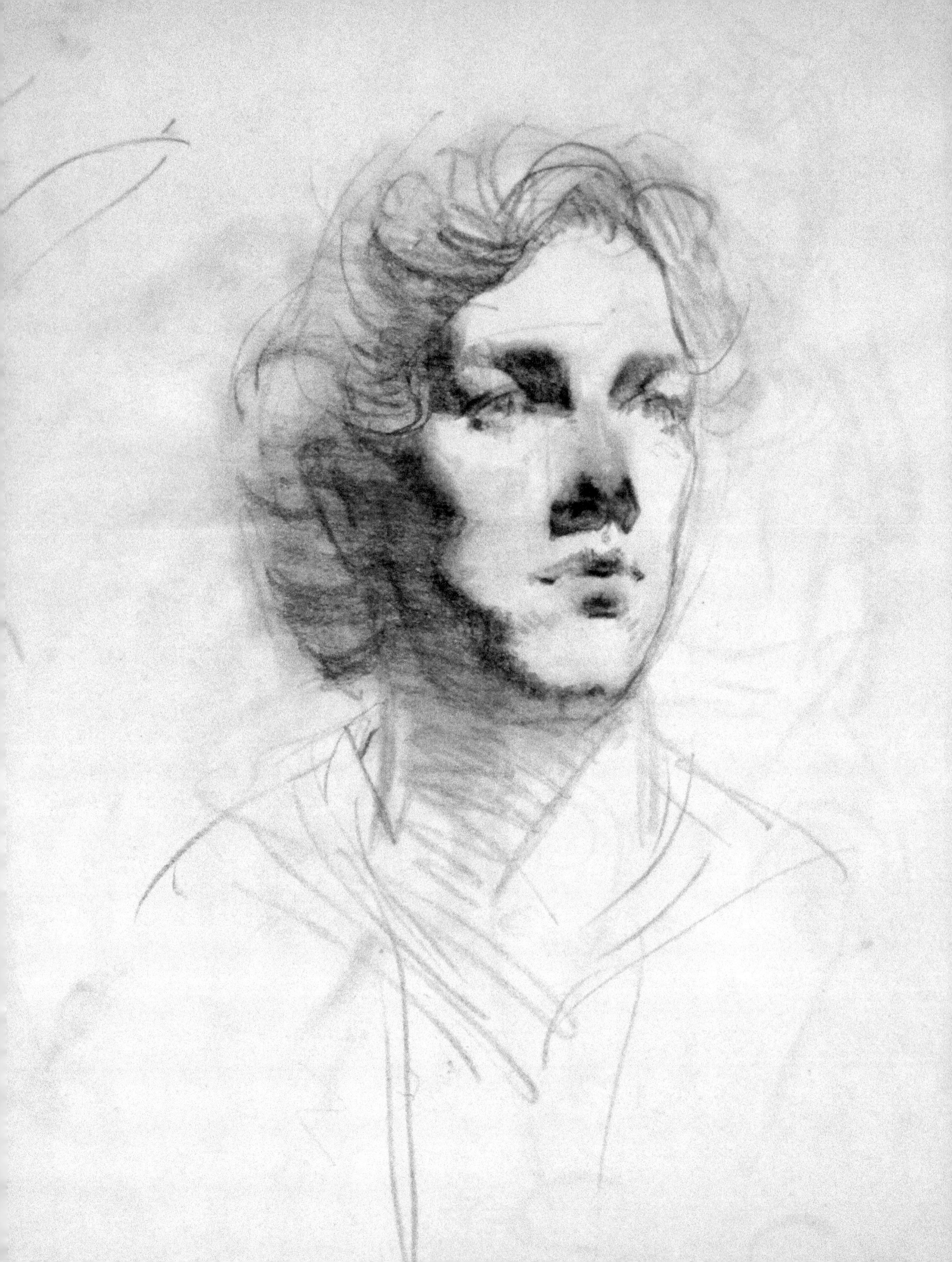

REMEMBERING FORESHORTENING

Heads are often drawn from a seated position where the artist is looking up at the model. With foreshortening in mind, the standard proportions in such instances will not remain evenly spaced. Remember that as objects go back in space, they get smaller. When sitting below the model, these standard proportions get closer together as they go up and back toward the top of the head. This also happens if the head is tilted backward in any way.

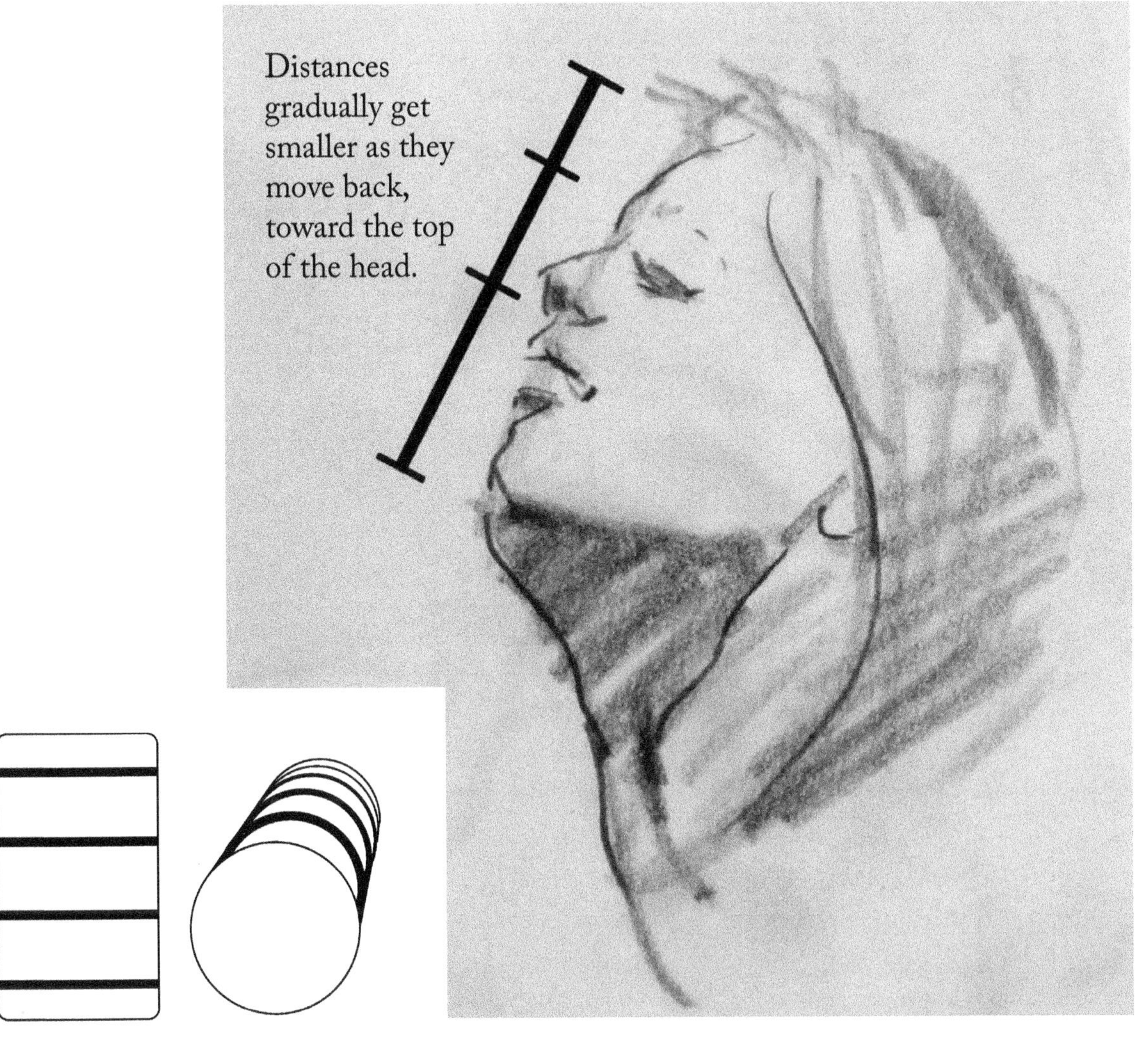

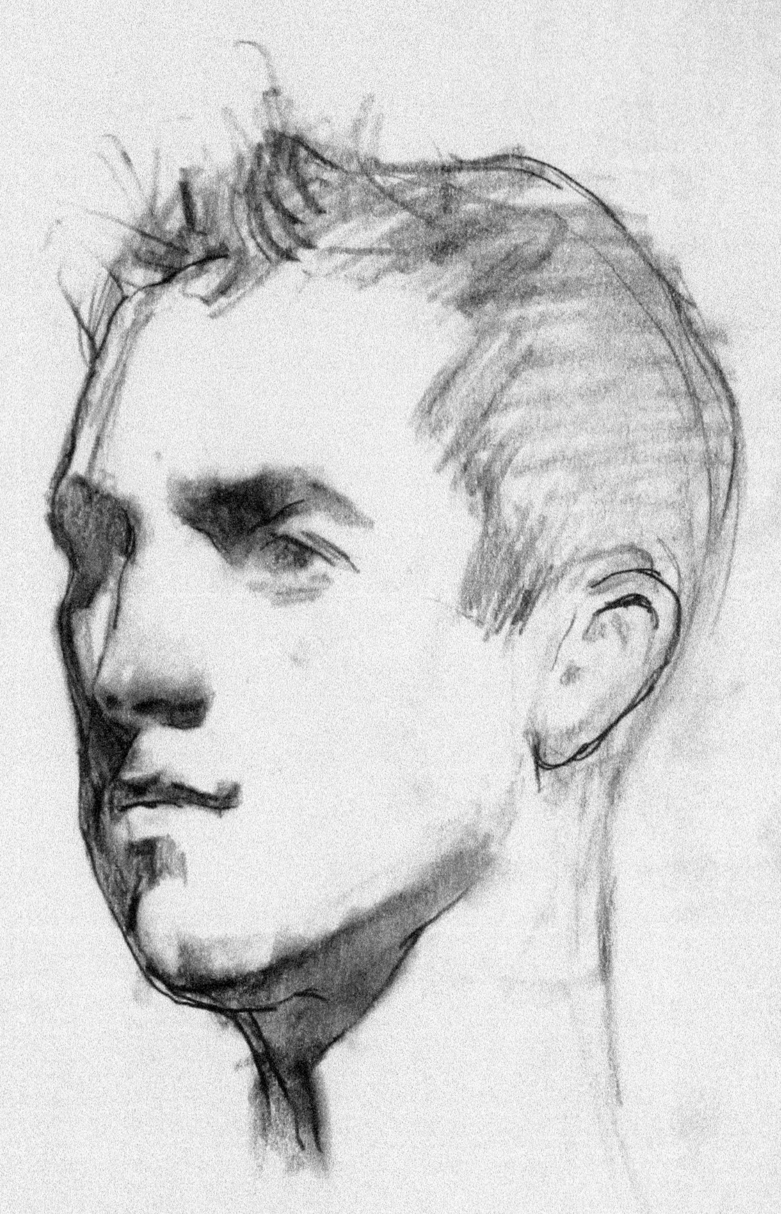

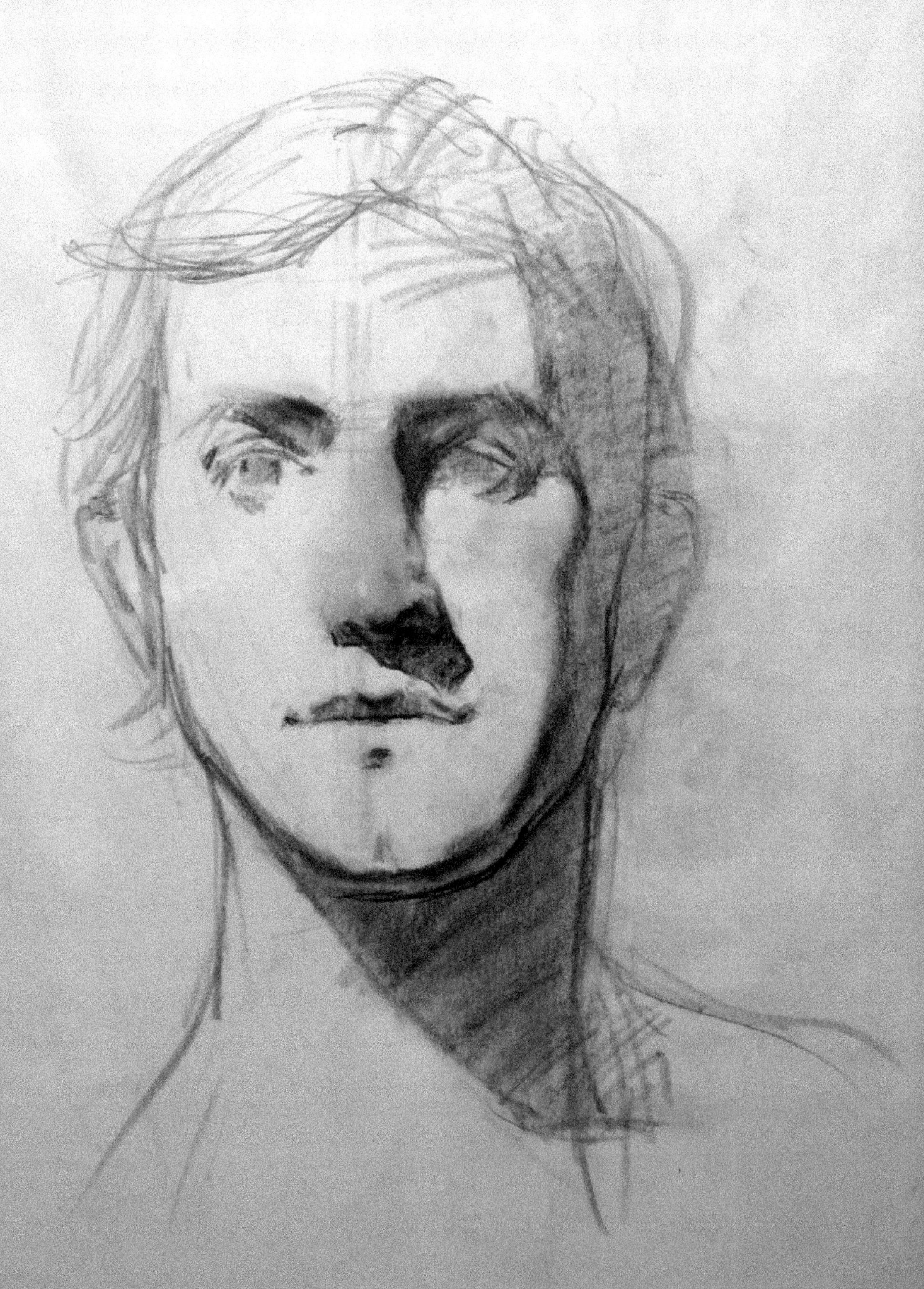

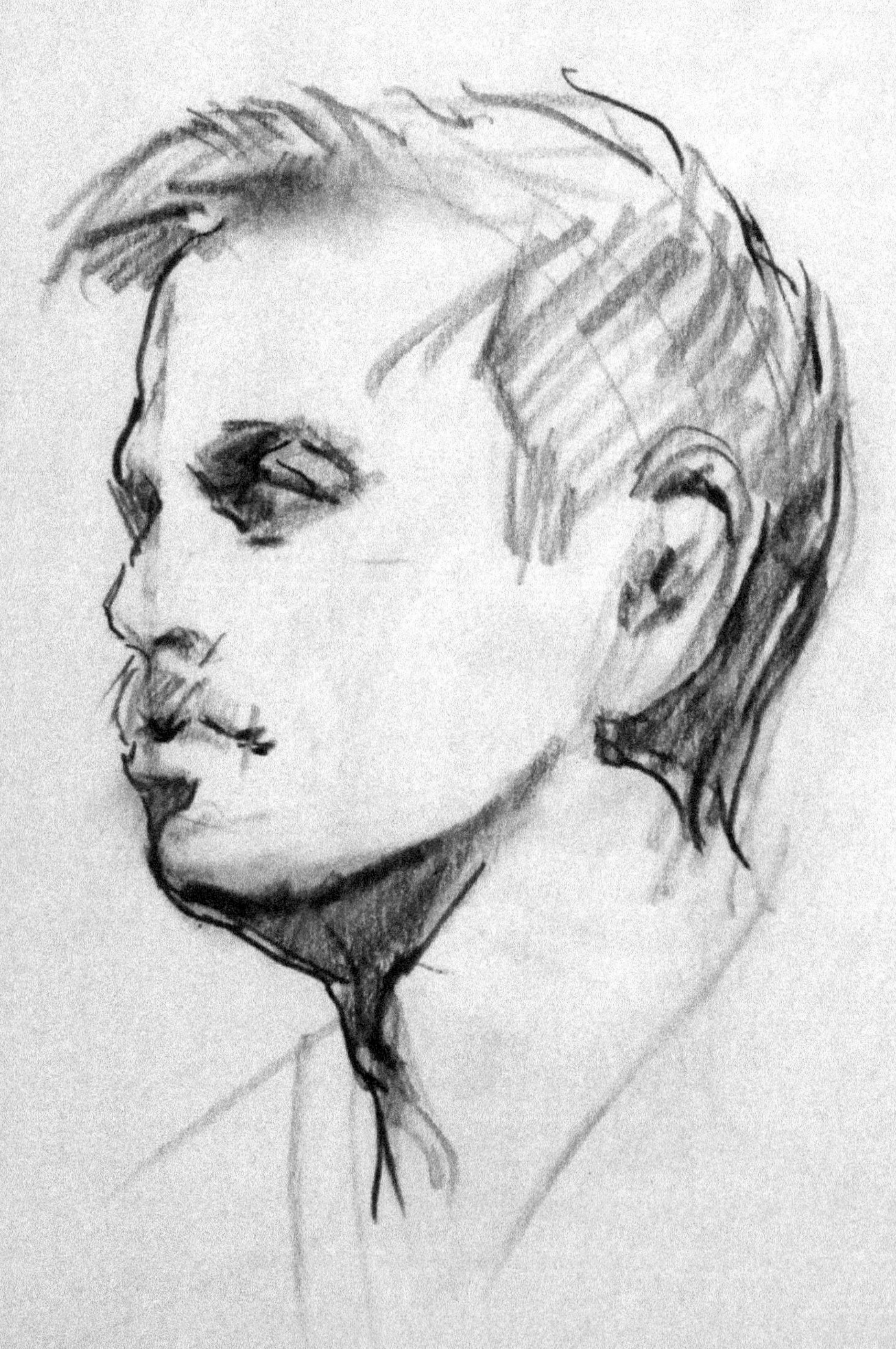

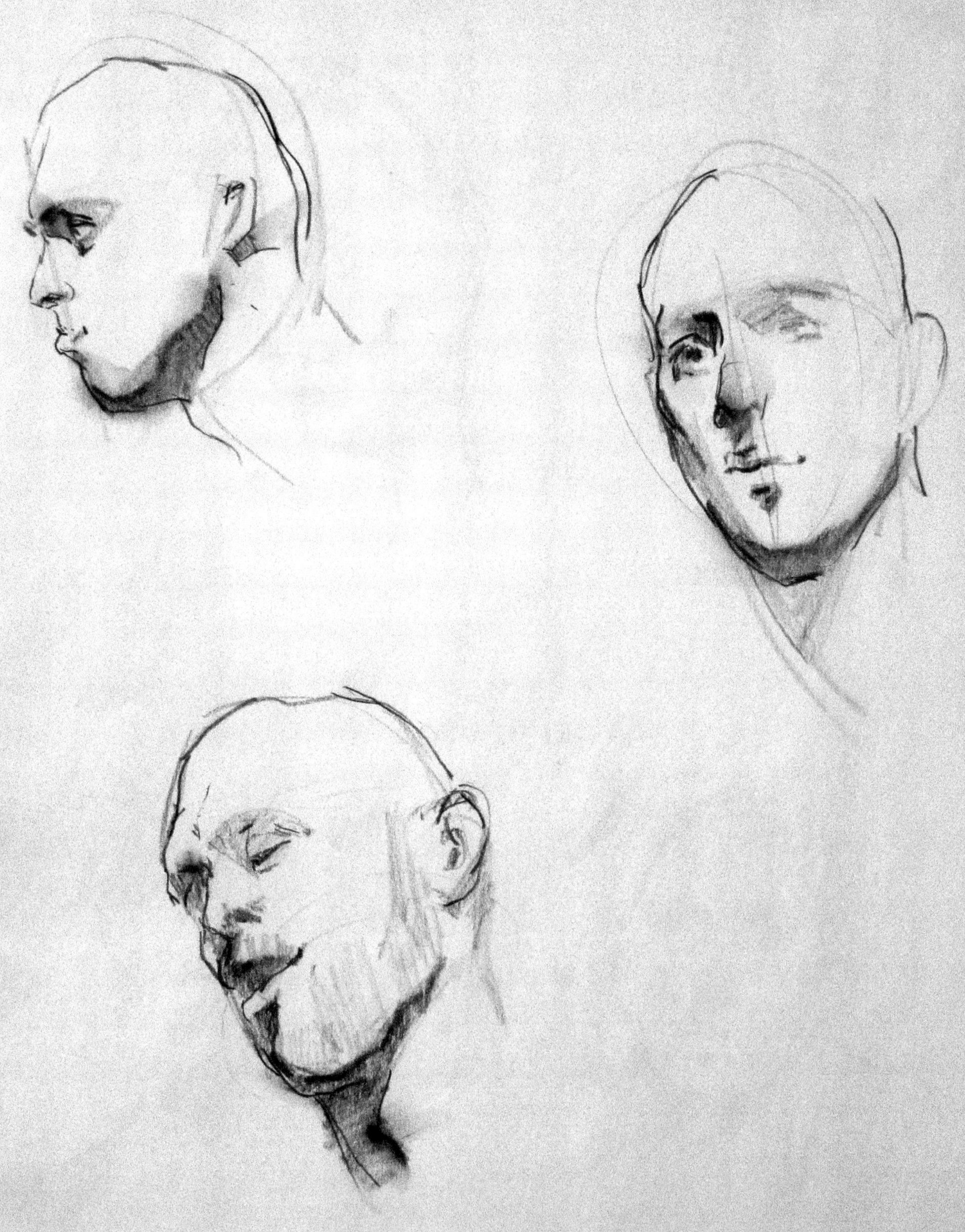

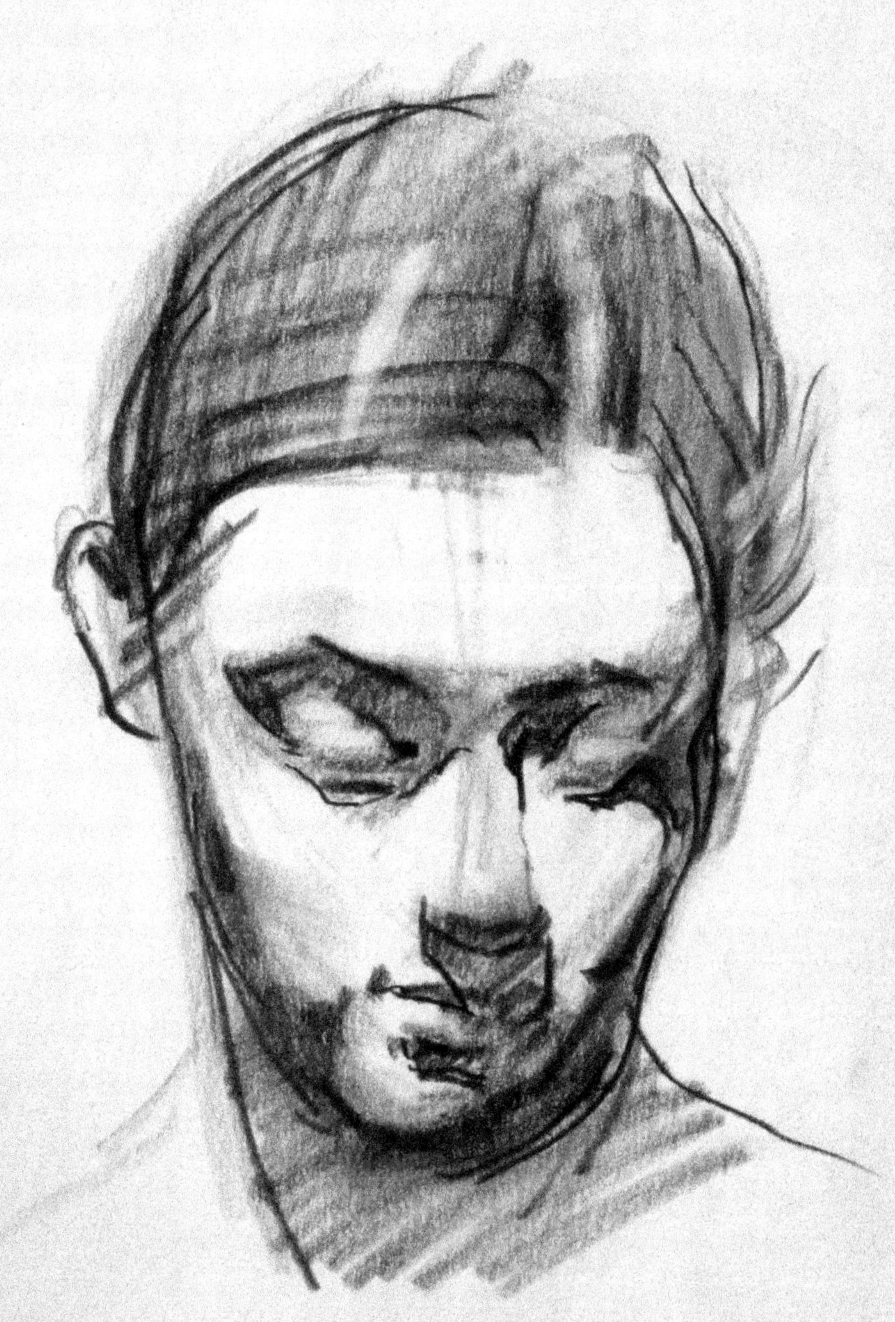

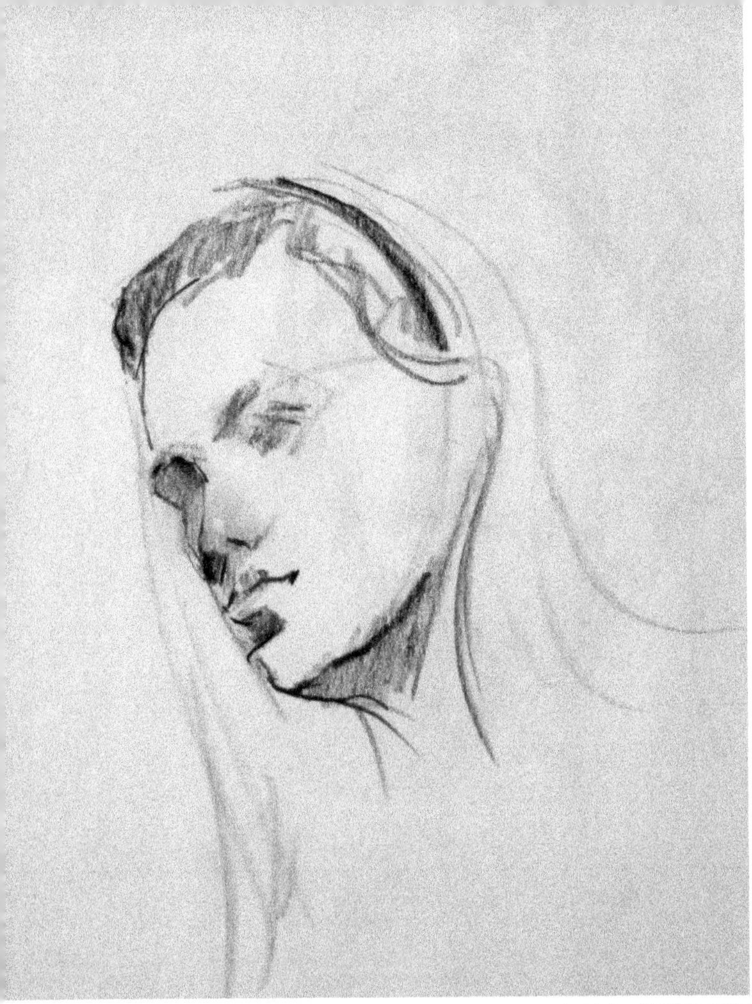

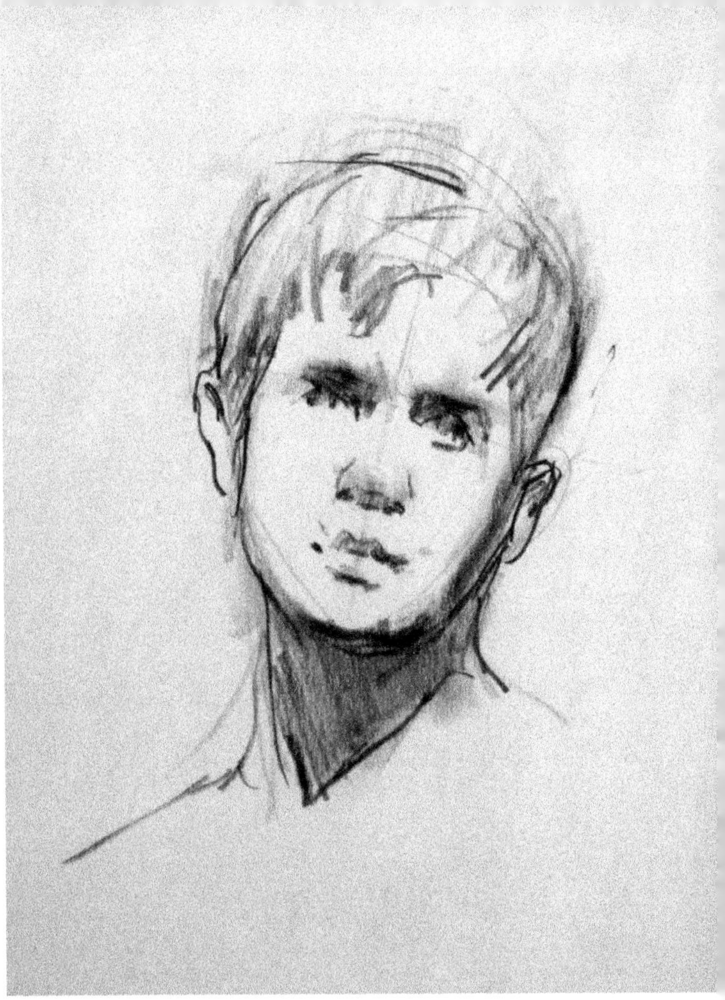

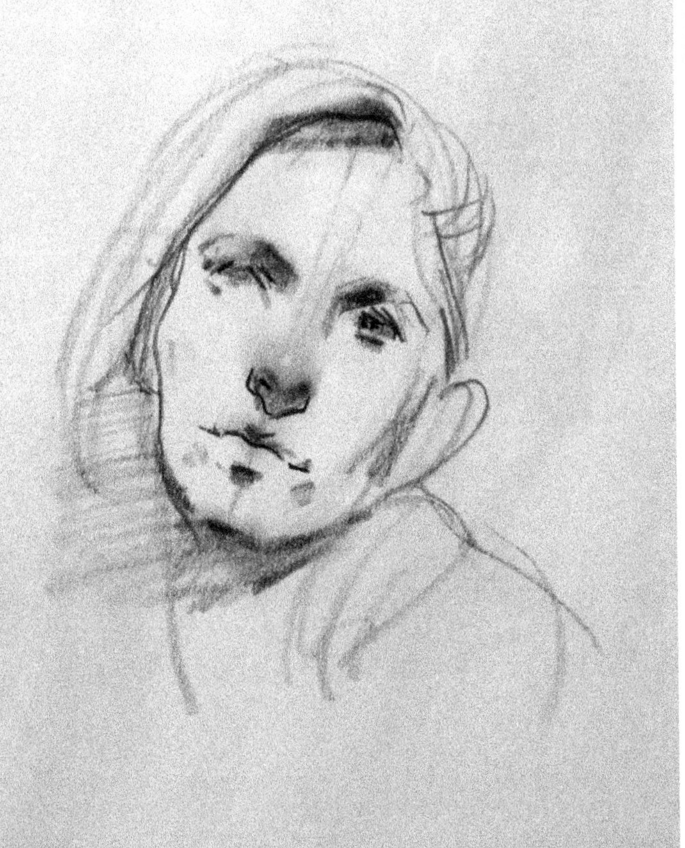
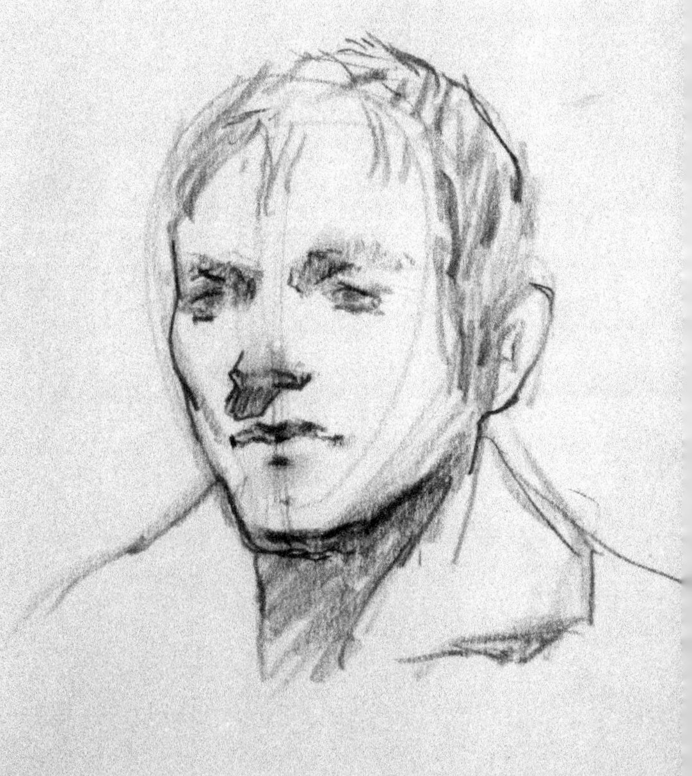

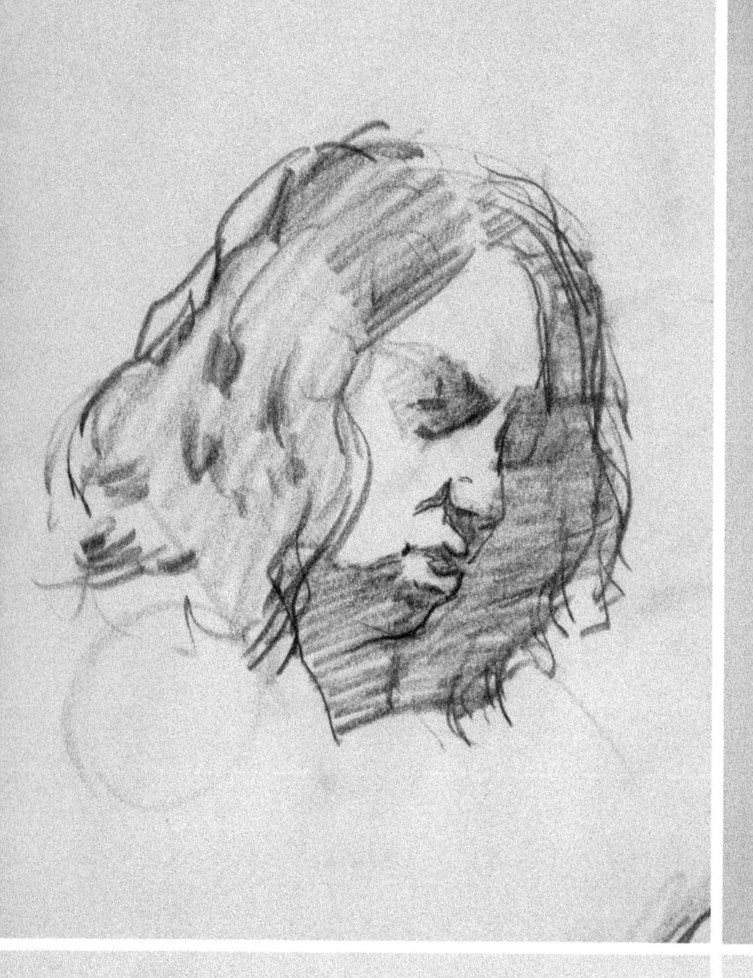
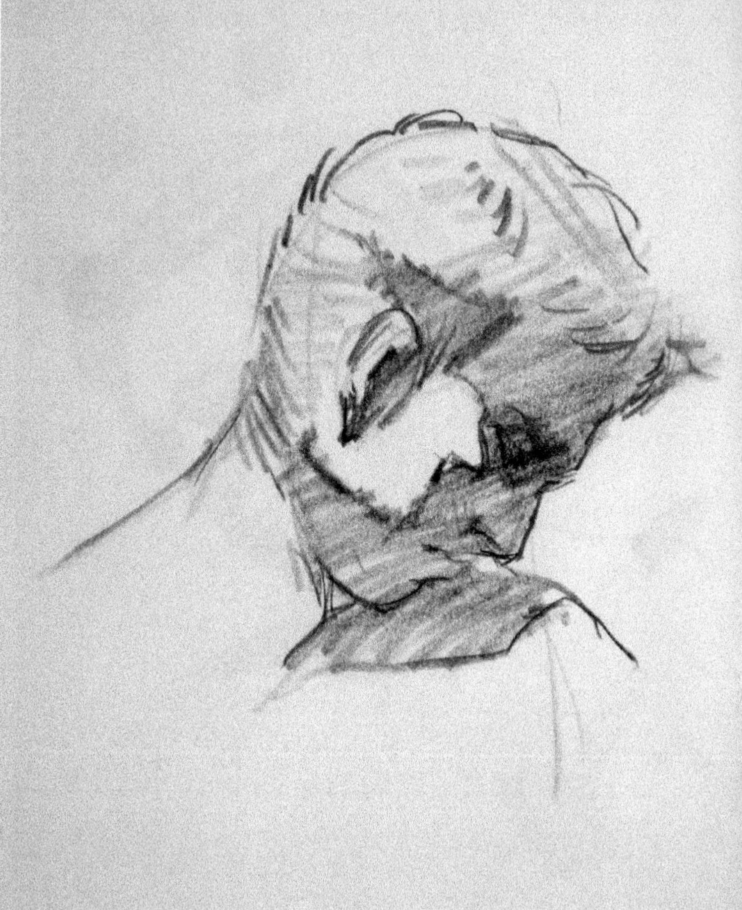
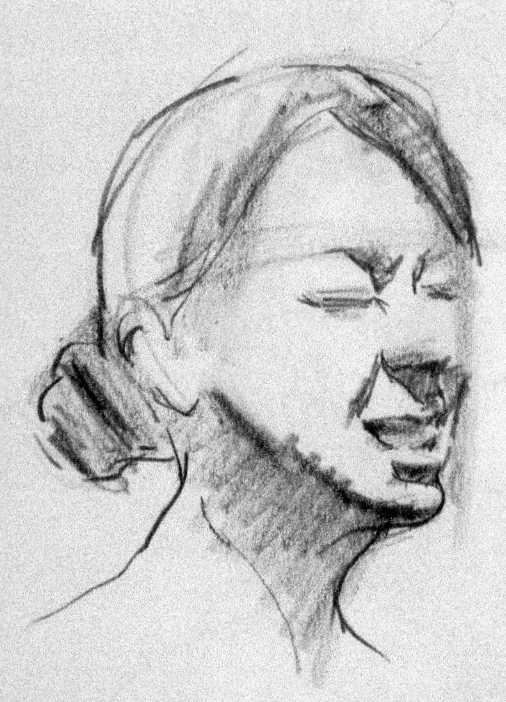
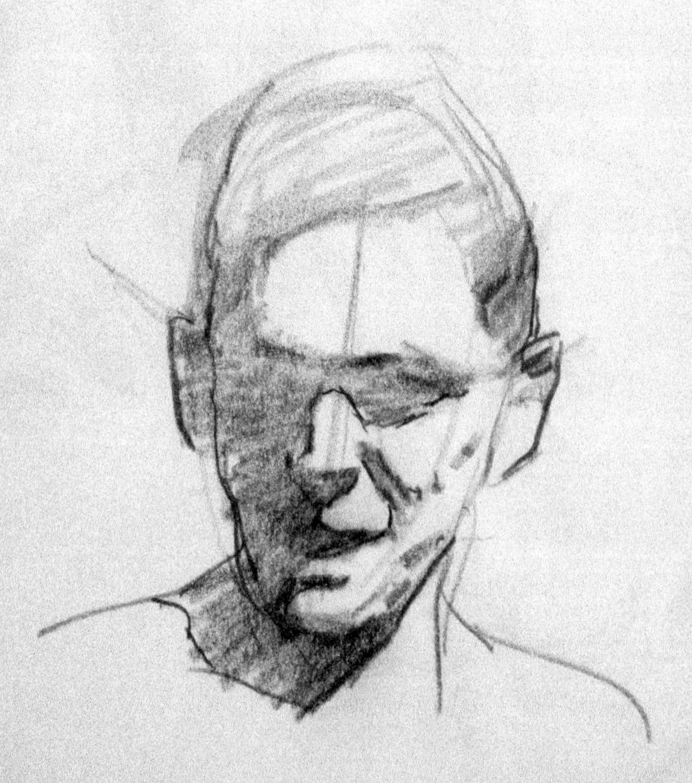

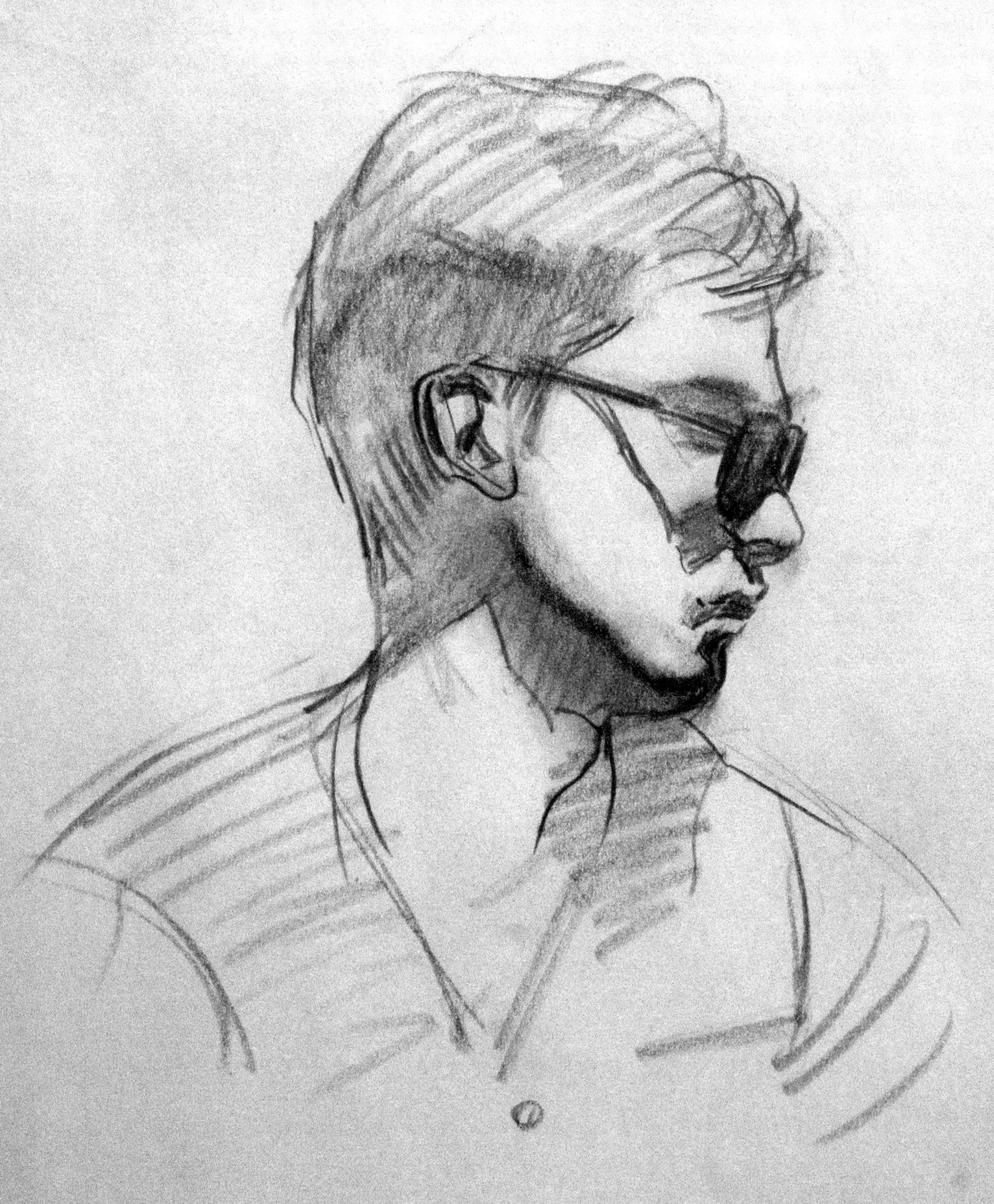

CLASS PROCEDURE

I like to start out with several two-minute head gestures in class. The students then take turns sitting for each other five minutes at a time. It is fun to draw people in the class for variety. If they are up to the challenge, some students even pull funny facial expressions, which are extra challenging. They learn to get a likeness by paying close attention to shadow shapes. These five-minute head studies are fairly small. I can fit about four on one page. My head drawings are larger when I have more time to draw them. However, I never draw heads any larger than life-size, which is about the size of your hand.

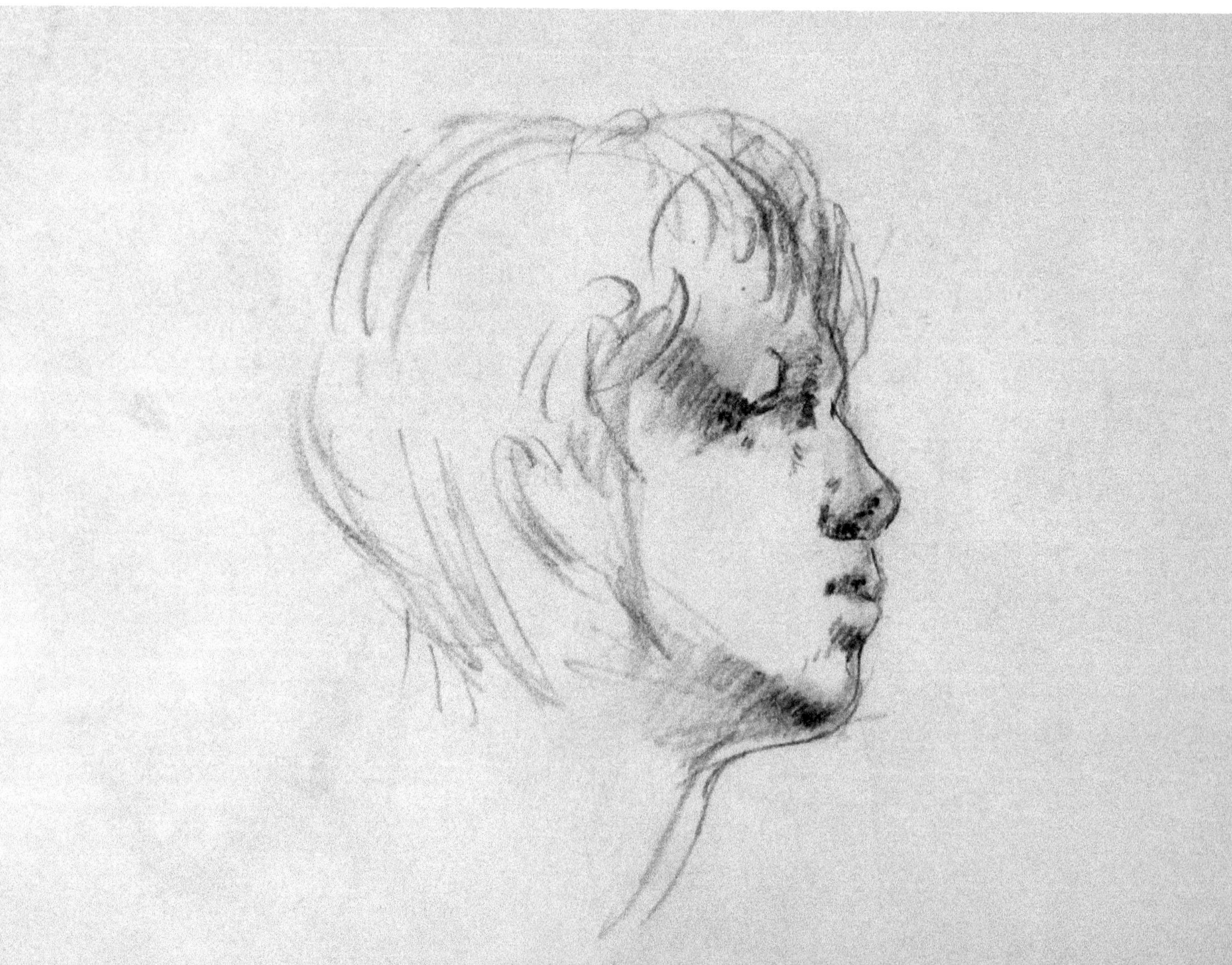

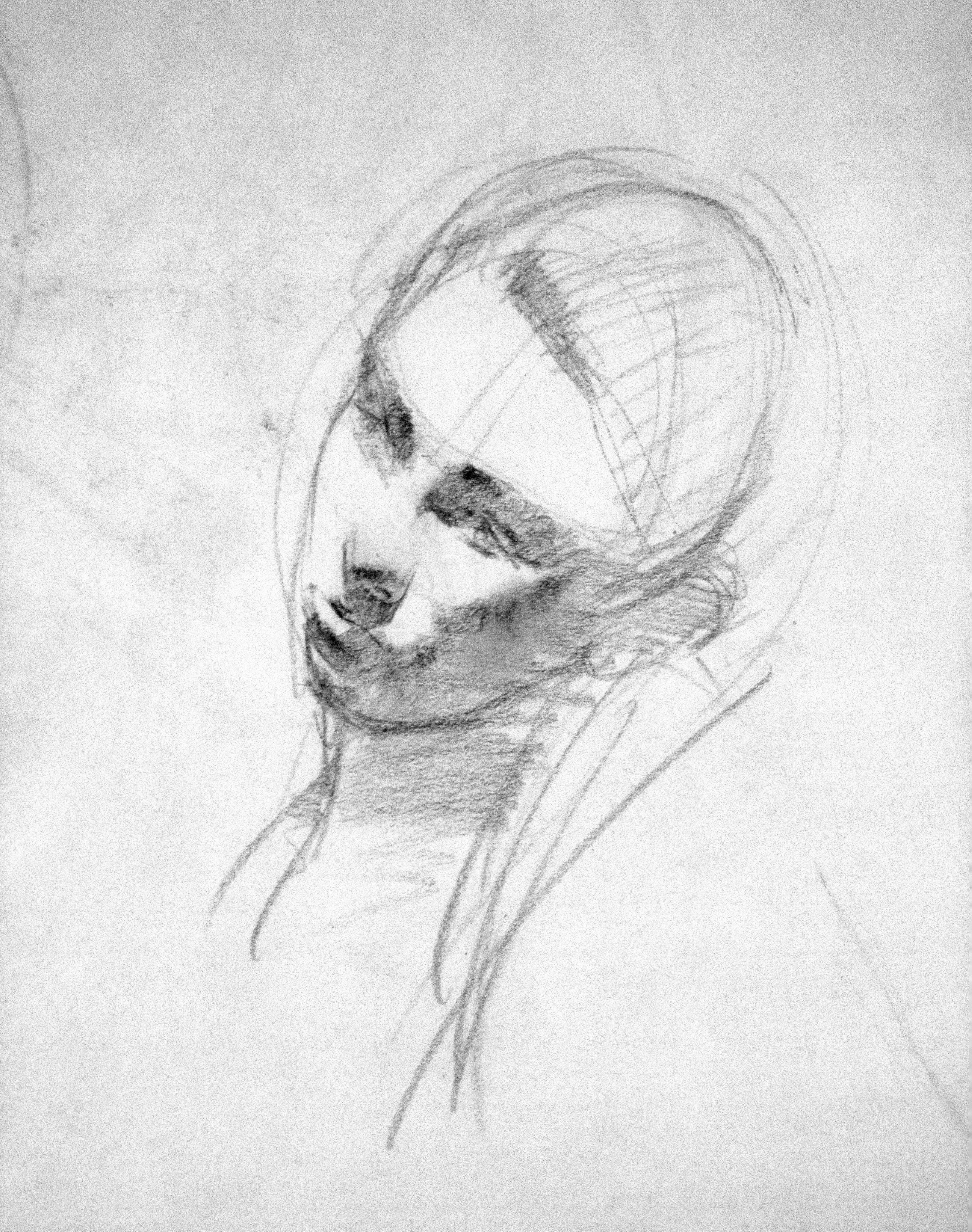

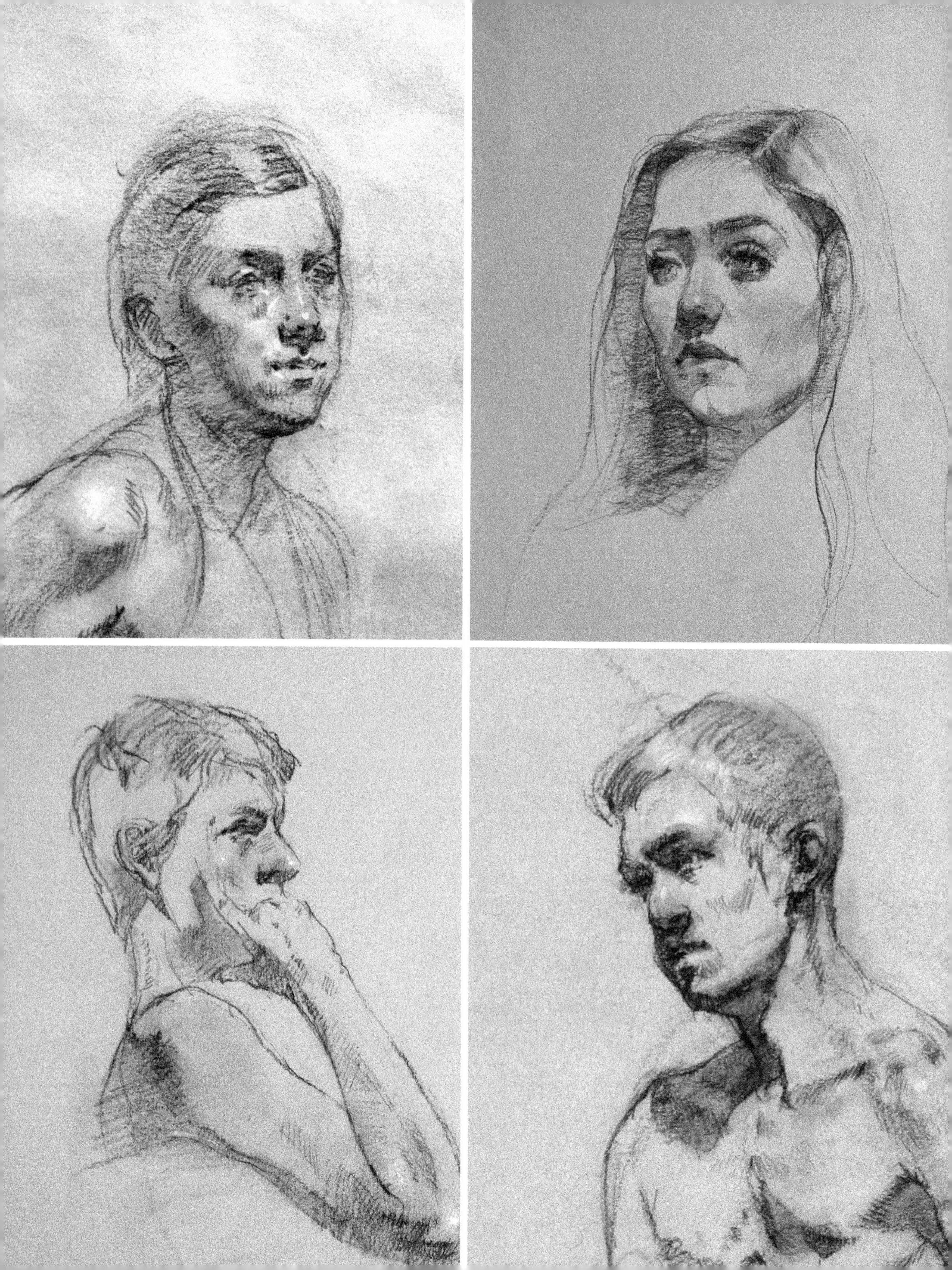

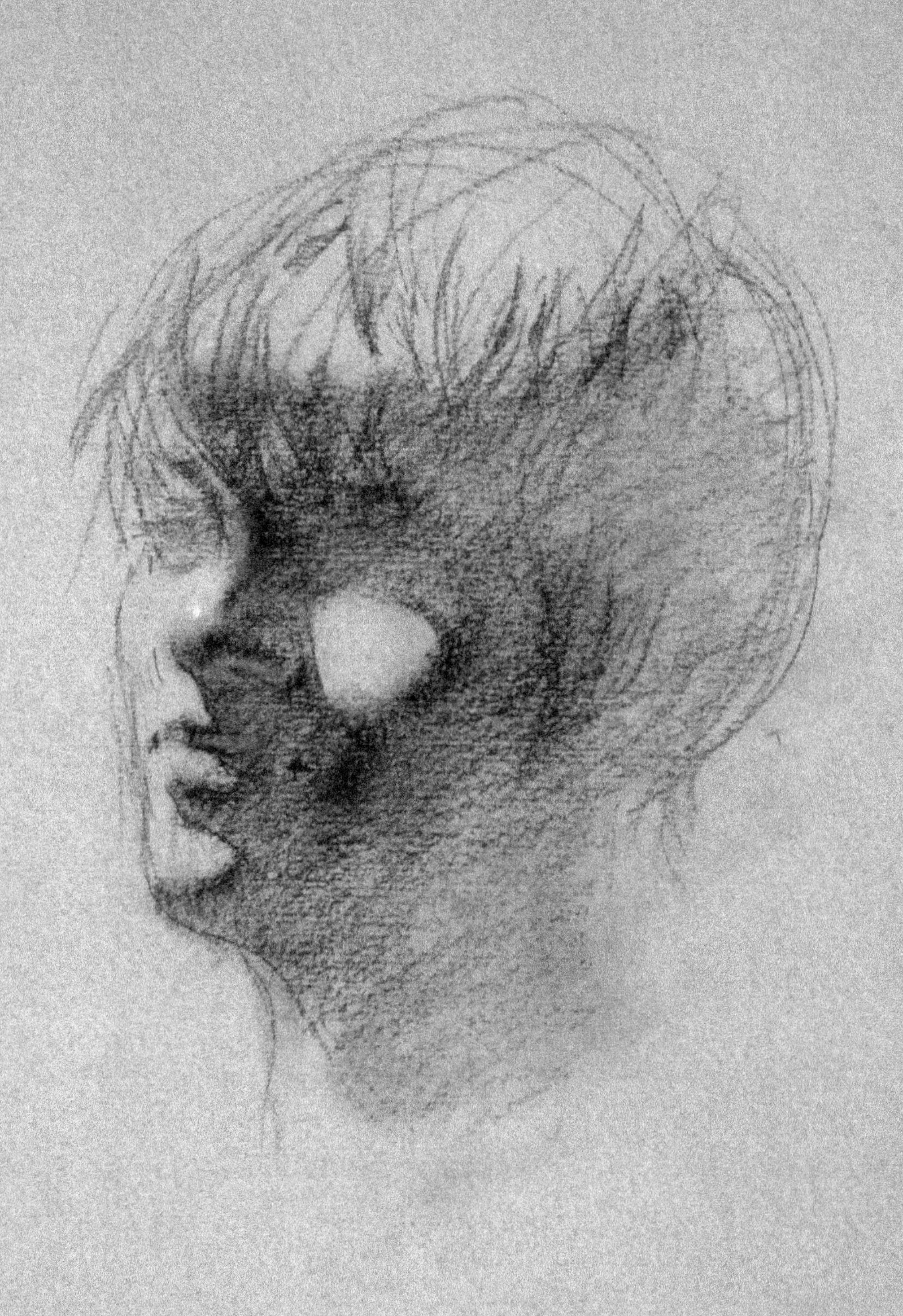

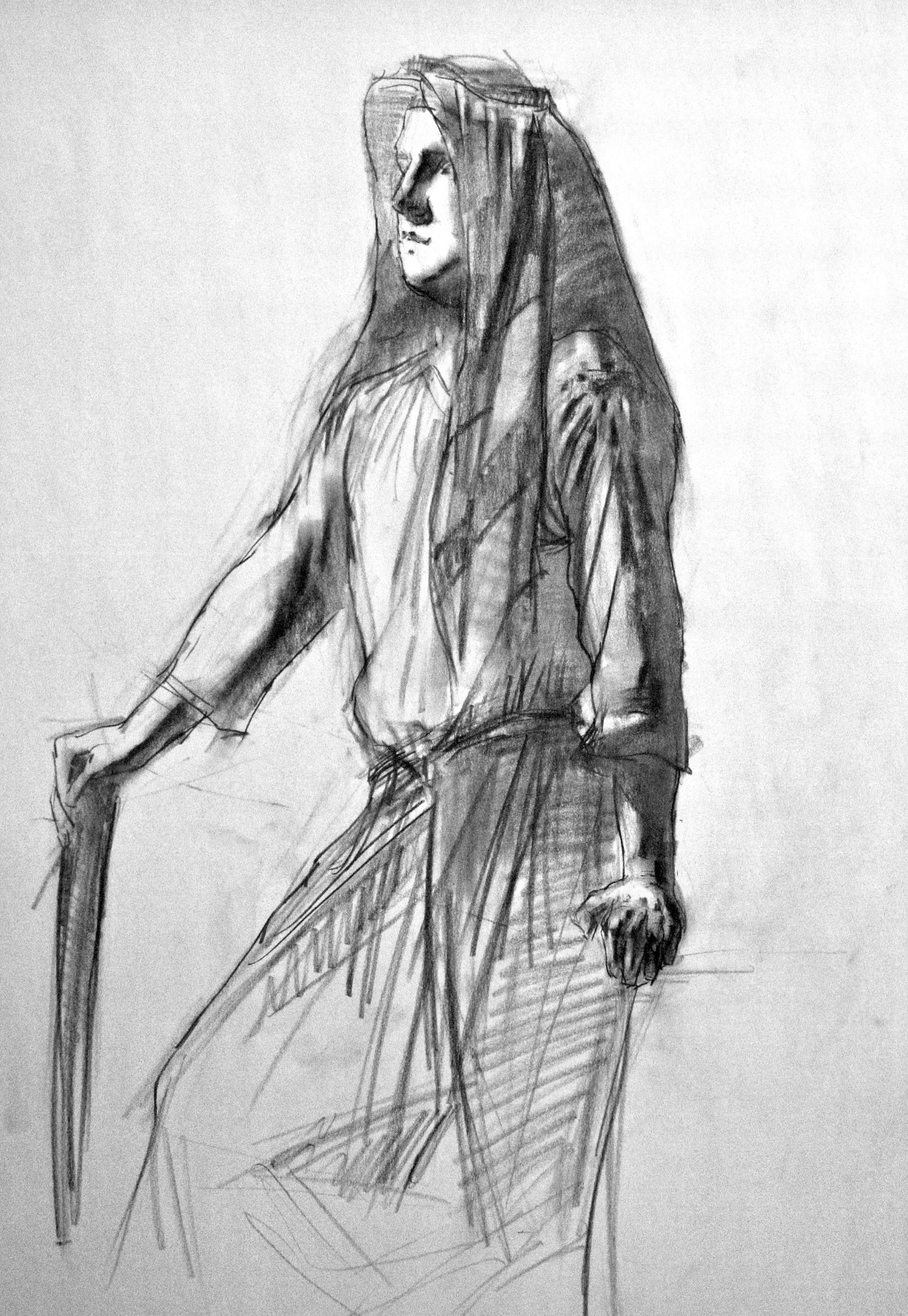

DRAPERY

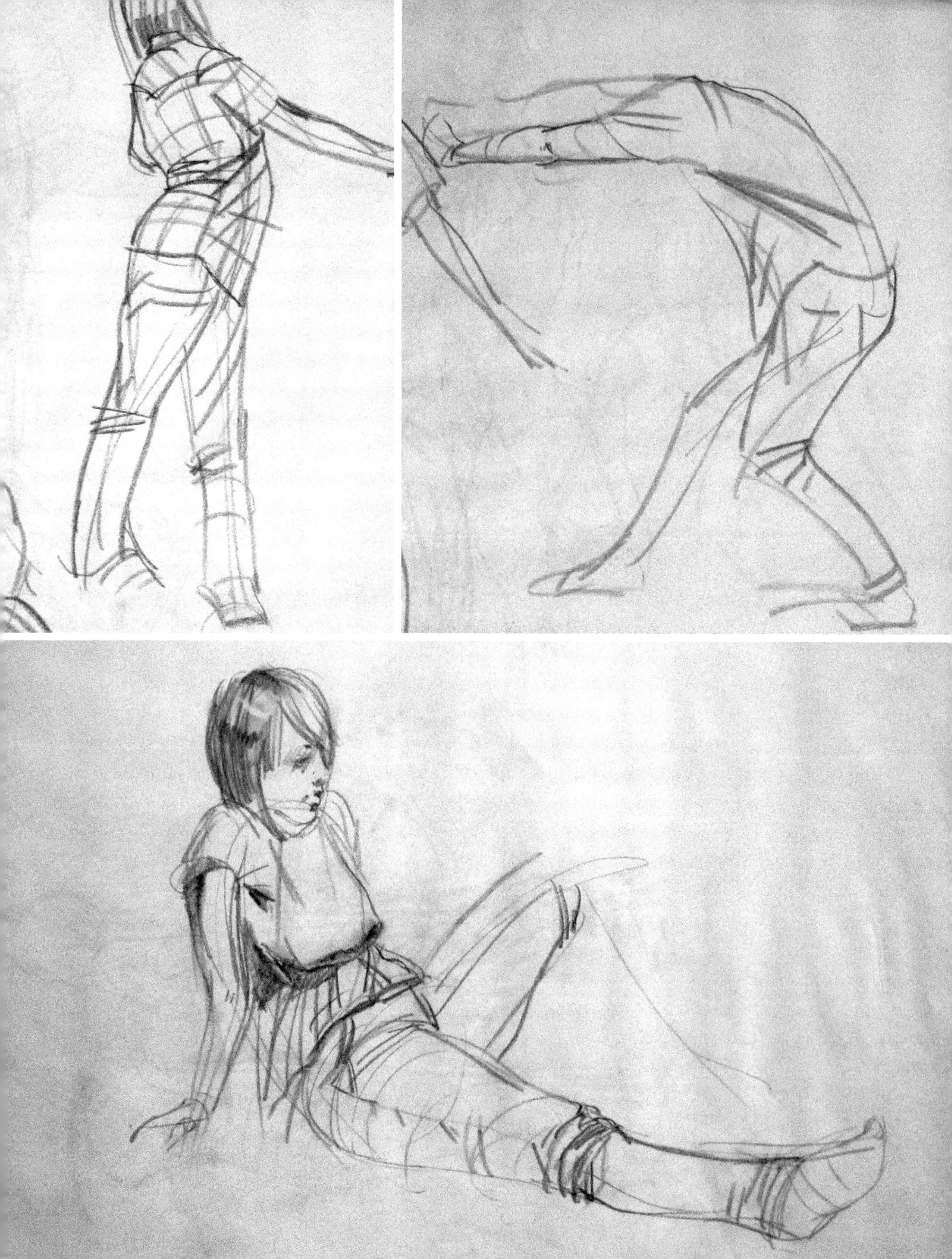

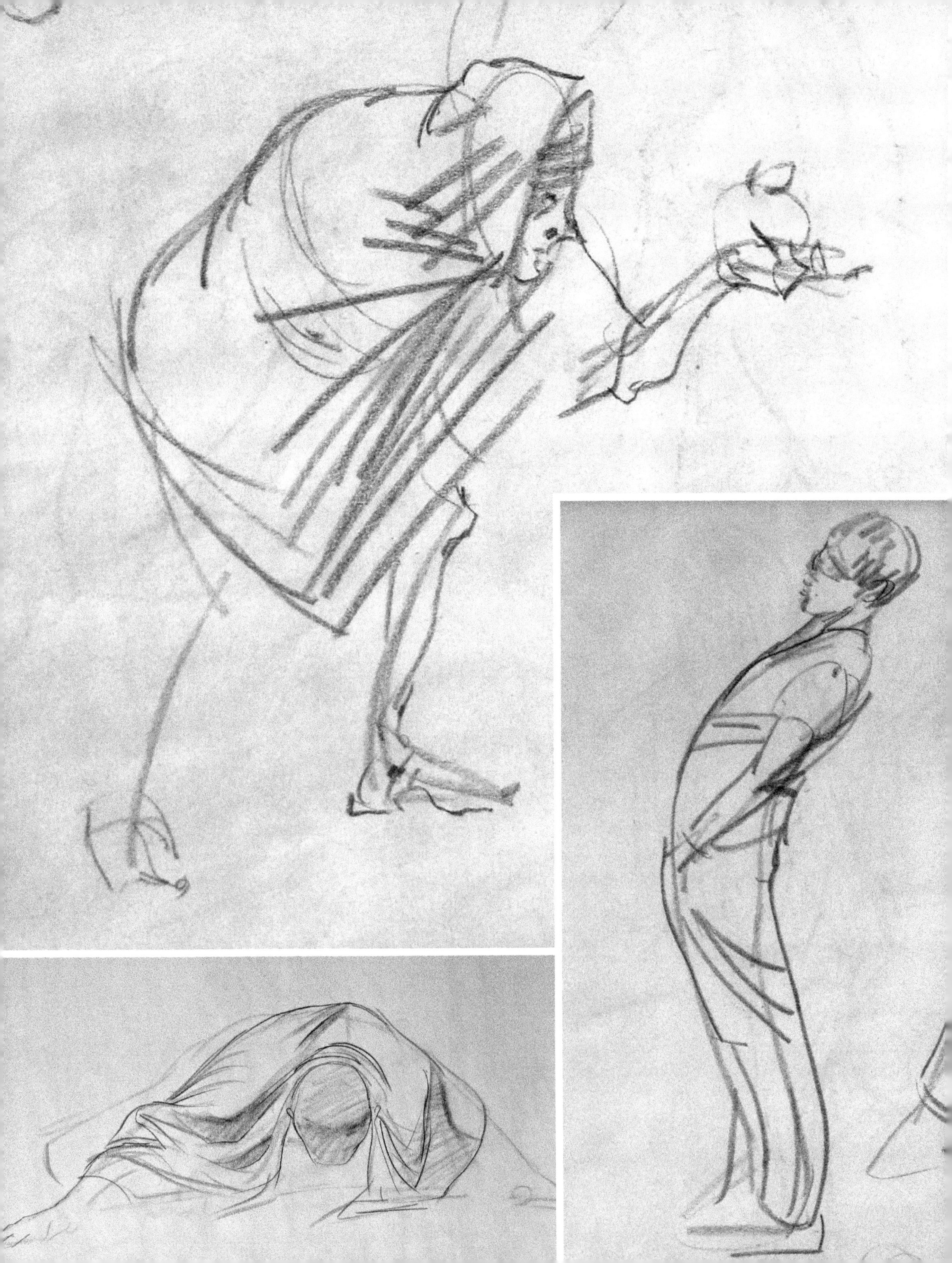

DRAPERY

Toward the end of the semester, we study drapery and the students get really excited. I think at this point, they look forward to adding some variety in their drawings. I feel it is important to study drapery because these animation and illustration students will most likely draw people in clothes or costumes for various work projects in their future careers.

Drapery often acts as an extension of the gesture. It can accentuate the feel of the pose and add diversity in texture and movement. It is important to understand the figure underneath the clothing because that affects the way clothing hangs. It is also important to study drapery in itself and to know the structure of different types of folds that most often occur. It is beneficial to know the different types of folds that frequently appear in order to predict how certain clothing or costumes might behave in different circumstances.

POINTS OF SUPPORT

The most important thing to remember that has to do with drapery is to identify points of support or tension. On the figure, these typically happen at head, shoulders, hips, and supports in the design of the costume such as belts, sashes, darts, etc. Once the points of support are identified, it is easy to create convincing folds. Of course, refer to the model, but also understand that a lot of designing will be required on the artist's part.

I often look at old master paintings and marvel at their drapery. I used to think their models must have held so still and never taken any breaks because the drapery seemed so perfect. It dawned on me one day as we were studying drapery in class that these old masters must have definitely understood the nature of folds, and I am sure they did a lot of designing and editing. Drawing is incorporating both what we *see* and what we *know*.

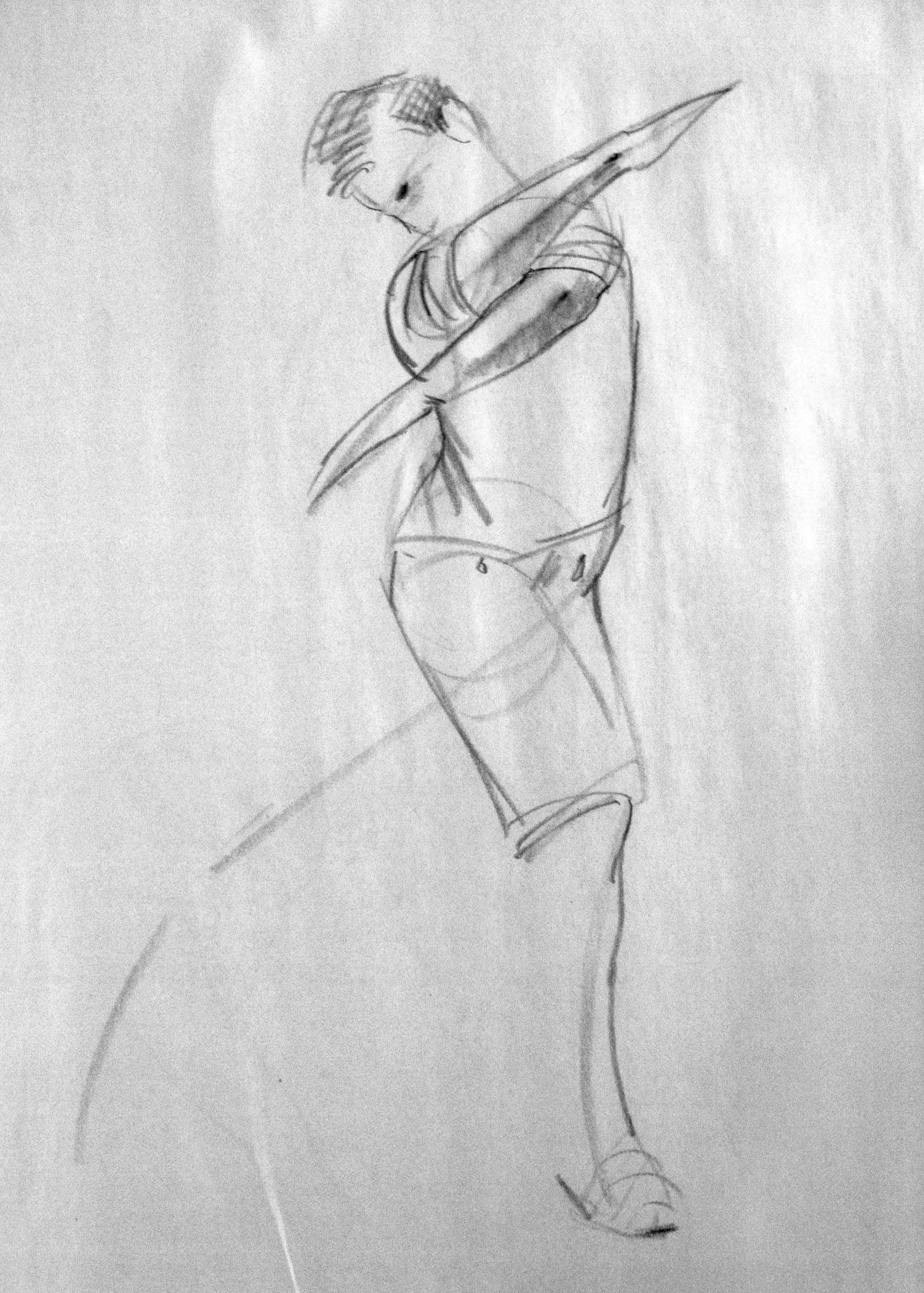

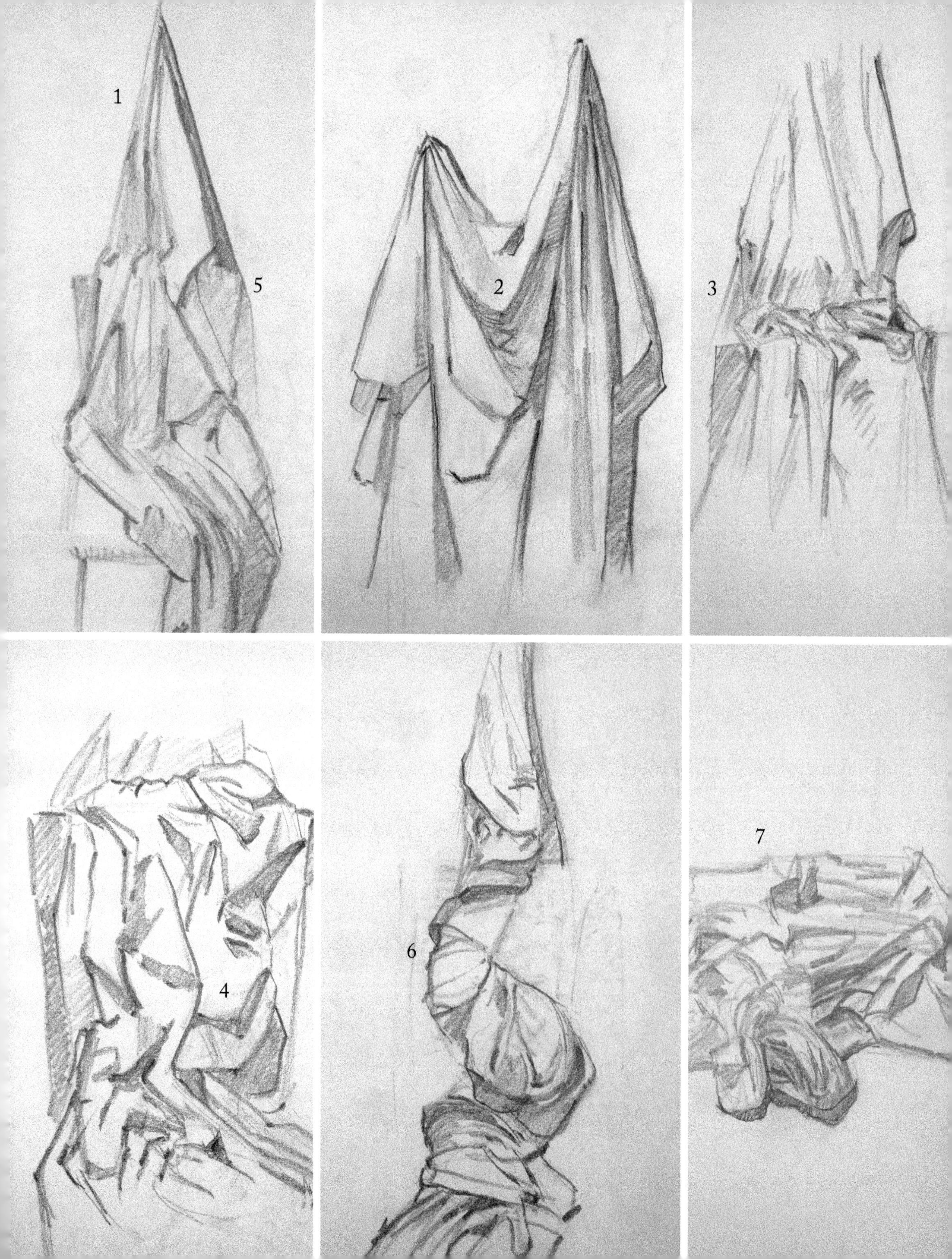

1
5
2
3
4
6
7

THE SEVEN FOLDS

Again, it is important to know the different types of folds in order to better anticipate where they will occur. The seven types of folds are listed below. Most of them are built off of the basic pipe fold. All are subject to gravity and have unique properties.

1. **Pipe Fold.** This fold has one point of support. The fold lines stem from the point of tension and create folds that look like pipes.

2. **Diaper Fold.** This fold hangs between two points of support. An example would be a cape that is draped around the shoulders and hangs a little lower in the back. Miniature pipe folds occur near the points of tension, and the diaper fold is what hangs in the center connecting the two.

3. **Half-Lock Fold.** This fold happens when the form underneath the material is bent, like at the elbow or the knee. The point of tension is where the bend happens, and the fold marks stem from there.

4. **Zig-Zag Fold.** This is a more inactive fold that often appears *after* a half-lock fold has occurred. A zig-zag pattern of folds is created, like when someone straightens his or her arm after having it bent at the elbow.

5. **Drop Fold.** This fold is very similar to the basic pipe fold, although instead of falling straight down, it cascades onto another form jutting out underneath as it goes down. It does not pick up slack like the diaper fold, however. Imagine a waterfall. An example of a drop fold might be a woman wearing a skirt. The skirt drops from the waist, flows down onto her bent knee, and falls to the floor.

6. **Spiral Fold.** This fold is fairly self-explanatory. It twists and spirals. This happens frequently along the sleeves of a shirt or can just be a single piece of fabric twisted on its own.

7. **Inert Fold.** This is an inactive fold. It usually happens when there is a lot of extra fabric, like at the bottom of a dress, or it could simply be a piece of cloth lying on the floor. Inert folds are usually horizontal in nature and often are made up of a combination of several different types of folds.

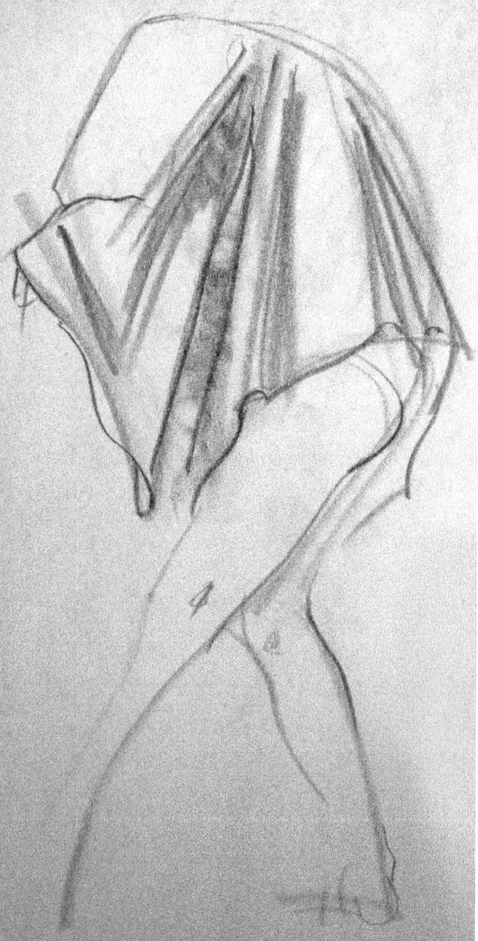

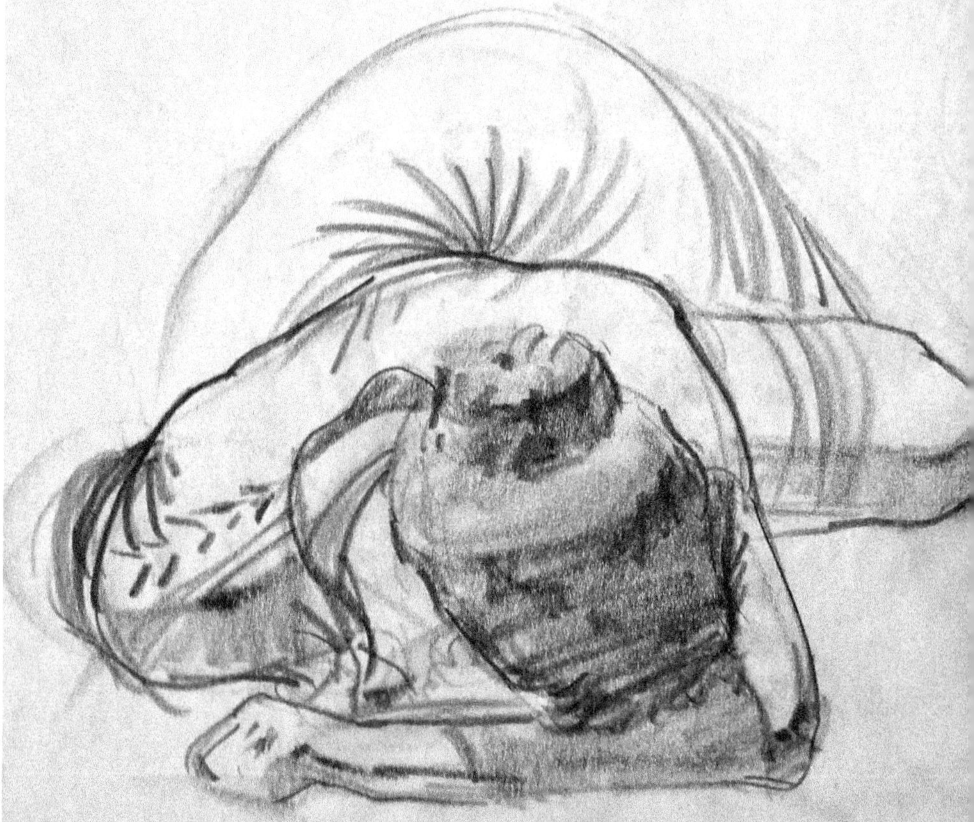

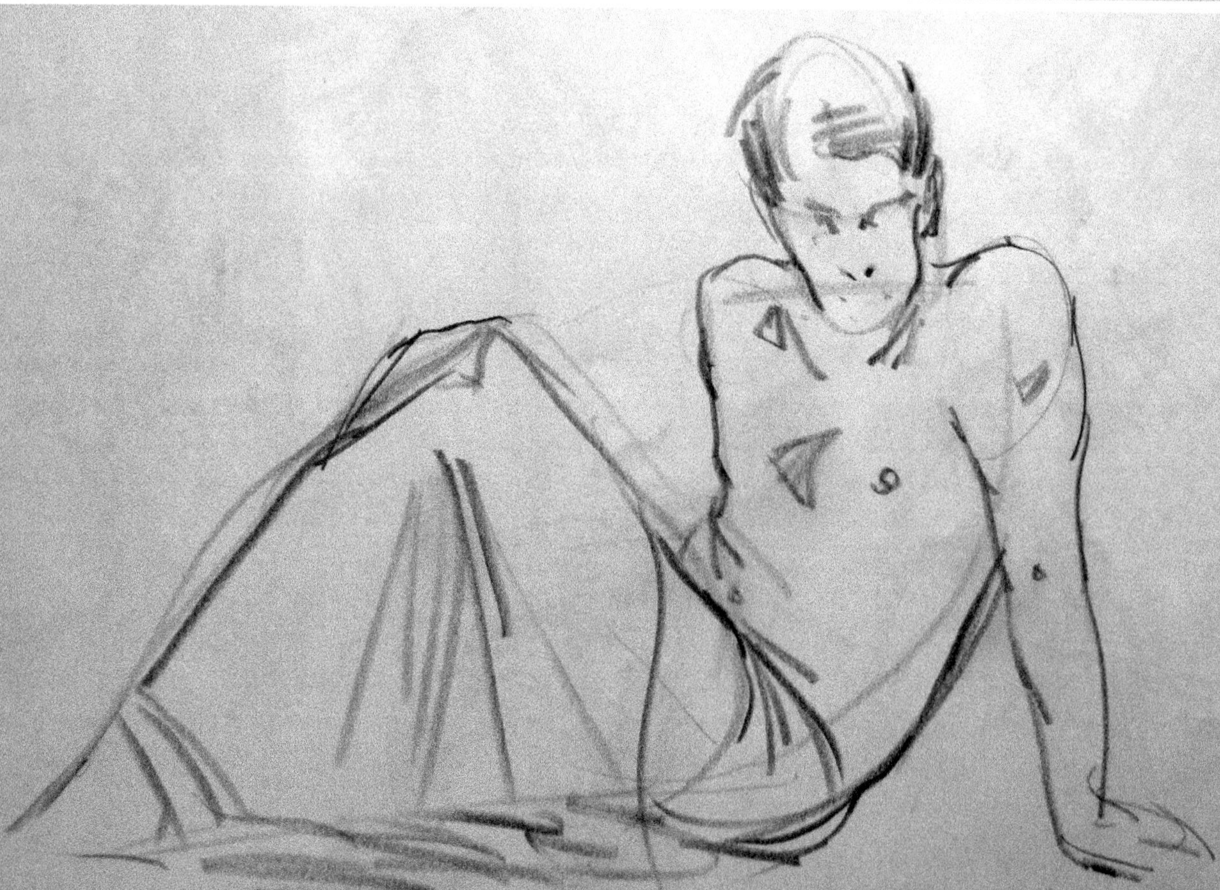

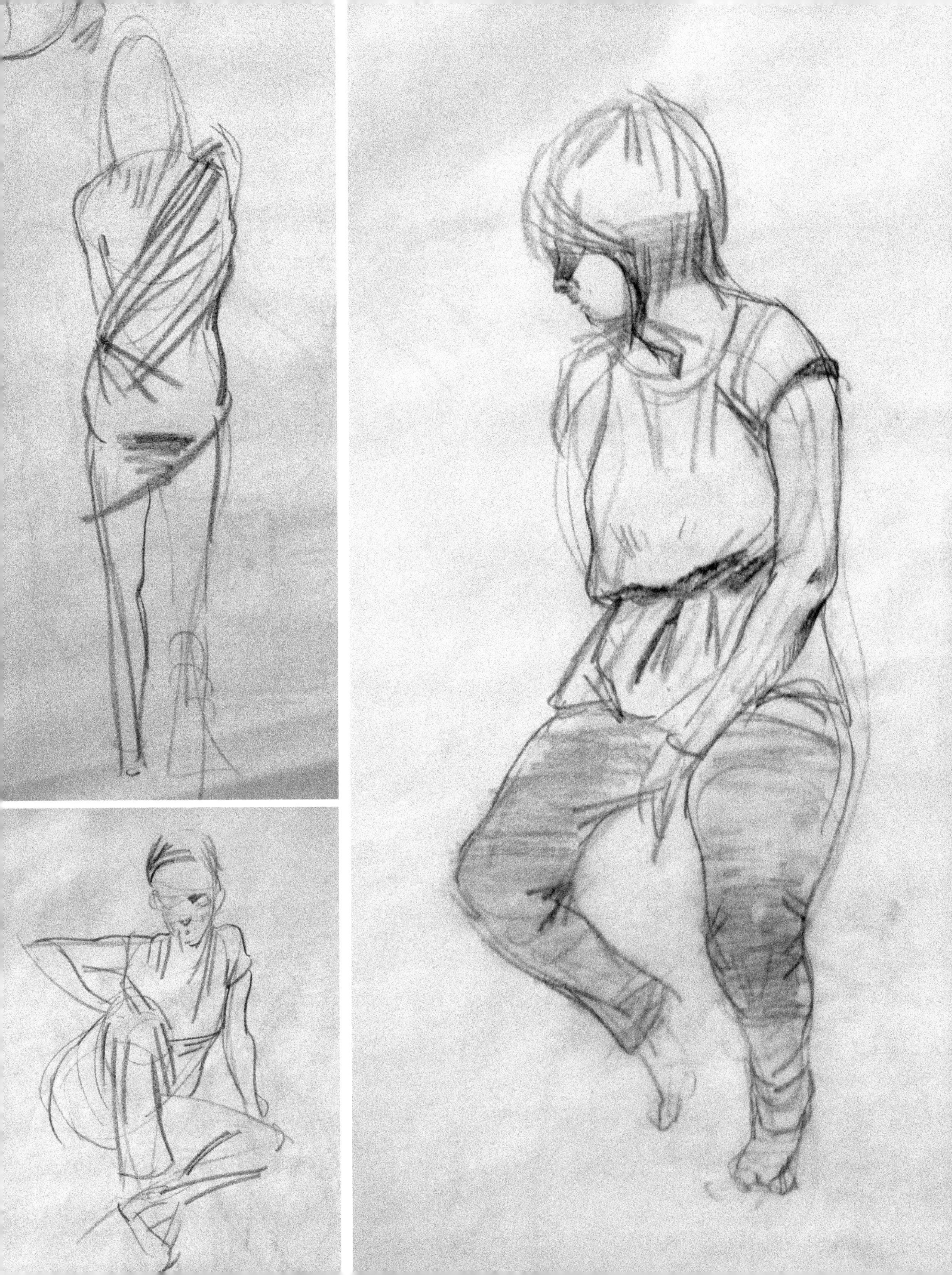

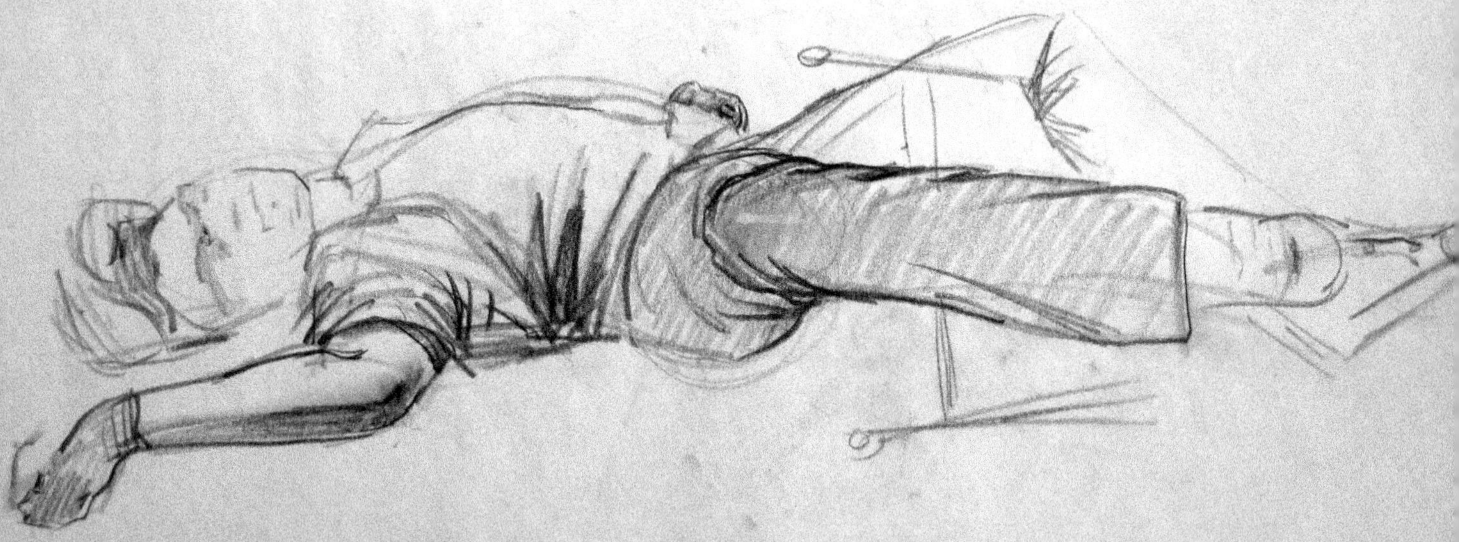

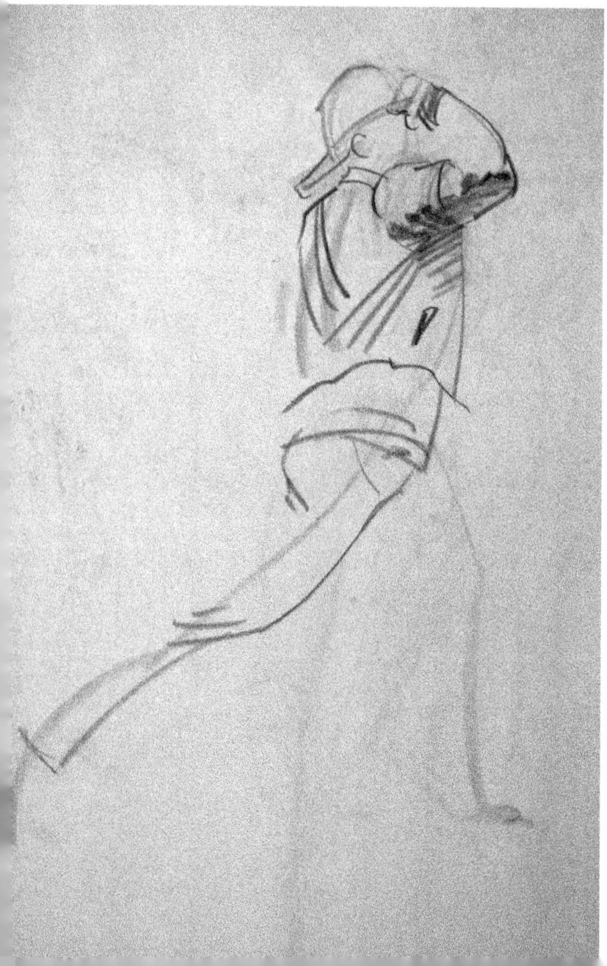

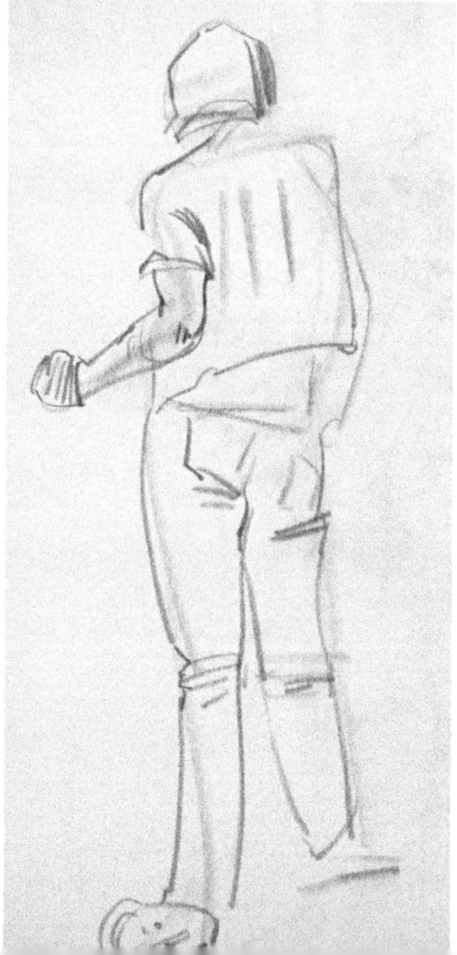

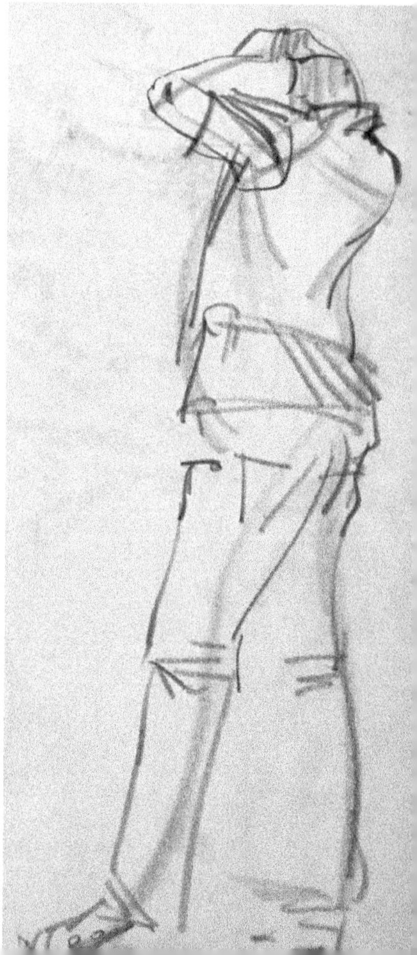

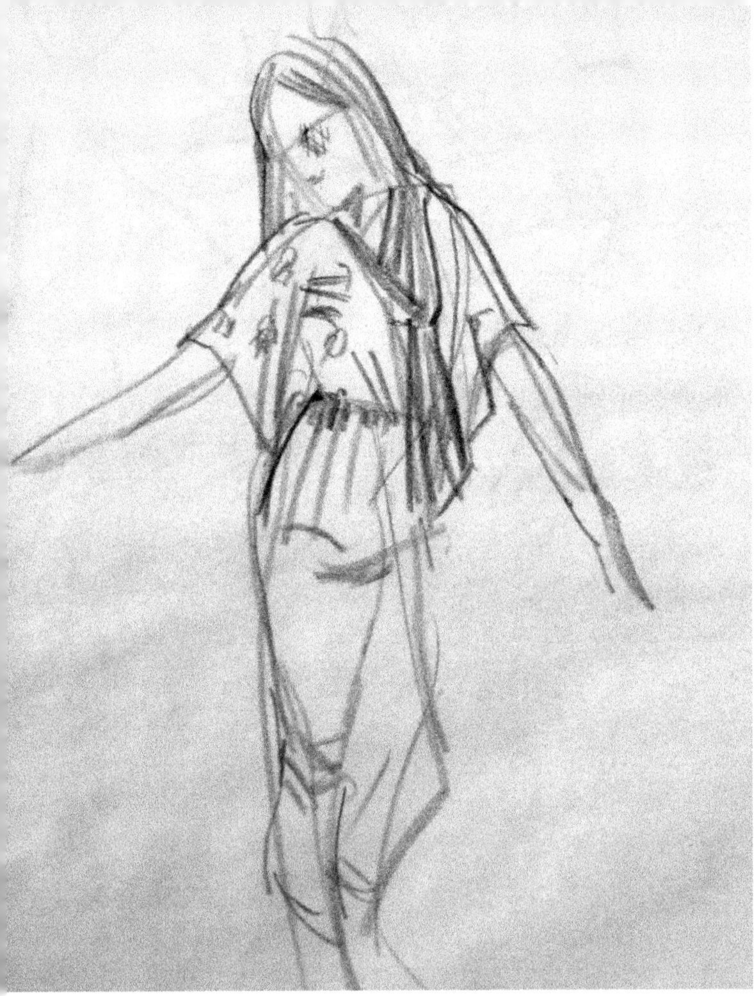

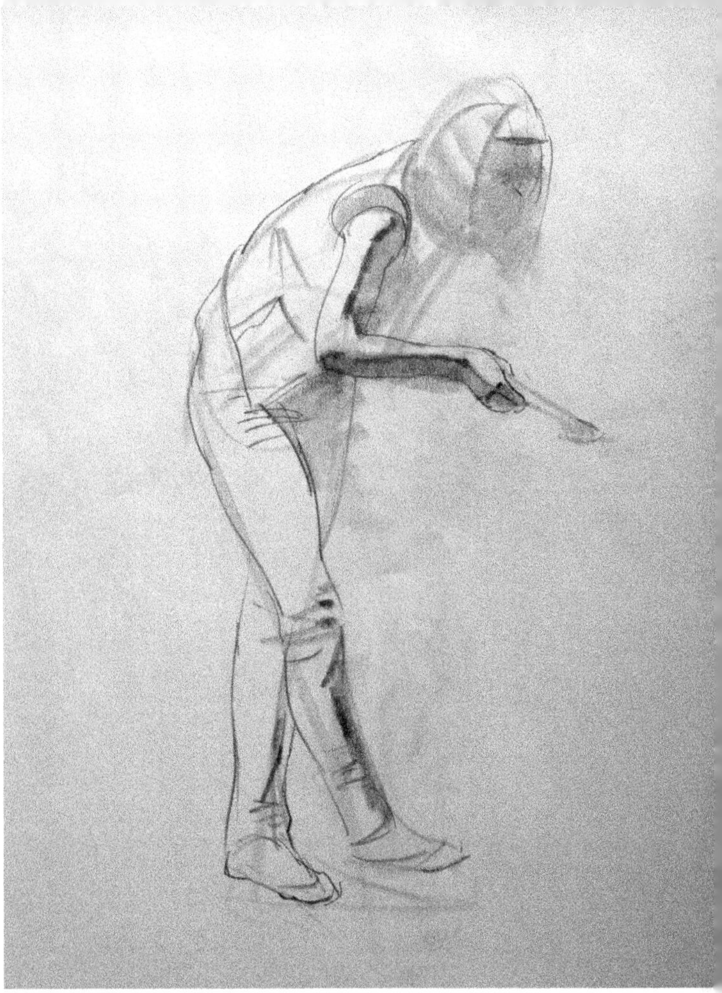

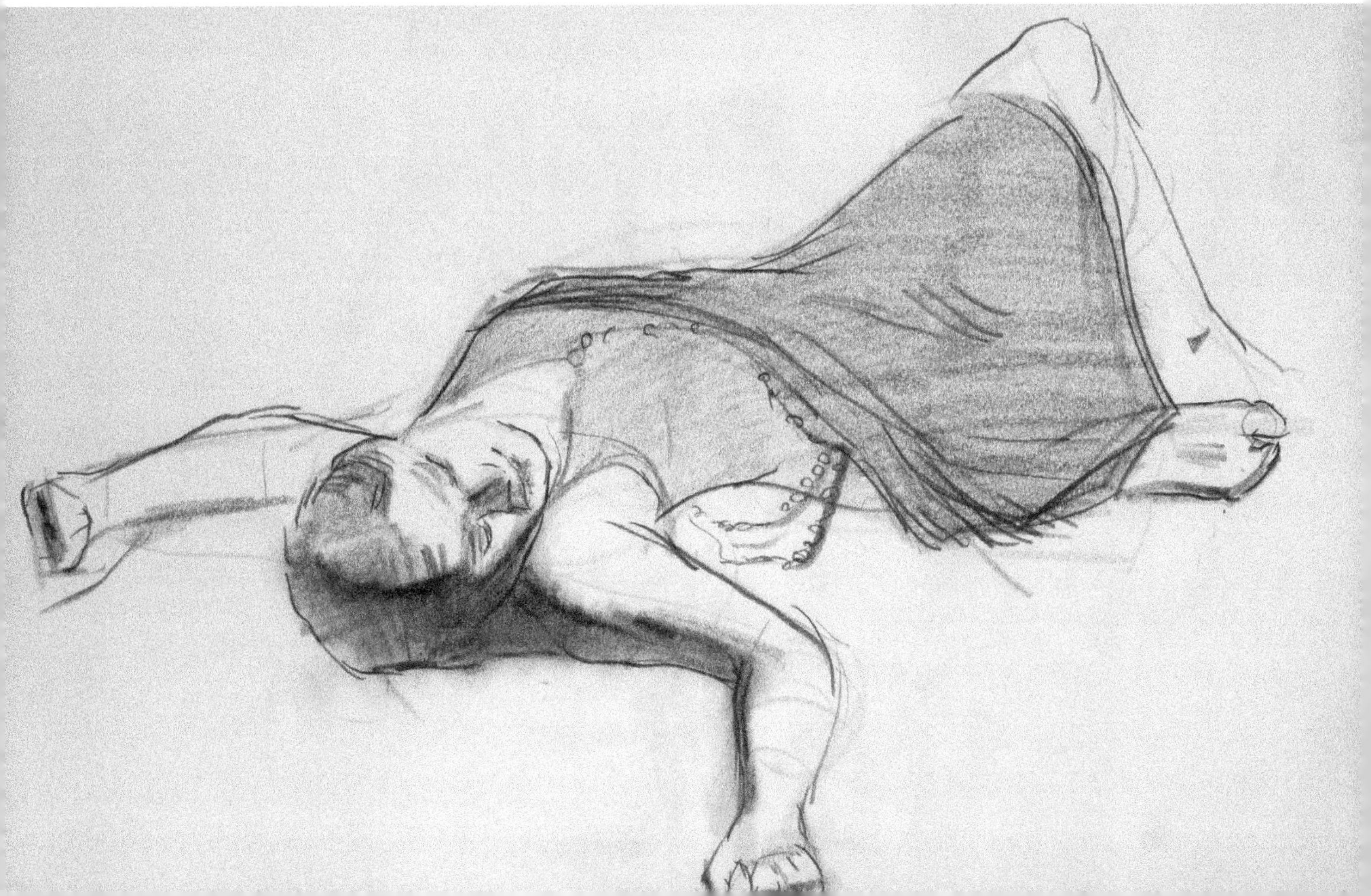

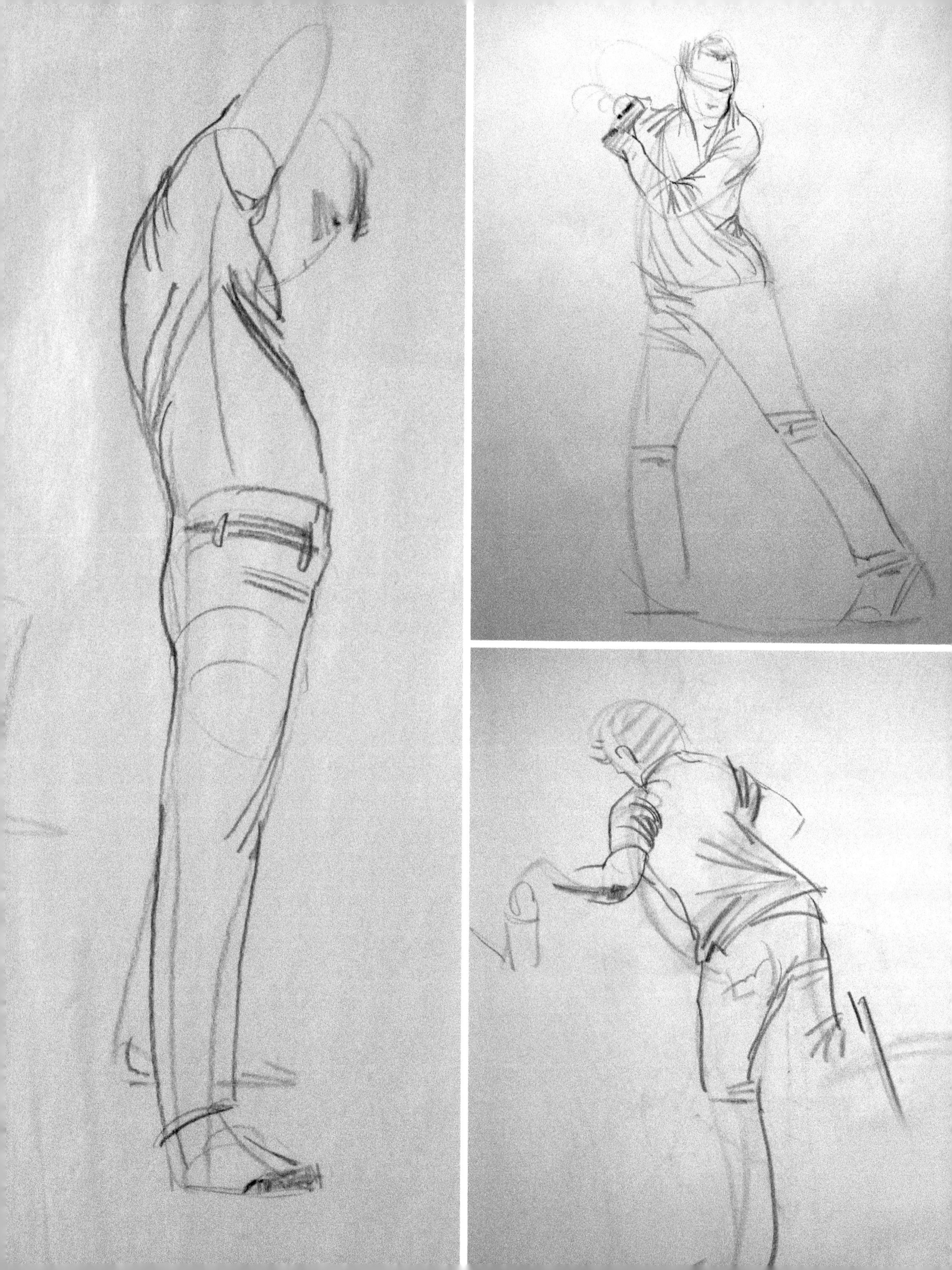

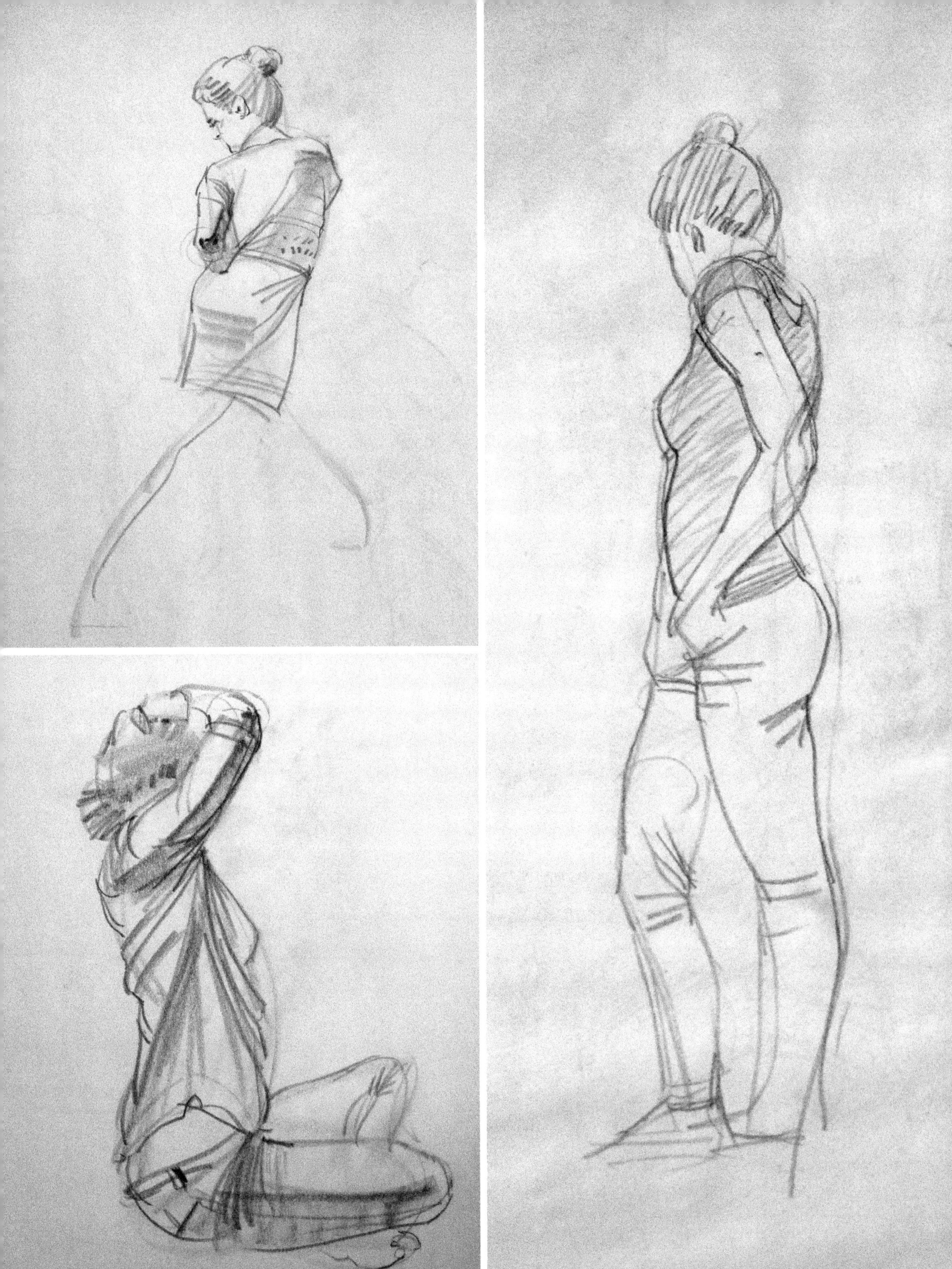

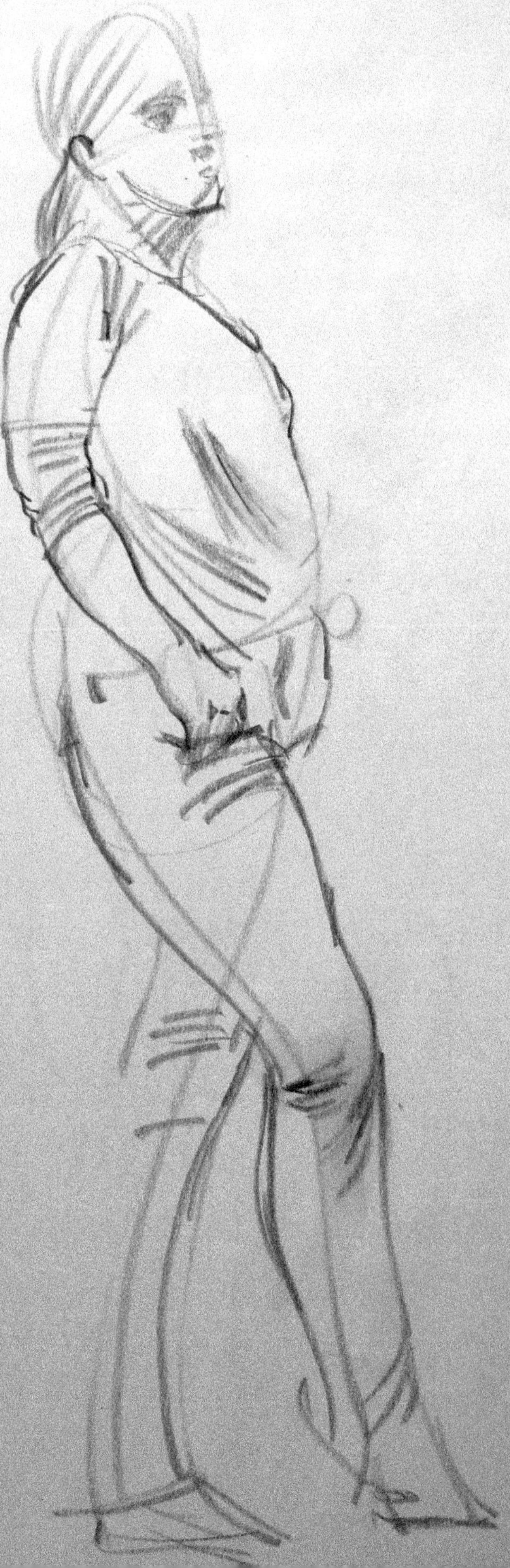

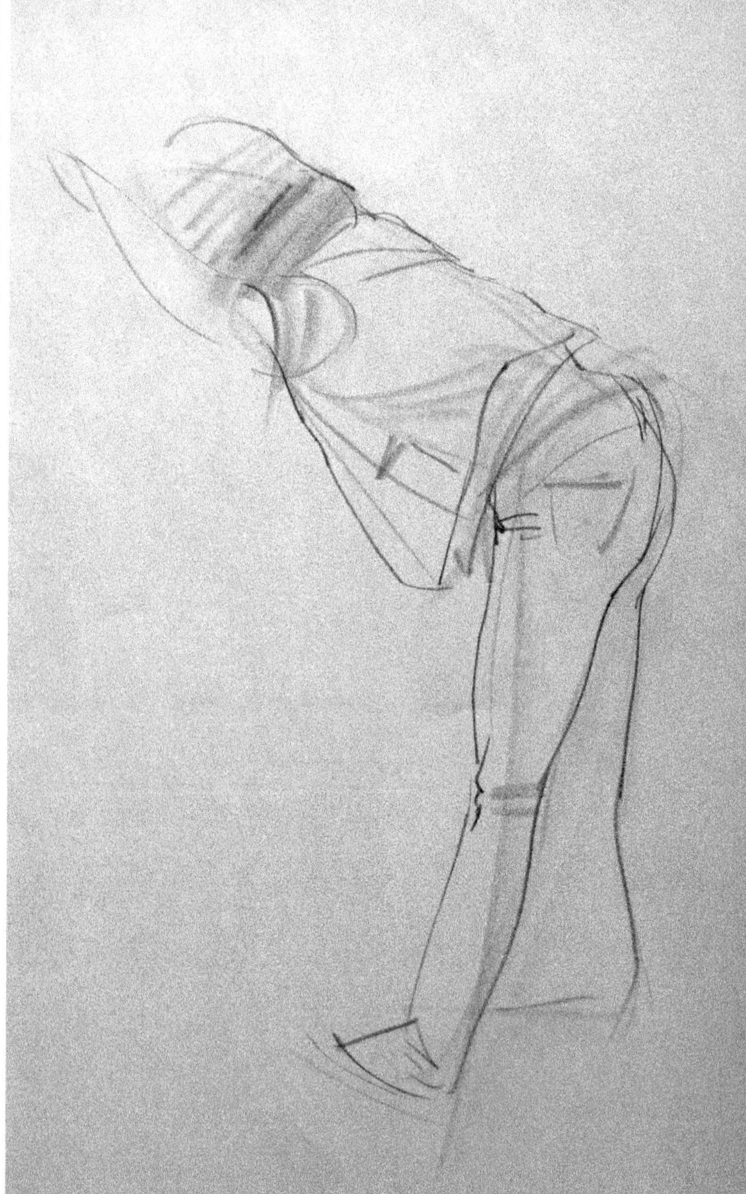
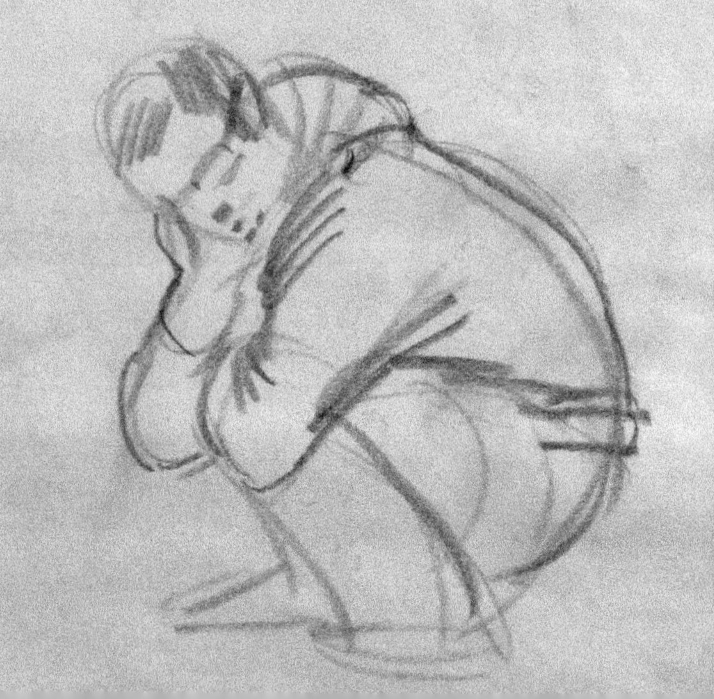

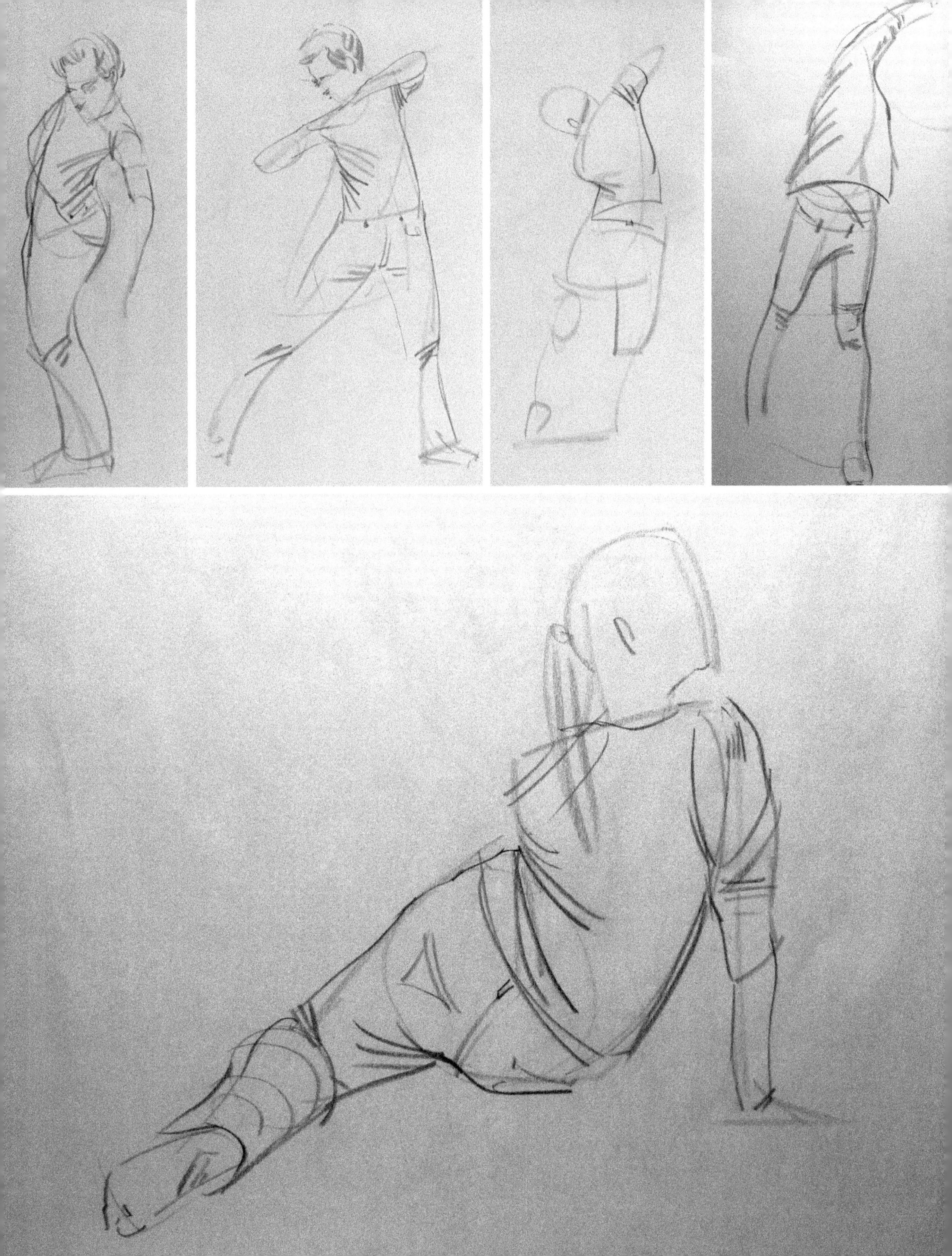

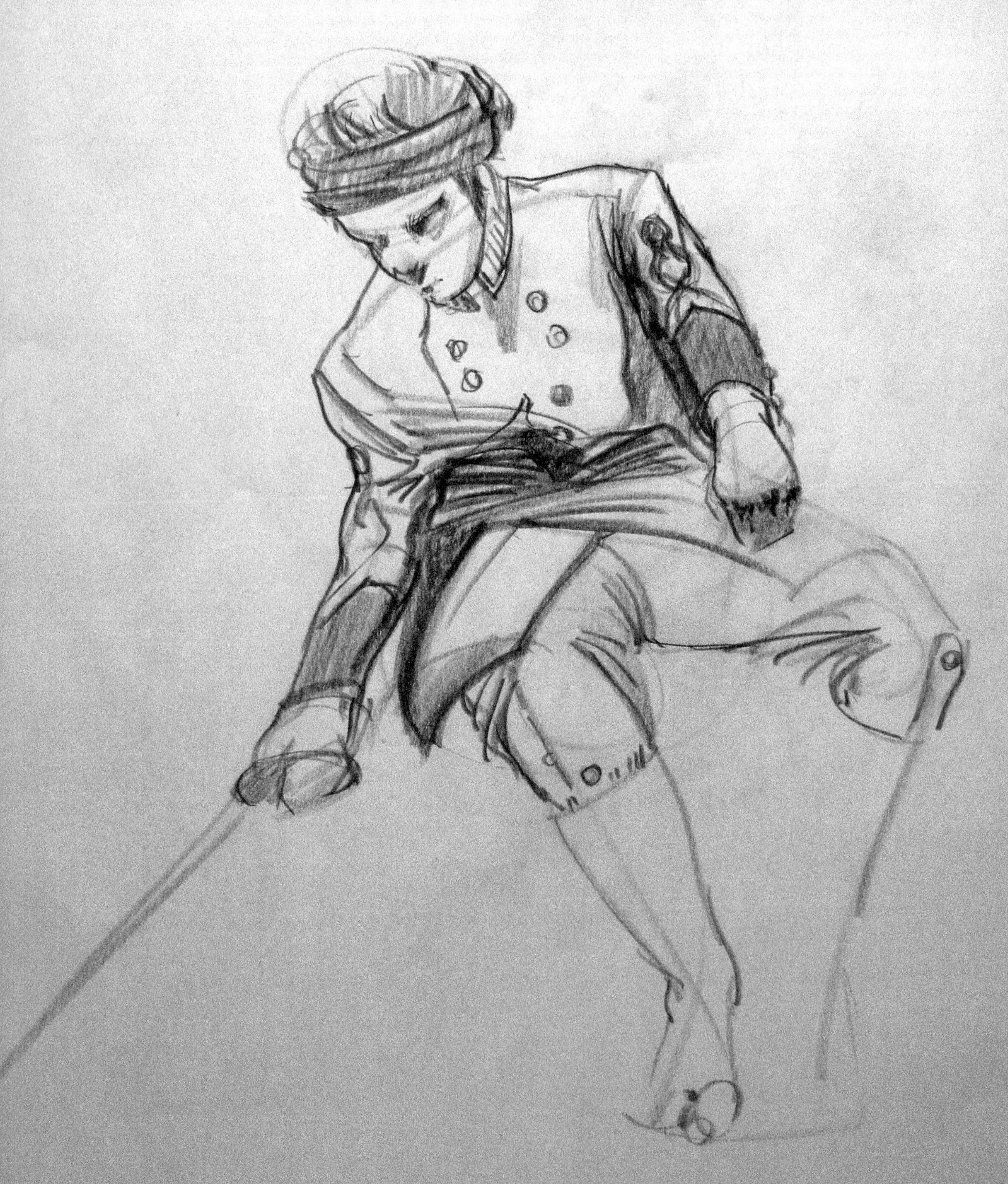

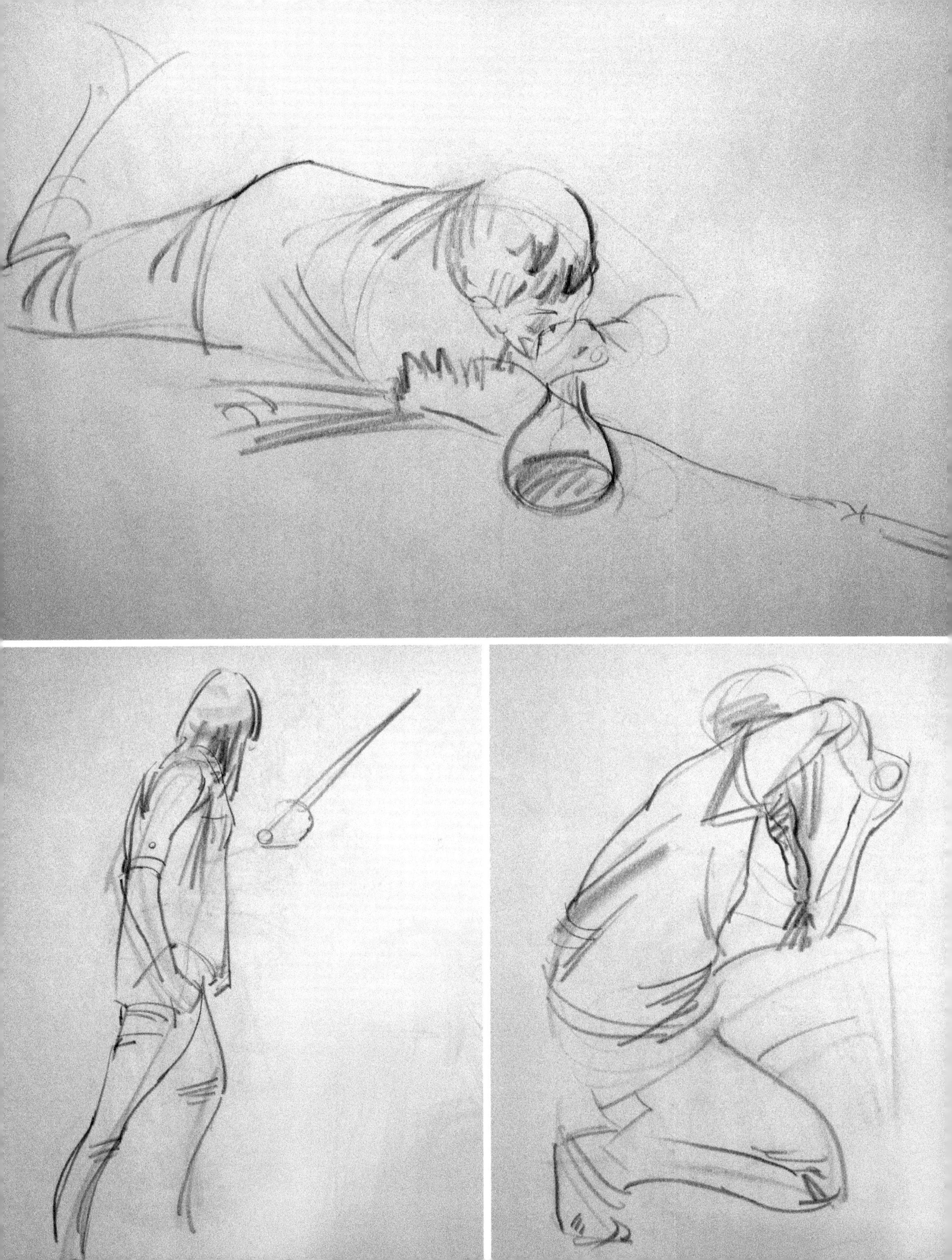

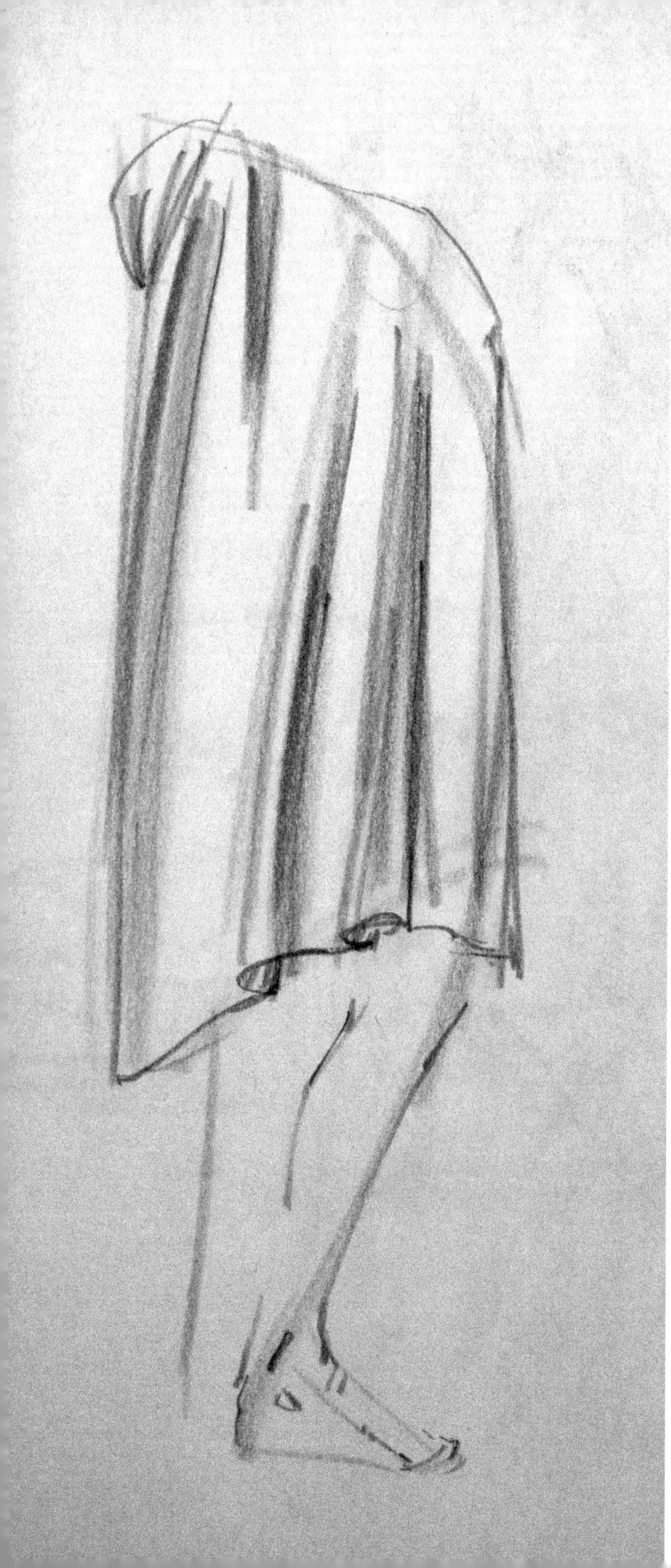

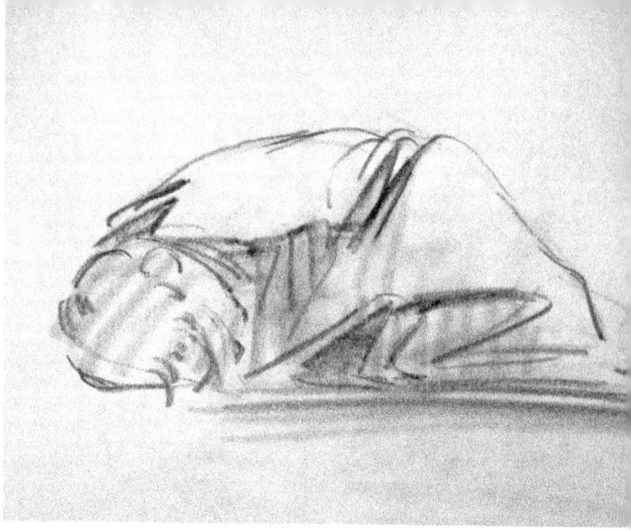

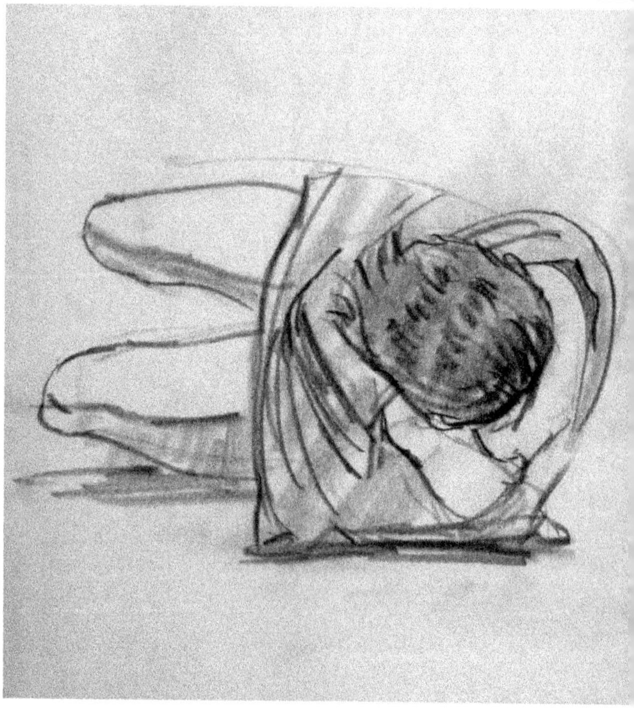

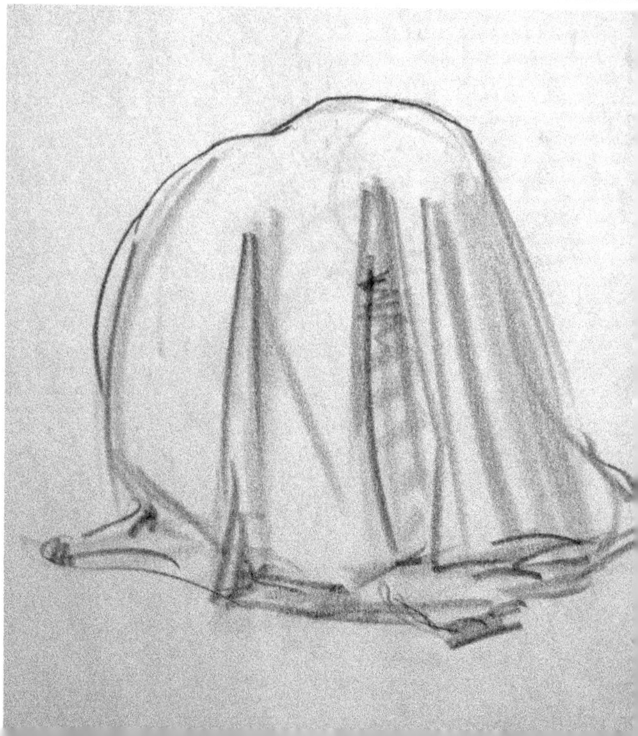

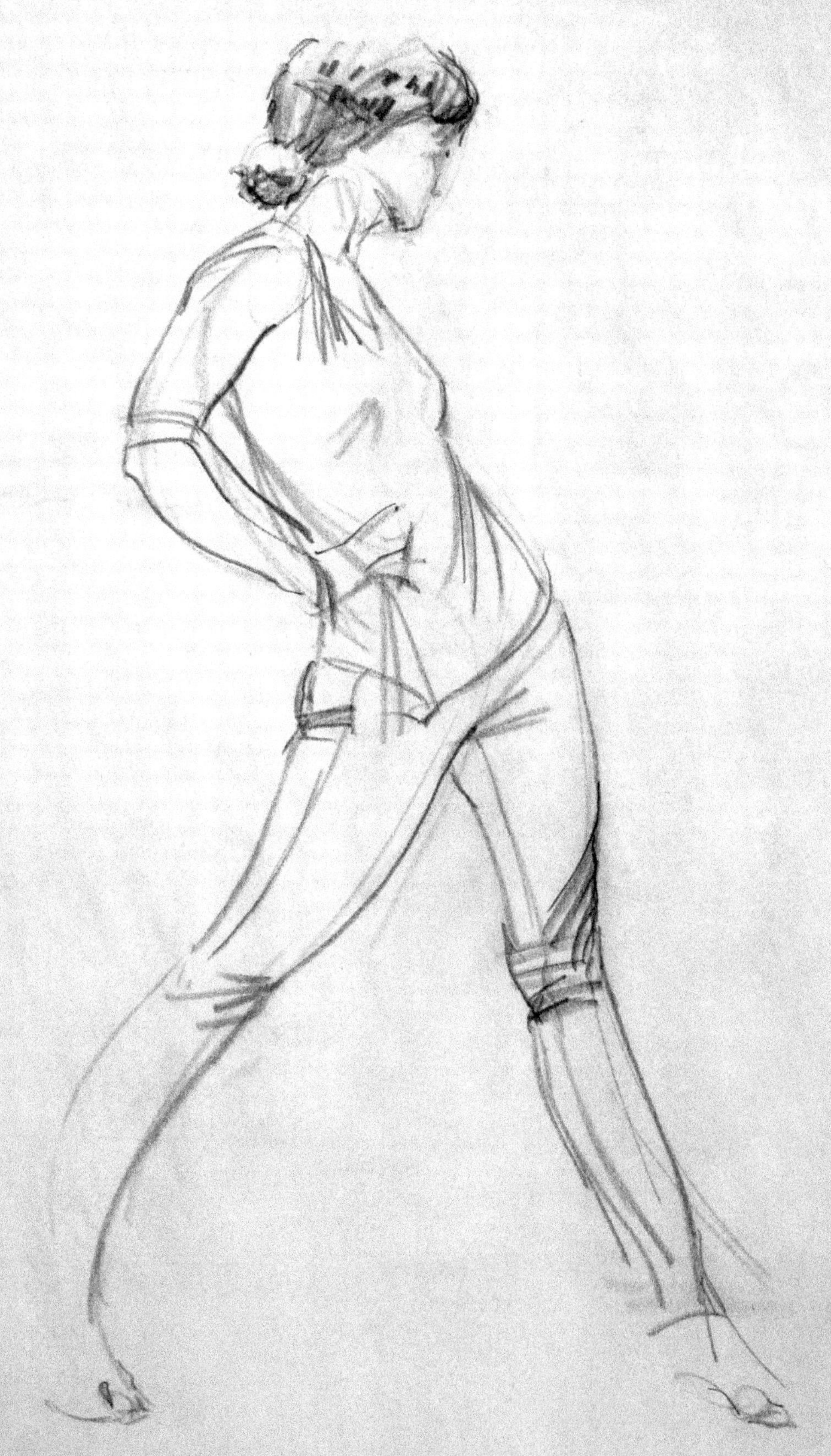

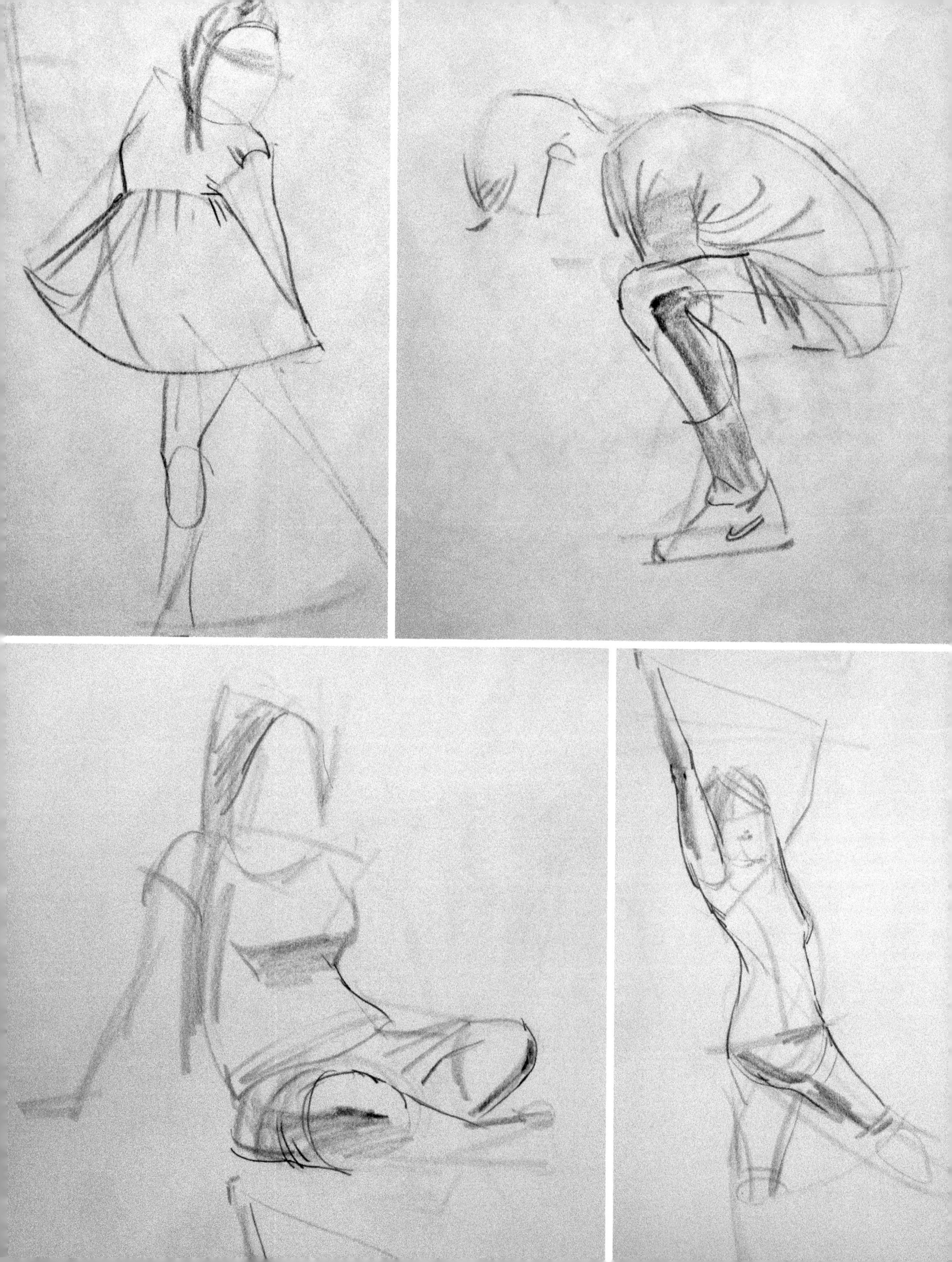

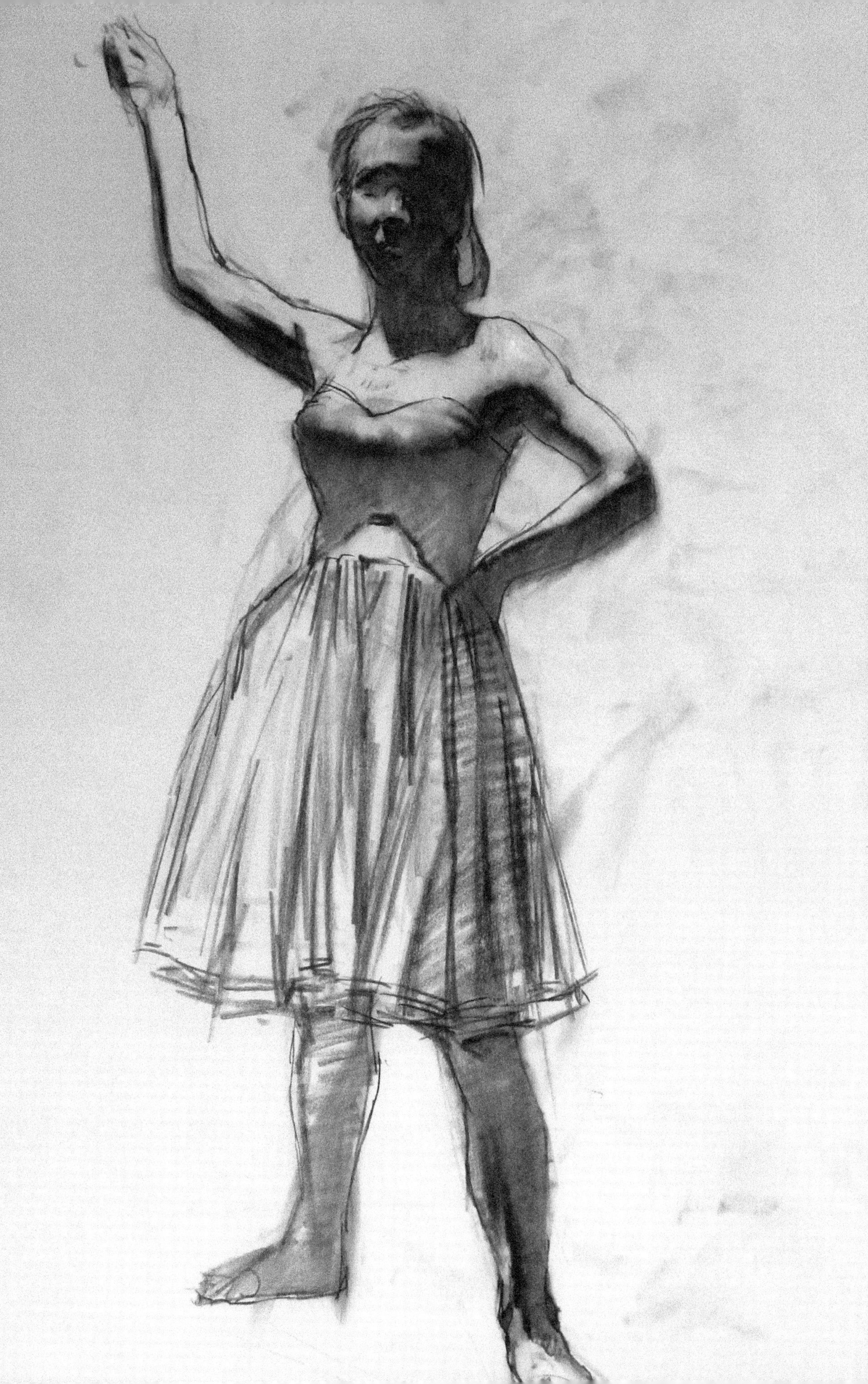

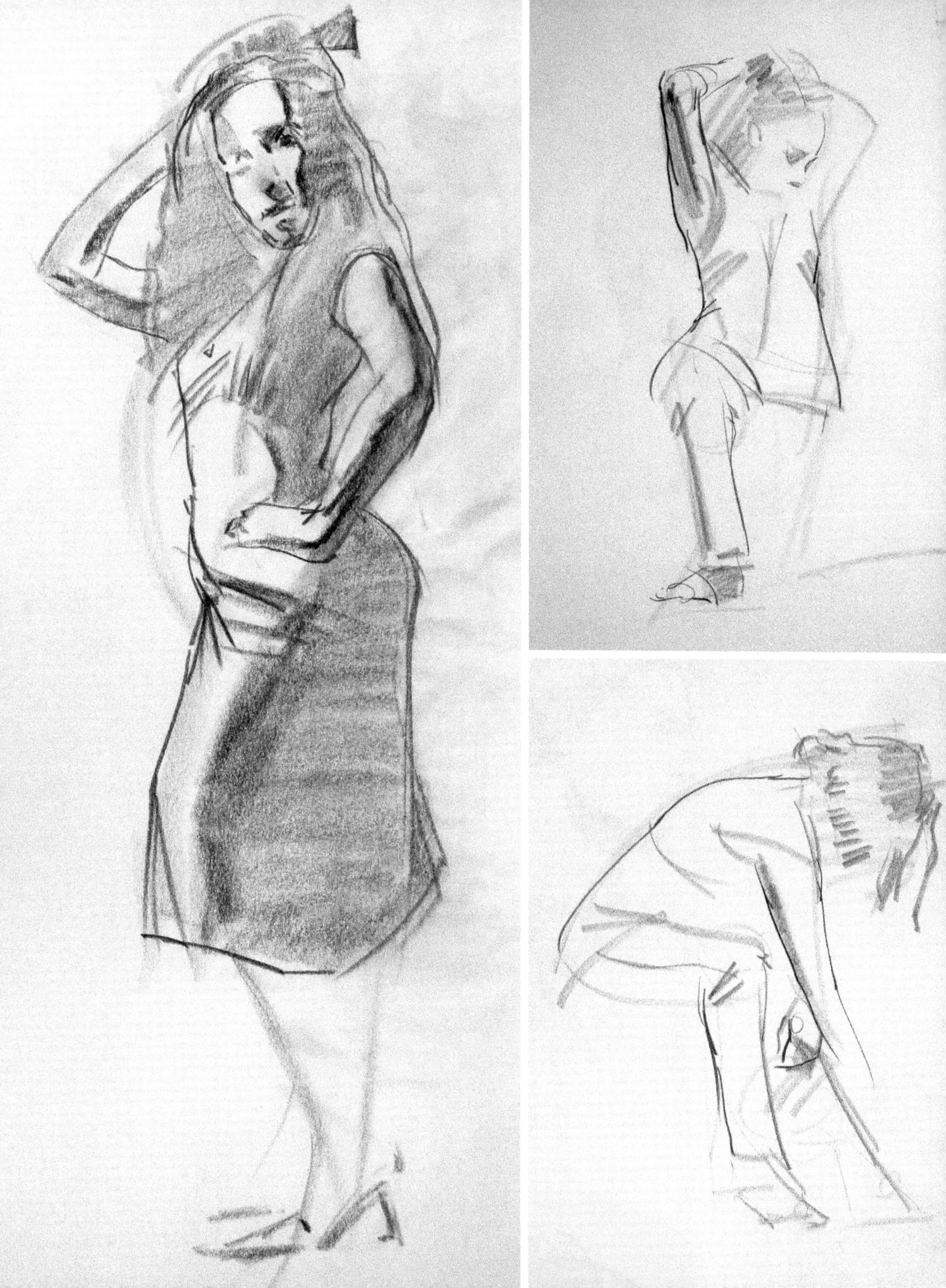

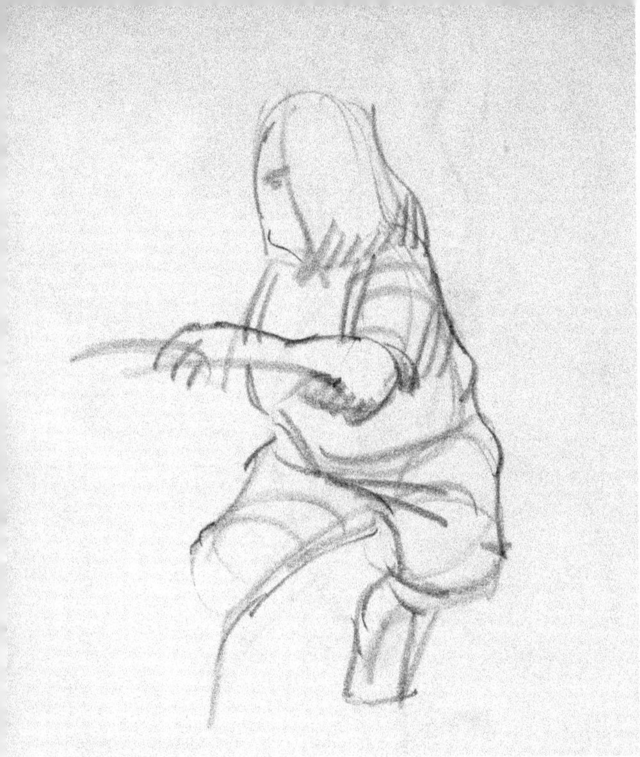

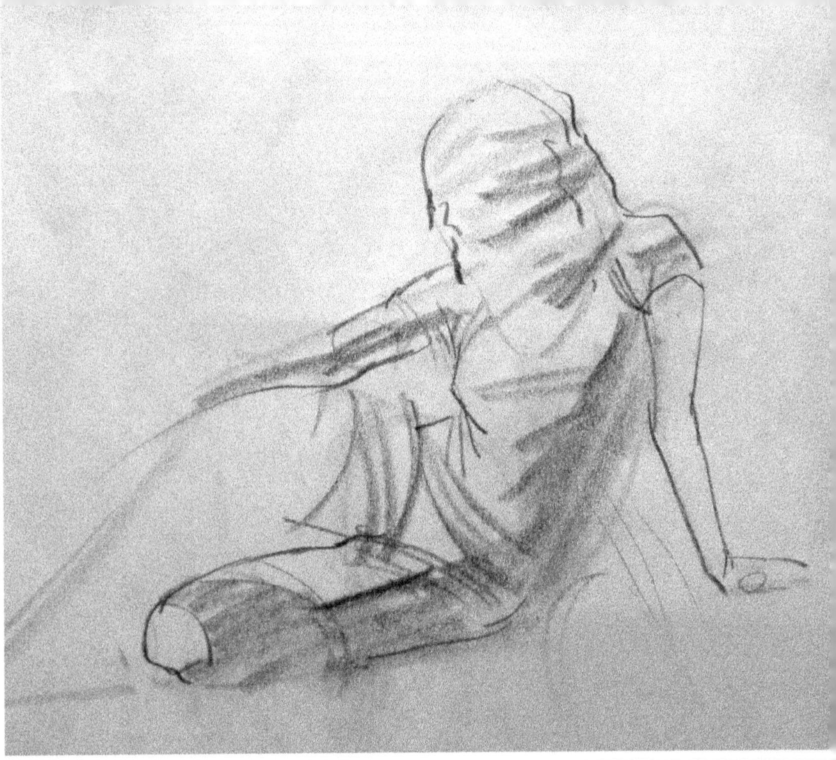

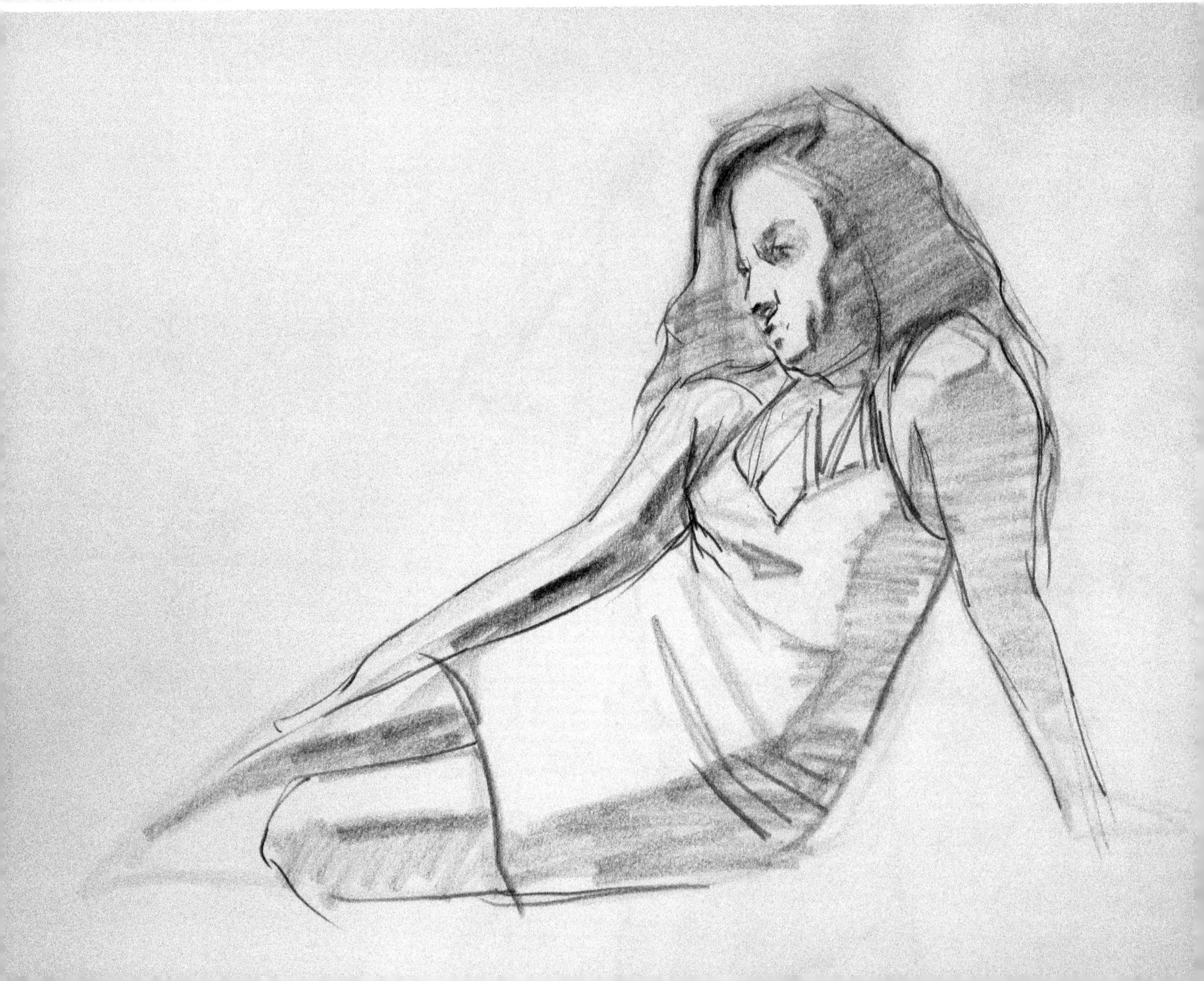

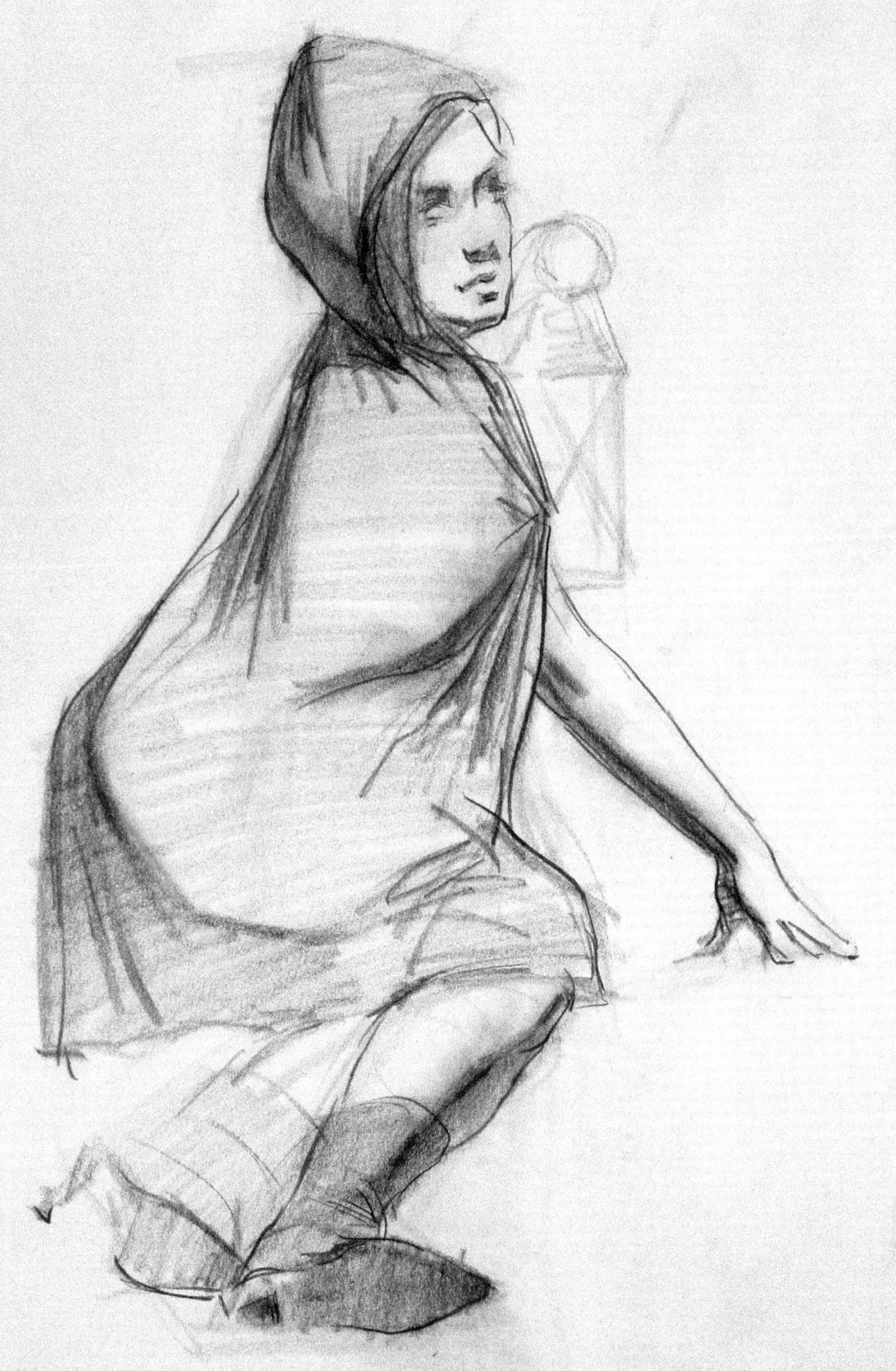

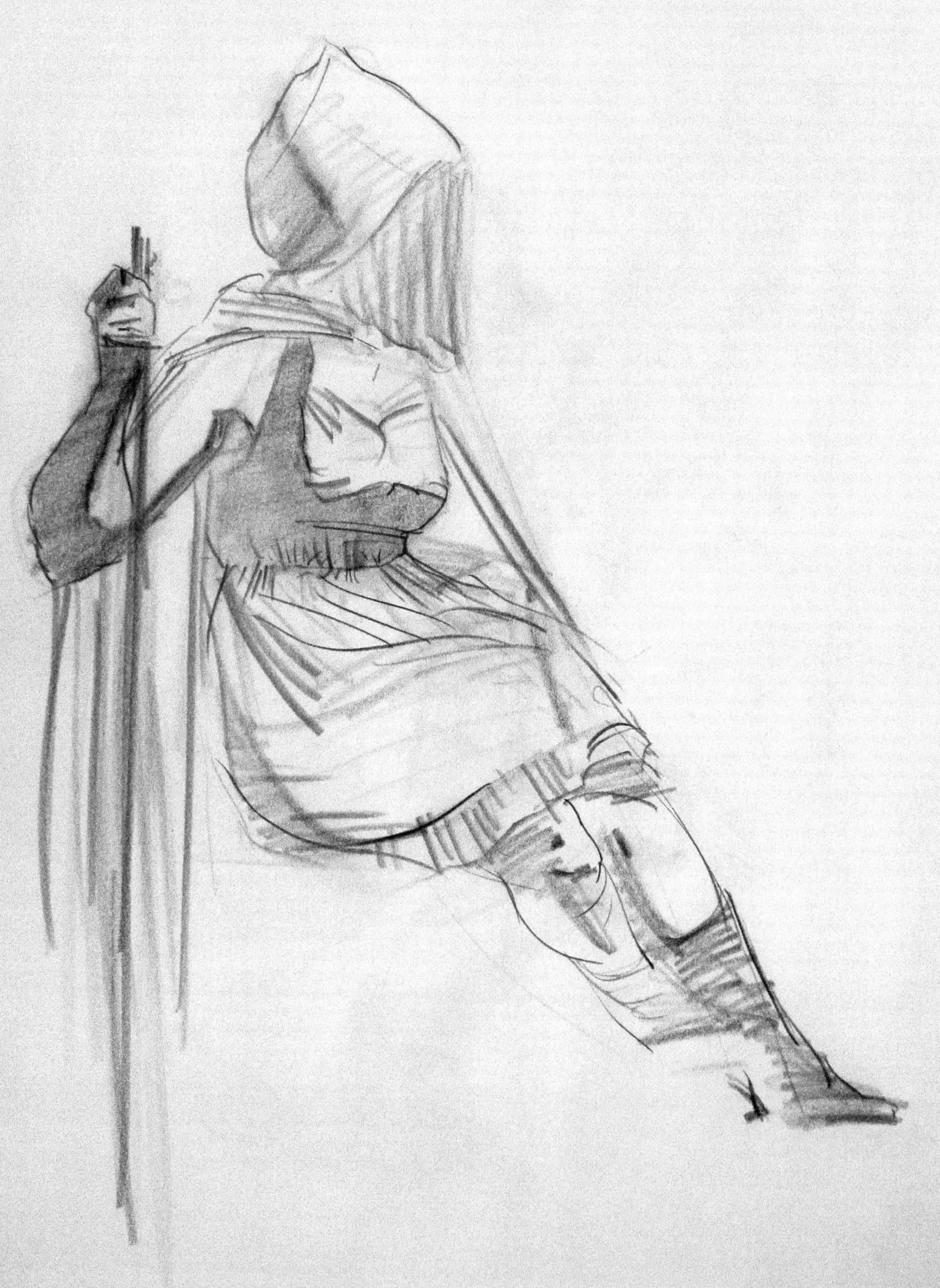

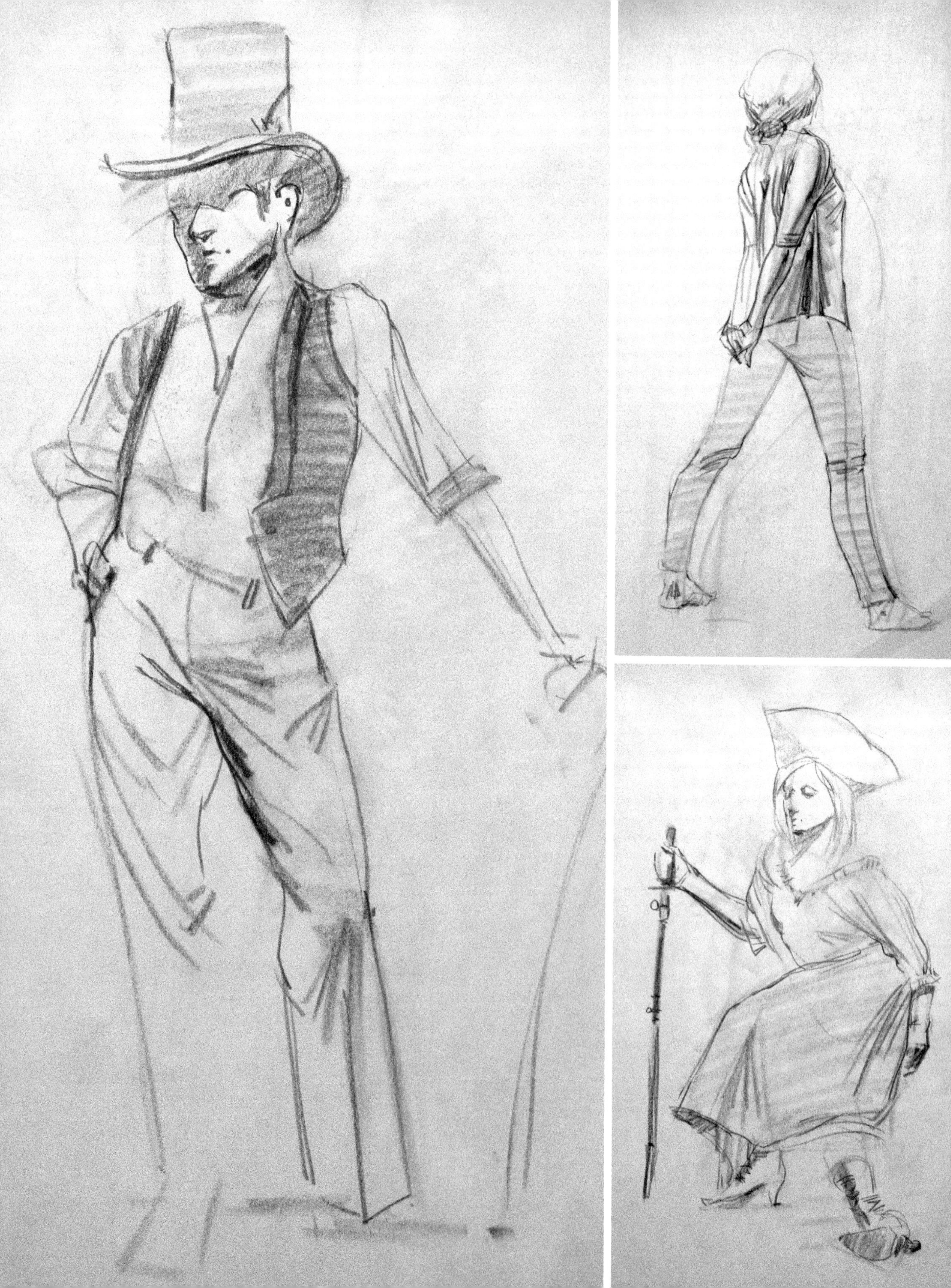

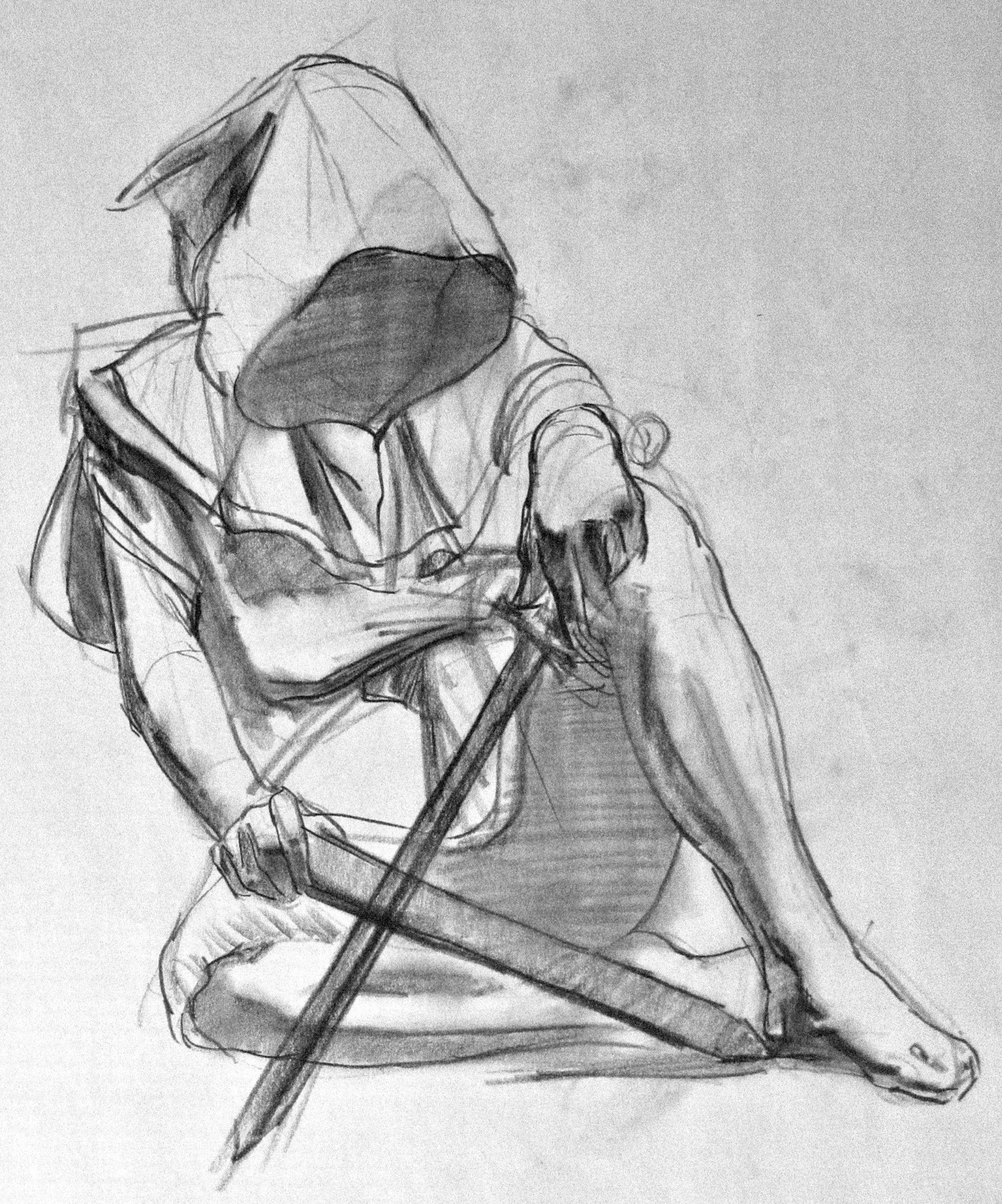

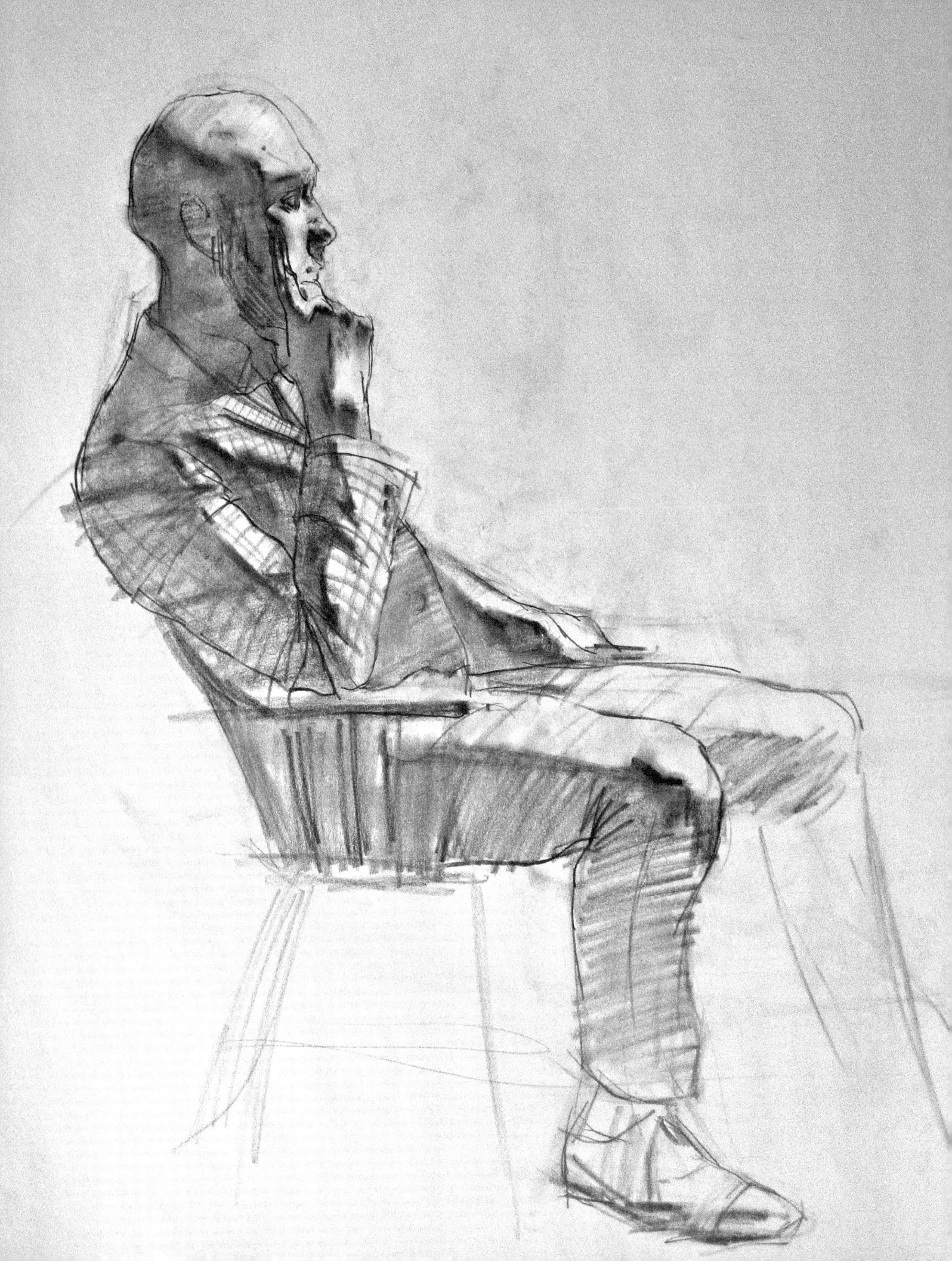

FINAL THOUGHTS

FINAL THOUGHTS

Figure drawing is definitely not as relaxing as one might think. It is actually a very brain-intensive activity. I know that when I am well rested and mentally prepared, my drawings are more successful. I see this in my students too. Those who are rushing to get to class and realize they don't have the proper materials, or are preoccupied in thinking about homework for other classes, do not see nearly the same amount of improvement as their classmates who are willing to learn and are prepared to take it all in when class begins.

INTENT

When I have a specific intent or purpose for being in a drawing session, I have found that figure drawing is much more rewarding. My drawing sessions are more productive and successful when I am specifically focused on improving an aspect of my technique (i.e. Weight & Balance, Symmetry, Light & Shadow, or some other topic addressed in this text). Sherrie McGraw, a well-respected draughtsman and painter, often uses a juggling analogy that I like to describe what artists may be feeling. In the beginning, we start out juggling with a couple of balls. Soon we add another and another and another. Inevitably we drop one here and there, but we try to keep going as best we can. Eventually we get pretty good at juggling more and more balls at once. With drawing, there are several things to think about simultaneously, especially when given a limited amount of time. But, the more you practice, the better you will become. Give yourself a chance to improve. Get yourself in front of a model and draw.

UNDERSTANDING

I believe drawing reveals the artist's understanding of the figure. I tell my students it is more important to understand the figure than to try to get an exact copy of it. I found in my own study that when I sought to understand the human figure and how to draw this three-dimensional being onto a two-dimensional surface, I saw improvement. My drawings felt stable and had more integrity. I began to see great improvement in my sketchbook as well when I took on this new mindset. Soon, I found I could draw believable figures from my head, whereas before, I was always so dependent on having an ideally lit model in front of me. As I drew more and more, I realized I was researching, and I was excited about building my personal reference bank each time I was exposed to a new pose.

LIFE LESSONS

I always encourage my students to draw as much as they can. Surprisingly, there are life lessons to learn along the way. As I draw and study the human figure, I often think of parallels and comparisons to my everyday life. For instance, the idea of deliberate mark making in figure drawing can be likened to the way we live our lives. Being deliberate and committed in this life will take someone much further than being hesitant or tentative. Just like in drawing, when an artist is unsure about making a certain line and holds back, the drawing lacks energy. There is no conviction. It is the same in our personal lives. When the artist commits, however, that vigor shows through. There is power in commitment. Do it with a surety, even if that surety is faith.

BALANCE

Balance is another parallel that can be applied in many aspects of both our lives and in drawing. It can be thought of in regards to the human body and how it is perfectly balanced. It is also present in our everyday lives as a healthy balance is crucial amidst work, play, and rest. A third and more subtle way in which balance is necessary is in the act of pursuing or practicing figure drawing itself. I believe people are given certain amounts of God-given artistic talent. Some are given more than others. That talent is what usually gets someone to take a drawing class in the beginning. From there, however, it is also about practice and hard work. The need for balance especially comes into play when faced with a quick pose, where the hope is for the drawing to look energetic, effortless, and flowing, yet accurate and representational of the model. While drawing, it is necessary to think about what you are doing, and yet let go just enough to allow that bit of intuition to kick in as well. That is when personal voice shows through. Stick with it. Constantly strive to understand and further comprehend the figure. I love figure drawing and find it to be absolutely rewarding. Yes, there are times break down will occur. Saddle up the drawing horse and try again.

Understand and try to accept that, interestingly, the mind's vision is usually at a level beyond the artist's physical capabilities to execute. Concepts and principles in drawing are often understood in your head, but then actually putting them into practice is a whole other story. It's frustrating, and it isn't easy, but keep on drawing. The more and more time spent figure drawing, the less and less those bad days will occur. There will still be difficult days and bad drawings; however, they will occur less often. Find joy in learning from the figure each session, and embrace the continual goal for understanding. This is when love for the activity grows, appreciation for the human figure expands, and your quality of work improves. Happy drawing!

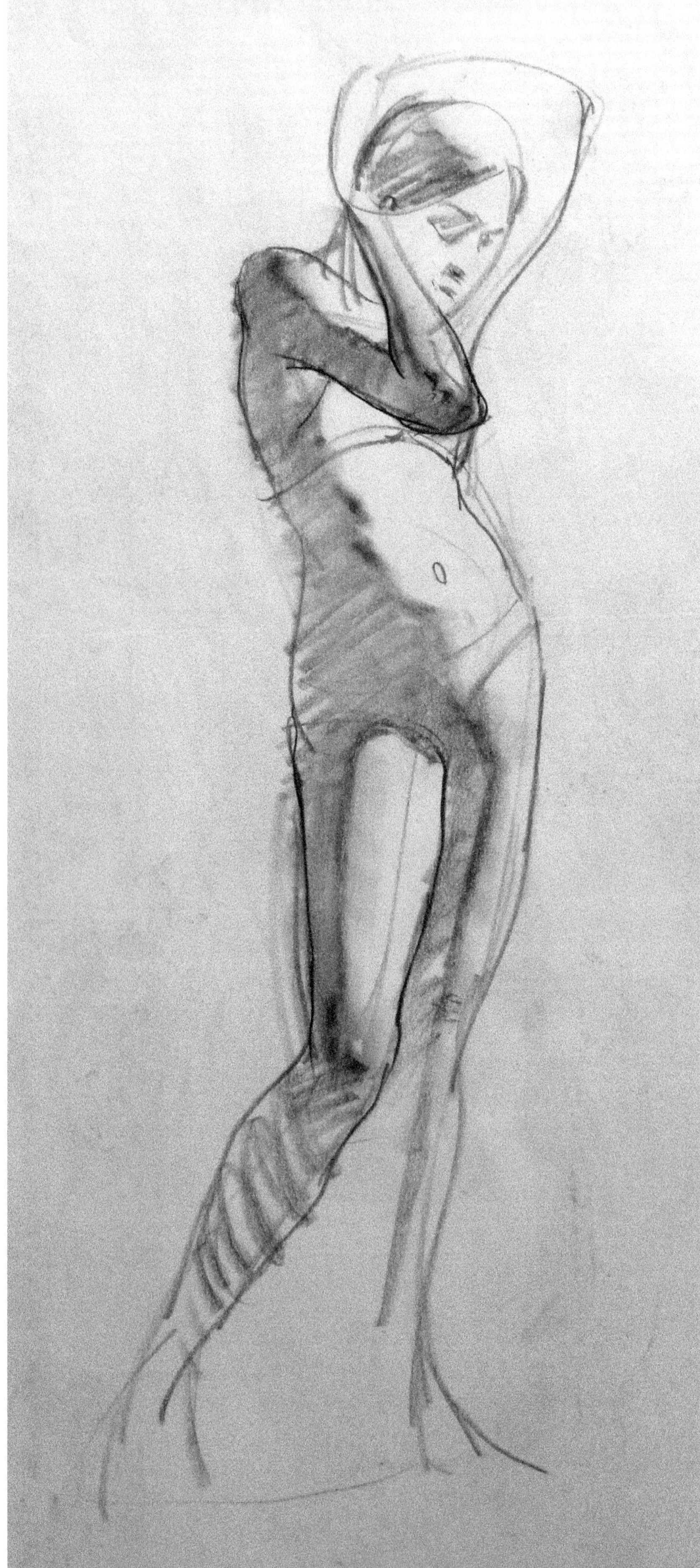

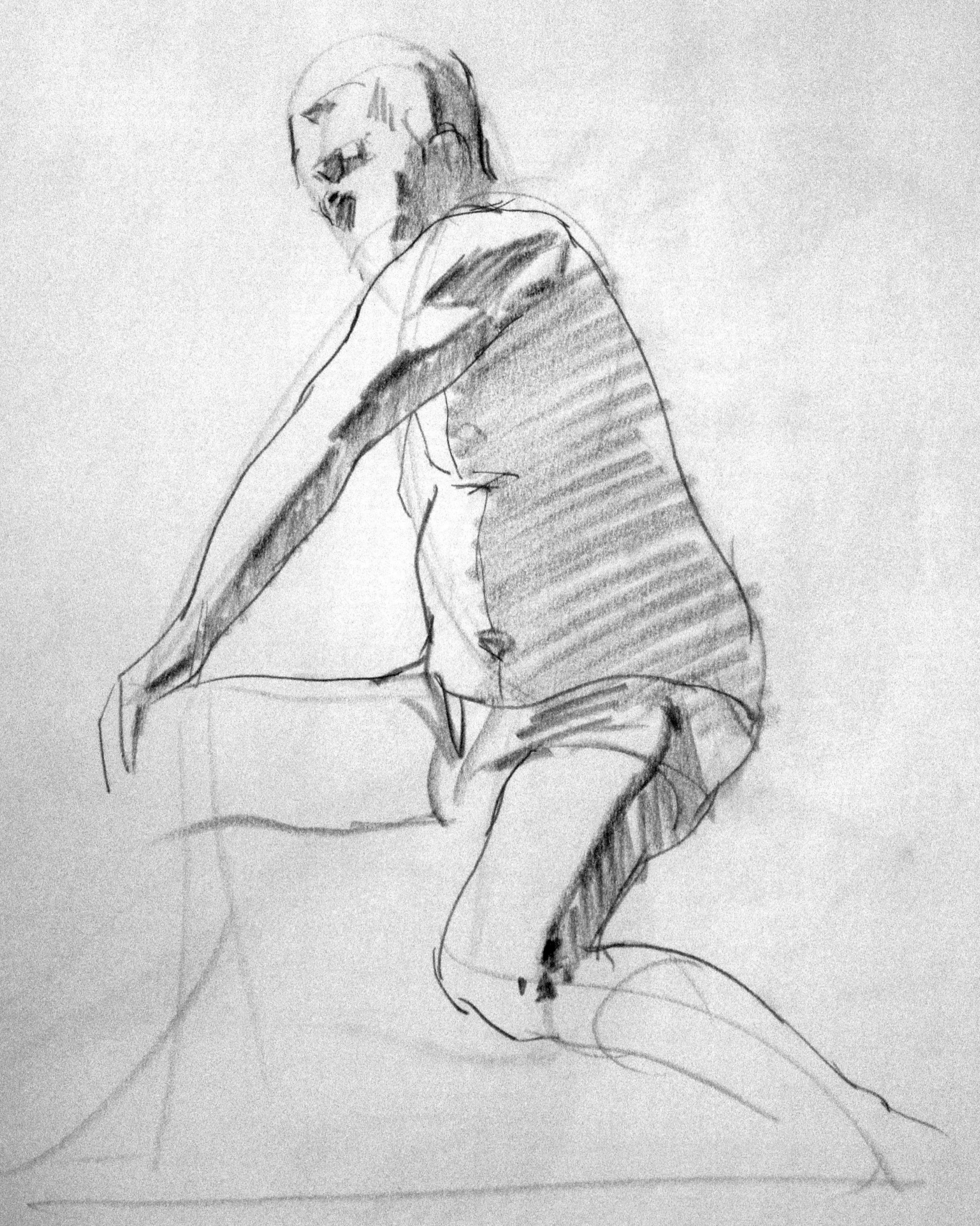

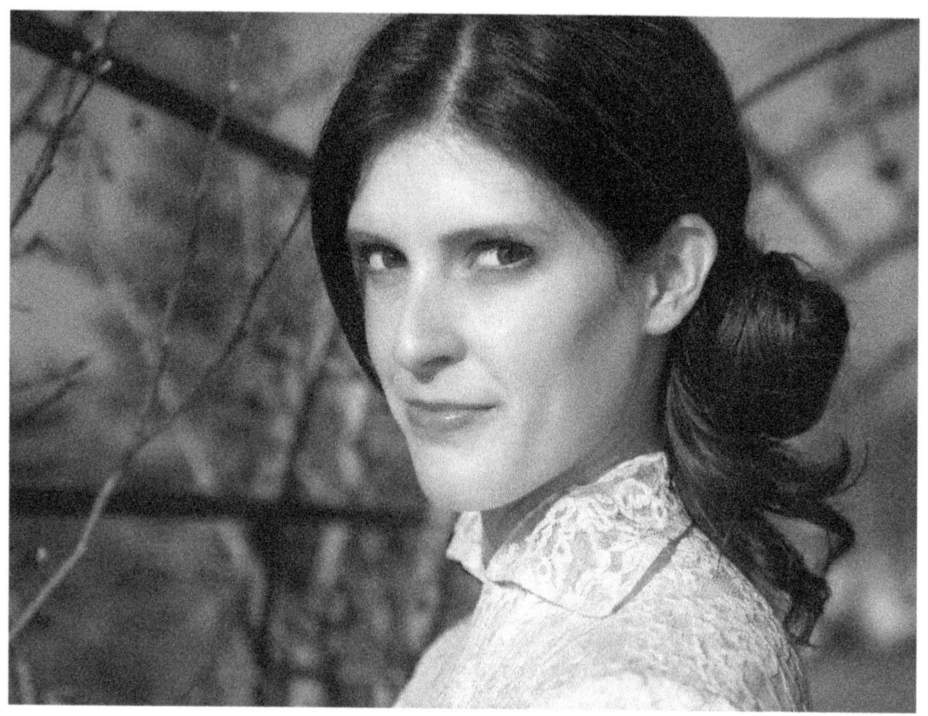

ABOUT THE AUTHOR

Erin was always interested in the arts as a child and in her youth, but it was not until college that she took an actual drawing class. She attended Dixie State College in St. George, Utah, where Del Parson introduced her to figure drawing. She initially went to Dixie to play softball, but decided to pursue art instead. She transferred to Brigham Young University in Provo, Utah, and completed a Bachelor of Fine Arts degree in Illustration. While there, she worked as a teaching assistant under area head Robert Barrett, and greatly valued the knowledge she gained as both his student and teaching assistant. While finishing her degree, she studied with William Whitaker at his home studio close to campus. After college, Erin and her husband moved around the United States for several years, where she was able to continue drawing and painting at a number of institutions including Zoll Studio School of Fine Art in Timonium, Maryland; The Art League in Alexandria, Virginia; The Art Students League of New York; and with Gregg Kreutz in his Manhattan studio. She has also studied with Sherrie McGraw at various workshop locations around the country, but most notably at the Scottsdale Artists' School in Arizona. Drawing and painting from life is important to her, and she tries to attend open sessions and workshops throughout the year. One of her favorite things about attending workshops, open sessions, lectures, and demonstrations is making new friends and acquaintances. She has taught drawing and painting at several locations including Brigham Young University, Bountiful Davis Art Center in Bountiful, Utah, and in her home studio. Besides drawing and painting Erin also enjoys yoga, cooking, reading, designing, learning new things, and spending time with family. Along with great artwork, she is especially influenced and moved by classical music, ballet, and her religious faith. She and her husband, Matt, and their daughter, Sicily, currently live in Mesa, Arizona.

NOTES

NOTES

NOTES

NOTES

NOTES

NOTES

NOTES

NOTES

NOTES

Other Dover Books in Art Instruction

THE PRACTICE OF ART: A CLASSIC VICTORIAN TREATISE, J. D. Harding. This comprehensive Victorian manual on the philosophy and principles of art is geared toward practicing artists. Twenty-four black-and-white plates accompany advice on composition, light and shade, drawing from nature, more. 208pp. 8 1/4 x 11. 0-486-81128-X

THE FANTASY ARTROOM, Written and Illustrated by Aaron Pocock. This richly illustrated guide presents new tricks and techniques for sketching and creating line art as well as working in watercolors. Step-by-step demonstrations offer easy-to-follow methods for drawing landscapes and characters. 160pp. 8 1/4 x 11. 0-486-80124-1

SECRET TEACHINGS OF A COMIC BOOK MASTER: The Art of Alfredo Alcala, Alfredo Alcala, Heidi MacDonald, and Phillip Dana Yeh. Introductions by Gil Kane and Roy Thomas. This unique work, full of insight on composition and other techniques, features interviews with the legendary comic artist as well as pages from his masterwork *Voltar*. It also includes Introductions by Gil Kane and Roy Thomas. 80pp. 8 1/4 x 11. 0-486-80041-5

HOW TO DRAW TATTOO STYLE, Andy Fish with Veronica Hebard. Along with background ranging from "old school" nautical motifs to tribal and Oriental styles, this well-illustrated guide offers expert tips on creating tattoo flash art of skulls, hearts, dragons, other images. 224pp. 5 3/4 x 7 11/16. 0-486-79678-7

HOW TO DRAW DOGS, CATS AND HORSES, Arthur Zaidenberg. A noted creator of art instruction books presents clear, step-by-step illustrations that demonstrate how to draw dogs, cats, and horses by placing basic shapes in proper relation to each other. 64pp. 6.14 x 9.21. 0-486-78048-1

ANATOMY, PERSPECTIVE AND COMPOSITION FOR THE ARTIST, Stan Smith. This volume of practical instruction in the foundations of art features many splendid color illustrations by the author. Perfect for intermediate-level and advanced artists wishing to take their work to the next level. 224pp. 8 1/4 x 11. 0-486-49299-0

LIGHT FOR THE ARTIST, Ted Seth Jacobs. Intermediate and advanced art students receive a broad vocabulary of effects with this in-depth study of light. Diagrams and paintings illustrate applications of principles to figure, still life, and landscape paintings. 144pp. 8 1/4 x 11. 0-486-49304-0

DRAWING OF THE HAND, Joseph M. Henninger. Numerous illustrations depict the anatomy of the hand and the forearm, in addition to a portfolio of related drawings by Old Masters and contemporary artists, many accompanied by the author's comments. 144pp. 10 7/8 x 8. 0-486-49302-4

DRAWING WHAT THE EYE SEES, Ted Seth Jacobs. Heralded as a revolutionary right-brain approach to figure drawing, this guide focuses on mentality rather than technique. More than 180 black-and-white drawings and eight pages of color illustrations. 136pp. 8 1/4 x 11. 0-486-49106-4

PEN & INK DRAWING, Frank J. Lohan. An inspiring sourcebook, this guide helps artists discover a wide variety of subjects and ideas. More than 140 of the author's drawings illustrate nostalgic scenes, old engravings, atmospheric effects, photographs, and landscapes. 128pp. 8 1/4 x 11. 0-486-49715-1

SKETCHING BIRDS: Pen, Pencil, and Ink Wash Techniques, Frank J. Lohan. Expert instructor presents 59 lessons accompanied by more than 350 easy-to-follow illustrations. Basic line drawings advance to pen, pencil, and ink wash techniques to produce texture and movement in realistic sketches. 144pp. 11 x 8 3/8. 0-486-49076-9

Browse over 10,000 books at www.doverpublications.com

Other Dover Books in Art Instruction

HOW TO DRAW NEARLY EVERYTHING, Victor Perard. Beginners of all ages can learn to draw figures, faces, landscapes, trees, flowers, and animals of all kinds. Well-illustrated guide offers suggestions for pencil, pen, and brush techniques plus composition, shading, and perspective. 160pp. 11 x 8 1/4.
0-486-49848-4

THE PRACTICE OF OIL PAINTING AND DRAWING, Solomon J. Solomon. New Introduction by James Gurney. This guide introduces not only the techniques of oil painting but also the underlying principles of figure drawing. A series of images by the Old Masters includes 32 full-color pages. 384pp. 5 3/8 x 8 1/2.
0-486-48358-4

THE INFLUENCE OF BONES AND MUSCLES ON FORM, Walter T. Foster. These succinct treatments on drawing muscles and bones were prepared by an expert artist and teacher. Each page features multiple illustrations with extensive explanations of bone and muscle placement, function, and artistic re-creation. 64pp. 9 x 12.
0-486-48285-5

THE ART OF ETCHING, E. S. Lumsden. An expert traces every step in the creation of etchings, from essential materials to completed proof, and presents a rich historical survey of the art. 200 figures and annotated plates. 384pp. 5 1/2 x 8 1/2.
0-486-20049-3

PEN & INK SKETCHING: Step by Step, Frank J. Lohan. Clear and concise guide to pen-and-ink work offers material for artists at every level. Thirty-seven step-by-step presentations illustrate the progression from pencil sketch to ink outline to shadows and details to completed work. 144pp. 8 1/4 x 11.
0-486-48359-2

PAINTING MATERIALS: A Short Encyclopedia, R. J. Gettens and G. L. Stout. An encyclopedia rather than a handbook, this five-part treatment covers mediums, adhesives, and film substances; pigments and inert materials; solvents, diluents, and detergents; supports; and tools and equipment. 368pp. 5 1/2 x 8 1/2.
0-486-21597-0

THE FIGURE IN COMPOSITION, Paul G. Braun. A valuable tool for intermediate artists, this volume treats the figure as a unit in the overall composition of a sketch or drawing. Discusses light and shade, draped figures, folds, movement, much more. 64pp. 6 1/2 x 9 1/4.
0-486-48155-7

THE DRAWING HANDBOOK, Frank J. Lohan. Clear, concise guide for beginners features more than 500 step-by-step illustrations. Topics include composition, tools, geometric shapes, and simple methods, plus exercises focusing on landscapes, architecture, animals, flowers, faces, more. 224pp. 8 1/4 x 11.
0-486-48156-5

VASARI ON TECHNIQUE, Giorgio Vasari. Sixteenth-century painter reveals technical secrets: gilding, stained glass, casting, painter's materials, much more. Most detailed, valuable sourcebook of Renaissance methods. 29 illustrations. 400pp. 5 x 8.
0-486-20717-X

SKETCHING THE COUNTRYSIDE: How to Draw the Vanishing Rural Landscape, Frank J. Lohan. Both experienced and aspiring artists can benefit from this practical guide. More than 400 detailed illustrations include fundamentals for drawing trees, rocks, buildings, mountains, lakes, and other scenic elements. 272pp. 8 1/4 x 11.
0-486-47887-4

Browse over 10,000 books at www.doverpublications.com